Construction Project Scheduling and Control

SALEH MUBARAK

PEARSON

Prentice Hall

Upper Saddle River, New Jersey
Columbus, Ohio

Library of Congress Cataloging-in-Publication Data

Mubarak, Saleh A. (Saleh Altayeb)
  Construction project scheduling and control / Saleh Mubarak.
    p. cm.
  Includes bibliographical references and index.
  ISBN 0-13-097314-9
  1. Building industry—Management. 2. Building—Superintendence. 3. Production
scheduling. I. Title.

  TH438.4.M83 2005
  690'.068—dc22
                                      2004014555

Executive Editor: Ed Francis
Editorial Assistant: Jennifer Day
Project Coordinator: *The GTS Companies*/York, PA Campus
Production Editor: Christine Buckendahl
Design Coordinator: Diane Ernsberger
Cover Designer: Ali Mohrman
Production Manager: Matt Ottenweller
Marketing Manager: Mark Marsden

This book was set in Stone Serif by *The GTS Companies*/York, PA Campus, and printed and bound by R. R. Donnelley & Sons Company. The cover was printed by The Lehigh Press, Inc.

Pearson Education Ltd.
Pearson Education Singapore Pte. Ltd.
Pearson Education Canada, Ltd.
Pearson Education—Japan

Pearson Education Australia Pty. Limited
Pearson Education North Asia Ltd.
Pearson Educación de Mexico, S.A. de C.V.
Pearson Education Malaysia Pte. Ltd.

10 9 8 7 6 5 4 3 2 1
ISBN 0-13-097314-9

To the soul of my father, a brilliant scholar and a noble person. He taught me the importance of knowledge, the art of teaching, and the spirit of giving. Best of all, he was a wonderful role model for me, being dedicated, altruistic, and humble.

■

To my mother, who always showed me the value of education and discipline.

■

To my wife, for her relentless encouragement, support, and patience during the years it took me to finish this book.

■

Contents

v

Chapter 5

Precedence Networks   83

Chapter 6

Chapter 7

Chapter 9

Reports and Presentations   227

Chapter 10

Scheduling as Part of the Project Management Effort 247

Chapter 11

Other Scheduling Methods 271

Chapter 12

Construction Delay Claims 305

Preface

The art of teaching requires two important components: knowledge of the subject and the ability to convey this knowledge to students. Having a love of the subject is a bonus that allows a teacher to take the classroom to an even higher level.

During my career as a structural engineer, as a construction professional, and as a professor, I have had to play many roles and wear many hats. There is no question that the different roles and different positions have provided me with rounded knowledge and a panoramic view of the construction industry. However, no subject has been more interesting and more intriguing to me than scheduling and project control. During my teaching career, I have acquired many books on this subject. Many of them are good or excellent books, but none has fulfilled my exact need. Some lack the detailed step-by-step approach, some have few examples and exercises, some are written by academicians with little real-world application, and some deal with the subject of scheduling and project control as if it were still the 1970s or 1980s. I have been looking for a book that does the following:

- Addresses the average student and details all steps clearly and without shortcuts
- Includes many solved and unsolved exercises that cover all the subjects in the book
- Relates to computer software programs used in the construction industry without making them the center of attention or overshadowing the theoretical principles
- Deals with precedence networks as the main and only scheduling method, having coverage of arrow networks only as part of the evolution of scheduling
- Focuses on scheduling as part of the overall project management effort (rather than as just one chapter in a book on project management)

Not having found such a book and after having taught scheduling for several years using four textbooks, I decided to write my own book. I started writing from scratch in early 2001. I also began living it: in my office, at home, when going to bed, in the shower, while driving the car, almost every waking moment. As ideas would come to mind, I would write them on a piece of paper or record them on my digital tape recorder. I did not want to let any idea escape me. Several experts also reviewed this book and provided me with invaluable critiques, and I made additional changes and improvements every time I read the text. Following is an outline of this textbook.

In chapter 1, planning, scheduling, and project control are defined, and the steps needed to build a schedule are described. In chapter 2, bar (Gantt) charts, the most common method used to display and report schedules, are introduced. This topic is revisited in chapter 9. Networks and the critical path method (CPM) are covered in the next four chapters. Chapter 3 covers arrow and node networks and their history, concepts, and structure. Chapter 4 addresses the CPM and its calculations. Chapter 5 covers precedence networks, an advanced form of node networks with its own calculations and concepts. I realize that this subject can become more complicated than field personnel or students can (or like to) handle. As a result, in this chapter, I offer two approaches: the simplistic approach, which leads to bottom-line results without becoming bogged in the details, and the detailed approach, for those who want to study the subject thoroughly. I further distinguish between continuous and interruptible activities, a subject I have not seen discussed clearly and sufficiently elsewhere in the literature.

Chapter 6 deals with resource allocation and leveling. This concept is explained clearly, more so in English than in mathematical terms. The mathematical model or algorithm for resource leveling is not discussed because it is complicated and unnecessary and because most schedulers never refer to it. Powerful computers and software have made this function feasible and practical.

Scheduling would be worthless without updating and project control, so chapter 7 covers this important subject. Chapter 8 addresses an interesting topic: schedule compression and time-cost trade-offs. In chapter 9, I explain some commonsense ideas about reports and presentations, in the context of scheduling. In chapter 10, I address scheduling as part of the project management effort. This chapter sheds some light on the interrelationships among scheduling, estimating, and other components of construction project management.

Chapter 11 covers a few other scheduling methods, such as the program evaluation and review technique (PERT) and the linear scheduling method (LSM). Chapter 12 provides brief coverage of delay claims, their avoidance, and their resolution. Because the coverage is brief, this chapter is not to be considered the ultimate reference on this subject.

Appendix A contains a computer project with multiple assignments that correspond to all subjects discussed in the book. Appendix B contains a few sample reports that the author created using Primavera P3e/c and SureTrak Project Manager software.

Throughout the book are not only illustrated examples for almost every concept, but also end-of-chapter exercises. Such exercises include both numerical-type exercises (covering the spectrum of difficulty) and conceptual questions. The latter type are mostly short, essay-type questions. Multiple-choice questions are not included because students need to know what the terms and definitions of construction scheduling are, rather than what they are not. Also, several exercise projects are provided so that students can use them for a computer project.

My intent was to introduce a scheduling book suitable for the 21st century. I hope that I have succeeded; however, I am sure that readers—construction professionals, educators, and students—will have suggestions and criticisms of this text. I encourage readers to send their corrections and suggestions to the publisher so that I can include any necessary changes in future editions.

In preparing this book, I relied on the help of many friends and associates. To them, I owe my gratitude. I give specific thanks to the reviewers of this text for their helpful comments: Michael J. Cook, University of Florida; Rocky Gerber, University of Washington; Charles R. Glagola, University of Florida;

James L. Jenkins, Purdue University; David Leo Lickteig, Georgia Southern University; and James Stein, Eastern Michigan University. Likewise, thanks to Attorney Barry Bramble, who provided me with his invaluable contribution to chapter 12, Construction Delay Claims.

—*Saleh Mubarak*

ABBREVIATIONS

IMPORTANT NOTE: Many of the following abbreviations are subject specific. In this book, they are used within the context of the construction industry. One abbreviation or acronym may mean one thing in one discipline and something entirely different in another.

AAA	American Arbitration Association
AACEI	AACE International (formerly known as the American Association for Cost Engineers); http://www.aacei.org/
AASHTO	American Association of State and Highway Transportation Officials; http://transportation1.org/aashtonew/
ABA	American Bar Association; http://www.abanet.org/
ABC	Associated Builders and Contractors, Inc.; http://www.abc.org/
AC	actual cost, air-conditioning (mechanical), or alternating current (electrical)
ACI	American Concrete Institute; http://www.aci-int.org/
ACWP	actual cost for worked performed
ADM	arrow diagramming method
ADR	alternate dispute resolution
A/E	architect or engineer
AFL-CIO	American Federation of Labor–Congress of Industrial Organizations; http://www.aflcio.org/
AGC	Associated General Contractors of America; http://www.agc.org/
AIA	The American Institute of Architects; http://www.aia.org/
ANSI	American National Standards Institute; http://www.ansi.org/
AOA	activity on arrow
AON	activity on node
ASAP	as soon as possible, a term to be avoided in contracts and construction agreements (a specific date should be specified); also, a type of constraint in MS Project software.

ASCE	American Society of Civil Engineers; http://www.asce.org/
ASME	American Society of Mechanical Engineers; http://www.asme.org/
ASTM	American Society for Testing and Materials; http://www.astm.org/
BAC	budget at completion
B/C ratio	benefit-cost ratio
BCWP	budgeted cost for work performed
BCWS	budgeted cost for work scheduled
CC	crash cost
CD	crash duration, or compact disk
CII	Construction Industry Institute; http://www.construction-institute.org/
CIP	cast-in-place (adj.)
CM	construction manager, or construction management (firm)
CMAA	Construction Management Association of America; http://cmaanet.org/
CMU	concrete masonry unit
CO	change order
CPI	cost performance index
CPM	critical path method
C/SCSC	cost/schedule control systems criteria
CSI	The Construction Specifications Institute; http://www.csinet.org/, or cost-schedule index
CV	cost variance
CY	cubic yards
D/B	design-build
DD##	design development (## is the percent complete; e.g., DD30 means design development at 30% complete)
DOD	Department of Defense
DOE	Department of Energy
DOT	Department of Transportation
DRB	dispute review board
DRF	double-restricted float
EA	each
EAC	estimate at completion
EBS	enterprise breakdown structure
EF	early finish time (or date)
EJCDC	Engineers Joint Contract Documents Committee
ENR	*Engineering News-Record* magazine

ES	early start time (or date)
ETC	estimate to complete
EV	earned value
EVA	earned value analysis
EVM	earned value management
FCV	forecasted cost variance
FF	finish-to-finish (relationship) or free float
FICA	Federal Insurance Contributions Act
FRP	formwork, rebar, place (for concrete members)
FS	finish-to-start (relationship)
FSV	forecasted schedule variance
GC	general contractor
GERT	graphical evaluation and review technique
HVAC	heating, ventilation, and air-conditioning
IAI	International Alliance for Interoperability; http://www.iai-na.org/
IEEE	Institute of Electrical and Electronics Engineers; http://www.ieee.org/
Ind. F	independent float
Int. F	interfering float
IPA	immediately preceding activity
IROR	internal rate of return (on an investment)
ISA	immediately succeeding activity
ISO	International Organization for Standardization (ISO 9000, ISO 14000); http://www.iso.ch/iso/en/ISOOnline.frontpage
IT	information technology
LC	least cost
LCD	least-cost duration
LF	late finish time (or date) or linear feet
LS	late start time (or date)
LSM	linear scheduling method
MARR	minimum attractive rate of return
MBF	1,000 board feet
MEP	mechanical, electrical, and plumbing
MGD	million gallons per day
MSDS	materials safety data sheet
NAHB	National Association of Home Builders; http://www.nahb.org/

NASA	National Aeronautics and Space Administration; http://www.nasa.gov/home/index.html
NC	normal cost
ND	normal duration
NLT	no less than
NSPE	National Society of Professional Engineers; http://www.nspe.org/
NTP	Notice to Proceed
NTS	not to scale
OBS	organizational breakdown structure
OSHA	Occupational Safety and Health Administration; http://www.osha.gov/
P3	Primavera Project Planner (software)
P3e	Primavera Enterprise (software)
P3e/C	Primavera Enterprise for Construction (software)
PC	percent complete
PCA	Portland Cement Association; http://www.portcement.org/
PCM	pure agency construction management
PDM	precedence diagramming method
PE	professional engineer
PEP	program evaluation procedure
PERT	program evaluation and review technique
PF	project finish
PM	project manager, or project management
PMI	Project Management Institute; http://www.pmi.org/
PMP	Project Management Professional (certified by PMI)
PS	project start
PV	planned value
QA/QC	quality assurance and quality control
R&D	research and development
RFC	request for change
RFI	request for information
RFP	request for proposal
RFQ	request for quotation
ROR	rate of return (on an investment)
SC	substantial completion
SD	standard deviation
SDK	software development kit

SF	start-to-finish (relationship), or square foot
SFCA	square foot contact area (unit of measure for concrete formwork)
SPI	schedule performance index
SQ	square (unit of measure for roofs; equal to 100 square feet)
SRF	single-restricted float
SS	start-to-start (relationship)
SV	schedule variance
TB	total (planned) budget
TCM	total cost management
TF	total float
TQM	total quality management
URF	unrestricted float
VAR	variance
VE	value engineering
WBS	work breakdown structure
ZTF	zero total float

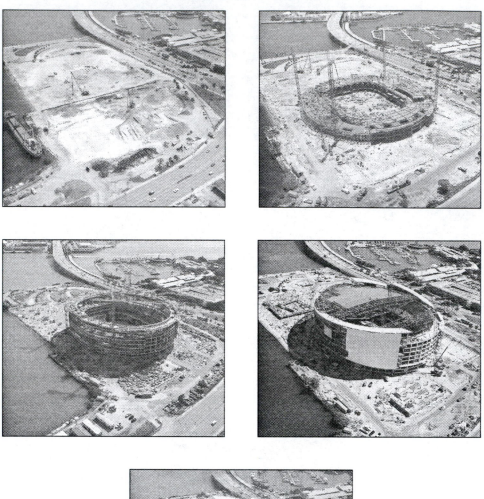

Five stages of the construction of the Miami Heat Arena in Miami, Florida. Courtesy of Smith Aerial Photos, Maitland, Florida.

Introduction

Bridge over Jacksonville, Florida. Courtesy of Smith Aerial Photos, Maitland, Florida.

PLANNING AND SCHEDULING

Planning and *scheduling* are two terms that are often thought of as synonymous. However, they are not. Scheduling is just one part of the planning effort. The term *planning* is used in many ways and different contexts. We commonly hear about *financial* planning, such as retirement planning and college education planning. Although this type of planning may include other aspects (such as what to do after retirement or which college to choose for your child), the main focus is on finance. The government, as well as large corporations, has planning units or teams in almost every department. At the individual level, a young person may have plans for marriage, a career, and so forth. However, in the context of this book, the term *planning* is restricted to meaning project planning, with an emphasis on construction projects.

Before we define project planning, we need to define a project. The Project Management Institute (PMI 2000) defines a **project** as "a temporary endeavor undertaken to produce a unique product or service" (p. 204). The key words in this definition are *temporary* and *unique*: any project must have a starting point and an ending point, and it must have a deliverable product or service that is unique. As a generic example, the Secretary of Education's saying "We need to improve our students' SAT scores" does not constitute a project. However, saying "We need to improve our students' SAT scores by an average of 15 points in 5 years" may qualify as a project.

Some government agencies have specific but ongoing work that they call a project, such as maintenance of a certain facility or park compliance with the Americans with Disabilities Act. Technically, these are not projects because they have no well-defined deliverable product or service and starting and ending points. Each could be called a *program*, instead, with several projects inside each program.

Some people may think of two construction projects as identical just because they have the same design. In project management, we may have similar projects, but every project is unique. Differences may come from a difference in location (soil type, weather conditions, the labor market, building codes, unforeseen conditions, etc.), in management type and experience, or in circumstances (and how much Murphy's Law is involved).

Project planning has been defined as "the process of choosing the one method and order of work to be adopted for a project from all the various ways and sequences in which it could be done" (Antill and Woodhead 1990, 8; Callahan, Quackenbush, and Rowings 1992, 2). Project planning serves as a foundation for several related functions, such as cost estimating, scheduling, project control, quality control, safety management, and others.

Scheduling is the determination of the timing and sequence of operations in the project and their assembly to give the overall completion time. As mentioned previously, scheduling focuses on one part of the planning effort.

Project planning answers the questions *What* is going to be done? *How*? *Where*? By *whom*? and *When* (in general terms, the project's start and end)? Scheduling deals with *when* on a detailed level.

To get an idea about the relationship between project planning and scheduling, assume you are planning a family vacation "project" for next summer. Your *plan* may include considerations such as these:

- Who will go on the trip?
- Which places do you want to visit? (You would like to visit many places, but your time and money resources are limited.)
- What is the time frame for the vacation (just the starting and ending dates)?
- What is the total budget for the "project" (including the contingency you did not tell other family members about)?
- What types of activities do you want to participate in during the trip (sharp differences among the family members)?
- What means of transportation do you plan to use (your car, a rental car, air, train, bus, RV, bicycles, etc.)?
- What other issues, such as accommodations, food, and clothing, need to be addressed?

The project *schedule* is simply the itinerary, such as this:

- Leave home in Tampa, Florida, on June 8, 2005.
- Arrive in Panama City on June 8, 2005.
- Leave Panama City on June 15, 2005.
- Arrive in Atlanta, Georgia, on June 15, 2005.
- Leave Atlanta on June 22, 2005.
- Arrive in Gatlinburg, Tennessee, on June 22, 2005.

    $\vdots$

- Return home to Tampa on July 7, 2005.

Note that not only the plan and the schedule are related, but also many of the elements of the plan are interrelated. For example, most of the choices in the plan (length of stay, type of accommodations, means of transportation, type of activities, food, etc.) affect the budget. Since different means of transportation have significant time durations, they may affect not only the cost but the schedule as well. Clearly, a lack of clarity of scope before the project starts may lead to heated arguments and dissatisfaction. In real projects, it may lead to huge budget overruns, schedule delays, and different parties' dissatisfaction. Therefore, it is important to decide who the "project manager" is—who makes the final decisions. Many issues are at stake in this example, but demonstrating the concepts of planning and scheduling is our objective.

In the context of construction projects, a typical plan for an office building may include the following:

- A *scope definition*, such as a five-story building for commercial use (offices) with a total area of about 30,000 square feet. The location is also part of the planning, although, in some cases, the exact location may be selected later or only a few sites are mentioned as candidates.
- A *schematic design*. This is not a must but helps you visualize the project. The final design may later differ significantly.
- A *budget number* (e.g., $4 million). The planner must be aware of all construction-related expenses, such as the cost of land, permits, design fees, and so forth.
- A *time frame* (i.e., when the project is expected to start and end).
- *Other pertinent information* that may be used to justify the project or clarify some of its aspects. If an investor is doing the planning, a **pro forma** helps predict the rate of return and helps in making the decision whether or not to build the project.

PROJECT CONTROL

Once a project starts, certain aspects can easily deviate or go astray. This deviation can be overspending, a schedule slippage, or something else. It is of utmost importance to know—at all times—where you stand in relation to where you planned to be (the baseline). If you find yourself behind schedule or over budget, you must know why, then take corrective action to get back on track, or, at least, minimize the deviation. If the deviation is positive (i.e., the project is ahead of schedule or under budget), actual performance was probably better than that expected in the baseline plan. This process exemplifies **project control.** Although the concept of project control covers all aspects of the plan (budget, schedule, quality, etc.), our main focus in this book is on budget and schedule control, which are related. (Extensive coverage of project control is provided in chapter 7.)

WHY SCHEDULE PROJECTS?

Scheduling may be important for many reasons, such as the following eight:

1. *To calculate the project completion date.* In most construction projects, the general contractor (GC), as well as other team members, is obligated to finish the project by a certain date specified in the contract. The contractor has to make sure his or her schedule meets this date. Sometimes, the contractor has an incentive (financial or other) to finish the project earlier than contractually required. Also, the schedule may show the stage of **substantial completion,** when the owner may start occupying and using the facility while the contractor is still doing some final touches.

2. *To calculate the start or end of a specific activity.* Specific activities may require special attention, such as ordering and delivering materials or equipment. For instance, the project manager may want special and expensive equipment to be delivered just in time for installation. Long-lead items may have to be ordered several months in advance. Delivery of very large items may need coordination or a special permit from the city so that such delivery does not disrupt traffic during rush hour. The schedule must show such important dates.

3. *To expose and adjust conflicts between trades or subcontractors.* In today's construction, the GC's role is mostly to coordinate different subcontractors. The responsibility of the GC may be to allocate the time of use of a tower crane among subcontractors or to just ensure adequate work space is available for all subcontractors. These tasks are in addition to coordinating logical relationships such as when a subcontractor's

activity depends on the completion of another subcontractor's activity. For example, the drywall contractor cannot start until the framing has been done; once the drywall is installed, the painter can start painting; and so on.

4. *To predict and calculate the cash flow.* The timing of an activity has an impact on the cash flow, which may be an important factor for the contractor (or the owner) to consider. The contractor (or the owner) must know his or her total spending in any month or time period. He or she may delay the start of certain activities, within the available *float* (this term is explained subsequently), to make sure the cash flow does not exceed a certain cap.

5. *To evaluate the effect of changes.* **Change orders** are almost inevitable, but well-planned projects may have few or minor change orders. Some owners like to know the effect of a change before authorizing it. This change may be an addition, a deletion, or a substitution. Cost estimators may estimate the cost of change orders, but schedulers can predict the impact of the change on the entire project schedule. Changes may not only affect the time frame but also have an impact on the overhead cost.

6. *To improve work efficiency.* By properly distributing workers and equipment (which is explained in chapter 6), the GC can save time and money.

7. *To resolve delay claims.* Construction **delay claims** are common. Lawyers often use expert witnesses who are professional schedulers. In most cases, only a **critical path method (CPM)** schedule can prove or disprove a delay claim, which can be a multimillion dollar claim.

8. *To serve as an effective project control tool.* Project control must have a solid and sound base with which current performance can be compared. Project control is achieved by comparing the actual schedule and budget with the baseline (as-planned) schedule and budget (this subject is explained in chapter 7).

The need for a CPM schedule varies with several factors. In general, it increases with the increase in size and complexity of the project. For example, a home builder who has built tens or hundreds of almost-identical homes may not have much need for a CPM schedule. Project control is still needed but may be conducted through simpler methods.

THE SCHEDULER

A Civil Engineer, a Computer Whiz, a Mathematician, a Project Manager, an Artist, or a Communicator?

An increasing trend—in all industries—is to use computer software and other high-tech tools. These software packages cover the entire spectrum of all industries, including some generic types of software, such as word processors and spreadsheets, that everyone uses. However, specialized software requires knowledge of both the software and the discipline. Scheduling is no exception to this rule.

Let us distinguish among three types of knowledge that a scheduler must have:

1. Knowledge of computer software and hardware
2. Knowledge of the principles of scheduling and project control (as part of project management)
3. Knowledge of the specific technical field, such as commercial building, industrial, transportation, and so forth

To efficiently operate a scheduling and control program such as Primavera Project Planner (P3) (Primavera Systems, Inc., Bala Cynwyd, PA), the scheduler must have the first two types of knowledge. The third type is a plus. Just because an individual knows computers and can surf the Internet does not mean he or she can operate a scheduling and project control program. Even if the individual can operate it, he or she may not understand its language and may have problems relating to and interpreting the technical information.

Currently, many high-tech innovations such as PCs, PDAs, digital cameras and scanners, and the Internet are available. They have become useful tools and an essential part of our daily life. Nevertheless, the human factor should never be underestimated. The combination of good tools and an educated, experienced operator is the only path to success in project planning.

SCHEDULING AND PROJECT MANAGEMENT

Planning, scheduling, and project control are extremely important components of project management. However, project management includes other components, such as cost estimating, cost control, procurement, project administration, quality management, and safety management. These components are all interrelated in different ways. The group of people representing all these disciplines is called the **project management team.** It is usually headed by the **project manager (PM).** In chapter 10, we discuss the relationships between scheduling and other project management components.

CHAPTER 1 EXERCISES

1. Define *project planning* and *scheduling*. Differentiate between the two terms.

2. Define a *project*. What makes planning and scheduling construction projects different from general planning? (*Hint*: Think of the key words in the definition of *project*.)

3. What is *project control*? Why is it important?

4. Think of a construction project you participated in or observed. Write down the steps involved in its planning and the steps involved in its scheduling (without much specificity).

5. List the benefits of CPM scheduling in construction projects.

6. Do all construction projects have the same need for CPM scheduling? Why or why not?

7. What characteristics must a scheduler of a building project have? Can the same person be a scheduler for an industrial project? Why or why not?

8. Go to a real construction site. Meet with the project manager. Ask whether he or she uses CPM scheduling. If so, discuss the benefits obtained from such scheduling. If not, politely ask why CPM scheduling is not being used.

9. Search for an article on a CPM scheduling topic (*ENR, Civil Engineering,* and *PM Network* are magazines that are good sources; avoid scholarly journals). Summarize and discuss the article.

Bar (Gantt) Charts

Lake excavation at a development site in Ft. Myers, Florida. Courtesy of Terra Excavating, Inc., Largo, Florida.

DEFINITION AND INTRODUCTION

A **bar chart** is "a graphic representation of project activities shown in a time-scaled bar line with no links shown between activities" (Popescu and Charoenngam 1995, 96). The bar chart was originally developed by Henry L. Gantt in 1917 and is alternatively called a **Gantt chart.** It quickly became popular—especially in the construction industry—because of its ability to graphically represent a project's activities on a time scale.

Before a bar chart can be constructed for a project, the project must be broken into smaller, usually homogeneous components, each of which is called an **activity,** or a **task.** No absolutely correct or incorrect way to break down a project exists; however, the scheduler should take a balanced approach and break it down into a reasonable number of activities that are easily measured and controlled without being overly detailed. (Project breakdown is discussed further in chapter 7.)

An activity, or a task, may be as large as laying the foundation of a building, as small as erecting the formwork of one footing, or anywhere between. The duration of each activity must be estimated. Bars are then drawn to show, for each activity, the duration and the starting and ending points. As mentioned previously, links between activities are not usually shown.

On a bar chart, the bar may not indicate continuous work from the start of the activity until its end. For example, the activity Getting a Building Permit may be represented by a 2-month-long bar. However, most of this time is a waiting period. Likewise, a Concrete Foundation summary activity may include several days of waiting for concrete to cure. Noncontinuous (dashed) bars are sometimes used to distinguish between real work (solid line) and inactive periods (gaps between solid lines) (Callahan, Quackenbush, and Rowings 1992).

Bar charts have become a vehicle for representing many pieces of a project's information. Many variations of bar charts have evolved; some simply show the start and end of each activity (Figures 2.1 and 2.2), some are loaded with resource or budget numbers (Figures 2.3 and 2.4), and others compare the **as-planned schedule** with the **as-built schedule** (Figure 2.5). Using Primavera Project Planner (P3) software (Primavera Systems, Inc., Bala Cynwyd, PA), we can show activities with interruptions as continuous bars or as "necked" bars (Figure 2.6).

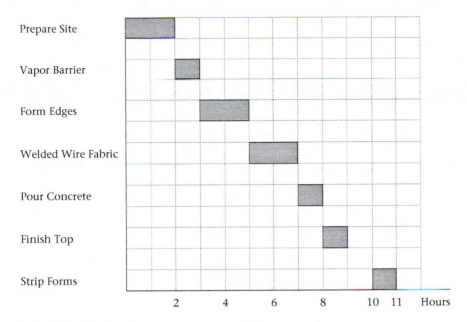

FIGURE 2.1   Bar chart for placing a simple slab on a grade

Since bar charts basically use the *x*-axis only (to depict time), the *y*-axis is used (in addition to showing individual activities) to represent a variable across time, such as man-hours (Figure 2.3), budget (Figure 2.4), percent complete (Figure 2.5), and so forth. This variable is usually shown as a curve superimposed on the bar chart.

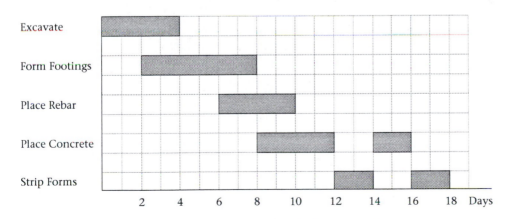

FIGURE 2.2   Alternative bar chart for placing a simple slab on a grade

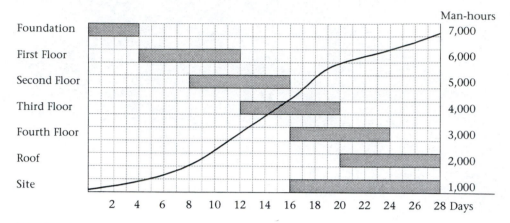

FIGURE 2.3   Bar chart—loaded with man-hours—for construction of a two-story building

In Figure 2.5, S curves (also called *lazy-S curves*) represent the percent complete for the project:

- The thin continuous line   (————)   represents the as-planned curve.
- The thick continuous line   (————)   represents the as-built curve.
- The thick dashed line   (------)   represents the predicted curve based on extrapolation from the as-built curve.

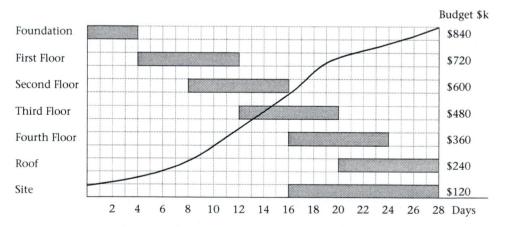

FIGURE 2.4   Bar chart—loaded with the budget—for construction of a two-story building

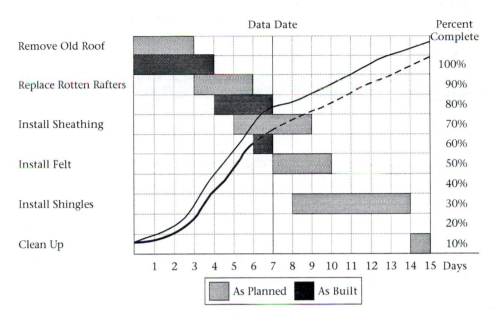

FIGURE 2.5   Bar chart for replacement of an old roof, showing a comparison between the percent complete of the planned (as-planned) activities (thin line) and that of the actual (as-built) activities (thick line)

Activity ID	Activity Description	Orig Dur	FEB
1000	Excavate	4	Excavate
1010	Form Footings	6	Form Footings
1020	Place Rebar	4	Place Rebar
1030	Place Concrete	6	Place Concrete
1040	Strip Forms	4	Strip Forms

FIGURE 2.6   Bar chart for placing a simple slab on a grade, with activities "necked" during nonwork periods

ADVANTAGES OF BAR CHARTS

Bar charts have gained wide acceptance and popularity mainly because of their simplicity and ease of preparation and understanding. No "theory" or complicated calculations are involved. Anyone can understand them. They can be prepared anywhere with just a pencil and paper. So, although bar charts can carry—or be loaded with—other information, the user must be careful not to overload them and thus eliminate their main advantage: simplicity.

Another advantage is that bar charts particularly appeal to persons who do not have a technical background. For example, some clients and upper-level managers may better understand the plan for carrying out a construction project by looking at a bar chart than by looking at a schematic of a logic network.

A final advantage of bar charts is that, with the advent of the critical path method (CPM) and the evolution of powerful computers, bar charts did not perish or lose importance. Instead, they evolved to a different supporting role that made them more valuable and popular. This role is explained in chapters 3 and 4.

DISADVANTAGES OF BAR CHARTS

The main disadvantage of bar charts is lack of logical representation (relationships): Why did this activity start on that date? Bar charts do not reveal the answer. It could be a logical relationship, a resource constraint, or a subjective decision by the project manager. Although some software programmers tried to depict logical relationships on bar charts, the result was not always clear. The logic lines would get tangled, and unlike networks, bar charts do not allow the length of the bars to be changed or moved around to make items clearer or look better.

Another limitation, rather than a disadvantage, for bar charts is the size and complexity of projects. Bar charts may not be practical for projects with large numbers of activities—*unless* you use them in two ways:

1. You show a subset of the work activities to maintain the simplicity of the chart. For example, the general contractor can produce bar charts for activities during only a certain period, for **critical activities** (activities that cannot be delayed or the entire project would be delayed; a full definition and discussion follows in chapter 4) only, for activities in a certain section of the project, or for activities under a certain subcontractor.

2. You show summary bars (each bar represents a group of activities combined on the basis of a certain criterion such as department, major component, or responsibility). This can be done during the early planning phase, when details are not available (see, for example,

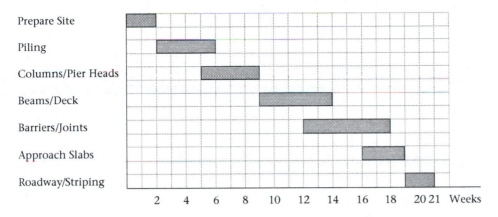

FIGURE 2.7 Bar chart representing the summary activities for constructing a bridge

Figure 2.7), and when you are reporting the information to high-level management.

New technology (computers, software, printers, plotters, etc.) has ameliorated some of the disadvantages of bar charts by enabling the user to organize, filter, roll up, summarize, or do almost anything to customize the bar chart. Bar chart reporting and presentation is discussed in chapter 10.

CHAPTER 2 EXERCISES

1. What is a *bar chart*? What other term is synonymous? How did the other term originate?
2. What are the main advantages of bar charts that made them so popular? What are their main disadvantages?

In the following exercises, draw a bar chart showing the time scale on the *x*-axis. Use engineering paper, or draw light vertical lines every certain interval (e.g., every 5 days) to help you read the starting and ending dates of any activity. Make simplifying assumptions whenever necessary. Be sure to mention these assumptions.

3. You are running out of space in your house, so you have decided to transform your two-car garage into a family room. In addition, you will build a simple carport in your driveway. Make a bar chart for this project, breaking your project into 10 to 15 work activities.

4. Think of college education as a project. You are advising a friend, a senior in high school who plans to attend college next year. Prepare a bar chart for him, depicting all the courses he must take from the start of college until graduation. Obtain the program course list. Make sure you do not overlook any prerequisite requirements. Make the following simplifying assumptions:

   a. Your friend is smart. He will not fail any course.
   b. All courses are available every fall and spring semester.
   c. No summer semesters are included. Your friend will work during the summer.
   d. The total load every semester should be no less than 15 credit hours and no more than 18. You can let him take as many as 20 credit hours in one semester only, and only during the last year.
   e. Your friend must graduate in eight semesters.

After finishing the bar chart, show it to your adviser and get his or her approval on your sequence of courses. Note that several correct solutions to this problem may be possible (which is often the case with construction projects).

5. Draw a bar chart for building a detached shed in your backyard. Break your project into 10 to 15 work activities.
6. You are given the task of changing the worn-out carpet in your office. Draw a bar chart showing all activities involved (including removing and reinstalling baseboards; removing and disposing of old carpet and the pad; selecting, purchasing, and delivering new carpet and a new pad; cleaning up before and after installing the new carpet; and any other relevant activity).
7. Prepare a bar chart for building an inground swimming pool. If you do not know the steps involved, ask a friend or a local contractor.
8. Contact a contractor and ask him or her whether he or she uses bar charts (they may be called *Gantt charts*). Ask about the main types of bar chart reports. Which groups of activities are included? Ask if the bar charts are prepared as bar charts or as an output for a CPM schedule.
9. To demonstrate the concept of summary bars, draw bar charts for building a new home. Use a few summary activities, such as laying the foundation, putting a slab on a grade, framing, doing electrical work,

putting in the plumbing, installing an HVAC (heating, ventilation, and air-conditioning) system, putting on the roof, installing doors and windows, and doing the finishing. You may need to show some of these activities (e.g., the electrical work, the plumbing) as discontinuous bars because you start the activity (do a rough-in), stop, then return and finish it. Take the chart to a specialized contractor and expand one of these bars. Expanding a summary bar means breaking it down into the detailed activities that compose the summary activity. For example, you can expand Framing to Installing First-Floor Bottom Plates, Installing First-Floor Studs, Installing First-Floor Blocking, Installing First-Floor Top Plates, Installing Second-Floor Joists, and so forth. Note that the total duration of the summary activity must equal the total duration (not necessarily the algebraic summation) of the detailed activities underneath the summary activity.

Basic Networks

Four Seasons Hotel & Tower, Miami, Florida. Courtesy of Smith Aerial Photos, Maitland, Florida.

DEFINITION AND INTRODUCTION

A **network** is a logical and chronological graphic representation of the activities (and events) composing a project. Network diagrams are basically of two types: arrow networks and node networks. Arrow networks were more popular in the 1960s and 1970s, then precedence diagrams (an advanced form of node diagrams) became the choice for network scheduling.

Network scheduling has revolutionized the management of construction projects. It has provided management with a more objective and scientific methodology than simply relying completely on the project manager's personal skills.

ARROW NETWORKS

Arrow networks are also called the **arrow diagramming method (ADM), activity on arrow (AOA) networks,** or the **I–J method** (because activities are defined by the *from node*, I, and the *to node*, J). In this book, we use the term *arrow networks*. Following are seven examples of arrow networks.

EXAMPLE 3.1

Draw the arrow network for the project given next.

ACTIVITY	IPA[a]
A	—
B	A
C	A
D	B
E	C, D

---

[a]Immediately preceding activity.

Solution

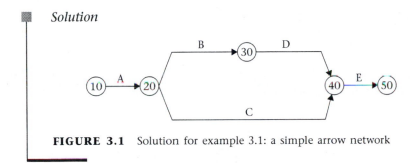

FIGURE 3.1   Solution for example 3.1: a simple arrow network

Brief Explanation

In the preceding example, the project has only 5 activities, each represented by an arrow. Each arrow connects two nodes (depicted by circles with numbers in them): the *from node* and the *to node*. These nodes represent events: an **event** is a point in time when an activity starts or ends. In computer software, events with significance can be created as **milestones,** * and they are either *start milestones,* such as Notice to Proceed, or *finish milestones,* such as Substantial Completion.

The Logic

In example 3.1, activity A starts the project. Activities B and C follow, but independently. In reality, depending on the availability of resources and other factors, activities B and C may occur concurrently, overlap, or occur consecutively. However, both B and C cannot start till A is complete. Activity D must wait till activity B is complete. Once both C and D are done, activity E can start. The end of activity E means the end of the project. Activity A is considered a **predecessor activity** to activities B and C. Similarly, activity B is a predecessor to activity D. Conversely, we can say that activities B and C are **successor activities** to activity A, activity D is a successor to activity B, and so on. Activity A has successors but no predecessors. Activity E has predecessors but no successors. All other activities have both successors and predecessors.

As mentioned previously, a node in an arrow network represents an event or a point in time. This event is the starting or ending point of an activity (or

*Primavera Project Planner, or P3, has two types of events: milestones and flags.

activities). Node 10 represents the start of activity A (and hence the start of the project). Node 20 represents the end of activity A and the start of activities B and C. Node 30 represents the end of activity B and the start of activity D. Node 40 represents the end of activities C and D, and the start of activity E. Node 50 represents the end of activity E and the project.

Notation

The arrow diagram is also called the *I–J method* because each activity is identified by the two nodes that define its start and end. For example, activity A is also known as 10–20, B as 20–30, C as 20–40, and so on.

Dummy Activities

Let us consider a simple project.

EXAMPLE 3.2

Draw the arrow network for the project given next.

ACTIVITY	IPA
A	—
B	A
C	A
D	B, C

Solution A

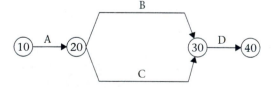

FIGURE 3.2a   Improper solution for example 3.2

The main problem in this case is that both activities B and C start from node 20 and finish at node 30. Hence, both are identified as 20–30.

This situation will create an identity problem. To solve this problem, we introduce a fictitious activity and an additional node. This fictitious activity is called a **dummy activity,** d. It is treated in the critical path method (CPM) calculations (discussed in chapter 4) and in computer programs as a real activity even though it is not.

Solution B

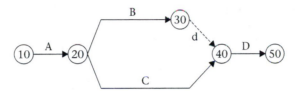

FIGURE 3.2b   Proper solution for example 3.2

In this case, activity B is identified as 20–30, whereas activity C is 20–40. Note that the dummy could be inserted in different positions, as shown next. They all serve the same purpose.

Other Solutions

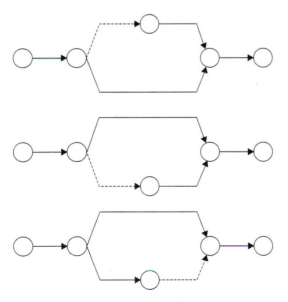

FIGURE 3.2c   Other proper solutions for example 3.2

Let us now consider another example.

EXAMPLE 3.3

Draw the arrow network for the project given next.

ACTIVITY	IPA
A	—
B	A
C	A
D	B
E	B, C

The problem in this example is how to draw the preceding logic correctly. We need to show that activity E depends on both activities B and C, whereas activity D depends on only activity B. The sole solution is also a dummy activity, as shown next. Figures 3.3a and 3.3b are examples of improper logic. Figure 3.3c shows the proper logic.

Solutions

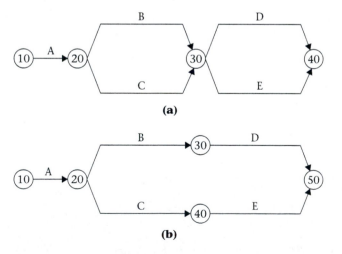

FIGURE 3.3 (a) Improper solution, (b) another improper solution, and

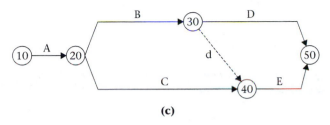

(c)

FIGURE 3.3   (*continued*) (c) proper solution for example 3.3

We can complicate example 3.3 just a little with one change.

EXAMPLE 3.4

Draw the arrow network for the project given next.

ACTIVITY	IPA
A	—
B	A
C	A
D	B
E	B, C
F	C

Solution
The solution requires two dummy activities (or simply *dummies*).

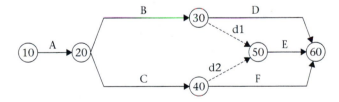

FIGURE 3.4   Solution for example 3.4

From the previous examples, we can define a dummy activity as a fictitious activity inserted in an arrow network to maintain proper logic or distinguish activities' identities. Two more examples demonstrate the need for
dummy activities to straighten up the logic.

EXAMPLE 3.5

Draw the arrow network for the project given next.

ACTIVITY	IPA
A	—
B	—
C	—
D	A, B
E	B, C

Solution

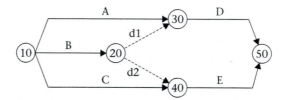

FIGURE 3.5   Solution for example 3.5

EXAMPLE 3.6

Draw the arrow network for the project given next.

ACTIVITY	IPA
A	—
B	—
C	—
D	A
E	A, B
F	A, B, C

Solution

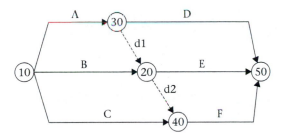

FIGURE 3.6 Solution for example 3.6

In larger projects, dummy activities may not only increase the number of activities, but also complicate the schedule. This fact is one of the main disadvantages of arrow networks. The following example demonstrates this disadvantage.

EXAMPLE 3.7

Draw the arrow network for the project given next.

ACTIVITY	IPA	ACTIVITY	IPA
A	—	H	C, D
B	A	I	D
C	A	J	E, F, G
D	A	K	F, G, H
E	B	L	H, I
F	B, C	M	K, L
G	C		

Solution

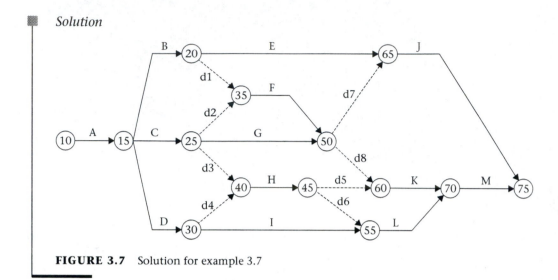

FIGURE 3.7   Solution for example 3.7

Redundancies

It is interesting to note that when you are building an arrow network, you can have not only a logically improper network, but also a proper one with redundant dummy activities. This fact is especially true for a complicated project. Redundant dummy activities are not logically improper: they are just redundant (Figure 3.8). (*Note:* Students may lose points on exams for having redundant dummies.)

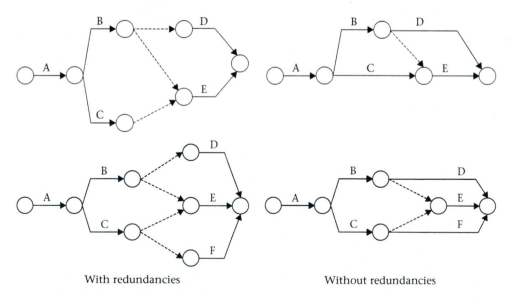

With redundancies   Without redundancies

FIGURE 3.8   Redundant versus nonredundant dummy activities

NODE NETWORKS

Node networks are also called **activity on node (AON) networks.** In node networks, we use a different notation for representation: a node represents an activity. Nodes (activities) are connected with arrows (or lines) that represent the logical relationships. For example, let us redraw Figures 3.1 and 3.2 as node diagrams (see Figures 3.9 and 3.10). There is no need in the node diagram for dummy activities. A scheduling novice can draw a node diagram much more easily than an arrow diagram.

For aesthetic reasons only, we like to start any network with one node (whether this node represents an event or an activity) and end it with one node. Doing so may require one or two fictitious activities in node diagrams that start or end with more than one activity. We call these activities *PS (project start)* and *PF (project finish)*, displayed as regular triangular or diamond-shaped nodes. For example, let us redo Figures 3.3 through 3.6 as node

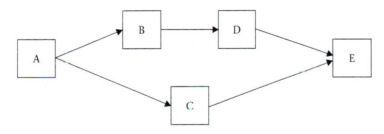

FIGURE 3.9   Solution for example 3.1 as a node network

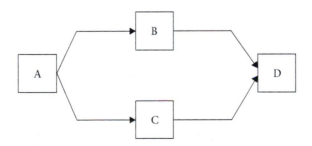

FIGURE 3.10   Solution for example 3.2 as a node network

diagrams. Figures 3.11 through 3.14 show the results. As shown in Figure 3.15, by using a node diagram, we can solve example 3.7 without using the annoying eight dummy activities.

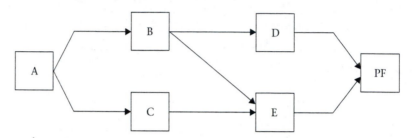

FIGURE 3.11   Solution for example 3.3 as a node network

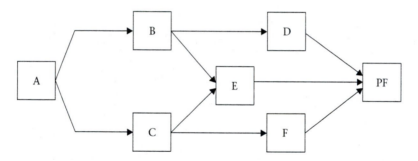

FIGURE 3.12   Solution for example 3.4 as a node network

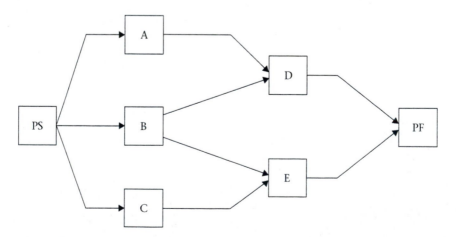

FIGURE 3.13   Solution for example 3.5 as a node network

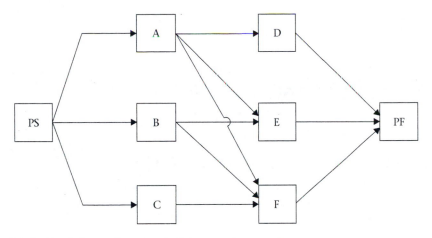

FIGURE 3.14   Solution for example 3.6 as a node network

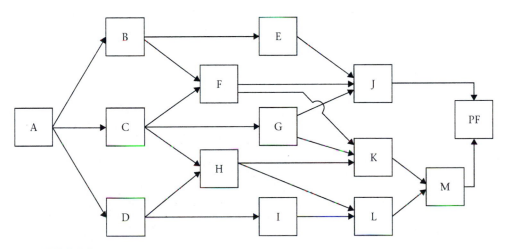

FIGURE 3.15   Solution for example 3.7 as a node network

Lags and Leads

In some situations, an activity cannot start until a certain time after the end of its predecessor. A typical example is concrete operations. Let us imagine this sequence:

1. Form the concrete column.
2. Install steel reinforcement (commonly known as *rebar*).
3. Place the concrete.

4. Wait for the concrete to set (attain sufficient strength).

5. Strip the forms.

Note that the fourth step is not a "real" activity, to which we must allocate resources and a budget. It is merely a waiting period, commonly known as a **lag.** A node network can accommodate such a lag if we simply put the lag on the relationship between Place Concrete and Strip Forms, as shown in Figure 3.16a. This 3-day lag means a minimum waiting period of 3 days. Waiting less than 3 days violates the preceding logic, whereas waiting more than 3 days does not violate the logic. In some networks, the lag number is put inside a little box for better visibility.

Thus, a *lag* is defined as a minimum waiting period between a start (or an end) of an activity and the end (or start) of its predecessor. Arrow networks cannot accommodate a lag. The only solution in such networks is to treat it as a real activity with a real duration, no resources, and a $0 budget (Figure 3.16b).

With arrow networks, an activity was defined as "a unique unit of the project which can be described within prescribed limits of time" (R. B. Harris 1978, 18) or "a time-consuming task" (Callahan, Quackenbush, and Rowings 1992, 29). Note that these definitions include "waiting activities" that have no real work or resources. With the current popularity of node (precedence) networks, the author of this book suggests changing the definition to "a resource-consuming task" since waiting periods are treated as lags rather than real activities.

The term **lead** simply means a negative lag. It is seldom used in construction. Lags and leads are covered in chapter 4, when we discuss CPM calculations.

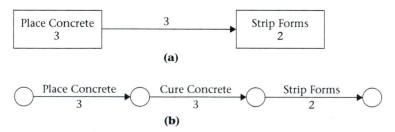

FIGURE 3.16   (a) A lag in a node network; (b) a lag in an arrow network

Recommendations for Proper Node Diagram Drawing

1. Since nodes in arrow diagrams (events) are always drawn as circles, we like to draw nodes in node diagrams (activities) as squares (rectangles). Doing so not only eliminates confusion between an arrow network and a node network, but, more important, defines the "start side" of an activity and the "end side." This distinction is important in precedence networks, which are discussed in chapter 5.

2. Do not connect nodes (in node diagrams) from the top or bottom (Figure 3.17). Connect sides only. The left side represents the start side, and the right side represents the end side.

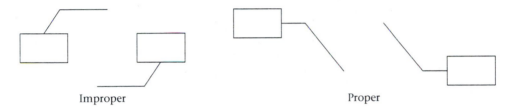

Improper   Proper

FIGURE 3.17   Node connection in node networks

3. Although networks are not time-scaled, in general, they should be designed from left to right in an almost chronological order. Try to avoid the situation shown in Figure 3.18.

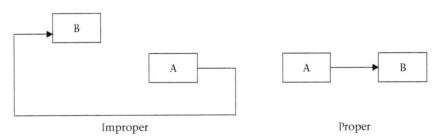

Improper   Proper

FIGURE 3.18   Node order in node networks

4. Do not combine relationship lines (Figure 3.19). These relationships are independent from their start to their end.

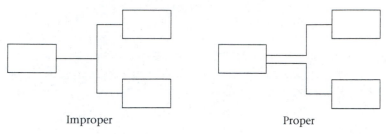

Improper   Proper

FIGURE 3.19   Relationship lines in node networks

5. Try to minimize line crossings (Figure 3.20). When two lines (relationships) must intersect, make a "jump" on one of them to indicate that they do not intersect or meet.

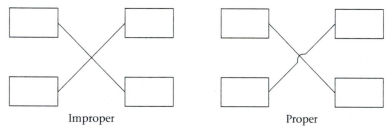

Improper   Proper

FIGURE 3.20   Intersecting relationship lines in node networks

6. In many cases of hand drawing, you will need to redraw the network after your first attempt. Although your first attempt may be logically proper, it may look awkward and confusing. Redraw it to minimize line crossing and relocate activities to be as near as possible to their predecessors and successors.

In most of the preceding points, the word *improper* may not mean "incorrect." However, following the preceding guidelines ensures a better and clearer drawing.

COMPARISON OF ARROW AND NODE NETWORKS

From our discussion of arrow and node diagrams, we find that node networks have the following five advantages over arrow networks:

1. Node networks are easier to draw.
2. Node networks do not require dummy activities to fix the activity identity problem.

3. Node networks do not require dummy activities to straighten up the logic.
4. Node networks can accommodate lags between activities without the addition of more activities.
5. In addition to the preceding advantages, node diagrams can be taken to an advanced stage in which they represent not just the traditional finish-to-start relationship, but also three other relationships (start to start, finish to finish, and start to finish). This subject is discussed in detail in chapter 5. However, we mention it here as one more advantage of node networks. Arrow networks can represent only the traditional finish-to-start relationship.

In fairness to arrow networks, they have one important advantage over node networks: they depict activities as well as events. Node networks do not contain provisions for events. This point is circumvented in node diagrams by creating milestone activities (such as in computer programs) with zero duration to represent important events such as substantial completion of a facility. In some cases, milestones in node networks may work better than event nodes in arrow networks. Milestones are tied to the start or end of the specific activity or activities we are considering. An event node in arrow networks may be tied to the end or start of two or more activities when we are focusing on just one of these events. To understand the point, consider the event of the completion of activity K in example 3.7. This event is shown in the arrow network of Figure 3.7 as node 70. However, node 70 also represents the completion of activity L, which may be later or earlier than the completion of activity K. Thus, the calculated event time for node 70 may not be accurate. In node networks, we create a milestone activity and tie it directly to the end of activity K. In this case, it will reflect the event of completion of activity K only.

NETWORKS VERSUS BAR CHARTS

When comparing bar charts with networks, we find that networks have three advantages over bar charts:

1. Networks show logic (i.e., the relationships among activities). Bar charts do not.
2. Networks can better represent large and complicated projects.
3. Networks can estimate, or predict, the completion date of the project, or other dates, on the basis of mathematical calculations of the CPM.

Bar charts predict the completion of the project, or other dates, on the basis of the creator's graphic skills.

In contrast, bar charts have these five advantages:

1. Bar charts are time scaled (i.e., the length of the activity bar represents the time duration of the activity). Both the node, in the node networks, and the arrow, in the arrow networks, are not time-scaled.
2. Bar charts are simple to prepare.
3. Bar charts are easy to understand.
4. Bar charts are more acceptable for presentation, especially for field people and people who are unfamiliar with the CPM.
5. Bar charts can be loaded with more information, such as cash-flow diagrams and man-hours. This advantage is partially a by-product of being time scaled.

Effective Use of Bar Charts with the CPM

Bar charts have an effective weapon CPM networks do not have: power of presentation. As mentioned in point 4 in the preceding list, bar charts can be used effectively for—mainly—two types of presentations:

1. *Presentation to field people.* The project manager produces customized reports that include only a small group of the project activities (e.g., bar chart reports for subcontractors for their particular activities, or for the activities that are supposed to start in the next 2 weeks). You can also isolate a group of activities that are to be done at a specific area of the project, or only critical activities. With the use of activity codes and the power of computer software, there is no limit for such uses.
2. *Presentation to high-level staff.* CEOs and senior managers are usually not concerned with the progress at the individual activity level. They like to get an overall idea about the project and the main components. Roll-up or summary bar charts have become a popular option in computer software. A group of activities is rolled up or summarized according to a common factor such as area, responsibility, phase, or the company's **work breakdown structure (WBS).** Instead of

looking at hundreds or thousands of activities, the top-level executive would be looking at a few bars that give him or her the overall picture of the progress of the project.

Time-Scaled Logic Diagrams

Some scheduling software vendors tried to take the advantage of networks (logic, or relationships) and impose it on bar charts in what some persons called **time-scaled logic diagrams**. The result was more like spaghetti. Depicting all relationships not only complicated bar charts (which eliminates their main advantage), but also did not make the logic as clear as it is in networks. This experiment was followed—in the software industry—by adding enhancing options such as "show only critical relationships" or "show only driving relationships." In some simple cases, this approach may work as a good and acceptable solution.

CHAPTER 3 EXERCISES

1. What does a node mean in an arrow diagram?
2. What does an arrow mean in an arrow diagram?
3. What does a node mean in a node diagram?
4. What does a line mean in a node diagram?
5. What are the main differences between bar charts and networks?
6. What are the differences between arrow and node networks?
7. Arrow networks have another name; what is it? What is the reason behind this name?
8. What are the main advantages of node networks over arrow networks?
9. What is the main advantage of arrow networks over node networks? How was it overcome?
10. What are *time-scaled logic diagrams*? Discuss their practicality.
11. What are the main advantages of networks over bar charts? How did bar charts manage to stay popular despite the advantages of networks?
12. Draw both the arrow network and the node network for the following project.

ACTIVITY	IPA
A	—
B	A
C	A
D	B
E	B, C

13. Draw both the arrow network and the node network for the following project.

ACTIVITY	IPA
A	—
B	—
C	A
D	A, B
E	C, D

14. Draw both the arrow network and the node network for the following project.

ACTIVITY	IPA
A	—
B	A
C	A
D	A
E	B
F	B, C
G	D, E, F

15. Draw both the arrow network and the node network for the following project.

ACTIVITY	IPA	ACTIVITY	IPA
A	—	F	D
B	—	G	D, E
C	—	H	C, F, G
D	A, B	I	C, G
E	B	J	H, I

16. Draw both the arrow network and the node network for the following project.

ACTIVITY	IPA	ACTIVITY	IPA
A	—	H	C, D
B	A	I	D
C	A	J	E, F, G
D	A	K	F, G, H
E	B	L	H, I
F	B, C	M	K, L
G	C		

17. Draw both the arrow network and the node network for the following project.

ACTIVITY	IPA	ACTIVITY	IPA
A	—	H	D, E
B	—	I	D, E, F
C	A	J	F
D	A, B	K	C, H, I
E	A, B	L	I, J
F	B	M	I
G	C	N	G, K

18. Draw both the arrow network and the node network for the following project.

ACTIVITY	IPA	ACTIVITY	IPA
A	—	L	E, G
B	A	M	F, G, H
C	A	N	F, G, H, I
D	A	O	H, I
E	A	P	M, N, O
F	B	Q	K, L
G	B, C	R	L, M
H	B, C, D	S	J, P
I	C, D	T	Q
J	E	U	Q, R
K	F	V	S, T, U

19. Convert the following arrow network into a node network.

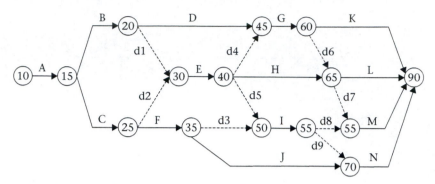

20. Find and correct the errors and redundancies in the following arrow network.

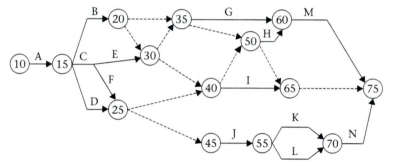

21. Convert the following node network into an arrow network.

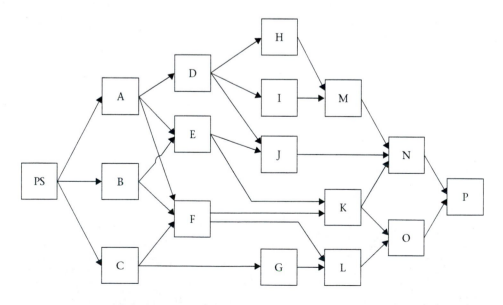

The Critical Path Method (CPM)

SR 429 (Western Beltway) ramp over Florida's turnpike, Ocoee, Florida. Courtesy of URS Corporation, Tampa, Florida.

INTRODUCTION

Suppose you meet with two friends and decide to go on a hunting trip. One friend will go to get the food, the other will go to get the hunting gear, and you will go to prepare your Jeep. After each person finishes his or her assignment, you will drive together to the hunting location. Also suppose that the first activity (getting the food) will require 2 hours; the second activity (getting the hunting gear), 3 hours; and the third (getting the Jeep ready), 4 hours. If all three activities would start at 8:00 a.m. (when each of you would leave to perform your task), the following activity (driving to the hunting location) could not start until all three of you had returned (i.e., all three preparation activities were complete). If everything would work according to plan, the first person would return with the food at 10:00 a.m.; the second, with the hunting gear, at 11:00 a.m.; and you, with the Jeep ready, at 12:00 p.m. (Figure 4.1).

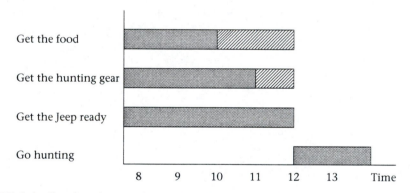

FIGURE 4.1   Bar chart for introductory hunting trip example

Now, ask yourself the following question: Which activity "drives," or controls, the schedule? The answer is the third activity (preparing the Jeep). Any delay in your return will delay the trip (past 12:00 p.m.). In contrast, your first friend will have 2 extra hours to "waste," and your second friend, 1 extra hour. They could choose to use the extra time however they like. For instance, they could do the following:

- Get an early start, finish early, then take a break
- Get a late start (10:00 a.m. for the first person and 9:00 a.m. for the second) and finish at 12:00 p.m.
- Take breaks between work periods

We will call this extra time **float.** Your friends will have to watch their time carefully so that they do not waste more time than the float that they have: 2 hours for the first person and 1 hour for the second. Any delay past these float times will result in a delay in the entire schedule. You, however, have no float. You are running on a tight schedule. Your activity is *critical*. This scenario provides a simplified example of the *critical path method (CPM)*.

STEPS REQUIRED TO SCHEDULE A PROJECT

For the planning, execution, and completion of a project, many steps are required that may not be part of scheduling. In this chapter, we discuss the role of the scheduler given that the project has been defined (and designed in most cases). Some schedules (especially those for **fast-track projects,** in which construction starts before design finishes) may include design steps as part of the schedule. In general, the preparation of a CPM schedule includes the following four steps:

1. *Determine the work activities*. Any project, no matter how large or small, must be divided into smaller entities, called *activities*, or *tasks*. An activity is a unique, definable element of work. In this step, there is no absolutely correct or incorrect breakdown. You may give the same project to 10 schedulers, and they may devise 10 significantly different breakdowns. In this regard, there are two schools of thought:

   a. *Restrict the number of activities for the simplicity of the project schedule.* In this case, activities become "major" components. However, there is a practical—and sometimes contractual—limit on how large an activity may be. For instance, it is impractical to have Concrete Operations as one activity with 300 days' duration. In addition, in many contracts, a maximum limit is set on the duration of any activity, usually about 14 to 20 days.

   b. *Break the project down into small activities.* This approach will result in a large number of activities. The main advantage of this approach is better control of the schedule during execution. You can easily tell the status (percent complete) of a small activity such as Place Concrete for Spread Footings No. 23 better and more objectively than you can for a large activity such as Building Foundation. The main disadvantage of having many activities is the additional work and hassle. However, this disadvantage may not be as important with the use of computers. Furthermore, you can roll up a group of activities into a major activity, as discussed in chapter 3.

Each activity must be given a unique identity (ID). In this book, we deal mostly with samples of small projects. We use the alphabet (A, B, C, etc.) as IDs for activities. Real-life projects may comprise hundreds—perhaps thousands—of activities. The ID must be chosen to follow a certain pattern consistently. In many cases, the breakdown must be coded according to the company's policy.

One way to break down a project is by using the **work breakdown structure (WBS).** The WBS is defined as a task-oriented, detailed breakdown of activities that organizes, defines, and graphically displays the total work to be accomplished to achieve the final objectives of a project. The WBS breaks the project down into progressively detailed levels. Each descending level represents an increasingly detailed definition of a project component. An example of the WBS can be seen in Figure 4.2. In construction scheduling, the components at the lowest WBS level are used as activities to build the project schedule. As mentioned previously, activities may be rolled up for summarization purposes.

2. *Determine activity durations.* Techniques for estimating **activity duration** vary from one situation to another, depending on the type of work, the estimator, and other factors. Most activity **durations** can be estimated as follows:

$$\text{Duration} = \text{Total quantity/Crew productivity.}$$

For example, for 10,000 CY (cubic yards) of excavation and a crew that averages 800 CY per day, the following is true:

$$\text{Duration} = 10{,}000 \text{ CY}/800 \text{ CY per day} = 12.5 \text{ days.}$$

This information could come from the project team (project manager, project superintendent), who receives feedback from field crew leaders; from the estimating department; or from other sources (e.g., subcontractors). It is given to the scheduler with the project manager's approval. Durations are, by no means, carved in stone. They are based on previous experiences, with adjustments for current conditions

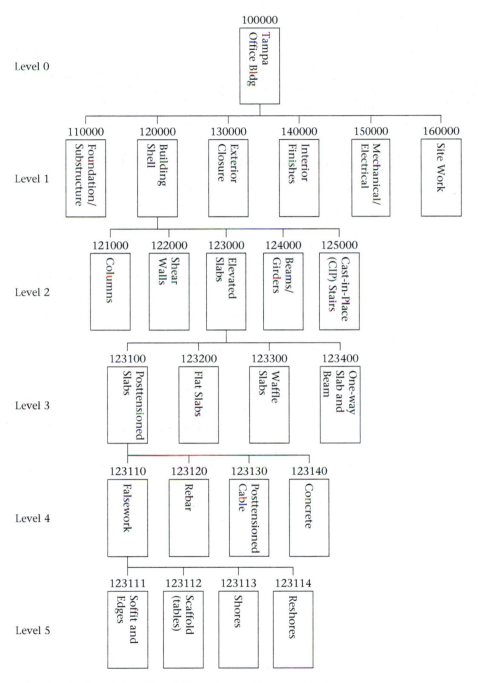

FIGURE 4.2 Sample work breakdown structure (WBS)

(such as weather conditions, design complexity, soil type, etc.). They are also subject to the crew size and the number of crews, if more than one. The durations of some activities are totally subjective and left to the project manager and the technical team, such as the mechanical or electrical repair team, to "guesstimate."

In most construction projects, durations are calculated in **workdays,** which usually, but not always, follow a 5-day work-week. In some cases, the project, or only certain crews, follow a 6- or 7-day workweek. In some other countries, a 6-day workweek may be the norm. In others, such as those in the Middle East, a workweek starts on Saturday, not Monday. The scheduler must be aware of such **calendars.**

The scheduler must also account for **nonworkdays,** such as holidays, rain days, shutdowns, and the like. The contract usually specifies official holidays and the allowed number of **rain days.** Rain days represent the number of days (per month) that work on the project is expected to be suspended because of weather delays. This prediction is usually calculated on the basis of past meteorological data for the location. It does not include unusual weather and disasters. (Delays due to unusual weather or disasters are discussed in chapter 12). The distribution of this time allowance is discussed in chapter 10.

Although the workday is the most-used **calendar unit** in construction projects, other units of time, such as the hour, the week, or the month, are not unthinkable. Industrial projects may have to be scheduled by the hour, especially with multiple-shift schedules. The scheduler, along with the management team leaders, must decide on the unit of time before preparing the schedule because changing the unit of time after the project starts is extremely difficult and confusing and can lead to unnoticeable errors.

3. *Determine logical relationships.* Again, this step is a technical matter. The scheduler should obtain this information from project managers and technical team leaders. Logical relationships should not be confused with **constraints:**

    a. A **logical relationship** exists between two activities when the start of one activity (or finish, as is explained in chapter 5) depends *physically* on the finish (or start) of another activity. For example, you cannot place the concrete until the formwork and reinforcement are erected. You cannot hang the drywall until framing is done.

b. A **resource constraint** (or restriction) is when you can theoretically do two tasks at the same time, but you have enough resources (labor, equipment) for only one activity at a time.

c. Another constraint is when an activity is subject to a (mostly subjective) constraint such as approval of an owner or a government agency or funding availability. Be careful not to confuse this type of constraint with a logical relationship. Typically, a project has few constraints of this type.

4. *Draw the* **logic network,** *and perform the CPM calculations.* If you are using a computer program, it will perform these functions for you, provided you have input the correct data. In this step, you will determine the calculated finish date of the project, the critical path, and the available float for all noncritical activities. It is important to check the input and the output and not to rely on the computer totally.

In most construction projects, subcontractors are involved, and their input into the schedule is important. The **schedule** is typically one topic discussed in preconstruction meetings of the owner, the general contractor (GC), and major subcontractors. Often, the GC provides an opportunity for the major subcontractors to supply him or her with schedules for work so that he or she can incorporate them into the overall schedule. Alternatively, the GC may create an overall schedule, then give it to the subcontractors for their approval (this topic is discussed further in chapter 10).

ADDITIONAL STEPS

The preceding four steps make up the "backbone" of the CPM. Following are four additional steps that are essential for a good, accurate, and successful schedule:

5. *Review and analyze the schedule.* First, review the logic and make sure every activity has the correct predecessors and no redundant relationships. Common errors are as follows:

a. *Wrong relationship.* A wrong relationship is when the relationship is connected to the wrong activity or to the appropriate activity but at the wrong end (e.g., you connect the end of an activity when the relationship is start to start).

b. *Missing relationship.* A missing relationship is when a predecessor of an activity is simply not shown. The possibility of this type of error is why we like to start a project with one activity and finish it with one activity. Computer programs such as Primavera Project Planner list all activities with either no predecessors or no successors. We typically like to see only one of each. Project managers and schedulers look at excessive float (explained later) as a red flag. Such float usually—but not always—indicates an activity not tied to any other activity, so the computer program gives it leeway till the end of the project.

c. *Redundant relationship.* When, for example, C requires B and B requires A, if you draw A and B as predecessors of C, A is a redundant predecessor for C (Figure 4.3a).

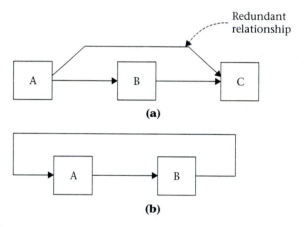

FIGURE 4.3   Common scheduling errors: (a) redundant relationship; (b) logic loop

d. *Logic loop.* A **logic loop** is when you leave a point on the network, then return to it later (e.g., A requires B, but B requires A) (Figure 4.3b). This error terminates the calculations in any CPM program. The author of this book strongly recommends that when drawing (or inputting) the relationships, you do so from one side only. This means looking at either predecessors or successors; not both at the same time. The author personally prefers dealing with predecessors. When reviewing the logic, you may look at both ends of an activity for accuracy of the logic.

6. *Implement the schedule.* Implementing the schedule means taking the scheduling from paper to execution. This step is important for fulfillment of the schedule. Every participating party must receive correct information at the appropriate time. Too little or too much information may be counterproductive. Three important points should be noted: First, the schedule must be realistic and fairly accurate. Second, the upper managers must take it seriously. Third, such implementation and commitment must continue throughout the project.

7. *Monitor and control the schedule.* As defined in chapter 1, *project control* means comparing the **baseline** (what was planned or what was supposed to have been done) with what has actually been done, analyzing any deviation from the baseline, and taking corrective action whenever and wherever needed. The main difference between the two terms (*monitor* and *control*) is the corrective action. *Monitoring* includes observing and reporting, and perhaps analysis. *Control* adds corrective action to this definition. The two terms are mentioned because the schedule may be monitored by the owner or the project management (PM) consultant. These two parties have no power to take direct corrective action during execution of the project. Only the party who is executing the work (usually the GC and subcontractors) can do control. As in the last step, keeping open communication channels among all involved parties and disseminating appropriate information are extremely important.

   An important part of the control effort is **forecasting.** Forecasting is done mostly by extrapolating actual performance for the remaining portion of the project. When actual performance is below the baseline, forecasting is used more as a warning. For example, the project manager may say, "We are 20% complete for the project and we are $10,000 over budget. If we don't make an adjustment, we'll finish the project $50,000 in the red."

8. *Revise the database and record feedback.* This process is continuous and iterative. All cost and time estimates for activities are based on past experience. This past experience must be documented in a well-organized, easy-to-retrieve fashion. Every new cycle should be a little more accurate than the previous one. Suppose you are estimating your new job on the basis of the past three jobs. After finishing this job and

inputting the new results, your database now has four jobs, and the next job will be based on the four previous jobs, and so on.

In addition to documenting and organizing, you must record any unusual results and explain any adjustment. For example, your productivity for a certain activity may be significantly below normal because of extreme weather, sticky soil, hard rock, equipment failure, low morale as a result of an accident, or some other reason. Your productivity may be above average because of an unusually "lucky"* work environment. Unusual recordings must be adjusted or normalized. If the job being estimated is expected to be completed under unusual circumstances, the estimate must be adjusted accordingly.

RESOURCE ALLOCATION AND LEVELING

In addition to the eight steps just discussed, another step may be implemented for a comprehensive approach to scheduling as part of project management:

9. *Implement resource allocation and leveling.* This topic is discussed in detail in chapter 6. For now, a definition of the concept will suffice. **Resources** in this context include labor, equipment, and materials. **Resource allocation** means simply assigning the correct amount of resources to each activity. **Resource leveling** is simply trying to maintain uniform daily use of a resource (or resources) for the entire life cycle of the project. The objectives of this step are as follows:

   a. To link scheduling with estimating and accounting. At any point in the project, you should be able to tell the total budget, the amount spent so far, an **estimate to complete (ETC),** and other financial criteria for each activity and for the entire project. You may also link spending to cost accounting.

   b. To improve the efficiency of resources (particularly labor and equipment) used by the process of leveling.

---

*We teach that good results and smooth, flawless work is no accident or coincidence. However, the term *lucky* is used in this instance to emphasize the reality of estimation.

BEGINNING-OF-DAY OR END-OF-DAY CONVENTION

In this book, for mathematical computations, and for the sake of simplicity, we follow the **end-of-day convention:** any date mentioned for an activity means the end of that day. In this convention, projects usually start at the beginning of day 1, which becomes the end of day 0. Almost all authors use this convention. Computer software, however, is more sophisticated: the start date follows the **beginning-of-day convention,** and the finish date follows the end-of-day convention. These conventions are explained further in the following examples.

THE CPM EXPLAINED THROUGH EXAMPLES

Example 4.1: Logic Networks and the CPM

EXAMPLE 4.1

Draw the logic network and perform the CPM calculations for the schedule shown next.

ACTIVITY	IPA[a]	DURATION[b]
A	—	5
B	A	8
C	A	6
D	B	9
E	B, C	6
F	C	3
G	D, E, F	1

[a]Immediately preceding activity.
[b]In days.

Solution: The Forward Pass
The project starts with activity A, which starts at the beginning of day 1 (end of day 0). It takes 5 days to finish activity A: it finishes on day

5 (end of the day). At this point, activities B and C can start. Activity B takes 8 days: it can start on day 5 (directly after activity A finishes), so it can finish as early as day 13. Similarly, activity C can finish on day 11 (5 + 6). Activity D follows activity B. It can start on day 13 (end of B) and end on day 22. Activity E must wait till *both* activities B and C are finished. Activity C finishes on day 11, but activity B does not finish till day 13. Thus, activity E cannot start till day 13. With 6 days' duration, activity E can then finish on day 19. Activity F depends on activity C only. Thus, it can start on day 11 and finish on day 14. The last activity, G, cannot start till activities D, E, and F are finished. Through simple observation, we can see that activity G cannot start till day 22 (when the last activity of D, E, and F finishes). Activity G takes 1 day, so it can finish on day 23. Figure 4.4 shows the completed logic network.

For this example, we have calculated two types of dates:

1) The expected completion date of the project: day 23.
2) The earliest date when each activity can start and finish. These dates are called the **early start (ES)** and the **early finish (EF)** dates for each activity. As we will soon learn, an activity cannot start earlier than its ES date and cannot finish earlier than its EF date, but it *may* start or finish *later* than these dates.

In mathematical terms, the ES time for activity j (ES_j) is as follows:

$$ES_j = \max(EF_i) \quad\dotfill\quad (4.1)$$

where (EF_i) represents the EF times for all preceding activities.

Likewise, the EF time for activity j (EF_j) is as follows:

$$EF_j = ES_j + Dur_j \quad\dotfill\quad (4.2)$$

where Dur_j is the duration of activity j.

The **forward pass** is defined as *the process of navigating through a network from start to finish and calculating the **early dates** for each activity and the completion date of the project.*

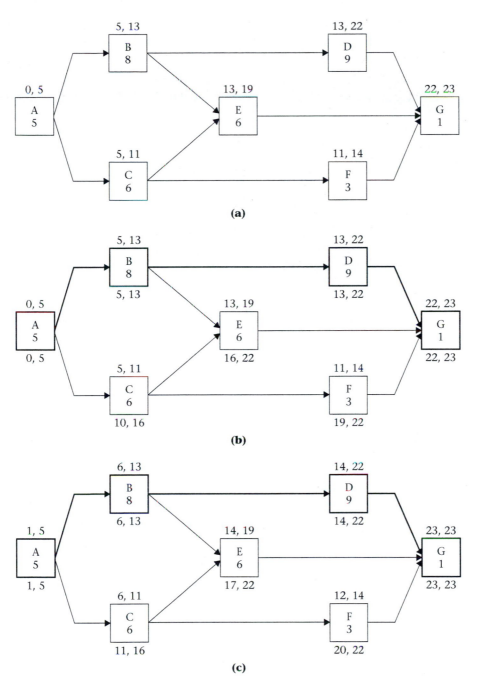

FIGURE 4.4   Completed logic network: (a) forward pass; (b) forward and backward passes; (c) computer generated

■ *Solution: The Backward Pass*

Now let us start from the end of the project and work our way back to the start. We already know the end-of-project date: day 23. Activity G must finish by day 23. Its duration is only 1 day, so it must start no later than day 22 (23 − 1) so that it does not delay the project. Similarly, activities D, E, and F must finish no later than day 22 so that they will not delay activity G. Through simple computations, we can find their late start dates: activity F: 22 − 3 = 19; activity E: 22 − 6 = 16; and activity D: 22 − 9 = 13. Activity C must finish before activities E and F can start. Their late start dates are 16 and 19, respectively. Clearly, activity C must finish by the earlier of the two dates, day 16, so that it will not delay the start of activity E. Thus, its late start date is day 10 (16 − 6). Similarly, activity B must finish by the earlier of its successors' late start dates: day 13 for D and day 16 for E. Therefore, the late finish date for activity B is day 13 and its late start date is day 5 (13 − 8). The last activity (from the start) is A: it must finish by the earlier of the late start dates for activities B and C, which are day 5 for B and day 10 for C. Consequently, the late finish date for activity A is day 5, and its late start date is day 0 (5 − 5).

In mathematical terms, the *late finish* (*LF*) time for activity *j* (LF_j) is as follows:

$$LF_j = \min(LS_k) \quad \dots\dots\dots\dots\dots\dots\dots\dots\dots\dots\dots\dots \text{(4.3)}$$

where (LS_k) represents the late start times for all succeeding activities.

Likewise, the **late start (LS)** time for activity *j* (LS_j) is as follows:

$$LS_j = LF_j - Dur_j \quad \dots\dots\dots\dots\dots\dots\dots\dots\dots\dots\dots\dots \text{(4.4)}$$

The **backward pass** is defined as *the process of navigating through a network from finish to start and calculating the **late dates** for all activities. This pass, along with the forward-pass calculations, helps identify the critical path and the float for all activities.*

If we refer to Figure 4.4b, we can see that for some activities (light lines), the late dates (shown under the boxes) are larger (i.e., later) than their early dates (shown above the boxes). For other activities (thick lines), late and early dates are the same. For the second group, we can tell that these activities have strict start and finish dates. Any delay in them will result in a delay in the entire project. We call these activities *critical activities*. We call the continuous chain of critical activities from the start to the end of the project the **critical path.**

Other activities have some leeway. For example, activity C can start on day 5, 6, 7, 8, 9, or 10 without delaying the entire project. As mentioned previously, we call this leeway *float*.

There are several types of float. The simplest and most important type of float is **total float (TF)**:

$$TF = LS - ES \quad \text{or} \quad TF = LF - EF \quad \ldots\ldots\ldots\ldots\ldots\ldots (4.5)$$

If we tabulate the results, we get the following table (boldface activities are critical):

ACTIVITY	DURATION	ES	EF	LS	LF	TF
A	**5**	**0**	**5**	**0**	**5**	**0**
B	**8**	**5**	**13**	**5**	**13**	**0**
C	6	5	11	10	16	5
D	**9**	**13**	**22**	**13**	**22**	**0**
E	6	13	19	16	22	3
F	3	11	14	19	22	8
G	**1**	**22**	**23**	**22**	**23**	**0**

With the backward pass, we have calculated two types of data:

1. The late dates for all activities, which indicate the critical path
2. The amount of float for each noncritical activity

The CPM with Computer Software Programs

If we plot the previous CPM network by using one of the commercially available computer software programs, such as Primavera Project Planner or Microsoft (MS) Project, Figure 4.4c will be the result. The only difference between the network shown in Figure 4.4b and that shown in Figure 4.4c is the start dates because, as mentioned previously, these computer programs use the start of the day when calculating start dates and the end of the day when calculating finish dates. This approach affects the forward-pass and backward-pass calculations. Equations 4.1 through 4.4 are thus rewritten as follows:

$$ES_j = \max(EF_i) + 1 \quad \ldots\ldots\ldots\ldots\ldots\ldots\ldots\ldots\ldots (4.1)'$$

$$EF_j = ES_j + Dur_j - 1 \quad \ldots\ldots\ldots\ldots\ldots\ldots\ldots\ldots (4.2)'$$

$$LF_j = \min(LS_k) - 1 \quad \dots\dots\dots\dots\dots\dots\dots\dots\dots\dots\dots \quad (4.3)'$$

and

$$LS_j = LF_j - Dur_j + 1 \quad \dots\dots\dots\dots\dots\dots\dots\dots\dots\dots \quad (4.4)'$$

The Critical Path

If we think about the situation in the project we just scheduled, we will notice that activities A, B, D, and G are "driving" the schedule. These activities are critical because any delay in their start or finish will delay the entire project. For example, if activity B takes 9 days instead of 8 days, it will finish on day 14. Activity D can then start and will finish on day 23. Finally, activity G can start on day 23 and will finish on day 24, which is 1 day past the originally scheduled date. This delay in the project completion date may not occur with a delay (within certain limits) in other activities, such as C, E, or F. Project managers usually focus on the critical path because of its criticality and direct impact on the project finish date. Knowing not only which activities are critical and which are not, but also the impact of the delay of one activity on other activities and on the entire project is the crux of the principle of scheduling.

Following are six observations about the critical path:

1. In every network, at least one critical path must exist.
2. More than one critical path may exist. Multiple paths may share some activities.
3. Any critical path must be continuous from the start of the project till its end.
4. Unless a constraint is imposed (which is discussed later), a path cannot be partially critical. The entire path must be either critical or noncritical.
5. If all paths in a network must go through one particular activity, this activity must be critical (e.g., activities A and G in example 4.1).
6. Some people like to define the critical path as the path with zero float. This definition is correct only if no **imposed finish date** is used in the backward-pass calculations (again, this point is discussed later). However, our definition—the longest path in a network, from start to finish—is more appropriate because it is always true.

Definitions Pertaining to Example 4.1

Activity, or task. A basic unit of work as part of the total project that is easily measured and controlled. It is time and resource consuming.

Backward pass. The process of navigating through a network from end to start and calculating the late dates for each activity. The late dates (along with the early dates) determine the critical activities, the critical path, and the amount of float each activity has.

Critical activity. An activity on the critical path. Any delay in the start or finish of a critical activity will result in a delay in the entire project.

Critical path. The longest path in a network, from start to finish.

Early dates. The early start date and early finish date of an activity.

Early finish (EF). The earliest date on which an activity can finish without violating the logic.

Early start (ES). The earliest date on which an activity can start without violating the logic.

Event. A point in time marking a start or an end of an activity. In contrast to an activity, an event does not consume time or resources. In computer software, events with significance can be created as milestones, and they are either start milestones, such as Notice to Proceed, or finish milestones, such as Substantial Completion.

Forward pass. The process of navigating through a network from start to end and calculating the finish date for the entire project and the early dates for each activity.

Late dates. The late start date and late finish date of an activity.

Late finish (LF). The latest date on which an activity can finish without extending the project duration.

Late start (LS). The latest date on which an activity can start without extending the project duration.

Total float (TF). The maximum amount of time an activity can be delayed from its early start without delaying the entire project.

Examples 4.2 and 4.3: Node Diagrams and the CPM

EXAMPLE 4.2

Draw the node diagram and perform the CPM computations for the schedule shown next.

ACTIVITY	IPA	DURATION
A	—	2
B	A	6
C	A	10
D	A	4
E	B	7
F	B, C	5
G	C, D	3
H	E, F	5
I	G, H	2

Solutions

Performing forward and backward passes yields the solution shown in Figure 4.5. The critical path is A, C, F, H, I. Activities B, D, E, and G have total floats equal to 2, 13, 2, and 7, respectively.

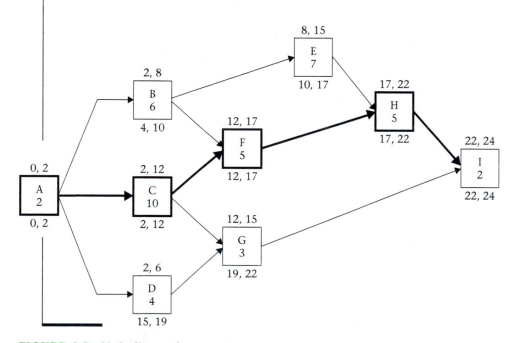

FIGURE 4.5   Node diagram for example 4.2

Free Float

Let us examine the impact that one activity may have on other activities when it consumes its total float or part of it. In example 4.2, if activity B is delayed by 1 day only and starts on day 3 (which is well within its available float), it will finish on day 9. (*Remember*: We always mean the end of the day.) Activity E then cannot start on its early start date (i.e., day 8). The earliest date E can start is day 9. If we delay activity B by 2 days, activity E cannot start till day 10 and thus becomes critical. This 1- or 2-day delay in the start of activity B will not affect the project completion date. However, if we delay activity B by more than 2 days, it will finish past day 10, which will affect the start of the critical activity H and thus delay the entire project. This discussion illustrates the concept of *total float*, which was defined previously as the maximum amount of time an activity can be delayed without delaying the entire project. Note, though, that this delay—within the total float—may (and did in this case) or may not delay the early start of the subsequent activities.

Now let us apply the same discussion to activity G. It has 7 days of total float. Delaying it by as many as 7 days will not affect the succeeding activity, I. The same argument applies to activity E, only with 2 days of total float.

Next, we discuss yet another type of total float. Consider the case of activity D. It has 13 days of total float. When we delay it by 1 or 2 days, for example, we notice that this delay does not affect the early start of the following activity, G, since G is waiting for the completion of activity C as well. However, when the delay of activity D exceeds 6 days, this observation changes. If we consider delaying activity D by 7 days, it finishes on day 13. Activity G then cannot start until day 13. It should finish on day 16, which will not delay activity I and the entire project. This 7-day delay in activity D delayed the early start of its successor (activity G) yet did not delay the entire project. We can increase this delay to 13 days (which is the total float for activity D) without affecting the completion date of the entire project but affecting the succeeding activity, G.

We can divide activity D's 13-day total float into two portions: The first 6 days will not delay its successor. This is called **free float (FF).** The other 7 days will cause a delay to its successor even though they will not delay the entire project. This is called **interfering float (Int. F).** We can look at the situation this way: Activities D and G share the 7-day interfering float. If the first activity in line uses it, it will be taken away from the next activity. Similarly, we can determine that activity B has no free float (total float is all interfering float). The free

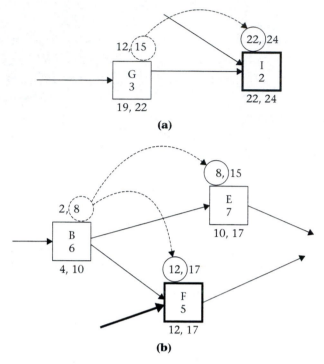

FIGURE 4.6 Free float with (a) one successor activity and (b) more than one successor activity

float of activity G equals its total float (no interfering float). To calculate free float, we need to compare the activity's early finish date with its successor's early start date. When there is only one successor activity (Figure 4.6a), the calculation is simple:

$$\text{Activity G's free float, } FF = 22 - 15 = 7 \text{ days}$$

When the activity has more than one successor (Figure 4.6b), you must pick the earliest early start date among the successors:

$$\text{Activity B's free float, } FF = \min(12, 8) - 8 = 0 \text{ days}$$

In general, *free float* is calculated by using the following equation:

$$FF_i = \min(ES_{i+1}) - EF_i$$

where min(ES_{i+1}) means the least (i.e., earliest) of the early start dates of succeeding activities.

EXAMPLE 4.3

Draw the node diagram and perform the CPM computations for the schedule shown next.

ACTIVITY	IPA	DURATION	ACTIVITY	IPA	DURATION
A	—	2	H	D	9
B	A	7	I	F, G	12
C	A	10	J	F	5
D	A	4	K	E, J	5
E	B	6	L	G, H	6
F	B, C	5	M	F, H	4
G	C, D	8	N	I, K, L, M	3

Solution

Performing forward and backward passes yields the solution shown in Figure 4.7.

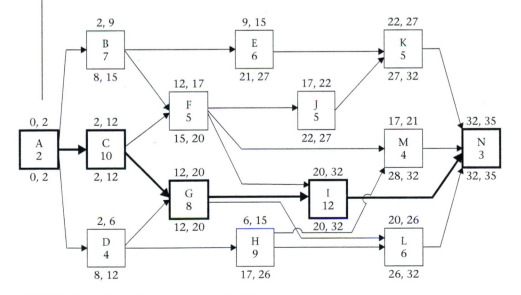

FIGURE 4.7 Node diagram for example 4.3

■ Performing the CPM calculations, we find the early dates, late dates, total float (TF), and free float (FF) for all activities, as shown in the following table.

ACTIVITY	DURATION	ES	EF	LS	LF	TF	FF
A	2	0	2	0	2	0	0
B	7	2	9	8	15	6	0
C	10	2	12	2	12	0	0
D	4	2	6	8	12	6	0
E	6	9	15	21	27	12	7
F	5	12	17	15	20	3	0
G	8	12	20	12	20	0	0
H	9	6	15	17	26	11	2
I	12	20	32	20	32	0	0
J	5	17	22	22	27	5	0
K	5	22	27	27	32	5	5
L	6	20	26	26	32	6	6
M	4	17	21	28	32	11	11
N	3	32	35	32	35	0	0

Definitions Pertaining to Examples 4.2 and 4.3

Free float may be defined as the maximum amount of time an activity can be delayed without delaying the early start of the succeeding activities. Some authors add "and without delaying the entire project." This statement is not incorrect, but it is redundant. The first condition "without delaying the early start of the succeeding activities" is more stringent than "without delaying the entire project."

We must always realize that $FF \leq TF$. In fact, free float is the part of total float that will not affect the early start of the following activities. The other part, interfering float, may be defined as the maximum amount of time an activity can be delayed without delaying the entire project but causing delay to the succeeding activities. It represents the part of the total float that remains after free float is deducted:

$$TF = FF + Int. F \qquad \text{or} \qquad Int. F = TF - FF$$

In some software scheduling programs, we may assign a start or finish constraint to a certain activity. Total float may then be calculated as the maximum amount of time we can delay the activity from its early start without delaying the entire project or the constraint. In example 4.3, let us assign a finish constraint on activity E: Finish No Later Than (also called *Finish on or Before*) Day 18. In this case, TF = 18 − 15 = 3 days. The computer program may still calculate the free float on the basis of the early start of the succeeding activities, *FF* = 7 days, without regard to the constraint. In such a situation, you may be confused about why the free float is greater than the total float. In reality, we are comparing apples to oranges. The two variables (*TF* and *FF*) are, in this case, calculated by using two criteria. Nevertheless, our earlier rule, *FF* ≤ *TF*, still stands as a general rule.

If we look further into free float, we find that it is calculated so as to not affect the succeeding activities, but it may be affected by the preceding activities. For example, in example 4.3, if activity B is delayed (within its total float), this amount will be taken away from the total float and the free float of activity E. Let B start on day 8 and finish on day 15 (using all its total float). Activity E will then start on day 15 and finish on day 21. This leaves activity E with only 6 days of total float, one of which is free float.

If we look at the **independent float (Ind. F)** of an activity, which is not shared or affected by any other activity, we may define it as the maximum amount of time an activity can be delayed without delaying the early start of the succeeding activities and without being affected by the allowable delay of the preceding activities. Independent float is calculated as follows:

$$\text{Ind. } F_i = \min(ES_{i+1}) - \max(LF_{i-1}) - Dur_i$$

For activity E in the previous example, *Ind. F* = 22 − 15 − 6 = 1 day. This equation may result in negative numbers, which should be interpreted as zero independent float. Independent float is part of free float, so make sure that *Ind. F* ≤ *FF*.

Interfering float and independent float are not used in construction scheduling or even calculated by commercially available software scheduling programs. They are sometimes used, although rarely, in delay-claims resolution.

Node Format

Since each activity has several data items, schedulers have been creative in depicting these data items inside the activity node. In the examples in this book, the author follows a simple node format in which the box contains the activity ID and original duration. The early dates are above the box, and the late dates under the box. Whether we are drawing the CPM network manually or by computer, we may follow one of many node formats or we may devise our own format. This is a matter of personal preference; there is no correct or incorrect format. Primavera Project Planner and MS Project provide ways to customize nodes. Two examples of node formats are shown in Figure 4.8.

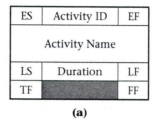

(a)   **(b)**

FIGURE 4.8   Node formats: (a) activity ID and name, duration, early start (ES), early finish (EF), late start (LS), late finish (LF), total float (TF), and free float (FF). (b) Activity ID and name, ES, EF, LS, LF, TF, original duration (OD), remaining duration (RD), and percent complete (PC). If early dates are followed by the letter *A*, they are actual dates, and late dates are not used.

It is not uncommon to include information such as activity codes (responsibility, area, phase, etc.) or cost in the activity box. The challenge becomes balancing the amount of information inside the box, the legibility of the information, and the size of the chart.

Examples 4.4 and 4.5: Introduction of Lags and Leads into CPM Networks

As defined in chapter 3, a *lag* is a mandatory waiting period between the completion (or start) of an activity and the start (or completion) of its successor, and a *lead* is a negative lag. Although lags are not "real" activities, they consume time and must be incorporated into the CPM calculations. They are shown as numbers above the lines of arrows: these numbers may be boxed (as in Figure 4.11) or not boxed (as in Figure 4.9).

EXAMPLE 4.4

Redo example 4.2 with the minor adjustments shown next.

ACTIVITY	IPA	DURATION	LAG
A	—	2	
B	A	6	
C	A	10	
D	A	4	4
E	B	7	
F	B	5	3
	C		
G	C, D	3	
H	E, F	5	
I	G	2	
	H		1

Solution

Performing forward and backward passes yields the solution shown in Figure 4.9. The 4-day lag between activities A and D means that

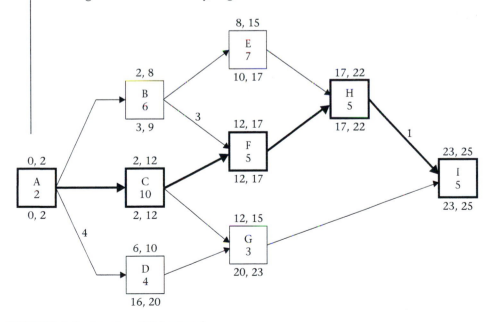

FIGURE 4.9   Lags in a CPM network

activity D cannot start until 4 days after the completion of activity A. The same principle applies to the lags between activities B and F and between activities H and I.

In this example, the critical path does not change, but it may in other cases. The 1-day lag between activities H and I adds 1 day to the project. In fact, if we look at the definition of *critical path* (the longest path in the project network from start to finish), we need to include the lags as part of the path. In this example, the critical path is A, C, F, H, I. Its length (i.e., the duration of the entire project) is 2 + 10 + 5 + 5 + (1) + 2 = 25 days (the lag is in parentheses).

Other lags in this example contribute to changes in the forward-pass and backward-pass calculations, causing total float and free float to change in some cases. Notice that in the CPM calculations, the lags must be added in the forward pass and subtracted in the backward pass.

EXAMPLE 4.5

Draw the node diagram and perform the CPM computations for the schedule shown next.

ACTIVITY	IPA	LAG	DURATION	ACTIVITY	IPA	LAG	DURATION
A	—		2	G	C		5
B	A	2	5	H	D, E		10
C	A		6		F	2	
D	B		6	I	E, F, G		8
E	B	3	7	J	D		7
F	B, C		4	K	H, J		1
					I	1	

Solution
Performing forward and backward passes yields the solution shown in Figure 4.10. The critical path in this example is A, B, E, H, K. Its length is 2 + (2) + 5 + (3) + 7 + 10 + 1 = 30 days. The solution to example 4.5 is summarized in the following table.

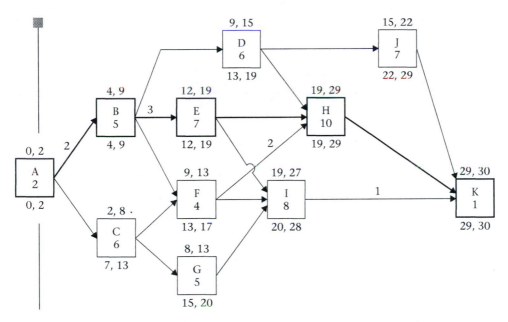

FIGURE 4.10 Lags in scheduling software

ACTIVITY	DURATION	ES	EF	LS	LF	TF	FF
A	2	0	2	0	2	0	0
B	5	4	9	4	9	0	0
C	6	2	8	7	13	5	0
D	6	9	15	13	19	4	0
E	7	12	19	12	19	0	0
F	4	9	13	13	17	4	4
G	5	8	13	15	20	7	6
H	10	19	29	19	29	0	0
I	8	19	27	20	28	1	1
J	7	15	22	22	29	7	7
K	1	29	30	29	30	0	0

Lags and Leads in Computer Software

In software scheduling programs, you may assign different calendars to different activities. For example, activity A follows a 5-day calendar, but activity B follows a 7-day calendar. Which calendar does the lag follow? Theoretically, it could follow A's, B's, or its own. Some software packages do not give you the choice and some do. You need to know which calendar the lag follows and whether you have any choices.

FIGURE 4.11   Two-day lag

One interesting scenario (Figure 4.11) may lead to a pitfall: There is a 2-day lag, but the scheduler timed activity A to finish on a Friday. The next activity, B, would start on the next business day (i.e., Monday). This leaves a "natural lag" of 2 days: Saturday and Sunday. A good example of this is concrete placement. Let us assume activity A to be Formwork, Rebar, and Concrete and activity B to be Strip Forms. The schedule works well unless a delay forces activity A to finish 1 or 2 days later. Activity B would then start the next day without any lag. Ideally, a 2-day lag must be entered. If there is a choice for the lag calendar, we should choose the 7-day calendar. If not, we may create a 2-day activity (Wait for Concrete to Set), in lieu of the lag, and assign the 7-day calendar to it. Such activity will have no resources or cost assignment.

Further Discussion of Float

From realistic observation, we can deduce the following five points about float:

1. In construction project scheduling, total float, TF, is the most- used type of float. Free float, FF, comes in a distant second. Interfering float and independent float are almost unheard of, except in some delay-claim-resolution cases. In fact, most commercially available computer software programs do not calculate these two types or even mention them.

2. The project manager should be responsible for distributing the total float and should understand that total float, in most cases, is shared among several activities. If the first activity in line consumes it, the remaining activities will be affected and may be left without float (or with less float) and become critical.

3. Total float may be used for resource leveling, which is explained in chapter 6. The project manager may choose a certain day on which to start an activity (between the early start and the late start) to satisfy certain resource or other needs. For example, an activity that includes

the installation of expensive equipment may have 60 days of float. The owner may elect to delay the installation as late as possible to defer the cost.

4. The question of float ownership is a wide and complicated subject. It is not only a technical subject but a legal subject as well. Some contracts spell out whether the contractor has granted the owner float ownership. If not, the float could be distributed in different ways. Some regulations give the right of "first come, first served." Others suggest distributing it in proportion to the duration, budget, a "priority code," or other criteria of the activities that share it. There are many publications on this subject, such as those by Pasiphol and Popescu (1994) and Ponce de Leon (1986).

5. The project manager may choose to hide or reduce the total float. Scheduling software provides several tricks for doing so, such as imposing a constraint on the activity to finish by a certain date. In computer programs such as Primavera Project Planner, you can do the following:

   - Reduce or eliminate the total float by imposing a finish constraint. For example, activity H in example 4.3 has an early finish date of day 15 and a late finish date of day 26, which gives it 11 days of float. If we impose the constraint Finish No Later Than Day 19, day 19 will replace the late finish date in the calculation of total float. Thus, $TF = 19 - 15 = 4$ days. Of course, if we impose the constraint Finish No Later Than Day 15, the total float will be zero and activity H will be critical. Different software packages provide different types of constraints: Some can override the logic and some cannot. For example, if we impose the constraint Finish No Later Than Day 13 (which is earlier than its early start date), will it then be forced to start on day 4 (before activity D is finished) and finish on day 13? You must check the definitions of constraints in the software.

   - Restrict the activity to its early dates and totally eliminate its total float. In MS Project, the constraint is called *ASAP (As Soon As Possible)*, and in Primavera Project Planner, it is called *ZTF (Zero Total Float)*. Note that the difference between this constraint and the one discussed previously is that this constraint is dynamic and the previous one is static. For example, if a delay in activity D causes it to finish on day 8, the ASAP or ZTF constraint will force activity H to finish on its *new* early finish date (i.e., day 17). The Finish No Later Than constraint will not adjust because of the change in the calculated dates.

- Delay the activity to its latest dates. Doing so may—and usually does—affect the float of the succeeding activities.
- Delay the activity as much as possible without affecting the succeeding activities. Both Primavera Project Planner and MS Project have such a constraint. In some programs, it is called *Zero Free Float,* and in others, *As Late As Possible.* For example, if we add a Zero Free Float constraint to activity E in example 4.3, it will be delayed by 7 days to start on day 16 and finish on day 22. It will still have 5 days of total float left (compared with 12 without the constraint). This type of constraint is particularly useful in procurement activities. When you have an equipment procurement activity with a lot of float, you may not want the equipment to be delivered too early or the contractor and the owner may have problems (the possibility of theft or vandalism, lack of storage space, tying up the cash, etc.).

Effect of Choice of Dates on Cash Flow

The effect of different dates on cash flow is shown in Figure 4.12. Early dates (———) and late dates (--------) provide a time frame within which the project manager can choose his or her planned dates (– - – - –). Conservative thinking

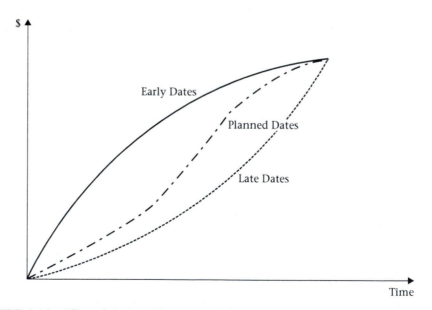

FIGURE 4.12   Effect of choice of dates on cash flow

leans more toward early dates (especially for the contractor). The owner's financial considerations may dictate late dates. The contractor may have other considerations for choosing planned dates, such as resource availability and cost, resource leveling (explained in chapter 6), other ongoing or potential projects, and so forth.

Example 4.6: Event Times in Arrow Networks

Event times in arrow networks are calculated in the following manner:

- The early event time, T_E, is the largest (latest) date obtained to reach an event (going from start to finish).
- The late event time, T_L, is the smallest (earliest) date obtained to reach an event (going from finish to start).

The preceding logic is similar to that of the forward and backward passes: When you are going forward, pick the largest number. When you are going backward, pick the smallest number.

EXAMPLE 4.6

Perform the CPM calculations, including the event times, for the arrow network shown in Figure 4.13a.

Solution
Early times, T_E. We start the project at node 10 with an early event time of $T_E = 0$ (Figure 4.13b). Event (node) 20 is reached when activity A is complete, which is on day 10. However, event 30 requires both A and B to be completed. In this case, we take the larger of $(0 + 10 = 10)$ and $(0 + 5 = 5)$, which is 10, for the early time. The early time for event 40 is $0 + 7 = 7$. Event 50 needs activities D, E, and F to be finished. We take the largest date of 18, 19, and 11 for the early time. The answer is 19. Similarly, early events 60 and 70 have early times of 24 and 27, respectively. *Late times,* T_L. Starting at event 70, the late time, T_L, is 27. Since all dummies have zero duration, event 60 has $T_L = 27$. For event 50, we must pick the earlier of the following: T_L of event 60 − Duration of G

(27 − 5 = 22) and T_L of event 70 − Duration of H (27 − 8 = 19). So, T_L for event 50 = 19. For event 40, T_L = 19 − 4 = 15. For event 30, T_L = 19 − 9 = 10. For event 20, pick the earlier of (19 − 8 = 11) and (10 − 0 = 10). Hence, T_L = 10 − 0 = 10. For event 10, pick the earliest of (10 − 10 = 0), (10 − 5 = 5), and (15 − 7 = 8). Clearly, T_L = 0.

Event float. We easily find that events 40 and 60 have floats of 8 and 3 days, respectively. All other events are critical.

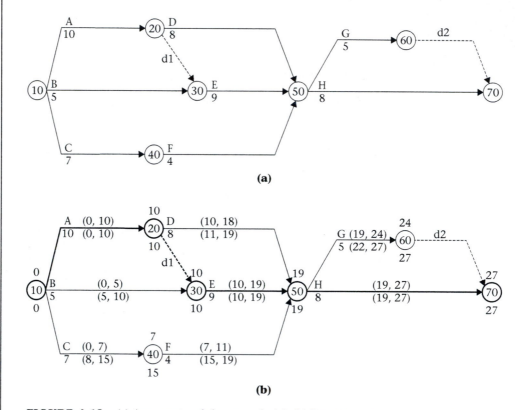

FIGURE 4.13   (a) Arrow network for example 4.6; (b) Event times in arrow network

Example 4.7: Effect of the Imposed Finish Date on the Schedule

So far, all calculations have been based on the duration estimate for each activity, along with the logic between these activities. The result is a **calculated finish date.** In many cases, the calculated finish date is different from that set by the owner. As a result, the contractor must adjust the schedule to meet the owner's imposed finish date. Doing so may require *accelerating* the schedule, a subject covered in chapter 8. In this section, we just study the effect that such an imposed date may have on the schedule.

The concept is simple: Do the CPM forward pass as usual. Then, on the backward pass, start with the imposed finish date and use this date for your backward-pass calculations. The imposed finish date may be earlier or later than the calculated finish date:

- If the imposed finish date is earlier than the calculated finish date, the activities on the critical path will have a negative float equal to the difference between the imposed finish date and the calculated finish date. Other activities may also develop negative float less than (in absolute value) the total float of the critical path. The contractor must accelerate the project (i.e., reduce its duration) by an amount equal to the negative float of the critical path. This acceleration, say 8 days, may be taken from several activities (e.g., 1 day from one activity, 2 days from another, and so on), with a total duration reduction equal to 8 days.
- If the imposed finish date is later than the calculated finish date, the contractor is in good shape. The difference between the two dates may be regarded as a **time contingency,** and the contractor may keep the calculated finish date as a target date. In such a situation, inserting the imposed finish date into the computer program will result in the "disappearance" of the critical path. This occurs because we gave each activity a "bonus float" equal to the difference between the imposed finish date and the calculated finish date. Since, by default, most computer programs define critical activities as those with zero float, no critical activities will be found. For this reason, the scheduler should not enter the imposed finish date until the calculated finish date is determined.

EXAMPLE 4.7

The owner of the project discussed in example 4.3 needs to have the project finished in 30 days. Use the imposed finish date to determine the effect on the entire schedule and on individual activities.

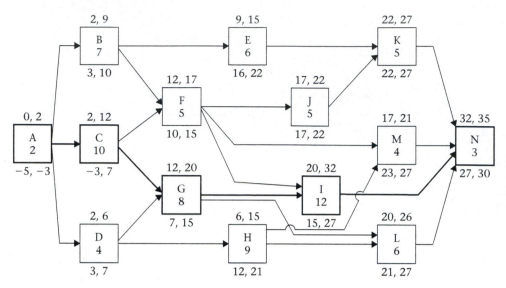

FIGURE 4.14   Effect of imposed finish date on the schedule

Solution

The results of example 4.7 can be tabulated as follows.

ACTIVITY	DURATION	ES	EF	LS	LF	TF
A	**2**	**0**	**2**	**−5**	**−3**	**−5**
B	7	2	9	3	10	1
C	**10**	**2**	**12**	**−3**	**7**	**−5**
D	4	2	6	3	7	1
E	6	9	15	16	22	7
F	5	12	17	10	15	−2
G	**8**	**12**	**20**	**7**	**15**	**−5**
H	9	6	15	12	21	6
I	**12**	**20**	**32**	**15**	**27**	**−5**
J	5	17	22	17	22	0
K	5	22	27	22	27	0
L	6	20	26	21	27	1
M	4	17	21	23	27	6
N	**3**	**32**	**35**	**27**	**30**	**−5**

Discussion of Example 4.7

We leave the details of project compression to chapter 8, but we note that in cases such as example 4.7, when the project needs acceleration, not all activities need to be shortened. This often-overlooked point may result in a lot of wasted money in construction projects. Shortening activities B, D, E, and so forth does no good. At the same time, we observe that activity F, which is not on the critical path, needs to be accelerated by 2 days. However, this may not be exactly true. If we accelerate any activity on the critical path, other than G, by at least 2 days, activity F will not need to be accelerated. Following is a numerical illustration of this point:

1. The critical path (A, C, G, I, N) is 35 days long.
2. The path (A, C, F, I, N) is 32 days long.
3. We need to shorten any path that exceeds 30 days.
4. Shortening a path is achieved by shortening the duration of an activity or a combination of activities by the desired amount of days—5 in this case.
5. Since the two paths share all activities except F and G, any reduction in the duration of any shared activity (A, C, I, or N) will result in a reduction in both paths.

This subject is discussed further in chapter 8.

LOGIC AND CONSTRAINTS

A trend among many schedulers and project managers is to "fix" the dates of activities rather than letting the software calculate them using the CPM concepts. For example, the project manager might ask the scheduler to make Door Installation start on 4/26/05. The scheduler would assign a constraint to this activity so that it would start on that particular date. This practice strips the schedule of its most important advantage: logic. The difference is simple: Logic is dynamic. Constraints are not. The author—when put in the shoes of this scheduler—would ask the project manager, "Why do you want to start that activity on 4/26/05?" The project manager would give an answer such as "That's when drywall will be finished." The scheduler can then tie Door Installation to Finish Drywall. To appreciate the advantage of logic over constraints, assume that the predecessor, Finish Drywall, is delayed. With the absence of logic, we need to go to Door Installation and manually move it. With logic, all we have to do is recalculate the schedule.

It is also possible to combine logic and constraints. Assume that an activity may be completed as early as 6/7/05, but the project manager wants to delay it till 7/14/05 for a reason that may have nothing to do with logic, such as cash-flow requirements. The scheduler may add a constraint (without taking out the logic) that will not allow it to start before 7/14/05.

The author believes that the overwhelming reason for using constraints in lieu of logical relationships is a lack of understanding of the mechanics of the CPM. Some contractors, especially those who work on small projects, used to make bar chart "schedules" by using a spreadsheet program or even by drawing a bar chart manually without any CPM calculations. In such schedules, the contractor would choose the start and finish dates for every activity rather than calculating them. Such a bar chart is subjective and not a real CPM schedule. Furthermore, it may not have much value in the court of the law. Consequently, using such schedules is strongly discouraged.

Nevertheless, constraints may be extremely important. The owner may have, in addition to the project completion date, other deadlines, such as Substantial Completion. Substantial Completion usually indicates the stage when the facility is completed to the point that the owner may use it while the contractor completes the final items (or **punch list**). Even though the deadline for Substantial Completion may be in the contract, the contractor must show it as a milestone on the schedule. The owner bears the responsibility of noting the absence of such milestones in the schedule before accepting it.

CHAPTER 4 EXERCISES

1. For the following schedule, draw the node network, perform the CPM calculations, mark the critical path, and complete the table.

ACTIVITY	DURATION	IPA	ES	EF	LS	LF	TF	FF
A	3	—						
B	7	A						
C	4	A						
D	5	B						
E	8	B, C						

2. For the following schedule, draw the node network, perform the CPM calculations, mark the critical path, and complete the table.

ACTIVITY	DURATION	IPA	ES	LS	EF	LF	TF	FF
A	7	—						
B	10	—						
C	15	A						
D	8	A, B						
E	4	C, D						

3. For the following schedule, draw the node network, perform the CPM calculations, mark the critical path, and complete the table.

ACTIVITY	DURATION	IPA	ES	EF	LS	LF	TF	FF
A	2	—						
B	4	A						
C	6	A						
D	9	A						
E	5	B						
F	7	B, C						
G	3	D, E, F						

4. For the following schedule, draw the node network, perform the CPM calculations, mark the critical path, and complete the table.

ACTIVITY	DURATION	IPA	ES	EF	LS	LF	TF	FF
A	6	—						
B	2	—						
C	8	A						
D	5	A, B						
E	3	B						
F	6	D, E						
G	5	C, D						
H	2	F, G						

5. For the following schedule, draw the node network, perform the CPM calculations, mark the critical path, and complete the table.

ACTIVITY	DURATION	IPA	ES	EF	LS	LF	TF	FF
A	6	—						
B	2	—						
C	9	—						
D	4	A, B						
E	7	B						
F	5	D						
G	10	D, E						
H	8	C, F, G						
I	3	C, G						
J	2	H, I						

6. For the following schedule, draw the node network, perform the CPM calculations, mark the critical path, and complete the table.

ACTIVITY	DURATION	IPA	ES	EF	LS	LF	TF	FF
A	2	—						
B	7	A						
C	10	A						
D	5	A						
E	4	B						
F	4	B, C						
G	3	C						
H	6	C, D						
I	3	D						
J	6	E, F, G						
K	8	F, G, H						
L	5	H, I						
M	3	K, L						

7. For the following schedule, draw the node network, perform the CPM calculations, mark the critical path, and complete the table.

ACTIVITY	DURATION	IPA	ES	EF	LS	LF	TF	FF
A	3	—						
B	5	—						
C	6	A						
D	9	A, B						
E	4	A, B						
F	6	B						
G	5	C, D						
H	12	D, E						
I	7	D, E, F						
J	9	E						
K	10	G, H, I						
L	6	I, J						
M	4	G, I						
N	2	K						

8. For the following schedule, draw the node network, perform the CPM calculations, mark the critical path, and complete the table.

ACTIVITY	DURATION	IPA	ES	EF	LS	LF	TF	FF
A	3	—						
B	10	A						
C	7	A						
D	6	B						
E	5	B, C						
F	4	C						
G	2	D						
H	4	D, E						
I	10	E						
J	6	E, F						
K	4	G, H, I						
L	2	H, I						
M	1	J, L						

9. For the following schedule, draw the node network, perform the CPM calculations, mark the critical path, and complete the table.

ACTIVITY	DURATION	IPA	ES	EF	LS	LF	TF	FF
A	5	—						
B	7	A						
C	10	A						
D	5	A						
E	9	A						
F	6	B						
G	4	B, C						
H	8	B, C, D						
I	2	C, D						
J	5	E						
K	8	F						
L	9	E, G						
M	7	F, G, H						
N	3	F, G, H, I						
O	6	H, I						
P	4	M, N, O						
Q	3	K, L						
R	5	L, M						
S	4	J, P						
T	6	Q						
U	4	Q, R						
V	1	T, U, S						

10. For the following schedule, draw the node network, perform the CPM calculations, mark the critical path, and complete the table.

ACTIVITY	DURATION	IPA	LAG	ES	EF	LS	LF	TF	FF
A	5	—							
B	6	A							
C	4	A	3						
D	5	A							
E	3	B							
F	2	C, B							

11. For the following schedule, draw the node network, perform the CPM calculations, mark the critical path, and complete the table.

ACTIVITY	DURATION	IPA	LAG	ES	EF	LS	LF	TF	FF
A	4	—							
B	9	—							
C	6	A							
D	4	A							
		B	2						
E	4	B							
F	2	B, C							
G	6	D							
		E	3						
H	3	F, G							

12. For the following schedule, draw the node network, perform the CPM calculations, mark the critical path, and complete the table.

ACTIVITY	DURATION	IPA	LAG	ES	EF	LS	LF	TF	FF
A	5	—							
B	6	A							
C	4	A	3						
D	5	A							
E	9	B							
F	7	B	2						
		C							
G	6	C							
H	8	C							
		D	4						
I	3	D							
J	7	E, G							
		F	2						
K	4	F, G, H							
L	1	H	3						
		I							
M	2	K, L							

13. What is the main reason for the overuse of date constraints? How do you minimize such use?

14. Create a WBS for building a house. Use four levels of details and provide activity codes for each breakdown element.

CHAPTER 5

Precedence Networks

Diplomat Resort, Hollywood, Florida. Courtesy of Smith Aerial Photos, Maitland, Florida.

83

DEFINITION AND INTRODUCTION

Precedence networks are node networks that allow for the use of four types of relationships: finish to start (FS), start to start (SS), finish to finish (FF), and start to finish (SF). To understand the idea of precedence networks, consider the simple project of laying 1,000 LF (linear feet) of a utility pipe. The logic is simple: dig a trench, provide a 6-inch-thick gravel subbase (bedding), lay the pipe, backfill, and compact—five consecutive activities. However, are they actually "consecutive"? Do you need to finish excavating the entire 1,000 LF before you can start the subbase? Do you need to finish the subbase completely before you start laying the pipe? If the answer is yes, your bar chart may look like the one shown in Figure 5.1.

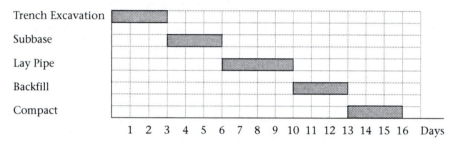

FIGURE 5.1   Bar chart for five consecutive activities

Most likely, though, the answer to the preceding questions is no. Practically, once you have dug a reasonable amount, say 100 LF, your second crew can start providing the subbase while the first crew continues digging. Once digging reaches about 200 LF (say 20%), the subbase is about 10% complete, and your third crew can start laying the pipe. As a result, the bar chart for the project looks like the one shown in Figure 5.2. Clearly, relationships exist among these activities, but not the traditional FS relationship. The activities are said to be

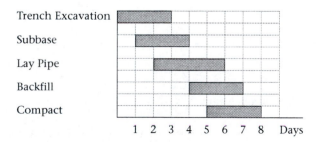

FIGURE 5.2   Bar chart for five overlapping activities

overlapping. This project may be represented in one of two common ways. A third method, using the Linear Scheduling Method, will be discussed in chapter 11.

1. *The stair-type relationship.* In this method, each activity is divided into two or more parts (Figure 5.3): After Excavation I is complete, both Excavation II and Subbase I can start. Once Subbase I is finished, Subbase II and Pipe I can start (probably Excavation III as well), and so on. This method is well known and widely acceptable. It is popular for projects such as heavy construction (highway, utilities, etc.) in which activities are few but large and have long durations. It is customary to divide the activities of these projects into phases, steps, or "subactivities." The main drawbacks of this method are the increase in the number of activities and the confusing similarity of their titles. For instance, in the example shown in Figure 5.3, a 5-activity project became a 15-activity project.

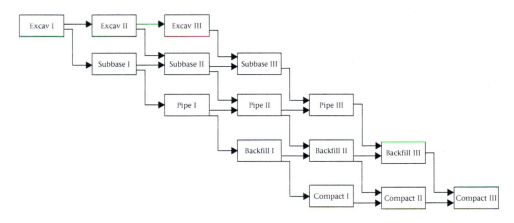

FIGURE 5.3   Stair-type schedule for utility pipe installation project

2. *The precedence diagramming method.* The project can alternatively be represented as shown in Figure 5.4. The activities in this network have SS relationships. This means Subbase cannot begin till Excavate has started, Lay Pipe cannot begin till Subbase has started, and so on. Theoretically, all five activities can start simultaneously (one immediately after the other), then the project can finish in 7 days (the largest single duration). However, this scenario may be a little too unrealistic. In real life, some amount of excavation must be done (say 20%) before Subbase can start. The same can be said of the other steps.

We can add lags to the network shown in Figure 5.4, as shown in Figure 5.5. In Figure 5.5, if Excavate starts on day 0 (*remember:* the end of day 0 means the

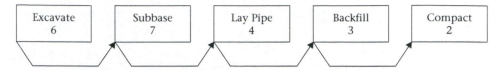

FIGURE 5.4   Precedence diagram, for utility pipe installation project, using start-to-start relationships with no lags

beginning of day 1), Subbase can start 1 day later, at the end of day 1. Lay Pipe can start 2 days later (on day 3), Backfill can start on day 4 (3 + 1), and Compact can start on day 5 and finish on day 7.

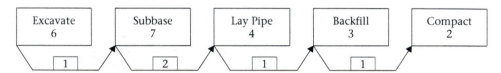

FIGURE 5.5   Precedence diagram, for utility pipe installation project, using start-to-start relationships with lags

With careful estimates of both durations and lags, this method can work well. However, what may result is an awkward situation in which a successor finishes before the predecessor.* For example, we just calculated the finish of the last activity in the project: Compact, on day 7. However, by that date, the second activity, Subbase, has not finished. This situation is unacceptable, so we must either increase the lags or add FF relationships, as shown in Figure 5.6. FF relationships ensure that no successor can finish before its predecessor. Thus, Subbase cannot finish till Excavate is finished, Lay Pipe cannot finish till Subbase is finished, and so on. Since we did not add lags to the FF relationships, theoretically two or more activities can finish at the same time. If this possibility is unacceptable, we can add lags, as shown in Figure 5.7. In the network shown in Figure 5.7, Subbase cannot finish till 1 day after Excavate has finished, and Backfill cannot finish till 1 day after Lay Pipe has finished.

One important note: These relationships are "binding in one way," which means you can exceed the lag in one direction but not the other. For example, Subbase cannot start till *at least* 1 day after Excavate has started. It is allowed to start *more than 1 day* after the start of Excavate. The same argument holds for

---

*This situation may be acceptable in some but not all cases. For example, if the predecessor is Clear & Grub and the successor is Excavate Foundation; you may have to lag the start of excavation a few days after starting Clear & Grub. However, you may finish excavation before finishing clearing and grubbing because the completion of the two activities is independent.

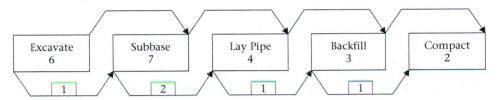

FIGURE 5.6   Precedence diagram, for utility pipe installation project, using a combination relationship and lags

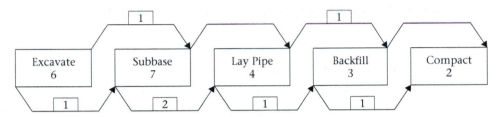

FIGURE 5.7   Precedence diagram, for utility pipe installation project, using a combination relationship and more lags

the FF relationship: Subbase cannot finish earlier than 1 day after the finish of Excavate, but it can finish more than 1 day after the finish of Excavate.

The relationships shown in Figures 5.6 and 5.7 are called *combination relationships*. In this type of relationship, two activities are related by two relationships. Some computer software, such as Microsoft (MS) Project, does not allow combination relationships.

THE FOUR TYPES OF RELATIONSHIPS

As mentioned previously, four types of relationships are possible in precedence networks:

1. ***Finish-to-start (FS) relationship.*** The most common type of relationship is the FS relationship. Many project managers still insist on using only this type. Many examples of this type exist, such as the following:
   - The concrete cannot be placed (poured) until the formwork has been built.
   - The doors cannot be hung until door frames have been installed.
2. ***Start-to-start (SS) relationship.*** The SS relationship is common and extremely useful. Examples of this type are as follows:
   - Excavation for the foundation cannot start until clearing and grubbing begins (usually with a certain lag; i.e., a certain percentage is finished).

- Laying felt on the roof cannot start until sheathing has started (also usually with a lag).
3. ***Finish-to-finish (FF) relationship.*** The FF relationship is also common and useful. Examples of this type are as follows:
   - Landscaping cannot finish until the driveway is finished.
   - Backfilling a trench cannot finish until the pipe in the trench has been laid.
4. ***Start-to-finish (SF) relationship.*** The SF relationship is uncommon and almost nonexistent in construction projects.

Important Comments About the Four Types of Relationships

1. Practically, the only two types of relationships that can be combined are SS and FF, as shown in the previous example.
2. You can always use lags and leads with the four relationships. In fact, you will have more need to use lags with SS and FF relationships than with the traditional FS relationship.
3. With regard to critical path method (CPM) calculations (discussed later in this chapter), when you are using a combination relationship (SS and FF), usually only one of the two relationships becomes binding (driving). This situation may change if some criterion—such as duration, lag, or logic—changes.

THE PERCENT COMPLETE APPROACH

O'Brien and Plotnick (1999, 138–140) suggested a slightly different approach. The relationship shown in Figure 5.8a means that activity B can start after A is at least 50% complete. In Figure 5.8b, the final 30% of activity B cannot progress until A is completely finished. Although this approach makes sense, it did not gain popularity. Perhaps the main reason is that in the CPM, early and late dates of an activity are calculated using lags that have a definite number of days (constant) rather than a percentage of completion of another activity (variable), although the conversion of this variable to a constant is simple.

We must note here that MS Project accommodates such relationships. For example, the relationship shown in Figure 5.8a can be entered as follows: B's predecessor is A, relationship: *SS* + 50%. Primavera Project Planner does not accept a relationship in this form: it must be in number of days.

In reality, the lags we use in the CPM are nothing but an estimate of the portion (percent complete) of the preceding activity that must be finished before the succeeding activity can start (or finish). For example, Figures 5.8a and 5.8b can be redrawn as shown in Figures 5.8c and 5.8d. Note that the relationship shown in Figure 5.8b is not equivalent to that shown in Figure 5.8d, but close enough. If you try to do CPM calculations for both, assuming activity A starts the project, you will find A's early dates are (0, 5). The last 30% of activity B is about 2 days. Thus, the last 2 days of B must follow A (i.e., occur on days 6 and 7). However, the early start of activity B is not restricted, so it can be zero (start of the project), in which case the early dates of B are (0, 7), which is also true in Figure 5.8d, unless activity B is contiguous. In this case, early dates for B are (1, 7). (Contiguous and interruptible activities are discussed later in this chapter.)

Another way we can redraw the relationship shown in Figure 5.8b is by splitting activity B. This redrawing is shown in Figure 5.8e.

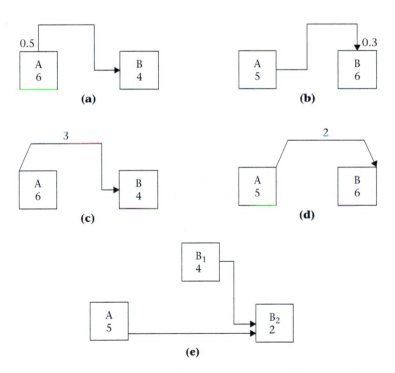

FIGURE 5.8   Percent complete approach: (a) activity B starts after activity A is at least 50% complete; (b) final 30% of activity B progresses only after A is complete; (c) Figure 5.8a with lags; (d) Figure 5.8b with lags; (e) activity B split

FAST-TRACK PROJECTS

The term *fast track* in the construction world means starting the construction process while the design is still under development. Under normal circumstances (i.e., the traditional way), the design must be complete before construction can start. In some situations, time may be so tight that the owner or project management team decides to "fast track" the project. In this case, the design portion is divided into several phases, and it proceeds along with construction, as shown in Figures 5.9a and 5.9b.

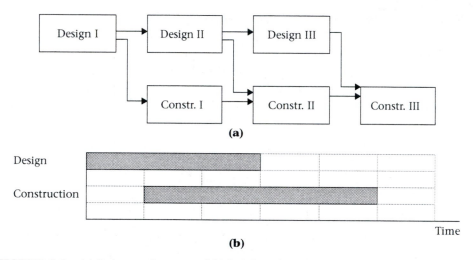

FIGURE 5.9 (a) Stair-type diagram and (b) bar chart for a fast-track project

In many cases, the design development (DD) stage is identified with a certain percentage, such as DD 30%, DD 60%, and so forth. The higher the percentage, the more well defined the design and the fewer assumptions must be made.

Fast tracking takes advantage of precious time, but with a cost. The concept is to start to build something which you have a general, but not an exact, idea of what it is (you have some preliminary ideas but not a complete design). Doing so minimizes the ability of the contractor, and other participants, to practice value engineering and constructability studies (see the definitions of *value engineering* and *constructability* in chapter 8). Fast tracking may also lead to more change orders and higher cost. For obvious reasons, contractors cannot take these types of projects on a lump-sum basis, so owners may not know the final cost of the project until it is complete. To counterbalance this unknown, the contractor may give the owner an estimate with a "guaranteed maximum budget." Refer to the project management books listed in the Bibliography for more discussion on this concept.

A PARALLEL PREDECESSOR?

We learned in chapters 3 and 4 that a predecessor is the activity that must happen before another one can happen. For example, if A is a predecessor of B, then A must happen before B can start, but not necessarily immediately after A (Figure 5.10a).

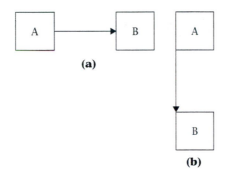

FIGURE 5.10   (a) Typical predecessor relationship; (b) parallel predecessor relationship

If A is a predecessor of B with an SS relationship, both may occur in parallel (Figure 5.10b). Would A still be called a *predecessor?* The answer is yes because A must start first (even with zero lag). If B starts several days after A starts, the logic is not violated. However, if B starts first—by any amount of time—the logic *will* be violated. Activity A thus controls activity B and is still called a *predecessor.* Note the direction of the arrow in Figure 5.10b: it points from the activity that controls to the activity that is controlled.

Realistically, a portion (maybe a small portion) of A must occur before B can start. Popescu and Charoenngam (1995) defined a *predecessor* as "an activity that has some measurable portion of its duration logically restraining a subsequent activity or activities" (p. 438). In reality, we may show two activities with an SS relationship and zero lag, but a certain—possibly small—portion of the predecessor must occur before the successor starts.

CPM CALCULATIONS FOR PRECEDENCE DIAGRAMS

The CPM calculations for precedence diagrams differ from those for standard arrow or node diagrams. However, before we start the CPM calculations, *we must make an important distinction: are the activities contiguous (continuous) or interruptible?* In other words, once an activity starts, can it be paused and then resume, or must it proceed continuously until it is finished? In real life, both scenarios are possible, but the assumption about whether the activities are contiguous or interruptible makes a substantial difference in the calculation method used and possibly in the calculated finish date of the entire project.

Interruptible Activities

Let us start with the simple three-activity project depicted in Figure 5.11. The three activities are tied with only SS relationships, with no lags. Theoretically, all three activities can start at the same time. The project finishes when the activity with the longest duration, A, finishes. Thus, activity A is critical. Activities B and C have floats equal to the difference between their duration and the duration of A (the float for B is $10 - 5 = 5$ and the float for C is $10 - 3 = 7$). Now, let us add some lags, as shown in Figure 5.12.

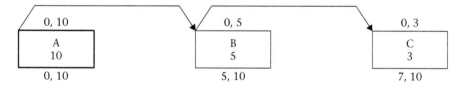

FIGURE 5.11   Three-activity project using a start-to-start relationship

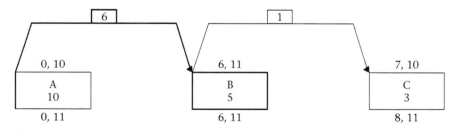

FIGURE 5.12   Three-activity project using a start-to-start relationship with lags

In Figure 5.12, we are forcing a delay in the start of activities B and C, maybe because we want to see a certain percentage of activity A finished before B can start, and a certain percentage of activity B finished before C can start. We find that, in this example, activity B is the critical activity since it takes 11 days to finish (6-day lag + 5 days' duration). The problem is that activity C may finish early, on day 10, which is 1 day *before* activity B is scheduled to finish (in reality, this situation may or may not be a problem). Consequently, let us try to tie the ends of the activities with FF relationships rather than the SS relationships (Figure 5.13).

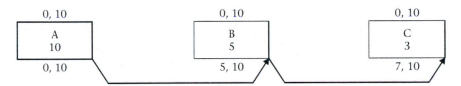

FIGURE 5.13   Three-activity project, with a 10-day duration, using a finish-to-finish relationship

In Figure 5.13, the finish of each activity is restricted to the finish of the predecessor. Activity B cannot finish till A is finished. Activity C cannot finish till B is finished. No restriction is put on their start other than the start of the project. Thus, not only activity A (the activity with the longest duration) is critical, but also the *ends* of activities B and C are. This criticality can change if, for example, activity B has 12 days' duration, as shown in Figure 5.14.

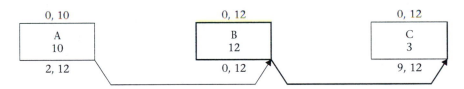

FIGURE 5.14   Three-activity project, with a 12-day duration, using a finish-to-finish relationship

In Figure 5.14, B has become the driving activity. It has no control over the completion of the predecessor (activity A), but it has control over the finish of activity C. Activity B automatically becomes critical (since it has the longest duration). The end of activity C is still critical since it is tied to (follows) the end of B. Activity A has 2 days' "unrestricted" float.

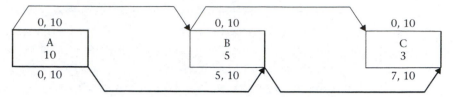

FIGURE 5.15   Three-activity project, with a 10-day duration, using a combination relationship

If we tie both the start and the end of the activities shown in Figure 5.13; we get Figure 5.15 The relationships shown in Figure 5.15 combine those shown in Figures 5.11 and 5.13. As mentioned previously, in the case of two activities tied with two relationships, in most cases, one of these two relationships governs (i.e., becomes driving). In less likely cases, both relationships govern (become driving.) The main difference between Figures 5.15 and 5.11 is that we did not allow activities B and C, in Figure 5.15, to finish before day 10, the finish date for activity A. There are no differences—so far as dates are concerned—between Figures 5.13 and 5.15. However, a logic difference occurs between the two cases, but as a result of the durations of the activities, the FF relationships control. This control can change with a change in duration, as shown in Figures 5.16 and 5.17.

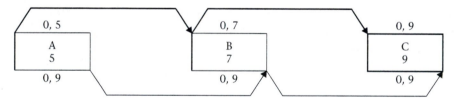

FIGURE 5.16   Three-activity project, with a 9-day duration, using a combination relationship

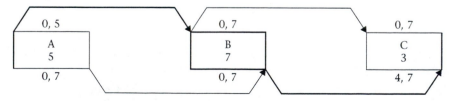

FIGURE 5.17   Three-activity project, with a 7-day duration, using a combination relationship

Note that, in all the preceding cases—Figures 5.11 through 5.17, the duration of any activity may be longer than the difference between its finish and start dates: $EF - ES$ or $LF - LS$. This means it may stretch across a period that is longer than its duration (i.e., started, stopped, and then resumed), which is in accordance with our assumption of interruptible activities.

The Simplistic Approach

CPM calculations for precedence diagrams are similar to, but not the same as, the CPM calculations discussed in chapter 4. The differences can be summarized by the following three points:

1. In chapter 4 (arrow and node diagrams), we had only the FS type of relationship. Activities were always connected in only one way: from the end of an activity's predecessor to its start, and from its end to the start of its successor. In precedence diagrams, we use four types of relationships. Thus, you must be careful about the type of relationship chosen. An activity can be controlled (driven) not only from its start, but from its end as well.

2. In precedence diagrams, we may use combination relationships (mainly SS and FF). Doing so creates a condition in which each relationship yields a different set of dates, but one set prevails. Let us go through the calculations for Figure 5.17, for example:

   a. In the forward pass, activity A starts the project. $ES = 0$; $EF = 0 + 5$ (duration) = 5.

   b. Activity B is connected to A by a combination relationship. The SS relationship (with no lag) means B can start just after A has started. This means activity B's $ES = 0$. However, its EF is controlled by the later of the following:

$$EF = ES + Dur = 0 + 7 = 7$$

   or

$$EF (B) = EF (A) + Lag \text{ (if any)} = 5 + 0 = 5$$

   The first, $EF = 7$, prevails.

   c. The same method applies to activity C. Its start is controlled by the start of activity B, so its $ES = 0$. Its EF is controlled by the later of the following:

$$EF = ES + Dur = 0 + 3 = 3$$

or

$$EF \, (C) = EF \, (B) + Lag \, (\text{if any}) = 7 + 0 = 7$$

The second, $EF = 7$, prevails.

d. In the backward pass, we start at the end of activity C with its finish no earlier than day 7: $LF = 7$; $LS = LF - Dur = 7 - 3 = 4$.

e. Activity B must finish no later than the LF of C; that is, $LF \, (B) = LF \, (C) - Lag = 7 - 0 = 7$. Its LS is controlled by the earlier of the following:

$$LS = LF - Dur = 7 - 7 = 0$$

or

$$LS \, (B) = LS \, (C) - Lag \, (\text{if any}) = 4 - 0 = 4$$

The first, $LS = 0$, prevails.

f. Activity A must finish no later than the LF of B; that is $LF \, (A) = LF \, (B) - Lag = 7 - 0 = 7$. Its LS is controlled by the earlier of the following:

$$LS = LF - Dur = 7 - 5 = 2$$

or

$$LS \, (A) = LS \, (B) - Lag \, (\text{if any}) = 0 - 0 = 0$$

The first, $LS = 0$, prevails.

3. Note that unlike in chapter 4, the durations may not be equal to $EF - ES$ or $LF - LS$. Furthermore, all or some of the total float may be restricted. This will be elaborated in the detailed approach (discussed subsequently). Total float is always calculated by using this simple equation:

$$TF = LF - Dur - ES$$

Free float (FF) is calculated the same way as in chapter 4 and is always less than or equal to total float.

General Notes About the Simplistic Approach

Two points about the simplistic approach should be noted:

1. The position of the relationships (i.e., from top or bottom) is left to the user's discretion and has nothing to do with the choice of early or late dates. For example, the network of Figure 5.17 can be redrawn as shown in Figure 5.18.

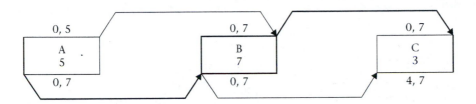

FIGURE 5.18   Figure 5.17 redrawn

2. We may have **dangling activities** in precedence diagrams. Dangling activities are tied from one end only. In other words, dangling activities have either no predecessors or no successors. As mentioned previously, we like to always start the network with one activity (e.g., Notice to Proceed) and end it with one activity (e.g., Final Completion). As an example of dangling activities, you may have a Clear & Grub activity with an SS relationship to the next activity, Excavation, with a 4-day lag (Figure 5.19). Nothing controls the end of the Clear & Grub activity (other than the end of the project). In this case, the LF date of the Clear & Grub activity is the end of the entire project. Another example is when the start of Order & Deliver Equip. is not tied logically to another activity, but its finish controls the Install Equip. activity near the end of the project (let us imagine the activities in Figure 5.20 at the end of a large project network). In this case, the ES of Order & Deliver Equip. is the start of the entire project (day 0).

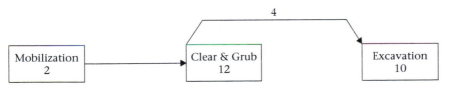

FIGURE 5.19   Example of a dangling activity

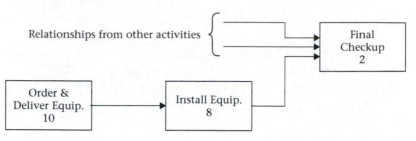

FIGURE 5.20   Another example of a dangling activity

You should not leave any dangling activities. Instead, tie them to the most reasonable predecessor or successor. For example, you can make Order & Deliver Equip. in Figure 5.20 a successor to Submittals or another activity. Scheduling software such as Primavera Project Planner lists all activities with no predecessors or successors in its scheduling report. Ideally, you should have only one of each, not a list of them.

Alternative Approaches

Let us consider the activities shown in Figure 5.21. After performing the calculations for the three sets, we get the same results: the dates for A are (0, 10) and the dates for B are (4, 12), for both early and late dates. However, are the three approaches similar? The answer is no. In Figure 5.21a, the finish of A may be delayed without delaying B (if A is interruptible). In Figure 5.21c, the start of both activities is independent. In addition, if the duration of A changes, the three scenarios will yield different results. The scheduler must be careful, when choosing the logical ties (relationships), to reflect the actual relationship as much as possible.

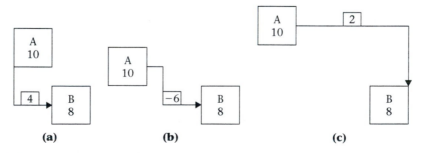

FIGURE 5.21   Three alternative approaches

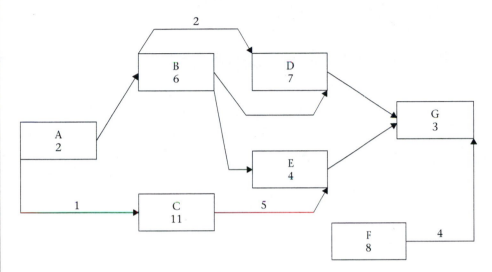

EXAMPLE 5.1

Perform the CPM calculations for the network shown in Figure 5.22.

FIGURE 5.22   Network for example 5.1

Solution

Forward Pass

1. Start the project at activity A. $ES = 0$. $EF = 0 + 2 = 2$.
2. Activity B can start as soon as activity A is finished. $ES = 2$.
   $EF = 2 + 6 = 8$.
3. Activity C can start 1 day after A has started. $ES = 1$.
   $EF = 1 + 11 = 12$.
4. Activity D can start 2 days after activity B has started.
   $ES = 2 + 2 = 4$. Use the later of $EF = 4 + 7 = 11$ and the
   EF (for B) = 8. We choose $EF = 11$.
5. Activity E can start as soon as B is finished. $ES = 8$. Use the later
   of $EF = 8 + 4 = 12$ and EF (for C) + 5-day lag = $12 + 5 = 17$. We
   choose $EF = 17$.
6. Activity F has no restriction for its start (dangling activity).
   $ES = 0$. $EF = 0 + 8 = 8$.

7. Activity G can start after both D and E are finished. *ES* (for G) = 17 (the later of 11 and 17). Use the later of *EF* = 17 + 3 = 20 and *EF* (for F) + 4-day lag = 8 + 4 = 12. We choose *EF* = 20.
8. The calculated early finish date for the project is day 20 (project duration is 20 days).

Backward Pass

1) Start at activity G. *LF* = 20. *LS* = 20 − 3 = 17.
2) Activity F must finish 4 days prior to the finish of G (i.e., *LF* = 20 − 4 = 16; *LS* = 16 − 8 = 8).
3) Activity E must finish before G can start. *LF* = 17. *LS* = 17 − 4 = 13.
4) Activity D must finish before G can start. *LF* = 17. *LS* = 17 − 7 = 10.
5) Activity C must finish 5 days before the finish of E. *LF* = 17 − 5 = 12. *LS* = 12 − 11 = 1.
6) Activity B must finish before D has finished, on day 17, and before E has started, on day 13. *LF* = 13 (the earlier). Use the earlier

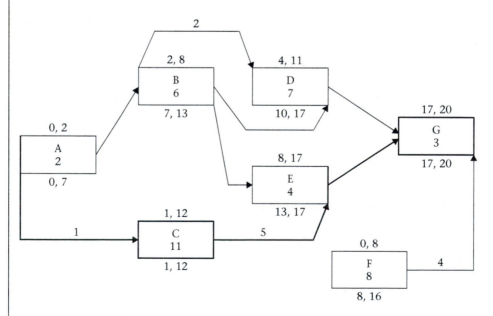

FIGURE 5.23   Solution for example 5.1

of $LS = LF - Dur = 13 - 6 = 7$ and 2 days before the LS for D (i.e., 8). We choose the earlier: $LS = 7$.

7) Activity A must finish before B can start. $LF = 7$. Use the earlier of $LS = 7 - 2 = 5$ and LS (for C) $- 1$-day lag $= 1 - 1 = 0$. We choose $LS = 0$.

8) The critical path is the start of A, all of C, the end of E, and all of G (Figure 5.23).

9) The total float equals 5, 5, 6, 5, and 8 for A, B, D, E, and F, respectively. Some of this float is restricted; some is not. This subject is discussed in the following section.

The Detailed Approach

Unlike the arrow and node diagrams in chapter 4, precedence diagrams may show the start or finish of an activity to be critical while the rest of the activity is not. This is the situation in Figures 5.12 through 5.21. Let us add a twist to this scenario, as shown in Figure 5.24.

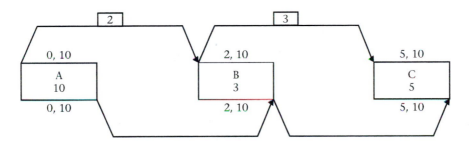

FIGURE 5.24 Network for the detailed approach

In this case, both activities A and C are completely critical. Activity B has a critical start and a critical finish but is not critical between.

Looking at Figures 5.12 through 5.24, we also notice that, contrary to arrow and node diagrams in chapter 4, the duration of an activity may not always be equal to its $EF - ES$ or $LF - LS$. What does this mean? In Figure 5.17, for example, activity A must start on day 0; otherwise, the start of activity B, which is critical, will be delayed. The only restriction on the finish of activity A is that it should not delay the LS of activity B, which is day 7. This leaves activity A with 7 days, but it has only 5 days' duration. Therefore, activity A has 2 days of *restricted float,* which we explain later in this chapter. The crew for activity A has two options:

1. Start the activity on day 0, work nonstop, and finish early on day 5.
2. Start the activity on day 0, finish a certain portion, take a break of 1 or 2 days, and return and finish the activity by day 7.

A third float option, which activity A *does not* have, is to delay its start. If its start is delayed, the start of B will be delayed, which will delay the whole project. This is why we call it *restricted float.* This particular type of restricted float is called **start-restricted float.** Looking at activity C in Figure 5.17, we also find that C has 4 days of float in its start. However, no matter when it starts, it must finish on day 7; not before, not after. We conclude that activity C has 4 days of restricted float, or **finish-restricted float.** The work crew has the following two options:

1. Start the activity on day 0, finish a certain portion, take a break (or breaks) of 1 to 4 days, and return and finish the activity by day 7.
2. Delay the start of the activity till day 4, work nonstop, and finish on day 7.

A third float option, which activity C *does not* have, is to start early *and* finish early on day 3. It cannot finish before activity B is finished.

Looking at Figures 5.14 through 5.16, we find activities A and B in Figure 5.16 with *start-restricted floats.* Activity C in Figure 5.14 and activities B and C in Figure 5.15 have *finish-restricted floats.*

Activity B in Figure 5.24 must start on day 2 and must finish on day 10. We note that it has only 3 days' duration but must fill an 8-day time interval. We call the difference $(8 - 3 = 5)$ *start-finish-restricted float,* or, for short, **double-restricted float.**

Activity B in Figure 5.11 has unrestricted float. The work crew can use this float in one of three ways:

1. Start the activity on day 0, work nonstop, and finish early on day 5.
2. Start the activity on day 0, finish a certain portion, take a break (or breaks) of 1 to 5 days, and return and finish the activity by day 10.
3. Delay the start by 1 to 5 days, work nonstop, and finish on or by day 10.

This type of float is similar to the total float discussed in chapter 4. We call it **unrestricted float.** *Total float* is the combination of all types of float, whether restricted or unrestricted.

Definitions

Start-restricted float (of an activity). The amount of time we can delay the rest of the work in the activity, after it has started, without delaying the entire project.

Finish-restricted float (of an activity). The amount of time we can delay the start of work on the activity, or the rest of it if it has started, then finish on time without delaying the entire project.

Double-restricted float (of an activity). The amount of time we have to delay the rest of the work in the activity after it has started, then finish on time without delaying the entire project.

Unrestricted float (of an activity). The amount of time we can delay all or part of the activity without delaying the entire project.

The Equations

For calculation purposes, let us put both *start-restricted float* and *finish-restricted float* under one category, **single-restricted float (SRF),** as compared with *double-restricted float (DRF)* or *unrestricted float (URF)*. As mentioned previously, in this chapter, *total float (TF)* includes all types of float, restricted or unrestricted.

For calculations, follow these steps:

1. Calculate the DRF:

$$DRF = \max[(EF - LS - Dur), 0] \tag{5.1}$$

2. If $DRF = 0$, apply these equations:

$$URF = \min[(LS - ES), (LF - EF)] \tag{5.2}$$

and

$$SRF = abs|(LS - ES) - (LF - EF)| \tag{5.3}$$

or

$$SRF = TF - URF^* \tag{5.4}$$

---

*See equation 5.6 for TF.

3. If $DRF > 0$, apply these equations:

$$URF = \min[(LS - ES), (LF - EF)] \qquad (5.2)$$

and

$$SRF = \max[(LF - LS), (EF - ES)] - Dur - DRF \qquad (5.5)$$

4. $TF(URF + SRF + DRF) = [LF - ES - Dur] \qquad (5.6)$

The preceding equations combine start-restricted float and finish-restricted float as single-restricted float. You can distinguish between the two types mostly by simple observation, or by the following rule:

If $(LF - EF) > (LS - ES)$, then SRF is start restricted.

However,

If $(LF - EF) < (LS - ES)$, then SRF is finish restricted.

Contiguous (Uninterruptible) Activities

Let us assume that our activities cannot be interrupted **(contiguous activities).** In other words, once they start, they must continue till they are finished.[†] All types of restricted float are eliminated. The activity becomes like an indivisible unit: if there is float, the whole activity slips or does not slip. In this case, activities become, simply, either critical or noncritical. Calculations are much simpler, but they may give you a different (later) project finish date than those for interruptible activities.

Let us return to Figure 5.12: with activity A as contiguous, it becomes entirely critical, with both early and late dates as (0, 10). Activities B and C in Figure 5.13 become entirely critical, with both their early and late dates as

---

[†]Even with this assumption, a real-life interruption can occur. In computer programs such as Primavera Project Planner or MS Project, there is a special (manual) function to suspend or pause an activity, then resume it. This type of manual suspension and resumption is not factored into the calculation. Programs still treat the activity as one unit. The suspension time may not count as part of the duration of the activity but will certainly affect the succeeding activities and possibly the entire project.

(5, 10) for B and (7, 10) for C. The same is true of activity C in Figure 5.14. Its early and late dates become (9, 12). In Figures 5.15 and 5.16, all activities also become critical.

In the preceding cases, the finish date of each project does not change, despite the change in assumption from interruptible to contiguous. The only change is that activities with restricted float lose their float and become totally critical. However, this may not always be the case. In Figure 5.24, if activities become contiguous, the dates change per Figure 5.25, and the entire project is pushed back 5 days. CPM calculations for such cases are similar to

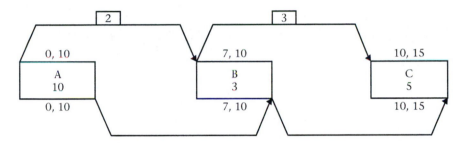

FIGURE 5.25   Network in Figure 5.24 with contiguous activities

those described previously for interruptible activities, with one exception: we must satisfy the following equation:

$$Dur = EF - ES = LF - LS$$

This can force the early dates to be pushed forward (to a later date) or late dates to be pushed backward (to an earlier date). In the previous example (Figure 5.24), we find that the early dates for activity B violate the preceding equation:

$$Dur = 3 < (EF - ES)$$

We have to move one of the two dates. Moving the EF date to day 5 will satisfy the equation but will violate the FF relationship between B and A. The only choice we have is to move the ES date to day 7. Then, the early dates for activity B are (7, 10). The same argument applies to late dates. All three activities in this case are critical and have no float of any type.

To formalize the rules, we can say that activities with a combination (SS and FF) relationship, say A and B, for example, will have two sets of early dates and two sets of late dates. One set will prevail:

a. In the forward pass, the SS relationship (plus lag if any) determines the ES_1 date for activity B, which is ES (for A) $+ 2$ (lag) $= 2$. The EF_1 for B is calculated as $EF_1 = ES_1 + Dur = 2 + 3 = 5$. The first set of early dates for activity B is $(2, 5)$.

b. The FF relationship (plus lag, if any) determines the EF_2 date for activity B. The EF date for activity A is day 10, which is the same for B (since the lag on the FF relationship is 0). The ES_2 for activity B is then calculated as $ES_2 = EF_2 - Dur = 10 - 3 = 7$. The second set of early dates for activity B is $(7, 10)$.

c. Pick whichever date set—(ES_1, EF_1) or (ES_2, EF_2)—is later; that is $(7, 10)$.

d. In the backward pass, the SS relationship (minus lag if any) determines the LS_1 date for activity B, which is LS (for C) $- 3$ (lag) $= 10 - 3 = 7$. The LF_1 for B is calculated as $LS_1 + Dur = 7 + 3 + 10$. The first set of late dates for activity B is $(7, 10)$.

e. The FF relationship (minus lag if any) determines the LF_2 date for activity B as LF (for C) $-$ Lag (0 in this case) $= 15 - 0 = 15$. The LS_2 for B is calculated as $LF_2 - Dur = 15 - 3 = 12$. The second set of late dates for activity B is $(12, 15)$.

f. Pick whichever date set—(LS_1, LF_1) or (LS_2, LF_2)—is earlier; that is $(7, 10)$.

The preceding process looks complicated in theory but is actually intuitive. Total float and free float are calculated the same as in chapter 4.

If we re-solve example 5.1 using contiguous activities, we will get the same finish date for the project; day 20. The only difference will be that activities A and E will be completely critical. As mentioned previously, this is not always true. Let us look at the following example:

EXAMPLE 5.2

Perform the forward and backward passes on the precedence network shown in Figure 5.26, on the basis of the following:

Interruptible activities
Contiguous activities

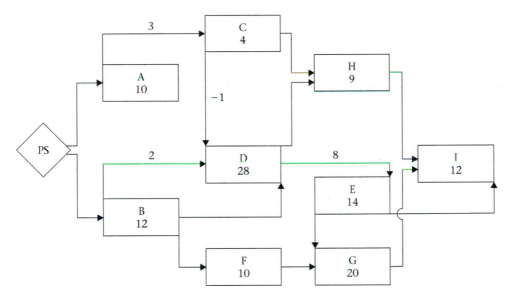

FIGURE 5.26 Network for example 5.2

Solution with Interruptible Activities

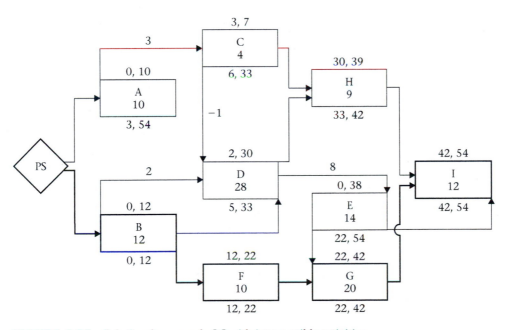

FIGURE 5.27 Solution for example 5.2 with interruptible activities

ACTIVITY	ES	EF	LS	LF	DRF	SRF	URF	TF
A	0	10	3	54	0	41	3	44
B	0	12	0	12	0	0	0	0
C	3	7	6	33	0	23	3	26
D	2	30	5	33	0	0	3	3
E	0	38	22	54	2	22	16	40
F	12	22	12	22	0	0	0	0
G	22	42	22	42	0	0	0	0
H	30	39	33	42	0	0	3	3
I	42	54	42	54	0	0	0	0

Solution with Contiguous Activities

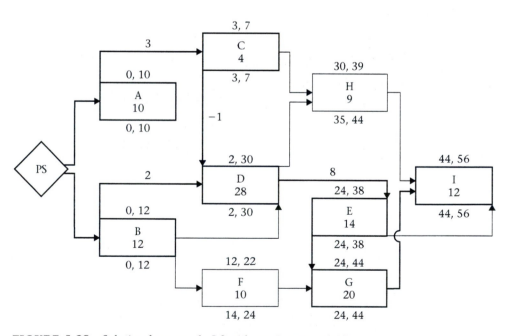

FIGURE 5.28 Solution for example 5.2 with contiguous activities

ACTIVITY	ES	EF	LS	LF	TF	FF
A	0	10	0	10	0	0
B	0	12	0	12	0	0
C	3	7	3	7	0	0
D	2	30	2	30	0	0
E	24	38	24	38	0	0
F	12	22	14	24	2	2
G	24	44	24	44	0	0
H	30	39	35	44	5	5
I	44	56	44	56	0	0

The simple difference between the two solutions is that in the case of contiguous activities, we do not allow restricted float. Once an activity starts, it must continue till it is finished. Calculations were going similar until activity E. The early dates (24, 38) were calculated from its FF relationship with activity D. This is not good enough for activity G, whose critical start on the 22nd day depends on the start of activity E. This forces a delay in activity G, which will delay the entire project by 2 days. As a result, two critical paths emerge: A, C, D, E, G, I and B, D, E, G, I. This leaves only two noncritical activities: H and F. They both increased their total float by 2 days (the same 2-day delay in the duration of the project): Activity F had zero total float (was critical) and now has 2 days of total float. Activity H had 3 days of total float and now has 5 days.

Note also that a relationship between two critical activities is not necessarily critical. For example, the FF relationship between activities B and D is not driving and, thus, not critical. The same argument applies to the FF relationship between activities E and I.

FINAL DISCUSSION

Four final points should be considered:

1. The subject of precedence diagrams can be somewhat complicated. It is easy for someone in the field to use the "sour grapes" excuse and

say, "Who uses these things anyway?" There is nothing wrong with making assumptions that simplify our life. However, if these simplifications mean avoiding a subject that we perceive as complicated or unfamiliar to us, we may be missing something important. Understanding the nature of relationships among activities is extremely important. Making the assumption of interruptible or contiguous activities is also important. It can result in several days' delay in the entire project. We just proved this when we compared Figures 5.24 and 5.25. Maybe the project manager does not need to discuss the types of float with his or her work crews, but he or she *must* understand—in layperson's terms—that some activities must start with a certain portion (but not all) of them finished before a succeeding activity can start. Failure to understand this point may result in an inaccurate schedule and a possible conflict between field operations and the office-prepared schedule.

2. In reality, most project managers and schedulers overlook the issue of interruptible or contiguous activities and may also overlook the type of relationship and lags. They try to compensate for the inaccurate logic by "correcting" it through schedule updates. For example, the baseline schedule may show a Clear & Grub activity with 12 days' duration followed by an Excavation activity (FS relationship). Once the project starts, you may indicate an Actual Start for Excavation only 4 days after Clear & Grub has started, a clear violation of the set logic. The scheduling report may indicate "Activity started; predecessor has not finished." The calculation of the updated schedule will depend on whether you want to apply **Retained Logic** (i.e., schedule the remainder of Excavation *after* the predecessor, Clear & Grub, has finished) or to apply **Progress Override** by allowing Excavation to continue independently of the Clear & Grub activity (this topic is explained in more detail in chapter 7). This option is available with some computer software programs, but the author's observation has been that many software users never pay attention to this choice. As a result, the program always uses the more conservative assumption—Retained Logic—which may result in a later calculated finish date for the project.

3. At the same time, the scheduler should use the KISS (keep it simple and smart, not stupid) approach as much as possible. Sometimes, instead of having a combination (SS and FF) relationship with lags, splitting the predecessor activity into two and then using the traditional FS relationship may be simpler and more acceptable. The

precedence diagramming method is an effective and powerful tool, but it should be used in a reasonable and effective way.

4. Computer programs, to the best of the author's knowledge, either do not give the user the choice of interruptible or contiguous activities or allow it at the entire project level only. In the latter case (such as in Primavera Project Planner), the user must decide whether *all* activities are interruptible or contiguous (although the user can choose the contiguous option then manually interrupt and resume certain activities). Real-life activities are not exactly one way or the other. This puts the responsibility back into the scheduler's hands (remember the discussion on the scheduler's qualifications at the end of chapter 1). He or she must make intelligent and informed decisions that should align the schedule assumptions with reality as closely as possible within the limitations of computer programs and practicality. Remember, the human being behind the computer makes the important decisions, not the computer.

CHAPTER 5 EXERCISES

1. Explain the main differences between the standard node diagram (covered in chapter 4) and precedence diagrams.

2. What is the *stair-type relationship?* What is the advantage of precedence diagrams over it? Draw a network for a roofing job (install trusses, install sheathing, install felt, install shingles), using each method (i.e., draw two diagrams, one for each method).

3. Give a practical example for each of the following:

   a. Start-to-start (SS) relationship only

   b. Finish-to-finish (FF) relationship only

   c. Combination SS and FF relationship

4. What does the following relationship mean?

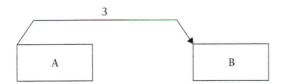

a. Activity B must start exactly 3 days after the start of A.

b. Activity B can start at least 3 days after the start of A.

c. Activity B can start at most 3 days after the start of A.

d. None of the above.

5. What does the following relationship mean?

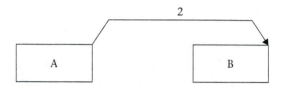

a. Activity B must finish exactly 2 days after the finish of A.

b. Activity B can finish at least 2 days after the finish of A.

c. Activity B can finish at most 2 days after the finish of A.

d. None of the above.

6. What does the following relationship mean?

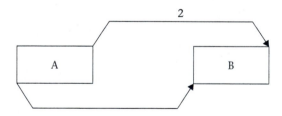

a. Activities A and B must start simultaneously, but B must finish exactly 2 days after the finish of A.

b. Activity B can start after the start of A but must finish at least 2 days before the finish of A.

c. Activity B can start before the start of A but must finish at most 3 days after the finish of A.

d. Activity B can start after the start of A but must finish at least 2 days after the finish of A.

7. What does the following relationship mean?

a. Activity A can start 2 days before the start of activity B.
b. Activity B can start 2 days after the completion of activity A.
c. Activity B can start 2 days before the completion of activity A.
d. Activity B has to start at least 2 days before the completion of activity A.

8. Define a *fast-track operation*. Briefly discuss its pros and cons.
9. Mention examples in which using fast tracking is bad, good, or a "must" option.
10. From the following table, draw the precedence network, perform the CPM calculations, and complete the table entries, assuming interruptible activities.

Activity	Duration	IPA	Type Rel[a]	Lag	ES	EF	LS	LF	TF	FF
A	3	—								
B	5	A	SS	3						
C	2	A								
D	6	B	FF							
		C								

---

[a]If the relationship type is not mentioned, it is finish to start (FS). If no lag is mentioned, it is zero.

11. From the following table, draw the precedence network, perform the CPM calculations, and complete the table entries, assuming interruptible activities.

Activity	Duration	IPA	Type Rel[a]	Lag	ES	EF	LS	LF	TF	FF
A	4	—								
B	3	—								
C	8	A	SF							
D	7	A, B								
E	6	D	SS	3						
F	3	D								
G	5	F	SS	2						
	2	F	FF							

[a]If the relationship type is not mentioned, it is finish to start (FS). If no lag is mentioned, it is zero.

12. From the following table, draw the precedence network, perform the CPM calculations, and complete the table entries, assuming interruptible activities.

Activity	Duration	IPA	Type Rel[a]	Lag	ES	EF	LS	LF	TF	FF
A	5	—								
B	7	A	SS	2						
C	8	A								
D	10	A	SS	3						
			FF							
E	4	B	FF	2						
F	6	C, D								
G	2	E, F								

[a]If the relationship type is not mentioned, it is finish to start (FS). If no lag is mentioned, it is zero.

13. Repeat exercise 10 using contiguous activities.
14. Repeat exercise 11 using contiguous activities.
15. Repeat exercise 12 using contiguous activities.

16. Prove that using interruptible activities in the following project allows the project to finish 5 days earlier than if the activities were contiguous.

Activity	Duration	IPA	Type Rel[a]	Lag	ES	EF	LS	LF	TF	FF
A	7	—								
B	6	A	SS	3						
		A	FF	4						
C	2	B	SS	1						
		B	FF							
D	6	C	SS							
		C	FF	4						
E	10	D	SS	3						
		D	FF	2						

[a]If the relationship type is not mentioned, it is finish to start (FS). If no lag is mentioned, it is zero.

17. Give real-life (not necessarily construction) examples for the following:

   a. An SS (start-to-start) relationship without lag. No FF (finish-to-finish) relationship is required.
   b. An SS relationship with lag. No FF relationship is required.
   c. An SS and FF combination relationship.
   d. An FF relationship, with or without lag.

18. A subcontractor must do the following:

   a. Framing (5 days)
   b. Drywall installation (4 days)
   c. Drywall finish and paint (3 days)

   Assuming he wants to make sure each activity finishes as least 1 day after its predecessor has finished, draw these three activities in a precedence diagram and calculate how much time the subcontractor would need to finish all three activities.

19. Look at your solution to the previous exercise. Is it a unique solution, or can you achieve the same result with different logic?

20. Mention an example for each of the following:

    a. Start-restricted float

    b. Finish-restricted float

    c. Double-restricted float

    d. Unrestricted float

Resource Allocation and Resource Leveling

Ocean Ridge Home, Palm Beach, Florida. Courtesy of Smith Aerial Photos, Maitland, Florida.

INTRODUCTION

The term *resource* is used in many fields and contexts. Most companies have *human resources* departments, which match the need for employees with the appropriate supply by hiring and laying off workers. The term *financial resources* is commonly used to indicate available monetary sources. In project management, we use the term *resources* to indicate three main categories: labor (human), materials, and equipment. Ultimately, everything is translated into a monetary quantity that may be—for the accounting department—a part of the financial resources.

THE THREE CATEGORIES OF RESOURCES

All expenses, in any construction project, can be classified under one of the three categories just mentioned.

Labor

Labor can be further classified into the following two subcategories:

1. *Salaried staff.* These individuals include the project manager, superintendent, project engineer, secretary, and any other person who is tied to the project but not tied to one particular activity or work package. Salaried persons usually get paid a fixed salary for the duration of the project or their assignment.
2. *Hourly workers.* These individuals are hired to perform a specific task or activity. Examples include carpenters, masons, ironworkers, electricians, foremen, and so forth. They are usually paid for actual hours worked.

Equipment and Materials

Equipment and materials can also be further classified into two subcategories:

1. *Construction equipment and materials.* This type of equipment and materials is used for the construction process but is not permanently installed in the project. Examples of *construction equipment* are bull-dozers, backhoes, cranes, power generators, forklifts, mechanical

trowels, heaters, and blowers. Inexpensive personal tools are usually treated differently (either as a lump sum for all tools or as the laborer's personal property). Examples of *construction materials* are formwork materials and scaffolding.

2. *Installed equipment and materials.* This type of equipment and materials stays permanently in the project after completion. Examples of *installed equipment* are heat pumps, emergency generators (in hospitals, industrial projects, and some other projects), equipment installed in kitchens, and many specialized equipment in industrial projects. Examples of *installed materials* are concrete, rebar, CMUs (concrete masonry units), brick, mortar, insulation, framing wood, shingles, floor tile and carpet, bathroom accessories, plumbing pipes and fittings, and electrical wires. Elevators and escalators may be classified as either installed equipment or installed materials, but in most cases, they are installed by the same vendor and in the estimate are considered a subcontractor cost.

For estimators, the *equipment* category includes mostly construction equipment. Installed equipment belongs in the *materials* category.

WHAT IS RESOURCE ALLOCATION?

Resource allocation is the assignment of the required resources to each activity, in the required amount and timing. Resource allocation is also called *resource loading.*

RESOURCE LEVELING

What Is Resource Leveling?

Resource leveling is minimizing the fluctuations in day-to-day resource use throughout the project. It is usually done by shifting noncritical activities within their available float. It attempts to make the daily use of a certain resource as uniform as possible.

Why Level Resources?

When the contractor adds the daily total demand for a specific resource for all activities, he or she must provide the required amount, or work will be delayed.

This daily demand naturally fluctuates depending on the work being performed that day and the resource demand for each activity. It is not practical or economical to hire, say, 10 carpenters for 2 weeks, then lay off 4 (or pay them for not working) for 1 week, then hire 8 extra workers for 4 days, then lay off 6 of them, and so on.

Leveling may also be necessary for an expensive piece of equipment (which may cost money not only in rental expenses, but in the cost of mobilization, setup, maintenance, and demobilization). Say, for example, two activities require a tower crane at the same time. If you can delay the start of the second activity till the first has finished, you will redirect your resource (the tower crane) to the second activity. By doing this, you will have reduced the maximum demand of tower cranes at any time to only one, which will save expenses.

Do All Resources Have to Be Leveled?

Not all resources need to be leveled. The main idea of resource leveling is to improve work efficiency and minimize cost during the life of the project. This concept applies to resources that are hired or rented—namely, labor and (major) construction equipment. The need for such resources may vary significantly as some activities start (they pull new resources) and other activities finish (they release their resources). Likewise, the resource requirement of some activities changes during their duration.

In general, materials do not need to be leveled. For instance, it is common practice to place 100 CY (cubic yards) of concrete 1 day, to place no concrete for 1 week, then to place more concrete the week after, and so on. Project managers mainly have to arrange small deliveries in an economical way. Materials must be managed using a completely different concept, as discussed at the end of this chapter.

Multiproject Resource Leveling

Some resources may be shared among projects. The question is which resources and how much of them. For small projects in a relatively close vicinity, for example, some staff (project manager, safety manager, quality manager, secretary, etc.) and equipment may be shared. Project managers must make decisions when the situation looks like a borderline case: for instance, would it be more efficient to have someone travel between two jobs or to hire another person even though the person will not be occupied 100% of the time? The same argument holds for equipment. In general, convenience and simple economics are mostly the driving criteria. However, other issues may be considered, such as the short- and long-term need; future market expectations; staff morale, fatigue, and satisfaction; relationships with vendors and subcontractors; and so forth.

EXAMPLE 6.1

Assume a project engineer earns $30 per hour. Two projects are within x miles of each other. The engineer travels at an average speed of 40 miles per hour and costs the company $0.35 per mile to travel between the two projects. Assume the following four statements are true:

1. The engineer is needed a minimum of 3 hours/day in each project,
2. travel between the two projects occurs only once a day (the engineer starts his or her day on job A, travels to job B, and then comes back home near job A),
3. overtime, if needed, is compensated at 1.5 times the regular rate, and
4. a second engineer costs the same amount as the first one.

What is the maximum distance between the two projects that makes sharing the same engineer efficient?

Solution
Let's consider two situations.

First—no overtime. No overtime means the engineer may travel between the two jobs (roundtrip) for no more than 2 hours (3 hours at job A + 3 hours at job B + 2 hours' travel = 8 hours per day).

Maximum distance = 2 hours · 40 mph = 80 miles roundtrip or 40 miles one way,

Mileage compensation = 80 · $0.35/mile = $28 per day,

Total cost per day = $30 · 8 + $28 = $268,

■ and

Average cost per hour = $268/8 = $33.50.

It is clearly much more economical to use one engineer than to hire two engineers at a combined cost of $60 per hour.

Second—with overtime. Let us assume the two jobs are 100 miles apart. The first engineer will have 5 hours of driving time (2.5 hours each way), or 11 hours of work per day.

Mileage compensation = 200 * $0.35/mile = $70 per day,

Overtime compensation = 3 * $30 * 1.5 = $135,

Regular-time compensation = 8 * $30 = $240,

and

Total cost per day = 70 + 135 + 240 = $445.

This cost is still less than $480 per day (the cost of two engineers, one at each job), but the difference is narrowing.

When the time needed at each job plus the travel time between the two jobs increases, hiring a second engineer may be more economical. Other factors influencing such decisions are length of need and future expected need. If the need is temporary, it may be more cost efficient to pay overtime to one engineer. Alternatively, some companies use temp(orary) workers to fill their short-term needs.

Staff members who do not have to be present at the job site every day may be spread out, either by dividing the day between two or more jobs or by assigning certain entire days to different jobs. Certain high-paid staff, such as safety officers, schedulers, and project control people, who need to spend only 1 day every week or every 2 weeks at the job site, may even fly hundreds of miles between jobs.

Assigning Budgets in Computer Scheduling Programs

Without going into accounting details, let us briefly cover budgeting in this chapter—only in the context of project control and resource leveling. In scheduling programs, two methods are available for assigning budgets to activities (this subject is discussed further in chapter 10):

1. Assigning a lump-sum amount without telling the scheduling program how the number is sliced or which resources used. You may still need to supply a cost account code in some software packages, which helps track the cost.

2. Assigning a number of units of certain resources (e.g., one bulldozer, one foreman, one equipment operator, two laborers, and one hydraulic excavator) to the activity. The program will calculate the budget for a particular activity from the "resource dictionary" in the project database.

The second method has four advantages:

1. You can level your resources only when you assign resources to the activity.

2. You can link your schedule with accounting (and estimating), match your demand with supply, and trace each expense in your project. You can do this, too, with the first method, but you will see only dollar amounts without any breakdown details.

3. In case there is a change in the cost or availability of a resource that is being used for one or more activities, the scheduling program will reflect the impact of the change at the entire project level.

4. **Resource-driven schedules** are possible. Under certain conditions, you can allow your resources to control the duration of an activity. For example, if a **resource-driven activity** requires four painters for 10 days, the program uses a total of 40 man-days, or 320 man-hours, for its basis. Depending on the painters' availability and logic, the scheduling program may assign a fluctuating number of painters to the activity to finish the job in the most efficient way (from a resource management perspective). The result may be an increase or a decrease in the duration, with the same bottom-line 320 man-hours. This option may also be turned off to maintain the original duration.

One interesting scenario that pertains to point 3 is when resources are priced through a certain date, then increase. Suppose a union contract calls for a carpenter's pay rate of $18 per hour through 6/30/05. After this, it will increase to $20 per hour. Assume a particular activity requires 128 carpenter man-hours and is scheduled to take place in June 2005. The total cost for the carpenters is 128 * $18 = $2,304. Now, suppose the activity schedule slips to July. The cost will increase by 128 * $2 = $256, for a new budget of $2,560. This extra cost may be in addition to other delay-related expenses. You have to be careful in such cases as to whether to allow the resource dictionary to drive the budget or to treat the budget as a fixed amount.

Leveling Resources in a Project

Resource leveling is a mathematically complex process. The resource-leveling method is called The *minimum moment approach,* as it was discussed by Robert B. Harris (1978) in his classic textbook, *Precedence and Arrow Networking Techniques for Construction.* Fortunately, computer programs eliminated the difficult part of this process. Let us deal with resource leveling manually for a small, simple example.

EXAMPLE 6.2

A subcontractor needs to install flooring in two areas:

1. *Area 1.* This area has old vinyl tile that must be removed and replaced with new vinyl tile.
2. *Area 2.* This area has a concrete slab that needs to be topped with ceramic tile.

This simple project is broken into the activities shown in the following table, along with the logic, the duration, and the required number of laborers for each.

ACTIVITY ID	ACTIVITY DESCRIPTION	IPA[a]	DURATION (DAYS)	LABORERS
A	Purchase & Deliver Materials	—	5	2
B	Remove Old Vinyl Tile	—	7	4
C	Install Ceramic Tile	A	3	3
D	Install New Vinyl Tile	A, B	5	3
E	Clean Up & Inspect	C, D	2	2

[a]Immediately preceding activity.

Do the following:

1. Draw the precedence network and perform the CPM calculations.
2. Allocate the required resources, then level them so that the subcontractor does not use more than six laborers at any time.
3. Find ways to improve the labor usage profile.

For the sake of simplicity, assume that any laborer can perform any task.

Solution

Figure 6.1 shows the precedence diagram for this example, and Figure 6.2, the bar chart and **resource usage profile,** or laborer, usage profile.

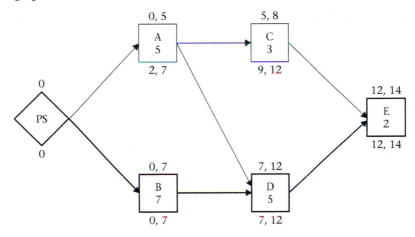

FIGURE 6.1   Precedence diagram for example 6.2 (PS, project start)

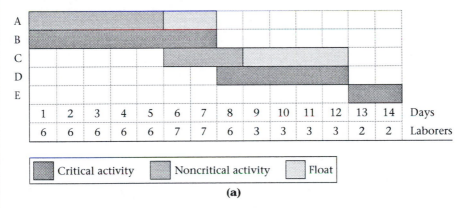

(a)

FIGURE 6.2   (a) Bar chart for example 6.2 with an unleveled labor assignment (typically following early dates);

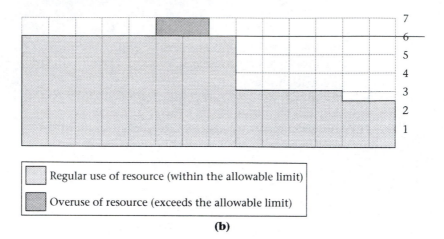

Regular use of resource (within the allowable limit)

Overuse of resource (exceeds the allowable limit)

(b)

FIGURE 6.2   *(continued)* (b) resource, or labor, usage profile for example 6.2, showing overallocation

Using the early dates, we note that on days 6 and 7, the subcontractor needs seven laborers, one more than the limit. He or she then decides to use 2 days of the float for activity C (Figure 6.3). This shift eliminates the labor-use spike on days 6 and 7 and increases the laborers' use on days 9 and 10 from three to six.

The subcontractor observes that even though he or she did not exceed the limit on the number of laborers per day (six) in Figure 6.3, he or she can improve the labor usage profile by minimizing the fluctuations, as shown in Figure 6.4.

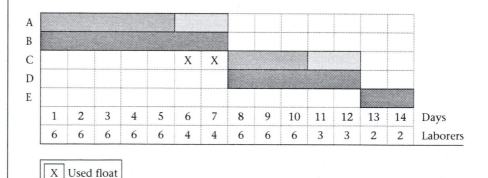

	1	2	3	4	5	6	7	8	9	10	11	12	13	14	Days
	6	6	6	6	6	4	4	6	6	6	3	3	2	2	Laborers

X Used float

(a)

FIGURE 6.3   (a) Bar chart for example 6.2 with a leveled labor assignment (within the allowable limit);

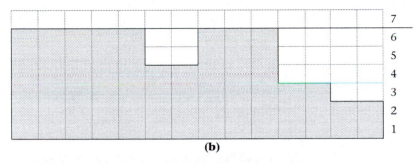

(b)

FIGURE 6.3 *(continued)* (b) resource, or labor, usage profile for example 6.2, with a labor assignment within the allowable limit

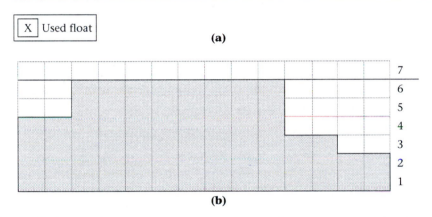

	1	2	3	4	5	6	7	8	9	10	11	12	13	14	Days
	4	4	6	6	6	6	6	6	6	6	3	3	2	2	Laborers

X	Used float

(a)

(b)

FIGURE 6.4 (a) Bar chart for example 6.2 with the labor assignment leveled and more efficiently distributed; (b) resource, or labor, usage profile for example 6.2 with the labor assignment efficiently distributed within the allowable limit

EXAMPLE 6.3

Let us consider a more complicated example, which is still far less complicated than real projects, which have hundreds of activities and tens of resources.

ACTIVITY ID	ACTIVITY DESCRIPTION	DURATION (DAYS)	IPA	LABORERS
A	Excavation & Foundation	6	—	4
B	SOG	3	A	3
C	Framing I	10	B	4
D	Plumbing	4	B	2
E	Electrical Wiring	3	C*	3
F	Drywall	5	C*	3
G	HVAC (heating, ventilation, and air-conditioning) rough-in	3	C*	4
H	Roof	5	C	3
I	Paint	4	F	2
J	HVAC Finish	2	G, H	2
K	Flooring	4	D, I	3
L	Electrical Finish	1	E, H	2
M	Punch List & Cleanup	1	J, K, L	2

*This is a combination SS + FF relationship.

For each of the following scenarios, determine how to level the resources:

   a. An unlimited number of laborers
   b. Only 10 laborers available at any time
   c. Only 8 laborers available but a peak use of 10 laborers is allowed for one time (day) only
   d. Only 8 laborers available at any time
   e. Only 8 laborers available at any time but activities may be interrupted
   f. Only 8 laborers available at any time but the laborer resource may drive the durations of activities

Solution

   a. *An unlimited number of laborers.* As shown in Figure 6.5, the project finishes in 28 days. Using the early dates results in a maximum labor use of 14 laborers per day on days 17, 18, and 19.

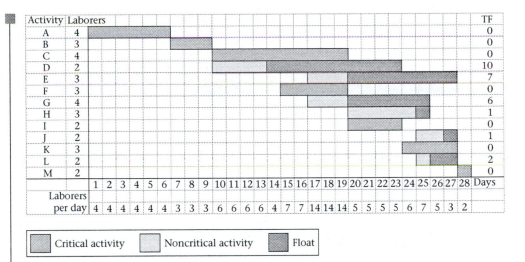

FIGURE 6.5 Bar chart for example 6.3 with an unleveled labor assignment

b. *Only 10 laborers available at any time.* Only one adjustment is necessary: delay activity G by 3 days (it had 6 days of total float), as shown in Figure 6.6.

c. *Only 8 laborers available but a peak use of 10 laborers is allowed for one time (day) only.* Another adjustment is necessary: delay activity E by 6 days (it had 7 days of total float), as shown in Figure 6.7.

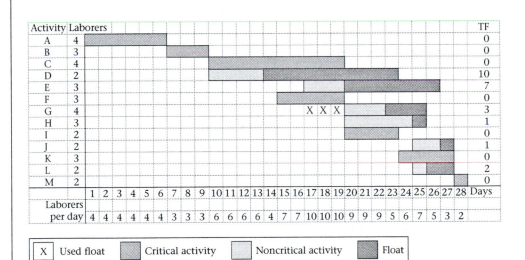

FIGURE 6.6 Bar chart for example 6.3 with the labor assignment leveled and a maximum of 10 laborers per day

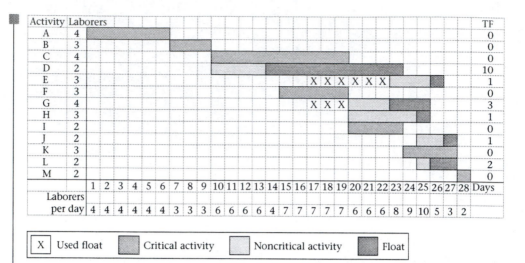

FIGURE 6.7 Bar chart for example 6.3 with the labor assignment leveled, a normal limit of 8 laborers per day, and a maximum of 10 laborers per day

d. *Only 8 laborers available at any time.* Note that in this case, the project must be delayed by 1 day (Figure 6.8). This is an example of **forward resource leveling,** in which resources are not available to both satisfy the demand for all activities and finish on time. This situation is discussed at the end of this example.

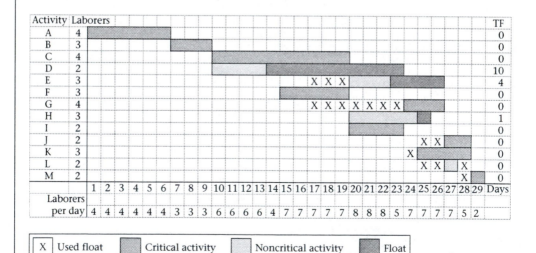

FIGURE 6.8 Bar chart for example 6.3 with the labor assignment leveled and a maximum of 8 laborers per day

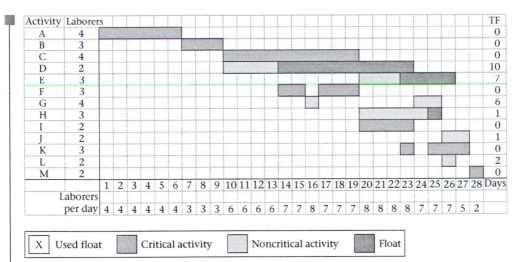

Activity	Laborers		TF
A	4		0
B	3		0
C	4		0
D	2		10
E	3		7
F	3		0
G	4		6
H	3		1
I	2		0
J	2		1
K	3		0
L	2		2
M	2		0

Days: 1 2 3 4 5 6 7 8 9 10 11 12 13 14 15 16 17 18 19 20 21 22 23 24 25 26 27 28

Laborers per day: 4 4 4 4 4 4 3 3 3 6 6 6 6 7 7 8 7 7 7 8 8 8 8 7 7 7 5 2

X	Used float		Critical activity		Noncritical activity		Float

FIGURE 6.9 Bar chart for example 6.3 with the labor assignment leveled, a maximum of 8 laborers per day, and interruptible activities

e. *Only 8 laborers available at any time but allow that activities may be interrupted.* Even with interruptible activities, we could not satisfy the activities' need for resources and maintain the total resource daily usage within 8 laborers, yet finish in 28 days. We need 29 days. In Figure 6.9, we managed to do it in 28 days with one minor violation of the logic: We allowed activity K to start one day before the completion of activity I.

f. *Only 8 laborers available at any time but the laborer resource may drive the durations of activities.* We show two scenarios in Figures 6.10a and 6.10b. Other scenarios can lead to the same project duration: 22 days. In this case, we "played with" activity resource allocations, allowing durations to fluctuate on the basis of supply (available resources) and demand (total resource requirements for activities). Even though we did not allow resource use to exceed 8 laborers per day, we were able to finish the project in 22 days (vs. 29 days in case d). Note also that we did not interrupt activities. If we allow activity C to start on the last day of activity B, we can cut the project duration to 21 days, as shown in Figure 6.11. Also, if we allow activity M to occur

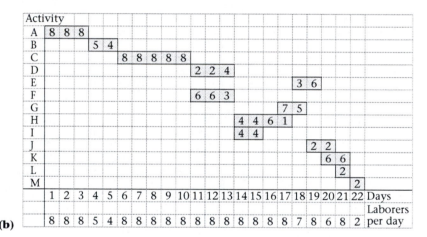

FIGURE 6.10   Bar charts for example 6.3 with the labor resource driving the durations of activities and a maximum of 8 laborers per day (a) for scenario 1 and (b) for scenario 2

on the second day of activity L, we cut another day of the duration without going over the 8 laborers per day limit. For example, we could have started activity E, F, or G on days 4 and 5 of the project, when the resource demand was low. Doing so would have cut out day 14 in Figure 6.10a (see Figure 6.11a) or day 18 in Figure 6.10b (see Figure 6.11b), which would have reduced the project duration to 21 days.

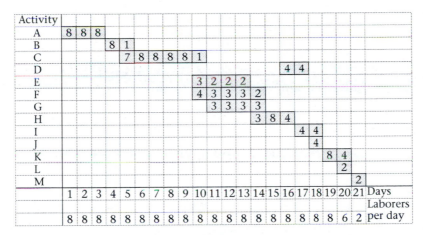

FIGURE 6.11 Bar chart for example 6.3 with labor resource driving the durations of activities, a maximum of 8 laborers per day, and activity C is allowed to start on the last day of activity B.

Discussion of Example 6.3 You may notice that in some of the figures of example 6.3 we did not use notation on the bars to indicate critical and noncritical activities. In fact, all activities may be considered "critical" in a way, but not necessarily unique. Moving an activity—even if doing so does not violate the logic—may disturb the resource allocation and may result in overallocation in certain periods. Therefore, logic and resource constraints must be met at the same time. You can use different combinations of resource allocations to maintain the following four criteria:

1. No more than 8 laborers used on any day
2. A correct total labor-day allocation for each activity
3. Unviolated logic
4. The earliest possible project finish date

If we classify activities as critical and noncritical and then try to use the total float of a noncritical activity, we may impair the resource leveling and cause a delay. The author of this book believes that this area of current commercial software needs more research and development before it can reach a stage at which the user is given all options, in a user-friendly way, to make educated decisions. The software should be able to display different scenarios (in plain English), such as the following:

- You can finish the project in 92 days with no resource leveling (unlimited resources) and no activity interruption.
- You can finish the project in 83 days with no resource leveling (unlimited resources) but allowing activities to be interrupted.
- You can finish the project in 98 days with a certain limit for resource use.
- You can finish the project in . . .

More Discussion   As defined previously, leveling resources involves shifting activities within their float to minimize the fluctuations in daily resource use. This "shifting" may involve any, or a combination of, the following:

- Delaying the start of an activity to any date up to and including its late start date.
- Interrupting an activity and resuming it later (breaking the activity into two or more segments) but finishing it no later than its late start date. The idea is to put "chunks" of the activity in the "schedule gaps" where resource use is low.
- Fluctuating the amount of resources assigned to an activity, day to day, according to resource availability, until the activity gets all the required resources.

Important   Note that the last two options often require special rules settings in computer programs. These programs may be set for default rules that do not allow such practices.

As mentioned previously, in some cases, staying within the available resource limits yet completing the project by the finish deadline is not possible. In such cases, the project manager must choose one, or a combination, of the following:

- Increase the limits on the available resources. This increase may be across the board (for the entire duration of the project), for one-time use, or for an assigned period. It may also be for one or more particular resources.
- Start the project on the planned start date but maintain the resource limits and allow the project to finish later than the finish deadline. This option is typically considered forward leveling.

- If feasible, start the project earlier than the planned start date by a number of days so that you can finish the project on the required finish date without raising the resource limits. This method usually levels resources starting from the project finish date, then working backward till the required start date. It is referred to as **backward resource leveling.**

- The preceding three practices are all based on the assumption that the logic cannot be changed. In reality, the relationships of some activities can be relaxed somewhat. The most common reason for this is when, for example, activity B requires only a portion of activity A to be finished before it can start. Project managers tend to assign finish-to-start (FS) relationships for all types of cases. A more in-depth inspection of the schedule by the scheduler and the project manager may reveal some of these cases. Changing the FS relationship to an SS relationship (possibly with a lag) may open the schedule a bit by giving some activities more float, and, hence, more flexibility. In Figure 6.12, the two-activity setup in part (a) takes 16 days, whereas the one in part (b) takes only 10 days.

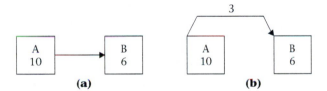

FIGURE 6.12   The effect of changing (a) an FS (finish-to-start) relationship to (b) an SS (start-to-start) relationship: a decrease in duration from 16 days to 10 days

- Make some activities interruptible. To the author's best knowledge, commercial software scheduling programs do not give the user the option of having certain (but not all) activities interruptible, then allowing the program to interrupt (split) them in the optimum way from a resource-leveling viewpoint. However, most programs allow manual interruption (stop, resume). Primavera Project Planner allows the choice of "contiguous" (the default value) versus "interruptible" at the entire project level. The interrupted activity does not show as a group of small bars. Rather, it shows as one long bar that starts (for early bars) with the earliest possible start date and ends with the earliest possible finish date (e.g., in Figure 6.9 the bars for activities F and K stretch more than their durations). The actual duration may be distributed within the bar without violating a logic constraint (such as finishing E, F, or G before finishing C).

- In Primavera Project Planner software, the resources (or budget) are distributed evenly throughout the duration of the activity. You may change this by assigning another distribution (e.g., triangular, normal). You may define any type of distribution by dividing the resource (or budget) into 11 increments throughout the duration of the activity. Increment 1 is usually assigned 0% because it represents 0% completion. The next 10 increments represent 10%, 20%, . . . , 100% completion. For example, increments of 0, 1, 3, 8, 15, 23, 23, 15, 8, 3, and 1 represent a bell-shaped curve. Note that the 11 increments must total 100%. With such a tool, you can concentrate the resources at the beginning, middle, or end of the duration of the activity. In the bell-shaped curve, the resources are concentrated in the middle. The contractor may use this feature to concentrate the budget at the beginning of the activity **(front-end loading the cost).**

Resource Leveling from the General Contractor's Perspective

Since the 1980s, subcontracting has increased to the point that many general contractors subcontract everything in a project (i.e., perform 0% of the project with their own workforce). Yet, the general contractor is still responsible for maintaining the schedule for the owner. In this case, resource leveling no longer becomes a concern to the general contractor because the resources are not his or hers. The general contractor instead must manage the overall work of his or her subcontractors. However, he or she may still be concerned with the following four issues:

1. Keeping up with the subcontractors' schedules and the number of workers each subcontractor has, each day, is one concern. The general contractor must make sure the site is not congested to the point of impeding work or causing safety problems. The general contractor must also be convinced that his or her subcontractors have sufficient resources to make adequate progress.

2. If the owner's purchased equipment and materials are to be used, the general contractor must be in full coordination with the relevant subcontractor with regard to the time and method of delivery.

3. When the general contractor is providing equipment such as a crane to the subcontractors, he or she must coordinate the use of this equipment and prioritize the subcontractors' needs.

4. For project control, the general contractor must enter the budget of each activity into the computer, then record and verify the progress of the activity so that the subcontractor is paid in a timely and accurate manner.

In such cases, each subcontractor may do his or her own resource leveling, with one important difference: the subcontractor's schedule is part of the general contractor's **master schedule.** As is typical of any critical path method (CPM) schedule, each **subschedule** may contain a range of dates for noncritical activities (i.e., early start, early finish, late start, and late finish). In many cases, the general contractor requires "scheduled dates" for certain activities (i.e., a single set of dates chosen between the early and late dates). This approach is used especially for activities that require coordination with the general contractor or other subcontractors. In such cases, the subcontractor loses the float for such activities and his or her scheduled dates become critical. The subcontractor must then be careful not to change the start or finish dates of these activities—for any reason—without consulting the general contractor.

MATERIALS MANAGEMENT

Materials management is defined as the planning and controlling of all necessary efforts to ensure that the correct quality and quantity of materials and equipment are appropriately specified in a timely manner, are obtained at a reasonable cost, and are available when needed (Construction Industry Institute [CII] 1986b). A materials management system includes the major functions of identifying (project planning and material takeoff), acquiring (vendor inquiry and evaluation, purchasing, expediting, and transportation), distributing (field material control and warehousing), and disposing of materials needed for a construction project (Construction Industry Institute

1986b, 1988b). Four important objectives of materials management are as follows (Construction Industry Institute 1988b):

1. Ensure that materials meet the specifications and are on hand when and where required.
2. Obtain the best value for purchased materials.
3. Provide efficient, low-cost transport, security, and storage of materials at construction sites.
4. Reduce any surplus to the lowest level possible.

Materials management is an important component of the project schedule. This function starts early with the planning phase of the project. When developing the materials plan, the general contractor must consider various factors, such as project size, scope, and location; cash-flow requirements; schedule and lead times of critical purchases; the owner's philosophy; owner approvals; the number of project participants; inspection roles; use of owner purchase agreements; acceptable bidders' or suppliers' list; and extent of prefabrication (Construction Industry Institute 1988b).

Some authors (Ahuja, Dozzi, and Abourizk 1994; Hendrickson and Au 1989) have identified four materials cost categories, as follows:

1. *Purchase costs.* Purchase costs are what the vendor charges for the materials, including transportation and freight costs. Usual practice is for vendors to give a volume discount as well as an incentive for quick payment. For example, the invoice may have the term *2/10 NET 30,* which means a 2% discount if the bill is paid fully within 10 days of the delivery date, or else the full amount is due in 30 days. After 30 days, interest and/or a penalty may apply.
2. *Order costs.* Order costs are the administrative costs for preparing the purchase order, which may not be a simple task. It may involve making requisitions, analyzing alternative vendors, writing purchase orders (with required specifications), receiving materials, inspecting materials, checking on and expediting orders, and maintaining records of the entire process.
3. *Holding costs.* Holding costs include held capital (interest or lost opportunity) and handling, storage, obsolescence, shrinkage, and deterioration costs. Many of these costs are difficult for the project manager to predict, especially those that involve high-tech items,

such as computers and computerized equipment. Insurance and taxes may be added to the holding costs as well.

4. *Shortage (unavailability) costs.* A shortage cost is the cost (or the loss as the result) of not having the required materials on the job site when needed. Shortages may delay work, which may result in the loss of labor resources or delay the entire project.

Theoretically, there are two extreme materials management theories:

1. The **just-in-time theory,** which calls for delivering materials at the time of installation only. Thus, materials are not stored at the site.
2. The **inventory buffer theory,** which calls for all materials to be purchased, delivered, and stored on-site prior to installation.

The advantages of the first theory are less handling, no storage, no frozen capital, and less vulnerability to theft, vandalism, obsolescence, shrinkage, and deterioration—in other words, fewer handling costs. The disadvantages are higher order costs (more orders) and higher shortage costs (higher probability of not having materials on time). Conversely, the advantages of the second theory are lower purchase, order, and shortage costs. The disadvantage is higher holding costs.

In real life, somewhere between the two extreme theories must be chosen for the general contractor to strike a balance that will result in the least total cost. This balance varies from one project to another, depending on several factors, such as the size of the project, the location of the project, the type and availability of materials, the locations of vendors, and weather. To illustrate this point, let us imagine two projects, one in the middle of nowhere (desert or countryside); call it *project A*. The other project is in the downtown of a major city; call it *project B*. Project A has plenty of space for organized storage and is away from urban areas. Thus, it is less vulnerable to theft and vandalism but far away from vendors and suppliers. In this case, ordering most or all materials in advance (as in the inventory buffer theory) makes sense. In the case of project B, we are in the downtown area of a major city, so storage space is scarce and theft and vandalism occur frequently. At the same time, plenty of vendors and suppliers are located within a 10-mile radius and can deliver on short notice and for little cost. In this case, we probably want to manage materials by using an approach closer to the just-in-time theory.

Other factors influencing which theory should predominate are the type and the availability of materials. For instance, ready-mix concrete must be delivered on time in all cases because it cannot be stored. In fact, for projects at remote locations it may be more practical and economical to have a concrete mix plant on-site, especially if the project is large. Similarly, expensive equipment may also need to be delivered on time for security reasons.

Weather (rain, snow, ice, wind, temperature, humidity) may be a factor that influences the delivery and storage decision. The 1976 Montreal Olympic Games experience reminds us of what can happen with poor planning. The precast posttensioned concrete beams were left on the ground (because of a labor strike), and water got into the tubes and froze before the cable had been threaded. Removal of the ice required expensive drilling and contributed further to a loss of time (Neil 1982).

Another interesting weather-related case was a large project in northern Canada. The location was remote from any urban area or even paved roads. Moving equipment and materials was possible only by air, which was expensive. Work was planned to take place only during the warm months because of the harsh winter conditions. An efficient plan was prepared to move equipment and materials on sleds during the winter. Some icy roads and bridges had to be prepared for this purpose, but the transportation cost was a fraction of the alternative: airlifting. The equipment and materials were kept in shelters till the weather permitted work to start.

For further information on materials management, refer to the books listed in the Project and Construction Management section of the Bibliography (especially see the Construction Industry Institute, 1986b, 1988b, books).

CHAPTER 6 EXERCISES

1. In the context of scheduling, what do we mean by *resources*?
2. What is *resource allocation*?
3. What is *resource leveling*?
4. Why level resources in construction projects?
5. Do all resources have to be leveled? Why or why not?
6. Discuss resource leveling in a multiproject environment.

7. Can you level resources in a multiproject environment? If so, what are the factors that influence your decision?

8. Two methods are used to assign a budget to an activity in the schedule. Explain both methods and mention the pros and cons of each method.

9. In the following network, manually level your resources so that you may not use more than nine laborers per day at any time.

ACTIVITY	DURATION (DAYS)	IPA	LABORERS
A	2	—	3
B	4	A	2
C	6	A	4
D	9	A	3
E	5	B	4
F	7	B, C	2
G	3	D, E, F	3

10. In the following network, try to reduce the maximum resource need to less than eight laborers per day. Can you do this? If not, can you manually shift activities so that you improve the daily resource use? (We try to start low, increase the resource use gradually till it peaks around the middle of the project, then gradually decrease it toward the end of the project.)

ACTIVITY	DURATION (DAYS)	IPA	LABORERS
A	6	—	2
B	2	—	3
C	8	A	3
D	5	A, B	5
E	3	B	4
F	6	D, E	3
G	5	C, D	2
H	2	F, G	3

11. In the following network, manually level your resources with a maximum of eight laborers per day. Also, improve the daily resource use

(start low, increase the resource use gradually till it peaks around the middle of the project, then gradually decrease it toward the end of the project).

ACTIVITY	DURATION (DAYS)	IPA	LABORERS
A	6	—	2
B	2	—	3
C	9	—	3
D	4	A, B	3
E	7	B	4
F	5	D	2
G	10	D, E	3
H	8	C, F, G	1
I	3	C, G	2
J	2	H, I	2

12. In exercise 9, can you improve the resource use by making the resources driving (i.e., they control the durations of activities)? Activities are still contiguous (noninterruptible).

13. In exercise 9, can you improve the resource use by making the resources driving and the activities interruptible?

14. In exercise 10, can you improve the resource use by making the resources driving (i.e., they control the durations of activities)? Activities are still contiguous (noninterruptible).

15. In exercise 10, can you improve the resource use by making the resources driving and the activities interruptible?

16. In exercise 11, can you improve the resource use by making the resources driving (i.e., they control the durations of activities)? Activities are still contiguous (noninterruptible).

17. In exercise 11, can you improve the resource use by making the resources driving and the activities interruptible?

18. In exercise 10, you are given only six laborers (rather than eight). Write a memo to the project manager discussing the situation and giving him or her the available choices (along with the consequences).

19. With regard to resource leveling, how does the role of a scheduler differ between working for a general contractor who does almost all his or her work with his or her own workforce and working for a general contractor who subcontracts everything?

20. Assume you are the scheduler for a large project. You work for the construction manager (CM), whose function is to manage the project and to coordinate the work of the subcontractors involved (there is no general contractor). You required each subcontractor to submit his or her schedule to you on a disk in Primavera Project Planner format. Where do you go from there? Write an itemized plan.

21. Why does materials management differ in principle from labor and equipment management? Briefly explain the concept of materials management.

22. What are the main objectives of materials management?

23. What types of costs are associated with materials management?

24. Materials management is a balance between two extreme theories. Explain this statement, mentioning the factors that influence your decision to lean more toward one theory than the other.

CHAPTER 7

Schedule Updating and Project Control

Baptist Hospital, Miami, Florida. Courtesy of Smith Aerial Photos, Maitland, Florida.

INTRODUCTION

If you have a powerful tool but never use it, it becomes ineffective or even useless. This description of the tool may be unfair, but the user is responsible for using the tool. Without a doubt, schedules are an extremely effective tool for managing construction projects, especially large and complex projects. However, schedules are not just for preparation and presentation to the owner before commencement of the work. Nor are they just a satisfaction of contractual requirements. Schedules are for day-to-day management operations. The most important use of schedules is *project control:* The scheduler compares actual performance with baseline performance and discerns any deviation. The project management team then deals with this deviation, analyzes it, and suggests solutions to bring the schedule back on track, if possible.

Using critical path method (CPM) scheduling as an effective tool requires a serious commitment from upper management to adopt and use the schedule throughout the project. There is a difference in attitude between a contractor who is using the schedule because he or she is convinced that it is an effective and powerful tool for project management and a contractor who is using the schedule because the owner requires doing so.

THE NEED FOR SCHEDULE UPDATING

Construction projects rarely—if ever—go as planned. Thus, we expect some deviation from the baseline. We need to know where and how much, then take corrective action whenever and wherever needed. Consider the following example: The army fires a long-range missile at a target about 500 miles away. The missile is given the coordinates of the target, so it flies at a certain, accurate angle. For various reasons, the missile goes astray by a fraction of a degree. Central command tracks and communicates with the missile, reads the actual location, and compares it with the destination location. Central command makes adjustments to the direction of the missile. This process occurs continuously to ensure the missile hits its target accurately. An early uncorrected error of a few minutes (a *minute* is 1/60th of a degree) in the direction may mean missing the target by a few hundred feet or even several miles.

PROJECT CONTROL DEFINED

Project control comprises the following continuous process:

1. Monitoring work progress
2. Comparing it with the baseline schedule and budget (what it was supposed to be)
3. Finding any deviations, determining where and how much, and analyzing them to discover the causes
4. Taking corrective action whenever and wherever necessary to bring the project back on schedule and within budget

Along with these four basic functions, another function of project control may be to help identify areas in which to improve work efficiency, to help accelerate the schedule, to help reduce cost, or to help the project in other ways.

Project control in the context of this book involves both budget control and schedule control. It can also include quality control and safety control, but they usually occur in separate departments and are analyzed differently. A significant correlation exists between budget control and schedule control, as described later in this chapter.

The term **project monitoring** is sometimes used in lieu of *project control*. Project monitoring, by definition, is passive. Although some people may use this term to mean more, it simply means "observation." The term **project tracking** is also used in the same context (Oberlender 2000). Depending on the intention and the role of the "tracker," tracking may or may not be equivalent to project control. The owner or construction manager (as a separate entity from the constructor) may "monitor" or "track" the project by observing the work progress and comparing it with the baseline budget, schedule, and quality. However, only the party who is physically doing the work—namely, the constructor—can "control" the project by not only monitoring or tracking it, but also taking corrective measures whenever and wherever necessary.

SCHEDULE UPDATING

Schedule updating is just one part of the project control process. Schedule updating must reflect actual work and involves incorporating approved changes into the baseline schedule.

What Is a Baseline Schedule?

A **baseline schedule** is a schedule prepared by the contractor, usually before the start of the project, and used for performance comparison. If approved by the owner, the baseline schedule usually becomes a part of the contract documents.

The baseline schedule is also called a **target schedule.** The *as-planned schedule* is the schedule submitted by the contractor—as usually required by the contract—and approved by the owner before the start of the project (and sometimes before the signing of the contract). Sometimes, the baseline schedule is the same as the as-planned schedule, but not always. In many situations, the as-planned schedule is submitted and approved, then some changes are implemented before the project starts, as a result of debugging, the owner's changes, or both. The baseline schedule should not be delayed beyond the start of the project, particularly if the contractor uses actual dates to build such a schedule. Otherwise, it will not be baseline.

The baseline schedule may be used by both the general contractor, who will execute the work, and the owner (or his or her representative), whose work is being executed. Sometimes both parties will use the baseline schedule for project control: each from his or her own perspective. A third party (professional construction management firm) may also monitor the schedule and compare it with the baseline. The baseline schedule, when part of the contract documents, binds not only the general contractor, but also all subcontractors, even if they were not part of the preparation of the baseline schedule. A general rule is that any condition or requirement in the contract between the owner and the general contractor automatically applies to all parties working under the general contractor and involved in the construction of the project.

In many cases, the as-planned schedule is also a part of the contract documents that bind both the owner and the contractor. It may provide a foundation for resolving any subsequent delay-claim disputes. It may also be used as a legal document in case of litigation.

In ill-planned projects, many change orders may be issued, and the baseline schedule will keep changing. Such changes may shift the critical path and thus the focus of effort. Such a situation may be counterproductive to the project management. The baseline schedule must incorporate design and other changes for fair and realistic comparisons. Therefore, a project may have two or more baseline schedules: one before and one after changes. It is strongly recommended that one of them be adopted for periodic comparison with actual performance. In some cases, it is possible and helpful to compare the current update with both the baseline schedule and the previous update. For example, if the current update shows the critical path with -10 days of float, this may be interpreted as bad news with regard to the "absolute measure" (as compared with the baseline schedule). However, if the previous update indicated -16 days of total float, the contractor is on the right track, bringing the project back to the baseline schedule.

Just like cost estimates, baseline schedules are a prediction. Slight and sporadic deviation is always expected in construction projects. An open eye and an expert mind can discern a serious deviation from a minor "normal" variation.

Baseline schedules are prepared on the basis of expectations and previous experiences. Thus, it is advisable to keep an accurate record of previous work to use for future estimates. As discussed in chapter 4 (in the Steps Required to Schedule a Project section), the scheduling team must not only crunch numbers (calculate durations), but also deal with real work conditions and make reasonable adjustments whenever and wherever needed.

Baseline schedules must be reasonable and realistic. They must take into consideration work and weather conditions; the size and complexity of the project; local codes and regulations; the location of and access to the project site; the labor market; materials and equipment availability, prices, and delivery; and other issues. Sometimes an overlooked activity such as Obtain Permits can hold up the entire project for a month or more. Likewise, a long-lead or custom item may need to be ordered several months before the required delivery date. A contractor's acceptance of an unrealistically ambitious schedule may hurt his or her reputation and pocket, even though his or her fieldwork may have proceeded at a normal and decent pace. The famous proverb "Expect the worst and hope for the best" can be modified in this context as "Be conservative in your expectations and strive for the best."

Baseline schedules may initially be prepared as summary schedules. A **summary schedule** may contain only a few major components; the details are left for a later stage. For example, a schedule prepared by the architect may include the different design activities and milestones, with Construction represented by a single 9-month activity. Later, when construction details are known, this activity is divided into reasonable-sized activities that have a combined duration of 9 months. Summary baseline schedules are not usually used for project control. However, such schedules may be prepared along with design development: the more we know about the project, the more details we have in the design, and the more detailed the schedule becomes. This case applies particularly to fast-track projects (discussed in chapter 5). With such projects, the project manager can use the following approach: The project is typically divided into several phases (see Figure 5.9), with the initial (preliminary) design done for the entire project. Later, when the detailed design for phase I is finished, the detailed construction plan, including scheduling, must be prepared for phase I while phase II is still being designed. In this case, the detailed schedule for any phase is done before actual construction starts on that phase. This process provides a baseline schedule, phase by phase.

The entire discussion on the baseline schedule applies to the **baseline budget,** with the obvious difference that a schedule deals with time, whereas a budget deals with money. The correlation between the two areas is explained subsequently, when the project control concept is discussed. Another difference is the level of details: In scheduling control, activities are connected by logical relationships. A delay in an activity may have an effect on other activities. In budget control, the effect of a budget overrun in an activity is mostly local and may not have a ripple effect on other activities (unless it is attributed to an increase in the price of resources, then all activities using these resources will be affected).

Primavera Enterprise (P3e), Primavera P3e/c, and Primavera TeamPlay (Primavera Systems, Inc., Bala Cynwyd, PA) create baselines as copies of project updates. These "baselines" are more snapshots than baselines. This concept, which Primavera Systems introduced, is extremely useful. It allows the scheduler to keep copies of the schedule at different points in the life of a project and to store them as inactive copies along with the active, most-updated schedule. The only caution is the name; Primavera Systems calls them *baselines*, but they are not baselines according to our—and the industry's—definition.

What Is an Updated Schedule?

Schedule updating is simply reflecting actual performance information—including time of occurrence and amount (or percentage) of work completed—on the schedule and indicating on the schedule any changes to future work. Popescu and Charoenngam (1995) defined an **updated schedule** as "a revised schedule reflecting project information at a given data date regarding completed activities, in-progress activities, and changes in the logic, cost, and resources required and allocated at any activity level" (p. 566).

What Is the Data Date?

The **data date** is the date as of which all progress on a project is reported. It is also called the **as-of date** and the **status date.** It is *not* the "current date" or the "time now" because the word *current* or *now* is moving along with time and is not tied to a specific time or date. For instance, the latest data date may be Friday, 2/4/05. This means the update contains all work completed up to and including that day. The report may not reach the scheduler till Monday, 2/7/05, or later, and the scheduler may not actually update the schedule till a day or more after that. Thus, it would be wrong to call the data date the *current date* or the *time now*. The data date is similar to the closing date on your checking account or credit card statement. By the time you receive the statement, several days have passed, and the statement reflects the account activities to that date. However, that date is not "current" or "now."

What Kind of Information Is Needed
for Updating Schedules?

Any new information that was not known for the previous update and relates to the schedule must be recorded on and implemented in the schedule. This information falls into two main categories:

1. *Past information.* What has happened since the last update? Past infor-mation includes the following:
    a. Activities that have started, and the actual start date, percent com-plete, and remaining duration of each
    b. Activities that are complete, and the actual completion date of each
    c. The actual budget spending or resource consumption for each activity

    This information can be further divided into *past* and *current* categories, in which *past* represents information about work that occurred prior to the previous update. Such information is considered history and must not be changed during this update.* *Current* repre-sents information about work that occurred between the last update and this update. This category is the main focus area for updating past information.

---

*Although sometimes project managers "revise" dates or other data that were reported previously, this practice may be considered falsification of records if the owner is not fully informed of such revisions.

2. *Future information.* The *future* category comprises any changes to the schedule or schedule-related items, such as the following:
    a. Any activities that have been added, along with their information (duration, logic, budget, resources, constraints, etc.)
    b. Any activities that have been deleted (the scheduler must be sure to maintain proper logic after the deletion)
    c. Activities that have changed in duration, logic, budget, resources, constraints, or otherwise
    d. Any change to the imposed finish date for the entire schedule or the constraint date for certain milestones
    e. Any schedule-related, but not activity-specific, change, such as a change in the cost or availability of resources, a change in calendar workdays, or a change in responsibility (e.g., a subcontractor took over a portion of the general contractor's work, or a subcontractor was replaced)

    Future changes are of two types:
    a. *Logic-driven changes.* Logic-driven changes are those that are not made directly by the scheduler but that occur as a result of changes in planned dates or logic.
    b. *User's changes.* User's changes are those that are made directly by the scheduler. They may not have anything to do with past events.

Frequency of Updating

Construction schedules may be updated monthly, biweekly, weekly, or according to another time interval. Weekly and biweekly are probably the most common frequencies. Project managers must achieve a delicate balance between a period between updates that is too long and one that is too short. The former case may yield negative consequences such as the following:

- Waiting too long to update a schedule may eliminate the effectiveness of updating as a control tool. By the time work progress is reported and analyzed, managers may not have the time or opportunity to take corrective action. This factor can be demotivating for them.
- The amount of work progress that occurred during the period may overwhelm the scheduler. Also, the superintendent or project manager may forget when an activity actually started or finished if the activity occurred a month ago and was not formally documented.

- Having a long reporting period may encourage procrastinators to put off corrective measures by using the logic "We'll do it later. There is plenty of time!"

Conversely, a reporting period that is too short may be costly in terms of time consumption and overhead and reporting costs. It may also become a nuisance to the management team.

Typically, the frequency of updating increases at certain times, such as in the last month or two of a project, or during a "crunch time," such as before a deadline.

Retained Logic or Progress Override

As explained previously, project managers often overuse the finish-to-start (FS) relationship. In many practical cases, an FS relationship is assigned to two activities, A and B, such that activity B cannot start until activity A is completed. In reality, when work starts, activity B starts shortly after activity A has started and prior to its completion. This situation violates the logic. In the "execution report" of Primavera Project Planner (P3) and Primavera's P3e, such a violation is reported (more as a warning than as an error). However, the question the user will be faced with is: Will the remainder of activity B depend on the completion of activity A, or is the FS relationship no longer required? For example, look at activities A and B in Figure 7.1a. Suppose that 6 days after the start of the project, 6 days worth of work is done on activity A (remaining duration = 4) and 2 days' worth of work is done on activity B (remaining duration = 6). Would we choose Retained Logic (the default value; Figure 7.1b) or Progress Override (Figure 7.1c)? The decision between the two choices may mean several days impact to the schedule. In this example, the decision means a 4-day difference in the completion date of activity B, and possibly the entire project.

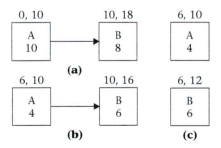

FIGURE 7.1 (a) Activities A and B of a project; (b) Retained Logic after 6 days' work; (c) Progress Override after 6 days' work.

Auto Updating

Some software scheduling programs offer an option for automated updating. Although this option makes updating easy and saves time, a potential danger exists. Along with such options comes the assumption that everything that was supposed to have happened, between the last and current updates, did happen—on the planned dates and within the planned budget and resources. This assumption may be true in most but not all cases. The potential danger is that the scheduler will become accustomed to using this convenient tool and use it all the time. The scheduler should exercise extreme caution in using such automated procedures.

Updating Schedules and Pay Requests

In many cases, project updating is tied to **payment requests** (*pay requests* for short). The subject of pay requests is a broad one that is discussed in detail in other project management books. What concerns us in this chapter is how pay requests tie to schedule updating. In general, a pay request is a document submitted by the contractor (using his or her own form, the owner's form, The American Institute of Architects [AIA] Document G702, or another form) to the owner, asking for payment for work actually performed (whether finished or not) during the period since the last pay request. Materials stored on-site but not yet installed are generally ineligible for inclusion in pay requests unless the contract allows for such payment. Typically, the owner verifies the amounts in the pay request (quantities and unit prices), then, after approval, issues a payment to the contractor that is equal to the approved amount minus any **retainage.***

Pay requests are usually done at the end of each month. Subcontractors usually submit their pay requests to the general contractor, who rolls these requests in with his or hers and submits it to the owner. The owner requests a lien release or waiver from the general contractor and all subcontractors and vendors before issuing the payment. This document assures the owner that the signer paid his or her subcontractors, workers, and vendors for work performed on the project for the period covered in the document. Once the general contractor receives payment, he or she pays the subcontractors.

---

*Retainage is a portion of the eligible progress payment that is held by the owner till the contractor fulfills his or her contractual obligations. The contract usually specifies the amount and conditions of a retainage.

When updating every 2 weeks, you could start by doing the pay request every other update (i.e., every 4 weeks). However, the problem with doing so is that the month is slightly longer than 4 weeks. Schedulers and project managers like to update schedules on a certain day of the week (e.g., Wednesday). To circumvent the conflict between the biweekly update and the monthly pay request, schedulers choose one the following five options:

1. If feasible for the project team, the updates are done on the 1st and 16th of each month. If any of these dates falls during a weekend or a holiday, the update is done on the closest workday.

2. When the update date is near the end of the month (say, within 1 or 2 days), the project manager estimates the work "to be done" between the current data date and the end of the month and counts this work as if it were done (with its real dates). The main drawback to this approach is approving an amount of work that is not yet physically done. If used within certain limitations, this approach may not cause a problem. However, the project manager and the owner must agree on this practice. One argument may be made in support of this approach: since reports take a few days and a payment check may take 2 to 4 weeks, the work done during that time almost always offsets the problem of projecting a few days' work.

3. Suppose the pay request must include work as of the end of day 30. The scheduler does the routine update on time—say, on the 28th of the month. A few days later, the project manager sends the work progress for days 29 and 30 to the scheduler for a "minor update" for the sake of the pay request. The scheduler must then separate "pure updates" and "pay request" schedules. This practice is not recommended.

4. When the update date is several days (say, 4 to 6) before the end of the month, the scheduler "skips" a week so that the next update is done during the first days of the next month. For example, an update is done on the 12th of the month. The next update is scheduled for the 26th of the month. It can be postponed to the 2nd or 3rd of the next month, on the same day of the week on which the 12th occurred.

5. If all contracting parties agree, the pay request may be a few days less or more than a month (i.e., you can close it on the 27th, 28th, or 29th of the month, or on the 1st, 2nd, or 3rd of the following month). In this case, the actual data date is reflected on both the updates and the pay request. However, this practice may not please the accounting

team because monthly accounts may not be accurate even though the bottom-line total will be correct.

When doing a pay request, you must start the month with a $0 amount for the **cost this period** by adding the amount remaining from last period to the total **cost to date** (in Primavera P3, it is called **Store Period Performance**).

"Degressing" an In-Progress Schedule to Create a Baseline Schedule

In some cases, the project schedule develops as work progresses. This is not a good practice. Some activities have already started or even finished when they are added to the schedule. In this case, only an as-built schedule exists; there is no as-planned or baseline schedule for comparison. The scheduler may need to create a baseline schedule at this late stage (better late than never). He or she may do so by taking a copy of the schedule and reversing all work progress in it to "go back in time" to the starting point. Doing so requires reversing progress on all activities, plus going back from the data date to the starting point of the schedule.

   This practice is acceptable (even though it is not the best). However, one important pitfall exists. When entering completed (or even started) activities, the scheduler may ignore their relationships since they are "history." Consider the following partial schedule, for example.

ACTIVITY ID	ACTIVITY DESCRIPTION	DURATION (DAYS)	IPA[a]
1000	Mobilize	2	—
1010	Clear Land	5	1000
1020	Excavation	6	1010
1030	Dewatering	20	1020
1040	Drive Piles	7	1030 SS-5
⋮	⋮	⋮	⋮

[a]Immediately preceding activity.

Suppose this schedule was being created after piles have been driven. The project manager or scheduler may just feed actual dates into the schedule without entering the relationships. He or she may also give actual durations as "original durations," not those estimated; see Figure 7.2a. Now, imagine that we "degress" the project; that is, reverse all work progress and take the data date back to the start date; see Figure 7.2b. In this case, you can see all these activities starting simultaneously at the beginning of the project. There is no need for an explanation; there is no logic. For this reason, the logic must always be input, along with estimated durations. Never forget that this schedule can be—and in most cases is—a legal document that may be dissected later to prove or disprove a delay claim. Accuracy is always important.

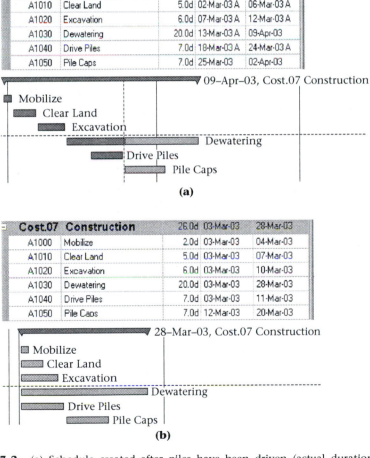

FIGURE 7.2 (a) Schedule created after piles have been driven (actual durations given as "original durations" and no relationships entered); (b) "degressed" schedule.

Effect of Adding or Deleting Activities on Logic

An activity in a schedule is usually like a link in a chain; removing a link may disturb the whole chain if it is not done properly. For example, deleting activity AS250 in the partial network shown in Figure 7.3 will remove any link

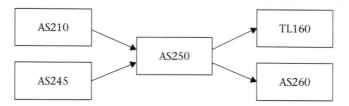

FIGURE 7.3   Effect of removing an activity from a schedule: removal of AS250 would disturb entire chain.

between activities AS210 and AS245 on one side, and activities TL160 and AS260 on the other side. This may have a devastating effect on the schedule if removing such links was not the scheduler's intent. Therefore, it is strongly recommended that the scheduler review the logic before making any change by first printing a logic report showing all predecessors and successors for the activity to be deleted. Some computer programs, such as Primavera Project Planner, have a function called **Dissolve an Activity,** which automatically assigns the predecessors of the dissolved activity to its successors (see Figure 7.4). The user must be careful when dissolving an activity that is tied to other

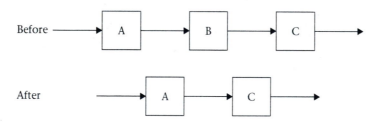

FIGURE 7.4   Dissolving activity B.

activities with relationships other than the FS relationship or that has lags. Regardless of the situation, the scheduler should neither let the computer make decisions for him or her nor let the computer execute commands with which he or she is unfamiliar.

Adding a new activity usually has less potential for harming the logic than does deleting an activity. The usual problem with adding an activity is redundant relationships. For example, we wanted to add activity FL225 to the partial network shown in Figure 7.5a. We assigned activity FL220 as a predecessor and activity FL230 as a successor but did not pay attention to the existing relationship between these two activities. The result was a redundant relationship, as shown in Figure 7.5b. As mentioned previously, redundant relationships are not logically incorrect. They are just meaningless pieces of information. The redundancy in our example can be removed as shown in Figure 7.5c.

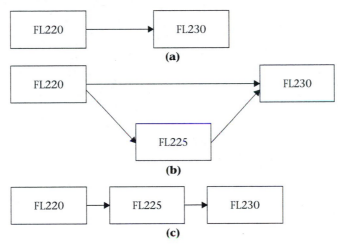

FIGURE 7.5 Adding an activity to the schedule: (a) original logic; (b) resulting redundant relationship; (c) redundancy removed.

EXAMPLE 7.1

In example 4.3, 10 days after the project has started, you receive the following report:

Activities A and D are complete (actual start and finish dates are given).

Activity B started on day 5. Remaining duration = 2 days.

Activity C started on day 2. Some problems were encountered. Remaining duration = 4 days.

The duration for activity F was adjusted to 8 days.

Activity J has been canceled.

The duration for new activity P is 4 days. IPA = E. ISA (immediately succeeding activity) = K.

Update the logic. *Note:* When we delete activity J, the schedule must verify whether we should assign its predecessor to its successor. In other words, would activity F become a predecessor to activity K?

Solution

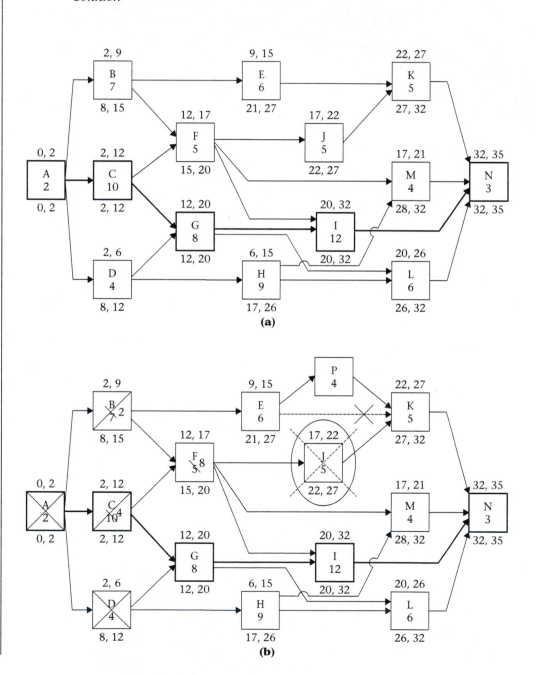

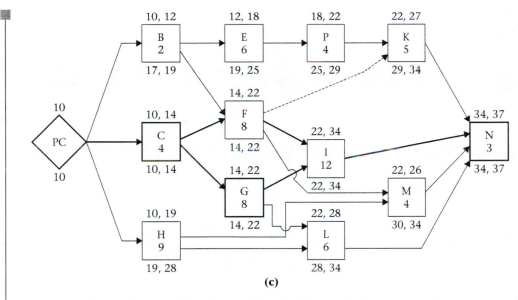

FIGURE 7.6   (a) Original schedule; (b) updating the schedule; (c) updated schedule.

Steps for Updating a Schedule

Updating a schedule includes the following six steps:

1. The project manager (or superintendent) prepares a list of actual progress, changes for individual activities, and all related information, as detailed previously.

    The author of this book has had experiences with both private companies and public agencies. In the private company experience, the scheduler represented the construction manager (CM)–at–risk (who is similar to a general contractor). The author used a simple tabular report with a project title, a data date, and a current date displayed at the top (Primavera Project Planner layouts, rather than reports, were used). The table contained columns for the activity ID, activity description, original duration, remaining duration, percent complete, and three empty columns with these titles: Actual Start, Actual Finish, and Notes (Figure 7.7 shows a sample report). Other columns could have been added, such as **Actual Cost This Period** or Resources Consumed This Period (Figure 7.8). Activities that were completed prior to this report are usually filtered out. The superintendent fills in (preferably in red ink) the percent complete and actual start and finish dates. Alternatively, he or she may cross off the remaining duration and provide the new remaining duration in lieu of the percent

Traffic control

Southbound Outer Lane

Northbound Outer Lane

Signage

General Construction

Earthwork

Southbound Outer Lane

Northbound Outer Lane

ACTIVITY ID	ACTIVITY DESCRIPTION	ORIG DUR	REM DUR	% COMP	EARLY START	ACTUAL START	EARLY FINISH	ACTUAL FINISH	NOTES
Traffic control									
Southbound Outer Lane									
P1N2100	PLACE CONST. BARRIER	12	3	75	06JAN00A		18JAN00		
Northbound Outer Lane									
P2N3100	PLACE TEMP. CONST. BARRIER	6	6	0	30MAR00		06APR00		
P2N3225A	REMOVE TEMP. CONST. BARRIER	5	5	0	07APR00		13APR00		
P2N2196	STRIPE ROADWAY	9	9	0	11AUG00		23AUG00		
P2N2198	REMOVE TEMP. BARRIER	4	4	0	24AUG00		29AUG00		
Signage									
General Construction									
P1NP100A	PROCUREMENT OF NOISE BARRIER POST &	10	3	70	02JUN99A		18JAN00		
P1N2190	INSTALL SIGN SUPPORT STRUCTURE	8	1	88	06JAN00A		14JAN00		
P1N2195	ERECT SIGNS	3	3	0	17JAN00		19JAN00		
Earthwork									
Southbound Outer Lane									
P1N2115A	GRUB & STRIP TOPSOIL	8	8	0	19JAN00		28JAN00		
P1N2105B	INSTALL EROSION CONTROL DEVICES	15	15	0	31JAN00		18FEB00		
P1N2200	INSTALL TEMP. SHEETING	12	12	0	21FEB00		07MAR00		
P1N2210	EXCAVATE RETAINING WALL	12	12	0	08MAR00		23MAR00		
P1N2240	PLACE POROUS FILL BEHIND WALL	9	9	0	23MAY00		02JUN00		
P1N2250	BACKFILL RETAINING WALL	7	7	0	05JUN00		13JUN00		
Northbound Outer Lane									
P2N2115B	REMOVE GUIDE RAIL	4	4	0	24MAR00		29MAR00		
P2N2125A	EXCAVATE FOR ELECTRICAL	10	10	0	30MAR00		12APR00		
P2N3110	REMOVE TEMP. PAVEMENT	9	9	0	07APR00		19APR00		
P2N3120	REGRADE AREA	7	7	0	20APR00		28APR00		

FIGURE 7.7 Updating a report without costs listed (most common type of report).

ACTIVITY ID	ACTIVITY DESCRIPTION	ORIG DUR	REM DUR	% COMP	EARLY START	ACTUAL START	EARLY FINISH	ACTUAL FINISH	BUDGETED COST	COST TO DATE	COST THIS PERIOD	NOTES
Traffic control												
Southbound Outer Lane												
P1N2100	PLACE CONST. BARRIER	12	3	75	06JAN00A		18JAN00		17,799.84	13,349.88		
Northbound Outer Lane												
P2N3100	PLACE TEMP. CONST. BARRIER	6	6	0	30MAR00		06APR00		9,999.12	0.00		
P2N3225A	REMOVE TEMP. CONST. BARRIER	5	5	0	07APR00		13APR00		8,332.60	0.00		
P2N2196	STRIPE ROADWAY	9	9	0	11AUG00		23AUG00		10,000.08	0.00		
P2N2198	REMOVE TEMP. BARRIER	4	4	0	24AUG00		29AUG00		6,666.08	0.00		
Signage												
General Construction												
P1NP100A	PROCUREMENT OF NOISE BARRIER POST &	10	3	70	02JUN99A		18JAN00		12,000.00	8,400.00		
P1N2190	INSTALL SIGN SUPPORT STRUCTURE	8	1	88	06JAN00A		14JAN00		6,895.36	6,033.44		
P1N2195	ERECT SIGNS	3	3	0	17JAN00		19JAN00		5,371.56	0.00		
Earthwork												
Southbound Outer Lane												
P1N2115A	GRUB & STRIP TOPSOIL	8	8	0	19JAN00		28JAN00		12,533.12	0.00		
P1N2105B	INSTALL EROSION CONTROL DEVICES	15	15	0	31JAN00		18FEB00		3,760.32	0.00		
P1N2200	INSTALL TEMP. SHEETING	12	12	0	21FEB00		07MAR00		9,347.04	0.00		
P1N2210	EXCAVATE RETAINING WALL	12	12	0	08MAR00		23MAR00		7,542.24	0.00		
P1N2240	PLACE POROUS FILL BEHIND WALL	9	9	0	23MAY00		02JUN00		11,107.08	0.00		
P1N2250	BACKFILL RETAINING WALL	7	7	0	05JUN00		13JUN00		7,770.84	0.00		
Northbound Outer Lane												
P2N2115B	REMOVE GUIDE RAIL	4	4	0	24MAR00		29MAR00		3,115.68	0.00		
P2N2125A	EXCAVATE FOR ELECTRICAL	10	10	0	30MAR00		12APR00		6,141.20	0.00		
P2N3110	REMOVE TEMP. PAVEMENT	9	9	0	07APR00		19APR00		6,772.68	0.00		
P2N3120	REGRADE AREA	7	7	0	20APR00		28APR00		6,902.84	0.00		

FIGURE 7.8 Updating a report for a cost-loaded schedule (less common type of report).

complete. Another option is to provide an expected finish date. One good practice is to adopt a *single criterion*—percent complete, remaining duration, *or* expected finish date—for updating activities. Software scheduling programs can calculate the other two variables. It is important for each page of the report to be numbered so that any missing pages can be discovered. Also, a ruler or a straightedge should be used to aid in reading the information. This hand-marked progress report stays with the superintendent as part of the project records, but the scheduler should keep a copy.

In the experience with the public agency, the author has been responsible for using Primavera P3e software to monthly update a large number of public works projects. The schedules are similar and do not contain much detail. Rather, they ensure—from the public agency's viewpoint—that the contractor meets important deadlines. The data date is the last day of every month. The scheduler sends an e-mail reminder about 2 workdays before the data date to all project managers and their section managers reminding them of the update. All update reports are due 2 workdays after the data date. A second reminder e-mail is sent on the morning of the due date. The monthly update includes two reports from each project manager:

a. A checklist (see Figure 7.9) that includes a list of all projects managed by the project manager. Next to each project, the project manager must check one of three choices: "As Planned," "Schedule Change," or "No Action." If he or she chooses the first or third choice, no further paperwork is needed for that project. The scheduler assumes that everything was planned to happen during this update period did happen, or that no work occurred in that project during that period.

b. If the project manager chooses Schedule Change, he or she must submit a Schedule Update Form (see Figure 7.10) for the project. The form lists all project activities, with a Start Date column, an A column, a blank Start Date Change column, and similar columns for the end date. If an activity started, the project manager writes an *A*, indicating an actual date, next to the start date. If the actual start date differs from the planned date, the project manager writes the updated start date in the Start Date Change column. If a future start date is changed (say, postponed for 2 months), the new start date is written in the Start Date Change column without writing an *A* in the A column. The same is done for the end date columns. The project manager may or may not use the Original Duration, Remaining Duration, and Percent Complete columns. Most project

Washington County, Florida

List of Projects by Project Manager

Data Date: 3/15/2003

Project Manager: John Doe

Project Manager Signature: _____ **Date:** _____

PROJ. NO.	PROJECT NAME	AS PLANNED	SCHEDULE CHANGE	NO ACTION
ABC1200	Washington Street Drainage Improvement, Phase I	×		
FGH3211	Road Resurfacing, Main St between 42nd and 52 Ave.		×	
LMN4500	Bridge No. 10345, US 41 over Hillsborough River	×		
XYZ7812	Traffic Signal at Intersection of Busch Blvd and Florida Ave.			×

FIGURE 7.9 List of projects by project manager.

Schedule Update Form

Data Date: 3/15/2003

Project Manager Signature: Date:

Scheduler Signature: Date:

PM: John Doe   Project No.: FGH2133   Project Name: Office Building, downtown Tampa

	ACTIVITY NAME	START DATE	A	START DATE CHANGE	END DATE	A	END DATE CHANGE	ORIG DUR	REM DUR	% COMP
1	NTP	1/3/2003	A					0	0	100%
2	Mobilize	1/6/2003	A		1/8/2003	A		3	0	100%
3	Dewatering	1/9/2003	A		1/19/2003	A		11*	0	100%
4	Excavation – North Side	1/20/2003	A		1/29/2003	A		9	0	100%
5	Excavation – South Side	2/3/2003	A		2/25/2003	A		10	0	100%
6	Drill Piles – North Side	1/30/2003	A		2/28/2003	A		13	0	100%
7	Drill Piles – South Side	3/3/2003	A		3/19/2003			13	3	77%
8	Concrete Piles – NS	3/3/2003	A		3/11/2003	A		7	0	100%
9	Concrete Piles – SS	3/20/2003			3/28/2003			7	7	0%
10	Pile Caps – North Side	3/12/2003	A		3/28/2003			13	10	23%
11	Pile Caps – South Side	3/31/2003			4/16/2003			13	13	0%
12	Footings – North Side	3/24/2003			4/4/2003			10	10	0%
13	Footings – South Side	4/7/2003			4/22/2003			12	12	0%
14	Elevator Pit – NS	3/31/2003			4/9/2003			8	8	0%
15	Elevator Pit – SS	4/14/2003			4/23/2003			8	8	0%

(*) This activity is on a 7-day-per-week calendar.

FIGURE 7.10   Sample Schedule Update Form.

managers prefer to give an expected finish date rather than the remaining duration or percent complete.

2. The scheduler feeds the information into the computer scheduling program and updates the schedule.

3. The scheduler discusses the new situation with the project manager and makes sure no more changes or adjustments are needed (in other words, he or she obtains the project manager's approval for producing the reports).

4. The scheduler prints new reports that show the updated schedule and delivers them to the project manager (who, in turn, distributes them

to the involved parties). The scheduler may also give the project manager a short descriptive analysis report. For example, if the expected finish date of the project was pushed back a few days, the scheduler may give the reason (e.g., a predecessor activity was supposed to finish by a certain date but did not). The scheduler tracks the delay from the end and works his or her way back to the activity or activities that caused the delay.

5. After producing the reports, the scheduler may receive feedback from different parties, some of which may have an impact on the schedule. The scheduler must filter any such feedback through the project manager. Only one point of contact (usually the project manager) should have the authority to approve any information before it is implemented in the schedule. Some schedule feedback received after the reports are printed may be kept till the next update.

6. When the next updating cycle is due, the same steps are repeated.

It is possible to include a cost estimate update in the process. In this case, the checklist will include two choices for each project: Cost estimate change or No cost estimate change. Similar to the process explained in part 1 earlier, if there is a cost estimate change for a certain project, the project manager must attach a cost estimate change form for that project.

Some commercial software programs on the market compare two schedules. For example, Digger (originated by HST Software, Simpsonville, SC, and acquired by Primavera Systems) can compare two Primavera Project Planner schedules. In this case, you can compare the current update with the previous (or another) update and summarize what happened between the two updates. You can select all or certain criteria for comparison, such as added activities, deleted activities, added relationships, deleted relationships, percent complete, used resources, budget, constraints, and so forth. Comparison with the baseline schedule is still important. It tells us where we stand now compared with where we are supposed to be (the baseline), which is—contractually—the bottom line. Nevertheless, comparisons with the previous update are important because they show whether we are moving in the proper direction.

Sometimes, after step 2 is complete, negative total float values appear on the schedule for certain activities. These are a red flag that must be addressed. A negative float for an activity means the activity is behind schedule by a number of days equal to the float amount. There could be one of two reasons for this:

1. The entire project (primarily, the critical path) is behind. If the negative float values vary—say, one activity has a total float (TF) of -12 and another has a TF of -8—the critical path is the path with the most

negative float.* This is the definition of the critical path (the longest path). You may argue that the activity with $TF = -8$ is "critical" as well. Primavera P3 even allows you to change the definition of critical activities from those on the longest path to those with a total float less than a certain value (usually 1). This issue is discussed further in chapter 8.

2. One particular activity is behind its constrained start or finish date. The entire project may still be meeting its expected completion date. For example, you could have the milestone Building Dry-In with an early finish constraint date of 10/12/01. If the calculated early finish date is 10/09/01, you will have $TF = -3$ for this activity.

These two scenarios are not mutually exclusive. They could occur simultaneously.

The project manager must find solutions to bring such activities back on schedule and not leave any negative total float. In many cases, the project manager meets with the scheduler to discuss some "what-if" scenarios to work out a solution to the problem. The meeting may include the subcontractors so that their consent can be obtained for any proposed recovery plan (see the *Recovery Schedules* section in chapter 8).

Change in the Critical Path

Sometimes, the critical path changes after updating. This happens if any of the following occurs:

- An activity (or activities) on the critical path took less time than originally planned or an activity on the critical path was deleted so the second longest path took over.
- An activity (or activities) not on the critical path (but on a near-critical path) took more time than originally planned so that path took over.
- An activity is added to a near-critical path so it became the longest path.

The project management team must then shift attention to the new critical path and determine why it became critical (particularly in the last two cases). For this reason, a wise idea is to inspect "near-critical" activities along with critical activities. In almost every scheduling software package, you can run a

---

*Mathematicians consider -4 greater than -8, but using this notion in construction may be confusing. In this book, if we say the "larger" negative float, we mean in terms of absolute value.

filter that selects only activities with a TF less than a certain value. In the absence of a negative float, a number between 3 and 5 is suggested for the filter. Any activity with $TF < 3$ is practically critical and has a better chance than others of becoming critical during construction.

Contractor-Created Float

When the general contractor, or a subcontractor, performs at a faster pace than planned, more float may be added to the remainder of the schedule. For example, if an activity finishes 2 days ahead of schedule, the result may be a float increase for some of the succeeding activities. If the activity was critical, the result may be an earlier finish date for the entire project. Some people call this type of float **contractor-created float.** This situation poses some interesting questions: Does the contractor or subcontractor who "created" this float own it? In other words, if he or she later "takes back" this float for a succeeding activity, is doing so allowed? If the float was created by a subcontractor working on a critical activity and resulted in an early finish for the entire schedule, who gets the "bonus," if any? Does it work both ways? If the subcontractor delayed work and this delay resulted in a delay for the entire project, is the subcontractor responsible for any liquidated damages? The answers to these questions depend on the contract. In many public projects, in which time is critical and the public's convenience is at stake, the government puts both "carrots" and "sticks" in the contract. In the aftermath of the Northridge earthquake, Caltrans (the California Department of Transportation) used this policy heavily. Penhall, an Anaheim-based demolition contractor, signed a contract that had a clause for a $75,000 bonus per day for each day finished ahead of schedule and a similar amount in liquidated **damages** for finishing late (Rosta 1994a; Tulacz 1994). C. C. Meyers received a $14.8 million bonus (the largest in the history of public contracts) for finishing 74 days ahead of schedule. This amount was based on a $200,000 per day bonus–liquidated damages clause in the contract (this story is discussed in more detail in chapter 8). In some bonus-penalty contracts, a limit is put on the bonus but not on the penalty. In 1995, Yonkers Contracting Co. Inc., Yonkers, New York, won the contract to modernize a four-lane, 2.5-mile stretch of the Northern State Parkway across Long Island. The contract included a $20,000 penalty for each day of delay after the deadline and a similar bonus amount for finishing ahead of schedule, with a $2.4 million cap on the bonus. There was no cap on the penalty (Cho 1997). You may want to refer to the legal references listed in the Construction Scheduling Law section of the Bibliography for more details.

Data and Information

Some people like to reduce the role of scheduling to just crunching numbers and producing colorful bar charts. In some simple, straightforward cases, the numbers may be sufficient. For example, suppose an activity was scheduled to take 6 days. When updating, you observe that 3 days of work have elapsed and the activity is 50% complete. Not much explanation is needed. However, other cases are not as straightforward. For example, suppose an activity was scheduled for 8 days; 6 days have elapsed but it is only 25% complete. Maybe an unforeseen condition occurred, maybe the work quantity was increased or underestimated, maybe the crew productivity decreased for some reason, or maybe another factor was involved. This observation must be recorded for project control and to prevent skewed estimates for future projects. Likewise, in some construction jobs, work may not be continuous. For instance, suppose an activity with only 3 days' duration shows an actual start date that is 20 days ago, yet the activity is not complete. Even though computer programs have provisions for such a work interruption, most schedulers and project managers do not show it on the schedule as an interruption. The important point is the necessity for explanation of the numbers, especially when a situation occurs that is not normal or average. Primavera's P3 and SureTrak Project Manager and Microsoft's Project all allow the addition of activity notes for this purpose. Primavera's P3e (and its siblings TeamPlay and P3e/c) allows notes for an activity and has multiple notebooks for each project.*

PROJECT CONTROL

Measuring Work Progress

Probably the single most important step in schedule updating is measuring work progress, because it has an effect not only on the schedule status, but also on progress payments to the contractor and subcontractors. Measuring work progress is mainly calculating or estimating the percent complete for each activity. It may also include estimating the percent complete for the entire project. This subject is broad. In this chapter, it is covered only briefly.

---

*Microsoft has developed Project Server 2003 and Microsoft Office EPM (Enterprise Premier Solution), in which the solution is customized by selecting certain Microsoft or partner components to fit the client's needs.

Methods for Determining Percent Complete for Individual Activities

As discussed in chapter 4 (in the Steps Required to Schedule a Project section), the project manager or superintendent can assign a percent complete to a small, simple activity easier and more objectively than he or she can do so for a large, complex activity. Several methods for measuring work progress are suggested. There are no correct and incorrect methods; there are only more and less suitable methods for the specific type of activity under consideration. Six of these methods are as follows (Construction Industry Institute 1987b):

1. *Units completed.* In the **units completed** method, Percent complete = Units completed/Total units. This method works well for activities with small, identical, repetitive components, such as laying bricks or CMUs (concrete masonry units), excavating, fishing electric wire, and so forth. In these activities, the type of work and pace are the same throughout the activity. Percent complete can be calculated simply by dividing units completed by the total quantity. For example, in an activity involving installing 4,000 concrete blocks, 1,200 have been installed. Percent complete = 1,200/4,000 * 100 = 30%.

2. *Cost or time ratio.* This method applies to those activities that are continuous and uniform throughout the project, such as Safety Inspection and project management–type activities. Percent complete is calculated by dividing time elapsed by total duration (if a **time ratio**) or cost to date by total budget (if a **cost ratio**). For example, a project management activity is scheduled for 12 months with a budget of $80,000. After 2 months, it is 2/12 * 100 = 16.7% complete, or if $20,000 are already spent, it is 20,000/80,000 * 100 = 25% complete. Another alternative is the **man-hour ratio** (actual man-hours consumed divided by total man-hours budgeted). The time ratio method for individual activities is similar to the duration percent complete and baseline duration percent complete methods for calculating the project percent complete. These methods are discussed in the next section.

3. *Start-finish.* This method works best for small activities or those with no or a short duration. The project manager may assign one of three stages: have not started yet (0%), started but not yet finished (an arbitrary amount; say, 40%), or finished (100%). When these activities sbecome too small, we can look at them as "almost events," with either 0% or 100% complete.

4. *Incremental milestones.* The incremental milestones method is more suitable for large and complex or multistage activities. Each stage of a given activity is assigned a "weight" that is approximately equal to its percentage share of effort in the total activity. Then, each stage is treated as "all or nothing." For example, a contractor is installing 25 doors. For 4 doors that have not yet been started, they are 0% complete. Eight doors had their frames erected. They are considered 30% complete. Another 6 doors have been hung. They are said to be 50% complete. Four more doors have been painted, making them 75% complete. The last 3 doors had the hardware installed. They are now 100% complete. Each door goes through the following stages:

TASK	WEIGHT (%)	CUMULATIVE WEIGHT (%)	NO. UNITS	% COMPLETE WEIGHT
Not Yet Started	0	0	4	$4 \cdot 0\%/25 = 0.0$
Erect Door Frame	30	30	8	$8 \cdot 30\%/25 = 0.096$
Hang Door	20	50	6	$6 \cdot 50\%/25 = 0.120$
Paint Door	25	75	4	$4 \cdot 75\%/25 = 0.120$
Install Hardware	25	100	3	$3 \cdot 100\%/25 = 0.120$
			25	Total $= 0.456 = 45.6\%$

5. *Supervisor's opinion.* The most subjective method is the supervisor's opinion method. It is used when no other method can suitably apply, such as in an engine tune-up or dewatering operation. This method relies totally on the foreman or superintendent's judgment. The contractor may use this method to exaggerate the percent complete for early payment. Because it does not require actual measurements, it has been considered the quickest (and dirtiest) and "most convenient" method. The scheduler must be careful not to overuse this method.

6. *Weighted or equivalent units.* The weighted or equivalent units method is used for large and complicated activities that usually comprise several consecutive or overlapping subactivities. The method involves the following five steps:

   a. Assign a weight to each subactivity so that Total weight = 100%.

   b. Multiply the weight of each subactivity by the quantity of the total activity. This is the "equivalent weight" in units for each subactivity.

    c. Determine the percent complete for each subactivity by using one of the previously discussed methods.

    d. Multiply the percent complete for each subactivity by its equivalent weight. The result is the "earned quantity."

    e. Add earned quantities for all activities and divide by total quantity. This is the percent complete for the total activity.

For example, for a wall-framing activity, with a total quantity of 3.5 MBF (1,000 board-feet), the following may be true:

ASSIGNED WEIGHT	SUBACTIVITY	UNIT[a]	TOTAL QUANTITY	EQUIVALENT MBF	COMPLETED QUANTITY	EARNED MBF
0.04	Bottom Plates	EA	20	0.14	20	0.14
0.40	Studs	EA	320	1.40	210	0.92
0.08	Corners	EA	12	0.28	8	0.19
0.12	Blocking	EA	160	0.42	92	0.24
0.14	Door Openings	EA	10	0.49	5	0.25
0.16	Window Openings	EA	12	0.56	5	0.23
0.06	Top Plates	EA	40	0.21	0	0.00
1.00		MBF		3.50		1.97
Percent complete = 1.97/3.50 = 56.3%						

[a]EA = each.

Only the weights (in the first column) are subjectively assigned. All other columns are either measured or calculated. Following is a sample calculation for the studs:

$$\text{Equivalent MBF} = \text{Assigned weight} * \text{Total MBF}$$
$$= 0.40 * 3.50 = 1.40$$

and

$$\text{Earned MBF} = \text{Equivalent MBF} * \text{Completed quantity} / \text{Total quantity}$$
$$= 1.40 * 210/320 = 0.92$$

The weighted or equivalent units method and the incremental milestones method are similar. Both are used for relatively large and complex activities that comprise several subactivities. The main difference is that subactivities in the incremental milestones method must occur in chronological sequence. So, when you assign a percent complete to a subactivity, you use the cumulative percent complete—that is, include the percent complete for the preceding steps (subactivities). In the weighted or equivalent units method, subactivities may be somewhat independent. Each subactivity has its own percent complete regardless of the percent complete for other subactivities.

You may wonder what the wisdom is for considering a wall-framing "activity" as a single activity with seven "subactivities" rather than simply having seven individual activities. One minor advantage is being able to tell the percent complete for the entire wall-framing activity. The author would prefer to treat the situation as seven individual activities. Many software scheduling programs can calculate the percent complete of a number of activities, grouped under certain criteria. Primavera Project Planner can do so in one of two ways: (a) you identify the wall-framing activities, for example, with an activity code (e.g., Step = Framing), then group activities by step, or (b) you create a "hammock" activity,* call it *Framing,* that encompasses all wall-framing activities. Another alternative is to use the WBS (an example of a WBS is provided in Figure 4.1), and then summarize the WBS at a certain level. In Microsoft's Project, you can "indent" activities to make them subactivities. If the major activity has a WBS code of 5, its subactivities will have WBS codes of 5.1, 5.2, 5.3, and so forth. In SureTrak, you can do this, too, by using the "outline" organization.

Methods for Determining Percent Complete for the Entire Project

We have shown how to estimate the percent complete for individual activities. The next question is what is the percent complete for the entire project? The answer is not clear. In fact, there might be several answers—substantially different but none "right" or "wrong."

Let us assume, for the sake of illustration, that a "project" has two activities: the first is Installing Interior Hollow-Core Wood Door, with a budget of $150 (including hardware). The other is Installing Hand-Carved Decorative Exterior Door, with a cost of $2,200. The first activity requires 2 man-hours for installation. The second requires 4 man-hours. Assume a man-hour costs $25. The total budget is $200, $2,300, and $2,500 for the first activity, second activity, and total, respectively.

---

*In P3e and its siblings (TeamPlay and P3e/c), it is called the *Level of Effort activity.*

Now, assume the first activity is completed and the second is not. Which of the following percent complete figures is true for the project?

1. *Units completed.* Units completed/Total units = 1 door/2 door = 50% complete (in this method, a door is a door).
2. *Budget spending.* Actual budget/Total budget = $200/$2,500 = 8% complete.
3. *Man-hours completed.* Actual man-hours/Total man-hours = 2 man-hours/ 6 man-hours = 33% complete.

Note that both method 2 and method 3 must be used carefully when there is a variance from the baseline. For example, we may have spent 60% of the budget, but the project is only 50% complete. We must differentiate among actual cost, earned cost, and scheduled cost. This concept is discussed in detail later in this chapter.

It is important to note that the man-hours unit is a measure of consumption of a labor resource, not a measure of time. Eight man-hours could be produced by one person during an 8-hour period, two persons for 4 hours, four persons for 2 hours, and so forth.

Since all the preceding criteria (units, budget, man-hours) are not absolutely required items for a CPM schedule, there must be a fourth method that estimates percent complete without the need for such criteria:

4. *Workday unit.* The workday unit method is based on the assumption that activities have weights proportional to their durations. For example, refer to the following schedule:

ACTIVITY	IPA	ORIGINAL DURATION (DAYS)	ACTUAL DURATION (DAYS)	REMAINING DURATION (DAYS)
A	—	7	7	0
B	A	12	9	3
C	A	6	4	2
D	B, C	5	0	5
E	D	9	0	9
Total		39	20	19

This method is used in software scheduling programs such as Primavera Project Planner. According to this method, the percent complete for this project is 20/39, or 51.3%. Note that two simplifying—but not necessarily realistic—assumptions underlie this method:

a. All activities have the same "weight per day."

b. Weight within the activity is distributed linearly. Some programs, such as Primavera's P3e, give the user the ability to change this assumption by dividing the activity into "steps" with different weights (similar to the weighted or equivalent units method). This division does not change the first assumption, that activities have weight proportional to their duration.

This method is simple and can be used by contractors who do not cost-load or resource-load their schedules.

5. *Duration percent complete.* The owner may not care about the details but rather thinks of the entire project as a "distance" and wants to know how far we have traveled. In this case, we can calculate percent complete as "how far we have gone compared with the total distance." In scheduling terms,

$$\text{Percent complete} = \text{Actual duration/Total duration}$$
$$= (\text{Total duration} - \text{Remaining duration})/\text{Total duration}$$
$$= (\text{Data date} - \text{Actual start date})/\text{Total duration}.$$

Thus, for the project shown in Figure 7.11, the percent complete is 16/33, or 48%.

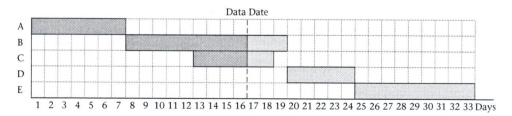

FIGURE 7.11   Duration percent complete method for percent complete estimation: Percent complete = Actual duration/Total duration = 16/33 = 48%.

Note that in this case the total duration is the time span between the actual (not planned) start date and the expected (i.e., updated) finish date.

6. *Baseline duration percent complete.* If the project is ahead or behind the baseline, we may be interested in measuring the percent complete by using the previous method, but with regard to the baseline schedule. In this case, we can calculate the percent complete as follows:

$$\text{Percent complete} = \text{(Data date} - \text{Baseline start date)} / \text{Total baseline duration.}$$

For the project schedule shown in Figure 7.12, the percent complete is $(19 - 0)/32$, or 59%. This percent complete indicates what the percent complete should have been if we were on schedule. It does not reflect reality.

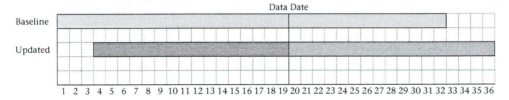

FIGURE 7.12 Baseline duration percent complete method for percent complete estimation: Percent complete = (Data date − Baseline start date)/ Total baseline duration = $(19 - 0)/32 = 19/32 = 59\%$.

The preceding equation uses workdays rather than calendar days or dates. The user must do the math or use a spreadsheet program, such as Excel, that can do this conversion automatically.

Discussion of the Methods The units completed method may work for the percent complete of an activity, but it is difficult to apply to the entire project because there is no single unit in common to measure. An exception to this statement is projects with simple and identifiable units of measure such as earthwork and highway construction. We can say 82 miles of a total 250 miles are finished. Then, the percent complete is 82/250, or 32.8%. In this case, we are assuming that "a mile is a mile" in the project (i.e., all paving effort takes the same amount of effort and duration throughout the project). We may still have a problem with "partially finished" units, but the project manager can make an assumption with a small error or apply the incremental milestones method.

Other types of projects, such as building and industrial projects, do not have a common unit of production. Do not confuse this "unit" (a unit of measurement, such as a cubic yard of concrete, a linear foot of electric wiring, or a square yard or foot of flooring) with "functional units" (finished usable units used mostly for design and estimating, such as a room in a hotel; a bed in a hospital; a pupil in a school; millions of gallons of water per day, or MGD, in a water project; and the like). For instance, if a hospital with 400 beds is built and costs $40,000,000, the cost of one bed (one functional unit) is estimated as $100,000. Functional units must go through multistage activities to get into their final form, and they are not appropriate, in most cases, as a measure of work progress, or project percent complete.

The budget spending and man-hours completed methods have their proponents, who believe such methods are the best way to control a project. They might be, if used with the proper understanding of what they mean. An important precaution is when project spending (in dollars or man-hours) differs from the baseline budget. For example, suppose the total baseline budget is $850,000. At a certain point in the project, the earned value is $235,000, but actual spending is $257,000. We must use the earned value and not the actual spending for a fair estimate of the percent complete: $235,000/$850,000 = 27.6%. Again, the subject of earned value is discussed later in this chapter. Also, when the baseline budget is adjusted as a result of approved change orders, it is important to use the adjusted baseline budget and not the original baseline budget for an unbiased percent complete. This entire discussion also applies to the man-hours completed method.

The workday unit method is generally a good and unbiased method. Its main pitfall is that activities such as procurement or obtaining permits, for example, may have much more weight than they deserve. Obtaining a permit may be a 40-day activity.* There may not be any work occurring on that activity during these 40 days and few or no resources allocated to it (not to underestimate the importance of the activity). It will have 20 times the weight of another activity with 300 CY of concrete placement that takes only 2 days.

The duration percent complete and baseline duration percent complete methods are good measures for what they represent—namely, the duration of the project. In this case, work in the project is treated as a linear variable (i.e., each day is the same). No consideration is given to the type and amount of work done per day. The two methods can (and should) be used together: one represents what is actually happening (till the data date), and one represents

---

*Some schedulers prefer to assign zero duration to such an activity but assign a 40-day lag or a fixed date (constraint) to it.

what should have happened. As mentioned for the budget spending and man-hours completed methods, when the baseline schedule is adjusted as a result of approved change orders, it is important to use the adjusted baseline schedule for an unbiased percent complete. It is also possible to use more than one baseline schedule comparison.

In the duration percent complete calculation, we presented the following equations:

Percent complete = Actual duration/Total duration, (A)

Percent complete = (Total duration − Remaining duration)/
Total duration, (B)

and

Percent complete = (Data date − Actual start date)/
Total duration. (C)

You must be careful in defining the total duration. In some software scheduling programs, total duration is taken as the original duration. The actual duration may significantly deviate from the original duration. This may lead to not only incorrect but also ridiculous results. Suppose, for the sake of illustration, an activity was originally estimated at 10 days. For some reason, work has taken much more time than estimated. After 13 days of actual work, we find that we still need 12 more days. If we keep the total duration as the original duration, which is 10 days, we will get the following results:

With equations A and C, the percent complete is 13/10, or 130%.
With equation B, the percent complete is (10 − 12)/10, or −20%.
The real percent complete is 13/(13 + 12), or 52%.

Most scheduling programs build "traps" so that any percent complete exceeding 100% will show as 100%, and any negative percent complete will show as 0%. The trap has only a cosmetic effect: it prevents ridiculous values from showing but does not correct any values. You must update or correct the total duration, as follows:

Total duration = At-completion duration

= Actual duration + Remaining duration.

This update may be possible by changing some of the software defaults. If not, you must do so manually or discard the calculated percent complete. The management team and any users of scheduling reports must be aware of such substitutions. The deviation between the at-completion duration and the original duration is worthy of studying and justifying.

So, which method—of the six—is better? Again, there is no unique answer; it depends on what you are looking for and what data you have in hand. It is important for the project manager to know the options and then select the appropriate percent complete method. From that point on, consistency is important. Once the management team picks one (or more) method for measuring the percent complete for the project, it should be used consistently throughout the life of the project for project control. The contractor may use more than one percent complete measure at the same time, each for a different purpose.

In reality, the project percent complete may not be very important. It can be used for a general idea about how close the project is to ending, but it is not normally used for project control or progress payments. The percent complete of individual activities is more important because it provides the basis for progress payments.

Progress Payments and Percent Complete

Pay requests depend completely on the percent complete for each activity and the unit prices submitted and approved in the **schedule of values.** The five standard steps for progress payment requests are as follows:

1. The project contract usually specifies the frequency of progress payments, usually monthly, and the closeout date for each period. This closeout date—say, the 25th of the month—is set for the general contractor to bill the owner. The general contractor sets another date, usually 2 or 3 days earlier, for his subcontractors to bill him or her. All charges that miss the closeout date must wait till the next billing cycle (i.e., next pay request).

2. The general contractor lists all activities that had work done on them. Each activity will have information such as the actual start, actual finish (if completed), percent complete (if > 0 but < 100%), original budget, cost this period, cost to date, and **cost to complete.** The owner might have stipulated some other information in the contract. The

general contractor must include work performed either by his or her own workforce or by his or her subcontractors.

Materials purchased but not yet installed may or may not be included in the pay request, depending on the contractual agreement between the owner and the general contractor.

3. This report goes to the owner, who usually verifies the information delivered in it. The owner's representative must verify the completed quantities, unit prices, and totals in the payment requests. Contractors often front-end load the cost, which means they get their money earlier than normal. This is done by two means: First, contractors increase the unit prices of early items and decrease the unit prices of late items, in a way that retains the same total. This is usually done when the general contractor submits the schedule of values to the owner and is called *bid unbalancing*. The other method of front-end loading the cost is by exaggerating the percent complete for certain activities. Most owners do not like, and may not approve of, such practices. Thus, the owner's verification of the numbers in the contractor's payment request is important.

4. The payment request can be approved as is or rejected with some numbers disapproved. Once the owner approves the payment request, it is processed and a check is issued payable to the general contractor for the total amount of the payment request minus any retainage.* The owner's verification of the pay request and the issuance of the check usually takes 2 to 4 weeks. When the owner pays the general contractor, he or she then pays the subcontractors.

5. The schedule of values must be updated with the cost of any change orders.

Standard forms for pay requests, such as AIA G702 (Application and Certification for Payment) and G703 (continuation to form G702), are used in the industry.

---

*As mentioned previously, *retainage* is a certain percentage of progress payments held by the owner, as specified in the contract, till the satisfactory completion of the project. In most cases, it is 10%. Some public projects start with 10% retainage until the midpoint of the project, then it decreases to 5%. In private contracts, owners have the right to waive the retainage requirement.

Earned Value Analysis

Earned value analysis (EV) is an integrated cost-schedule approach used to monitor and analyze the progress of a project. Popescu and Charoenngam (1995) defined it as "the performance measurement to report the status of a project in terms of both cost and time at a given data date" (p. 252).

Earned value management (EVM), started in the 1960s as a method for integrated project cost and schedule control, was designed by the Air Force and named the *cost/schedule planning and control system*. In 1967, it became Department of Defense (DoD) policy and was renamed the **cost/schedule control systems criteria (C/SCSC).** The objectives of the C/SCSC policy were (a) for contractors to use effective internal cost and schedule management control systems, and (b) for the government to be able to rely on timely data produced by these systems for determining product-oriented contract status. C/SCSC implementation was governed by DoD Instruction 7000.2, "Performance Measurement for Selected Acquisitions," issued by the comptroller in 1967 in the financial management regulatory series. The C/SCSC and DoD Instruction 7000.2 had several implementation problems and went through several cycles of research and redefining. The name changed several times, from cost/schedule planning and control system to cost/schedule control systems criteria, or C/SCSC, then to earned value management.*

The concept of **earned value (EV)** is simple; at any given point, take the following five steps:

1. Determine how much work you have done and how much you planned to have done by this date
2. Determine how much money you have earned and how much money you have spent
3. Calculate the time (schedule) and money (budget) deviations (variances) so far
4. Analyze the causes for the major deviations and determine possible remedies
5. Extrapolate these deviations to the end of the entire project

*For more information, see the Earned Value Management Web site (http://www.acq.osd.mil/pm) and the papers "Earned Value Management and Acquisition Reform" (http://www.acq.osd.mil/pm/paperpres/standown.html) and "Earned Value Management Rediscovered" (http://www.acq.osd.mil/pm/newpolicy/misc/abba_art.html), both by Wayne Abba.

To understand the math involved in EV analysis, consider the following simplistic example.

EXAMPLE 7.2

A contractor agreed to build 30 doghouses in 90 days at a price of $800 per unit. Twenty days later, the contractor has finished 8 doghouses with an actual total cost (that includes his overhead and profit) of $6,800. What is the status of the project?

Solution
The following analysis applies only if work is sequential and not parallel (i.e., the contractor works on one unit till it is finished then starts the next unit and so on). Linearity of production and no learning curve effect are also assumed.

$$\text{Total planned budget (TB)} = 30 \text{ units} \cdot \$800 \text{ each} = \$24,000,$$

$$\text{Daily planned production} = 30 \text{ units}/90 \text{ days} = 0.3\overline{3} \text{ units/day (or 3 days per unit)},$$

$$\text{Daily planned budget} = \$24,000/90 \text{ days} = \$266.67$$
$$= 0.3\overline{3} \text{ units/day} \cdot \$800 \text{ each} = 266.67,$$

and

$$\text{Percent complete} = 8/30 = 26.7\%.$$

After 20 days, the contractor's plan calls for $0.3\overline{3}$ units/day $\cdot$ 20 days = $6.6\overline{6}$ units to be finished, with a total cost of $6.6\overline{6} \cdot \$800 = \$5,333$. We call this amount the **budgeted cost for work scheduled (BCWS)**. In other words, if everything (schedule and budget) worked according to plan, in 20 days the contractor would have finished $6.6\overline{6}$ units and earned $5,333.

The contract price was $800 and the contractor actually finished 8 units, so he earned $8 \cdot \$800 = \$6,400$ from the owner (disregarding what it actually cost him). This is called the *earned value (EV)*, or **budgeted cost for work performed (BCWP)**.

However, the contractor's actual cost was $6,800. This is called **actual cost for work performed (ACWP)**.

Cost Variance (CV) = BCWP − ACWP = 6,400 − 6,800 = −$400

Schedule variance (SV) = BCWP − BCWS = 6,400 − 5,333 = $1,067

Schedule variance in days (SV, days) = SV ($)/Daily planned budget
$$= \$1,067/\$266.67 = 4 \text{ days}$$

Cost performance index (CPI) = BCWP/ACWP = 6,400/6,800 = 0.94

Schedule performance index (SPI) = BCWP/BCWS
$$= 6,400/5,333 = 1.20$$

Forecasted cost variance (FCV) = CV/% Complete −$400/26.7%
$$= -\$1,500$$

Forecasted schedule variance (FSV) = SV/% Complete = 4/26.7%
$$= 15 \text{ days}$$

The results are tabulated as follows:

ACTIVITY	Dog houses
TOTAL BUDGET ($)	24,000
% COMPLETE	26.7
ACWP ($)	6,800
BCWP ($)	6,400
BCWS ($)	5,333
CV ($)	−400
SV ($)	1,067
SV (DAYS)	4
CPI	0.94
SPI	1.20
FCV ($)	−1,500
FSV (DAYS)	15

From simple observation, we can tell the following:

- The project is 26.7% complete.
- The project is ahead of schedule by 4 days (planned to finish 6.6$\overline{6}$ units in 20 days but finished 8).
- The project is over budget by $400 (earned $6,400 but spent* $6,800).

*The contractor's overhead and profit are part of the "expenses."

- If work continues at the same pace and pattern, the contractor will finish this project 15 days ahead of schedule but with a budget deficit of $1,500.

  Several factors must be taken into consideration when you are interpreting the preceding numbers. One factor is the learning curve. It is possible that slightly below-average productivity is expected and acceptable if the crew is "learning" this task and the project manager expects an improvement later that will erase this negative variance.

The BCWS represents the baseline schedule and budget. The BCWP represents the "earned value" (i.e., the contract earning for performed work). The ACWP represents actual budget spending.

Both the variances and performance indexes are measures of deviation from the baseline. The variances are absolute measures in units of dollars and days. The performance indexes are relative measures in percentages. To "dramatize" the difference between absolute and relative measures, let us consider two activities: the first with a $100 budget, and the second with a $10,000 budget. If we have a variance of −$25 in *each* activity, the CPI for the first is 0.75 (seriously low) and 0.998 for the other (consider it perfect). Contractors strive for a nonnegative cost and schedule variances, and cost and schedule performance indexes at or exceeding 1.0.

It is important to note that EV analysis and schedule updating may yield conflicting results. The schedule variance (SV) may be positive, but the schedule update may show that the project is behind, or vice versa. This situation occurs mainly because the EV analysis is budget driven, whereas schedule updating focuses on the critical path, without regard to monetary issues.

In most cases, the forecasted amounts are used to raise a red (or yellow) flag rather than to accurately predict future amounts. For example, in the previous example, the contractor can tell his crew, "We are running $400 over budget and we are just 27% complete. If we don't do anything about it, we will end up with a $1,500 deficit." In projects in which a penalty is imposed for finishing late and/or a bonus for finishing early, forecasting can be a key tool for making a decision to accelerate the project.* Analysis of the causes for

---

*For example, see the discussion on *contractor-created float* previously in this chapter or the introduction to chapter 8.

variance is beyond the scope of this book. However, it is important to point out four issues:

1. Minor variances are usually expected and tolerated (although discouraged when negative). Major variances should be investigated.

2. For a negative variance (schedule or budget), something must have gone wrong in the actual work or in the baseline. For example, labor productivity may have been lower than expected. This could be due to uncontrolled circumstances (whether forgivable or not) or due to underestimation in the baseline. Materials prices could have risen unexpectedly or waste may have taken a larger-than-expected percentage. This causes major concern, especially in fixed-price contracts.

3. A large positive variance may not be a reason for celebration. It may indicate an error or an overestimation in the baseline budget and/or schedule.

4. Schedule performance and budget performance are independent. The contractor may find him- or herself operating under the conditions in one of the four quadrants shown in Figure 7.13. Quadrant I means the project is ahead of schedule and under budget (where you want to be). Quadrant II gives you bad news (you are behind schedule) and

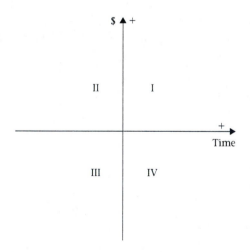

FIGURE 7.13   Schedule performance versus budget performance: quadrant I, ahead of schedule and under budget; quadrant II, behind schedule and under budget; quadrant III, behind schedule and over budget; quadrant IV, ahead of schedule but over budget.

good news (and under budget). Quadrant III is the worst: you are behind schedule and over budget. Quadrant IV is the opposite of quadrant II: you are ahead of schedule but over budget.

Another parameter that was suggested is the cost-Schedule Index (CSI), which is the product of the CPI and the SPI. The main problem with this parameter is the possibility that good performance in one area masks substandard performance in the other. For example, in our previous sample project, the CSI was $0.94 \cdot 1.20 = 1.13$, which is good but misleading.

S Curves

Earned value (BCWP) and actual cost (ACWP) may be plotted against the baseline (BCWS), as shown in Figure 7.14. Both curves, representing the ACWP and the BCWP, are usually extrapolated to forecast an **estimate at completion (EAC)** and the date of completion.

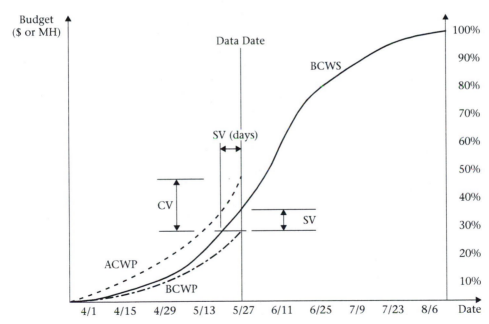

FIGURE 7.14 Earned value (budgeted cost for work performed, or BCWP) and actual cost (actual cost for work performed, or ACWP) plotted against the baseline (budgeted cost for work scheduled, or BCWS). INMH, man-hours; CV, cost variance; SV, schedule variance.

EV Analysis at Different Levels

When using the WBS, project managers may look at work at different summary levels.

EXAMPLE 7.3

The total estimated duration of the mass excavation activities in an office building project is 40 days. After 15 days, the project manager receives the following information:

TYPE OF EXCAVATION	TASK NO.	TOTAL QUANTITY (CY)	UNIT PRICE ($)	TOTAL BUDGET ($)	ACTUAL CY	ACTUAL COST ($)
Mass Excavation	TOB11110	39,000	—	176,500	12,900	59,300
Common Earth	TOB11111	20,000	2.50	50,000	7,800	17,950
Clay	TOB11112	8,000	5.50	44,000	1,200	5,850
Rock	TOB11113	11,000	7.50	82,500	4,200	35,900

Perform an EV analysis.

Note that the "Mass Excavation" line is a summary of the 3 lines below.

Solution

The solution, using the equations given in example 7.2, is tabulated as follows:

ACTIVITY	TOB11110	TOB11111	TOB11112	TOB11113
TOTAL BUDGET ($)	176,500	50,000	44,000	82,500
% COMPLETE	32.63	39.00	15.00	38.18
ACWP ($)	59,700	17,950	5,850	35,900
BCWP ($)	57,600	19,500	6,600	31,500
BCWS ($)	66,188	18,750	16,500	30,938
CV ($)	−2,100	1,550	750	−4,400
SV ($)	−8,588	750	−9,900	562

(continued)

SV (DAYS)	−1.95	0.17	−2.24	0.13
CPI	0.96	1.09	1.13	0.88
SPI	0.87	1.04	0.40	1.02
FCV ($)	−6,436	3,974	5,000	−11,524
FSV (DAYS)	−5.96	0.44	−14.96	0.33

In the analysis of the results, we can make the following six comments:

1. Looking at the overall budget, we find that the Mass Excavation operation is slightly ($2,100) over budget. With further investigation, we find that the main reason for this budget overrun is the Rock excavation, which is $4,400 over budget. In fact the other two excavation activities, Common Earth and Clay, are slightly under budget. This is an example of when above-standard performance masks below-standard performance. The CPI for Rock excavation is 0.88 (substantially low), when it is 0.96 for the whole operation.

2. When we look at the schedule, the only meaningful number is the overall schedule variance, which tells us that the Mass Excavation operation is almost 2 days behind schedule. Looking at individual schedule variances may be misleading. It is possible that the contractor planned to focus effort on one area at the expense of other areas. In this case, both Common Earth and Rock are on schedule; Clay is behind.

3. Let us consider the Mass Excavation activity as part of the total excavation operation, TOB11100, which includes, in addition to TOB11110 Mass Excavation, TOB11120 Special Excavation, as shown next:

WORK BREAKDOWN ELEMENT	LEVEL
TOB10000 Tampa Office Building	1
TOB11000 Substructures	2
TOB11100 Excavation	3
TOB11110 Mass Excavation	4
TOB11111 Common Earth Excavation	5
TOB11112 Clay Excavation	5

(continued)

TOB11113 Rock Excavation	5
TOB11120 Special Excavation	4
TOB11121 Confined Areas Excavation	5
TOB11122 Other Special Excavation	5

If the same subcontractor is in charge of the TOB11120 Special Excavation operation, he or she may also be concentrating effort on one operation at the time expense of the other (Mass Excavation and Special Excavation). In this case, we will not be able to tell how much the contractor is ahead or behind schedule till we look at the entire excavation operation, TOB11100. In contrast, the cost variance is activity specific and is a true indicator at any level.

4. Looking at forecasted variances indicates that, if work continues at the same pace and in the same pattern, the Mass Excavation operation will finish 6 days behind schedule and with a $6,436 deficit. This situation is certainly a reason for concern for the project management team. The project manager must try to prevent this outcome.

5. In the WBS shown in comment 3, we have five "levels of control." A typical superintendent or project manager may want to look at earned value at level 4 or even 5. Someone in upper management may look at level 2 or 3, but when he or she spots an unsatisfactory number, he or she may want to go to a lower level, such as level 4 or 5, for the particular operation with unsatisfactory numbers to pinpoint the trouble spot. It is very important to look at EV numbers as part of, but not the entire, picture. They are only indicators and possibly red flags. Once a flag is raised, more information must be collected to explain the substandard results. Once that analysis is done, and the source of the problem is identified, a remedy must be prescribed.

6. We can describe activities with negative variance as "substandard performance" as compared with "above-standard performance" for those with positive variances. We do not use the term *bad* or *good* performance because the analysis may show—for an activity with negative cost variance—that the performance was satisfactory but another reason caused the negative variance. The reason could be an unexpected work problem (not caused by the field crew in charge of the activity), an error

or unrealistic assumption in the original estimate, or something else. The possibility of poor performance also exists.

1. Define *schedule updating*.
2. Why is schedule updating needed for construction projects?
3. Define *project control* and discuss the roles of schedule updating as part of project control.
4. Are the terms *project monitoring* and *project tracking* equivalent to *project control?* Explain.
5. Why is project control needed in construction projects?
6. What is a *baseline schedule?* Discuss how to adopt a *balanced* baseline schedule—one that is not too optimistic and not too pessimistic.
7. What is an *updated schedule?* What does *schedule updating* mean?
8. What is the *data date?* What other names are used for it? Which are inaccurate? Why?
9. What kind of information is needed for updating schedules?
10. How frequent should schedule updating be performed?
11. Why is schedule updating important for progress payments?
12. What does the term *degressing a schedule* mean?
13. When you are updating a project, an activity may be added or deleted. What are the mishaps that may occur and how do you avoid them?
14. What are the steps involved in updating a schedule?
15. Refer to exercise 4 in chapter 4. Ten days after the start of the project, the following information is received:

Activities A and B	Completed on time.
Activity C	Started; 3 days left.
Activity D	Started; 2 days left.
Activity E	Has not started yet but duration adjusted to 5 days.

Draw the updated network. Calculate the new project completion date. Check whether any change in the critical path occurred.

16. Refer to exercise 5 in chapter 4. Fifteen days after the start of the project, the following information is received:

Activity A	Completed 2 days later than planned.
Activity B	Completed on time.
Activity C	Started; 4 days left.
Activity D	Completed. Took 5 days to finish.
Activity E	Completed.
Activity F	Canceled.
Activity G	Started 3 days late. Project manager hopes to cut 1 day of its duration.
Activity K	Added. Duration = 4 days. IPA = C.
Activity L	Added. Duration = 3 days. IPA = K, G.
Activity I	Adjusted: IPA = L.

Draw the updated network. Calculate the new project completion date. Check whether any change in the critical path occurred.

17. Refer to exercise 6 in chapter 4. Twelve days* after the start of the project, the following information is received:

Activities A and D	Completed on time.
Activity B	Completed by end of day 11.
Activity C	Started on time; finished 1 day late.
Activity E	Not started yet.
Activity F	Duration changed to 7 days.
Activity G	Canceled
Activity I	Started; 1 day left.

A change order was issued with three new activities:

Activity N	Duration = 4 days. IPA = None.
Activity O	Duration = 3 days. IPA = N, H.
Activity P	Duration = 5 days. IPA = O, L. No successor.

---

*Assume this project is updated biweekly but the crews are working 6 days per week.

Draw the updated network. Calculate the new project completion date. Check whether any change in the critical path occurred.

18. "If the logic used in creating this schedule was accurate, there should be no difference between the Retained Logic and Progress Override options." How much do you agree with this statement? Explain.

19. How is project updating tied to pay requests?

20. Explain what is meant by the term *contractor-created float.*

21. Explain the steps usually taken in a monthly update of a schedule.

22. Does the scheduler have to "explain" the results of the update to the project manager? When? Why or why not?

23. During the life of a project, the scheduler receives a lot of feedback on the schedule from different parties such as the architect, the engineer, the owner, the subcontractors, and others. As a scheduler, how would you take and implement or reject such feedback?

24. Can the critical path in a project change during the life of the project? How can such a thing happen?

25. Management must pay attention not only to critical activities, but also to near-critical activities. Explain this statement from a practical point of view.

26. List each of the six methods for measuring the work progress of a certain activity. Under what conditions would each be recommended? Give an example for each method.

27. A roofer is working to cover a 2,500-square-foot roof. He must first install rafters, then sheathing, then felt, and finally shingles. He assumes the previous tasks compose 35%, 20%, 15%, and 30% of the total roofing activity. At a certain point, he gets the following information on the subtasks:

SUBTASK	UNIT[a]	TOTAL QUANTITY	INSTALLED QUANTITY
Rafters	EA	150	102
Sheathing	SF	2,720	1,200
Felt	SQ	27.2	10
Shingles	SQ	27.2	5

[a]EA = each; SF = square feet. A square, SQ, is 100 square feet; a unit used mostly in roofing jobs.

Calculate the estimated percent complete for the roofing activity.

28. Which method of measuring work progress is suitable for each of the following activities?

    a. Laying bricks for an exterior wall
    b. Safety inspection
    c. Installation of a furnace
    d. Project supervision
    e. Multiple reinforced concrete footings
    f. Setting up a patented formwork system for a wall
    g. Hydration of a concrete slab on a grade (assume a small slab)
    h. Fishing* an electric wire for an entire floor
    i. Excavation of earth (assume one type of soil)
    j. Excavation of earth (assume several types of soil)
    k. Dewatering
    l. Installing ceramic tile for a large area (involves a few subactivities)

29. When you are calculating the percent complete for an entire project, more than one answer might be possible. The project manager says the percent complete is about 60%, the cost engineer says it is 65%, the computer program says 57%, and the owner says it should be 50% (according to his or her representative's feedback). You calculate it on the basis of how much time has elapsed and how much time is given in the contract; your result is 70%. Can you explain these confusing and "conflicting" numbers?

30. On the basis of the information given in the previous exercise, do you think the project is in trouble (with regard to the budget and the schedule)? How did you conclude this?

31. Explain the procedure for initiating and processing pay requests.

32. This exercise is for persons who use Primavera Project Planner software: You created a project without feeding the program any budget or resources information. After the first update, the scheduling report says the project is 16.7% complete. Do you know how the program determined this number? How accurate is this number?

33. The earned value (EV) analysis involves comparing what happened with what should have happened. Explain this statement with regard to both the budget and the schedule.

---

*To run an electric wire through a conduit by using resilient "fish tape" or a "snake."

34. A mason contracted with a general contractor to build an exterior wall from 8-inch CMUs. The wall is 82 feet long and 8 feet high.* The mason must finish the wall in 3 days and gets paid $4 per block. At the end of day 1, the mason has installed 220 blocks. His or her actual cost (including overhead and profit) was $836. Analyze the situation with regard to both the budget and the schedule.

35. Can you draw the S curve for the masonry job in the previous exercise?

36. A flooring subcontractor must install three types of flooring in an existing building:

TYPE	QUANTITY (SF)[a]	UNIT PRICE ($/SF)	TOTAL PRICE ($)
Carpet	2,600	2.30	5,980
Vinyl tile	1,200	2.95	3,540
Ceramic tile	3,330	4.95	16,484
Total	7,130		26,004

[a]Carpet is usually sold and installed by the square yard. We used square foot (SF) here for conformity with the other flooring types.

The subcontractor is given 10 days to finish all the work. Assume he has crews to start all three jobs concurrently. Four days after the start of the work, he discovers the following:

TYPE	QUANTITY INSTALLED (SF)	ACTUAL COST ($)
Carpet	1,500	3,150
Vinyl tile	800	2,488
Ceramic tile	750	3,638

Perform an EV analysis of the preceding task:

a. Analyze each subtask (carpet, vinyl tile, ceramic tile) individually; determine its status with regard to the budget and the schedule.

---

*Do not forget the CMU face dimension (including the mortar joint): 8 inches by 16 inches.

b. Analyze the entire flooring activity as one unit; determine its status with regard to the budget and the schedule.

c. How do you combine the answers for parts A and B?

d. On the basis of performance so far, do you believe the subcontractor will finish the job on time? within budget? Justify your answer.

e. Draw the S curve for the entire task.

CHAPTER 8

Schedule Compression and Time-Cost Trade-Off

Pedestrian bridge, Lake Mary, Florida. Courtesy of Smith Aerial Photos, Maitland, Florida.

197

On January 17, 1994, a 6.7-magnitude earthquake caused heavy damage and many casualties in Northridge, California. The immediate major concern for Caltrans (the California Department of Transportation) was reopening the public highways in one of the busiest areas in the United States.* Part of the damaged highways was two sections of Interstate 10 in Santa Monica. C. C. Meyers, Inc., of Rancho Cordova, California, was awarded the contract to repair these sections. C. C. Meyers' bid of $14.7 million was significantly less than the Caltrans engineer's $22.3 million estimate. The contract gave the contractor 140 days to finish the project and included a **liquidated damages**[†] *clause of $200,000 for each day of delay and a similar bonus amount for each day finished early. The contractor finished the project in only 66 days, 74 days ahead of the stipulated deadline. This early finish was possible because the project was fast tracked. In addition, C. C. Meyers worked around the clock, putting large amounts of resources into the project, making this project the focus of the company. Excellent cooperation between Caltrans and the contractor also helped. Caltrans did its part to help push the project, assigning 10 engineers on the day shift and 4 on call at night to inspect work and answer questions.*

In the process of expediting the schedule, C. C. Meyers may have gone over the original budget, but with about a $14.8 million bonus, the company was certainly ahead of the game. Despite the large bonus paid, Caltrans seemed pleased with the results. The public's convenience was well worth the effort and the money. Caltrans and C. C. Meyers both believe that despite the **schedule compression,** *work quality was not compromised.*

INTRODUCTION

Construction projects almost always have finish deadlines assigned by the owner and stipulated in the contract. Some of these projects have strict deadlines that do not allow for any slippage. An example of such a project is the facilities built for the Olympic Games or international exhibits or conferences. Any slippage in the schedule in such a case could literally mean a

---

*The next major concern for Caltrans was retrofitting bridges and other structures to be earthquake resistant.

[†]*Liquidated damages* are a stipulation in a contract of a monetary amount that must be paid by the contractor if he or she fails to satisfactorily complete the project by the contract finish date. They are discussed in more detail in chapter 12.

disaster: an international embarrassment and a loss of large sums of money. Other, mostly public, projects have strict deadlines because of the interest of or inconvenience to the general public. An example is a highway, a school, or a water treatment plant. Any delay in such a project may not be assessed by a monetary amount; however, the consequences are still serious. Other projects may have deadlines that are rigid, but a slippage would not result in such disastrous outcomes. An example of such projects is a hotel or a shopping center for a certain tourist shopping season. Finishing late in this case would mean a loss of revenue for the season. Still other projects, not tied to a specific event or season, may have "normal" finish dates, which means the contractor can work at a "normal" pace. In most cases, a normal schedule means 5 days per week, 8 hours a day, but the schedule depends on the contract. Slipping a few days or weeks in this case may be acceptable to the owner and may not cause serious consequences.

For all these types of projects, the contract may or may not contain a liquidated damages clause. The damages usually include an estimated loss of revenue as a result of a delay and may include **punitive damages.** Punitive damages are difficult to recover in courts, especially in the case of mere breach of contract. To recover punitive damages (also called **exemplary damages**), the owner must prove that the breach was committed maliciously or that an intentional tort or another illegal or wrongful act such as fraud was committed (Wickwire, Driscoll, and Hurlbut 1991, § 11.19).

SETTING PRIORITIES

Finishing on—or ahead of—schedule is an important objective of the contractor and the owner. Finishing on—or under—budget is another important objective. Achieving these two objectives simultaneously is desirable—and usually possible—but often the contractor must rank them in order of importance: one before the other. As is shown later in this chapter, the project manager may, at a certain point, be faced with a situation in which shortening the duration costs more money. At this point, a decision must be made between two alternatives:

1. Do not shorten the duration anymore and keep the cost to a minimum.
2. Keep compressing the schedule even though the cost will continue to rise.

ACCELERATING A PROJECT

What Is "Accelerating" a Project?

Accelerating a project means shortening the normal duration of the project schedule (also called **schedule acceleration**). It does not necessarily mean aiming for the shortest possible duration. The term *compressing the schedule* is synonymous and is used throughout this book. The term **schedule crashing** is generally used to indicate maximum acceleration, although it is sometimes used in lieu of accelerating.

Why Accelerate a Project?

A contractor may want to accelerate a project for many reasons, such as the following five:

1. The contractor's "normal" finish date in the baseline schedule does not meet the imposed finish date of the contract. The contractor usually knows this situation before starting construction, or, sometimes, even before bidding. In many cases, the owner requires the contractor to submit a construction (critical path method, or CPM) schedule that shows a satisfactory finish date. Many government agencies even restrict the contractor from using specific scheduling software.

2. After starting construction and completing a certain percentage of the project, the contractor realizes that the project is behind schedule. He or she needs to accelerate the remainder of the schedule to make up for lost time and avoid finishing late. In many contracts, penalties (mostly liquidated damages) may be levied on the contractor for a late finish.

3. In some cases, the contractor may have a contractual monetary incentive to finish ahead of schedule. The case study mentioned at the beginning of this chapter is an example.

4. Sometimes, especially when the economy is doing well, finishing early means—to the contractor—starting another job earlier and thus making more profit. In many cases, the contractor knows the date when he or she is supposed to mobilize to the next project. This time frame may require him or her to compress the current project to free certain resources so that they can be reallocated to the new project.

5. To a certain point, accelerating a project may prove profitable to the contractor, as is discussed subsequently.

Acceleration can be planned before the start of the project, as in points 1 and 3 and possibly 4 and 5. In other cases, it is not planned but sometime during construction the work situation necessitates it.

How Can the Duration of a Project Be Shortened?

Construction projects may take more or less time than planned (usually more than less) for reasons that may be within or beyond the contractor's control. Reasons beyond the contractor's control, such as **force majeure,** differing site conditions, and change orders, draw time extensions from the owner in most cases. These situations are not discussed in this chapter. Instead, the discussion is restricted to the ways the contractor can influence the duration of the project. The Construction Industry Institute (1988a) suggested more than 90 techniques for schedule compression. It further classified them by project phase or function:

    I. Ideas applicable to all phases of a project
   II. Engineering phase
  III. Contractual approach
  IV. Scheduling
   V. Materials management
  VI. Construction work management
 VII. Field labor management
VIII. Start-up phase

A review of these techniques underscores the importance of early planning. For some projects, the decision to compress the schedule may be made during the construction phase. Other projects, such as the Northridge case study, are carefully planned from the moment the project is conceived through completion.

The author suggests 10 techniques (not in any particular order):

1. *Revisit or study the schedule thoroughly to find any errors or unnecessary logic or constraints.* The most common pitfall is using the finish-to-start (FS) relationship when a start-to-start (SS) relationship with a

reasonable lag can work. For example, suppose the logic is that activity B in Figure 8.1a cannot start until activity A is finished (i.e., day 10). After checking the situation, we find that activity B can start only after a certain portion of activity A is finished (e.g., 40%). In this case (Figure 8.1b), activity B can start as early as day 4, which saves 6 days.

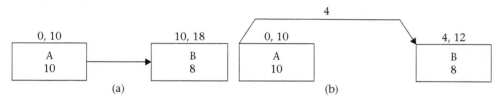

(a)   (b)

FIGURE 8.1   Time savings difference between (a) finish-to-start (FS) and (b) start-to-start (SS) relationships

2. *Fast track the project (as mentioned in chapter 5). Fast tracking* means starting construction before the design is completely finished. Conceptual design must first be done; detailed design follows in stages. Construction of each phase (or component) follows the detailed design of the phase while the next phase is being designed (see Figure 8.2). This option is not usually available in the middle of construction. It is a major decision that must be made with the agreement of the owner, the designer (architect or engineer, A/E), and the contractor prior to starting the project.

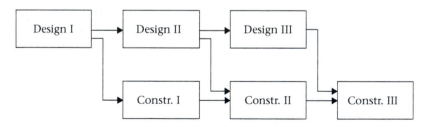

FIGURE 8.2   Fast tracking

3. *Conduct value engineering and constructability studies.* **Value engineering (VE)** has been defined as "a science that studies the relative value of various materials and construction techniques. Value engineering considers the initial cost of construction, coupled with the estimated

cost of maintenance, energy use, life expectancy, and replacement cost" (R. S. Means 2000, 611). **Constructability** has been defined as "the optimum use of construction knowledge and experience in planning, design, procurement, and field operations to achieve overall project objectives" (Construction Industry Institute 1986a, 2).

VE is considered an optimization study answering the question "Is it fit or overfit?" It focuses on functional analysis and life-cycle costs. It can be done by the designer (A/E), the professional construction manager, and the contractor. In some cases, the contractor may have a VE suggestion for modifying or changing the design that will achieve the same objectives with less cost, less time, a better product, or a combination of these. Contracts often include a reward clause for contractors who submit creative suggestions. In such clauses, the savings are usually split.

Constructability is mostly a feasibility study done by the contractor to check for any difficulties with or obstacles to carrying out the design. This type of study does not cover the "after construction" functions such as operation, maintenance, upgrading, and so forth.

VE and constructability can coexist and even complement each other (Construction Industry Institute 1993).*

4. *Work overtime—more hours per day and/or more days per week*. The results of some studies suggest that productivity declines with more hours worked per week than the basic 40 hours. The Business Roundtable[†] (1980) suggested an immediate, significant drop (1st week, as a result of the initial pattern change), followed by a partial recovery (2nd and 3rd weeks, when the person is starting to adapt to the overtime schedule), then a gradual, slight decline (4th through 9th weeks, as a result of work fatigue), and finally a leveling off (after the 9th or 10th week) (see Figure 8.3). R. S. Means (2001) showed a more "linear" approach. It gave declining productivity numbers from week 1 to week 4. For example, for 6 days per week and 10 hours per day, productivity was assumed to be 95%, 90%, 85%, and 80% for weeks 1 through 4, respectively. Some researchers (Larew 1998) questioned the reliability of these overtime studies.

---

*You may also want to refer to the summary in two Construction Industry Institute reports (1986a, 1987a).

[†]Now The Construction Users Roundtable (CURT).

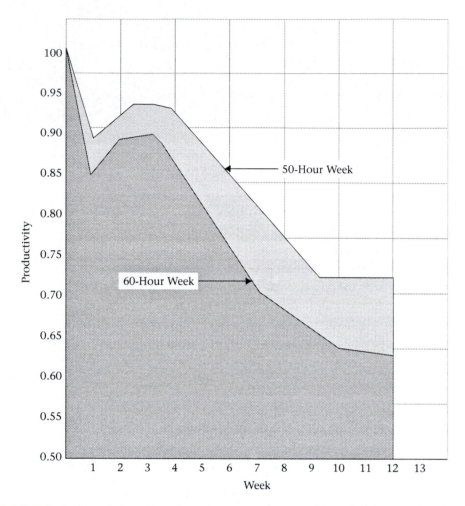

FIGURE 8.3 Cumulative effect of overtime on productivity (50- and 60-hour workweeks). (From The Business Roundtable, *Scheduled Overtime Effect on Construction Projects* [New York: The Business Roundtable, November 1980], Report C-2, p. 10. Reproduced by permission from The Construction Users Roundtable [CURT; formerly the Construction Committee of The Business Roundtable]; http://www.curt. construction.com/1_0_home.html)

As far as cost, overtime pay is almost always more than regular-time pay. If the workers have a union contract, overtime is compensated according to the collective bargaining agreement between the contractor and the labor union. In most construction contracts, hours exceeding 40 per week and any hours on Saturday are compensated at 1.5 times the regular rate. Other hours, possibly Sunday and night hours, may be compensated at twice the regular rate. If the project involves open-shop labor, overtime pay depends on the contractor's company policy but is always subject to government regulations. For hourly workers, hours in excess of 40 per week almost always cost more than regular hours. In contrast, salaried employees may not receive overtime compensation.

The Business Roundtable (1980) studied the combined effects of reduced productivity and increased cost resulting from overtime. The curves in Figure 8.4 show these effects.

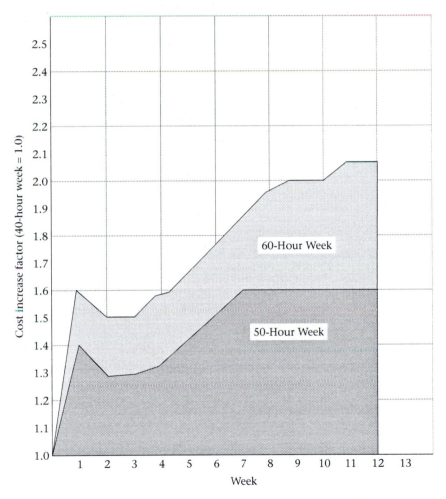

FIGURE 8.4   Cumulative cost of overtime = Successive weeks' productivity loss + Overtime premiums.
(From The Business Roundtable, *Scheduled Overtime Effect on Construction Projects* [New York: The Business Roundtable, November 1980], Report C-2, p. 11. Reproduced by permission from The Construction Users Roundtable [CURT; formerly the Construction Committee of The Business Roundtable]; http://www.curt. construction.com/1_0_home.html)

5. *Offer incentives to workers or crews for improving productivity.* The contractor usually has an incentive to compress the schedule (i.e., avoid a penalty or earn a bonus). Workers do not directly pay the fine or get the contract bonus. The contractor must offer them an "internal" incentive, which could be more symbolic (a plaque, certificate, party, baseball cap, bomber jacket, T-shirt, coffee mug, etc.), monetary, or a combination of the two.

6. *Acquire more workers and equipment.* Usually, the number of workers and the amount of equipment allowed on-site are limited. Saturating the job site may lead to site congestion that would adversely affect productivity and safety, which would defeat the purpose of acquiring more workers and equipment. Several factors must be balanced in this regard: the cost of the "extra" resources, the cost of not having these resources when needed, and the important consideration of what to do with the extra resources after the peak need ends.

7. *Hire a second, and possibly a third, shift.* A turnover time is always associated with multiple shifts: when a worker starts his or her shift, he or she must take some time to identify the work elements (i.e., what has been done and what needs to be done). Supervisors must ensure work consistency and that all shifts conform to the same standards. As in point 6, several factors must be balanced when such a measure is undertaken.

8. *Acquire special materials (such as accelerators for concrete) and equipment that help speed up the work process.* Difficult choices may have to be made in this regard—mainly, justifying the cost of such materials and equipment.

9. *Improve project management or supervision.* In some cases, the contractor may recognize a problem in the project team. Replacing the project manager or superintendent in the middle of the job is not an easy decision. However, under certain circumstances, doing so may be the lesser of the two evils, the other evil being the status quo.

10. *Improve communications among parties, particularly during the submittal process.* Sometimes a structural subcontractor may have an inquiry about a structural detail. The contract stipulates a chain of command that requires the subcontractor to submit his **request for information (RFI)** to the general contractor, who sends it to the architect, who in turn forwards it to the structural engineer. The response then must come in the reverse order across the same chain. Many contracts now allow the subcontractor to send an RFI directly to the structural engineer (or whoever the responsible party is) but require him or her to send copies to the contractual parties between (the general contractor

and the architect). The structural engineer, in turn, can answer the structural subcontractor directly but must also copy the architect and the general contractor.

Because of technology, the process of reviewing and approving drawings is faster than ever. Some companies do so online by uploading their drawings to a (usually exclusive) Web site. All parties are informed by e-mail about the new drawings. In many cases, the review can take place online. The entire process can now be completed in a few hours rather than in several days with a high accompanying delivery cost. Management software also speeds up the RFI process if all parties have immediate access to the software.*

The earlier the need to accelerate the schedule is known, the more options the contractor has and the less the cost may be.

How Does Accelerating a Project Work?

The duration of the entire project is equal to the duration of the critical path. Thus, to shorten the duration of the entire project, we must shorten the duration of the critical path. Let us consider a project that has eight paths (whether dependent—e.g., they share some activities—or independent), as shown in Figure 8.5. Path 4 is the critical path, with a duration of 27 days. To accelerate the project, we do the following:

1. We start accelerating the project by shortening the longest (critical) path (i.e., path 4).

2. To shorten the duration of a path, we cut the duration of an activity on the path. As a rule of thumb, we choose the activity with the least acceleration cost.

3. We accelerate path 4 by 2 days (we may have to do so in two steps—one day at a time—or we may be able to do so in one step; this point is explained later). Now, the duration of the project is 25 days.

4. If the shortened activity falls on more than one path, all the paths with the activity will also be shortened.

---

*Most project management software packages provide access to users on the company's server, with the possibility of providing limited access to others (outside the organization) through the Internet.

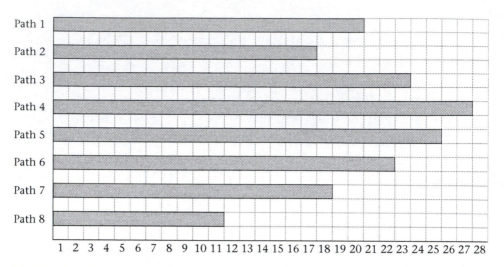

FIGURE 8.5   Project with eight paths

5. Assuming that the shortened activity was not on path 5, we now have two paths with 25 days' duration: path 4 and path 5. To accelerate the project further, we must shorten *both* paths. If the two paths share an activity or several activities, cutting the duration of a shared activity will shorten both paths. Otherwise, we must cut the duration of an activity on *each* path. We cut 2 days from each path. Now, the duration of the project is 23 days.

6. Three paths are now tied as the longest: paths 3, 4, and 5. We repeat step 5 for these paths to cut 1 day from each path and subsequently cut 1 day from the duration of the project. The duration is now 22 days.

7. Note again that when we cut the duration of an activity, several paths may be affected. For example, if we cut an activity that is on both path 4 and path 2, path 2 is now cut—unintentionally—from 17 days to 16 days.

8. Path 6 has now "joined the club" and become critical. We repeat step 6.

9. Clearly, the further we accelerate the project, the more paths must be shortened and the more activities must be involved. Consequently, we may need to compress six or seven activities to cut only 1 day from the project duration. This fact is why the direct cost of accelerating is not linear (although it may be linear for short intervals).

It is interesting to note that an increase in the duration of the critical path by *x* days will result in an increase in the duration of the project by *x* days as well. However, the reverse is not necessarily true. A decrease in the duration of the critical path by *x* days will result in a decrease in the duration of the project by *y* days, where

$$0 < y \leq x$$

DIRECT AND INDIRECT COSTS

A contractor's main expenses are as follows:

I. **Direct costs**
   A. *Labor*, particularly hourly workers, for whom a labor expense can be directly linked to a particular work item
   B. *Materials*, such as concrete, rebar, bricks, lumber, nails, paint, drywall, carpet, structural steel, and *installed equipment*, such as elevators, air-conditioning units, and kitchen equipment
   C. *Equipment*, particularly construction equipment (bulldozers, excavators, cranes, concrete pumps, etc.)
   D. *Subcontractors* (even though subcontractors' charges comprise labor, materials, equipment, overhead, and possibly subsubcontractors, the general contractor treats these charges as a direct cost)
   E. *Other costs*, such as government permits and fees, and fees for lawyers and consultants hired for a specific task in a project

II. **Indirect costs**
   A. Project overhead (or **job overhead**), such as the following:
      1. Project staff (project manager, project superintendent, project engineer, receptionist or secretary, clerk, etc.)
      2. Office trailer and other temporary structures
      3. Cars and trucks assigned to the project team
      4. Office equipment (copying machine, fax machine, computers, etc.)
      5. Temporary utilities (electricity, water, drinking water and ice, telephones, cell phones, gas, portable toilets, etc.)
      6. Other indirect project-related expenses

B. **General overhead,** such as the following:

1. Main office expenses (rent, lease, maintenance, utilities, etc.)
2. Main office personnel
3. Main office equipment and vehicles
4. Main office services, such as lawyers and accountants (not working exclusively for a specific project)
5. Other main office expenses, such as advertising and charity contributions

C. *Profit* (usually estimated by the contractor before he or she takes on the project; it usually ranges between 5 and 10%, although it can and does occur outside this range; the profit percentage depends on many project-specific factors, prevailing economic conditions, and the contractor's financial status)

D. **Contingency fees** (an additional sum of money allocated for the unknown events that will most likely occur during the life of the project; they are directly proportional to the risk taken in the project)

The main criterion for differentiating between direct and indirect expenses is that a direct-expense item must be directly linked to a specific work item. For example, if you pay someone to set up concrete forms for a shear wall, the expense is direct. If you pay a security guard to look after the project, the expense is indirect. The same simple rule applies to differentiating between project overhead and general overhead. Any overhead expense directly linked to one specific project is project (job) overhead; otherwise, it is general overhead. General overhead is usually distributed among all projects in proportion to their cost. In some cases, certain overhead expenses are shared by multiple, but not all, projects undertaken by a specific contractor. For example, a scheduler or a safety officer may be assigned to two or three projects of the many projects on which the company is working. Most likely, this cost is treated as job overhead and divided between the two or three projects.

Cost Concepts as They Relate to Schedule Compression

As the schedule is compressed, an impact on direct costs and a different impact on indirect costs will occur. Let us start with what we define as the normal duration and the normal cost for a project. Although the term *normal* may be vague and may be interpreted differently by different people, we define **normal duration** as *the amount of time required to finish the project under ordinary circumstances without any deliberate delay or acceleration*. **Normal cost** is *the cost of a project that is performed within the normal duration*. These definitions also apply to individual activities.

How to Choose the Best Method for Project Acceleration

Using accelerating methods that incur minimal cost (or have the lowest cost-benefit ratio) generally makes sense. Let us consider some of the different methods.

Overtime costs more per hour and, according to the studies mentioned previously, might contribute to lower productivity. This fact does not automatically disqualify overtime as a means for accelerating projects. However, all the pros and cons should be considered before a decision is made to use this method.

Acquiring more workers and equipment may lead to site congestion and less efficiency. In addition, it may create a problem for the human resources and equipment departments: what to do with excess resources after the peak need ends.

Hiring a second, and possibly a third, shift may lead to more turnover time, result in more communication problems, and require more careful management coordination. Extended work hours, because of the second and possibly the third shifts, may require artificial lighting or special nighttime arrangements (e.g., security). In addition, second and third shifts may also create a problem for the human resources department: again, what to do with them after the peak need ends.

Acquiring special materials or more efficient equipment must be evaluated on its merits on a case-by-case basis. Such acquisition almost always costs more, but the contractor must look at the cost-benefit ratio and other related factors (e.g., public relations, customer satisfaction, long-term impact). A classic case is when the contractor owns expensive equipment (e.g., an excavator) that is not the most efficient for the job. He or she is faced with the decision to use it even though it is not the most efficient for the job or to acquire the more or most efficient piece of equipment at an extra cost. The market is full of materials, equipment, tools, software, and other gadgets that allegedly make work simpler, faster, or more efficient. All these products come with a cost that may or may not be justified.

Effect of Acceleration on Direct Costs

As explained previously, direct costs almost always increase during project acceleration. However, the more we accelerate, the more the cost of accelerating per day increases. There are two reasons for this phenomenon:

1. At the activity level, accelerating more becomes more difficult and may require different and more expensive techniques. Consider a CIP (cast-in-place) concrete suspended slab activity. Its normal duration is 12 days, but we want to compress it to 6 days. Assume this activity includes setting up the formwork, placing the rebar, placing (pouring) the concrete, finishing the slab, stripping down the forms and reshoring, and removing the reshores. Compressing the schedule from 12 days to 11 days may be achieved with a simple and inexpensive adjustment such as having the laborers work 10 hours per day (still no work on Saturday and Sunday). If overtime hours are compensated at 1.5 times the regular rate, workers will work 10 hours per day but get paid for $8 \cdot 1$ (straight time) $+ 2 \cdot 1.5$ (overtime) hours, or 11 hours. The increase in labor cost will be 10% (we ignored the effect of overtime on productivity). Going from 11 days to 10 days may require working Saturdays (at 1.5 times the regular pay). The increase in labor cost will be 17%* (we again ignored the effect of overtime on productivity). To accelerate more, we may have to make adjustments to the concrete mix (accelerators) or method of placement (pumping in lieu of using a crane and bucket). In other words, when we start accelerating, we may have many options, and we select those that are least expensive. As we accelerate, we run out of inexpensive options, and we may be left with only those that are expensive.

2. At the entire project level (or, rather, the critical path level), we may have many activities from which to choose. We always choose the activity that has the least cost for crashing. As accelerating progresses, we may have fewer and more expensive choices. Also, as demonstrated previously, in the early stages of acceleration, the compression of one activity may result in the compression of the whole project. In later stages, when multiple paths are tied as critical, we may need to compress several activities (each on a different path) to reduce the project duration by only 1 day.

*In a typical 10-hours-per-day, 6-days-per-week situation, the worker works 60 hours, 20 of which are overtime. If overtime is compensated at 1.5 times the normal rate, the worker will receive 70 hours' worth of pay for the 60 hours' work. The additional pay ratio is $70/60 \cdot 100\% = 116.7\%$.

For the preceding two reasons, direct costs usually increase nonlinearly, as shown by the curve in Figure 8.6. Note that the *x*-axis represents the total duration of the project in days. For this reason, as we accelerate the project, we move from right to left on the *x*-axis.

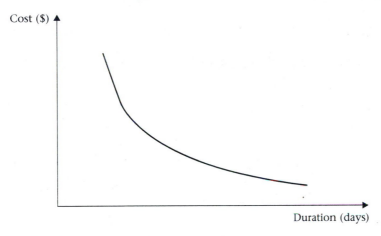

FIGURE 8.6   Nonlinear increase in direct costs with project acceleration

Effect of Acceleration on Indirect Costs

Indirect costs include mainly overhead items, such as the job trailer, equipment in the trailer (copier, fax, etc.), utilities, staff members (salaried employees, not hourly workers), and insurance. These expenses are directly and linearly proportional to the duration, as shown in Figure 8.7.

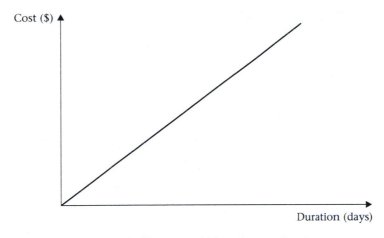

FIGURE 8.7   Linear decrease in indirect costs with project acceleration

Effect of Acceleration on Total Cost

Depending on the shape, slope, and real values, when we combine the curves for direct and indirect costs, we obtain a curve like that shown in Figure 8.8.

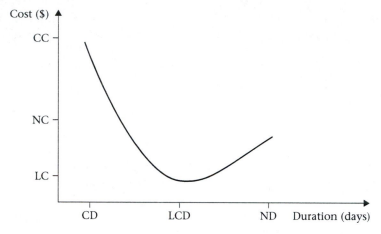

FIGURE 8.8   Effect of project acceleration on total cost: the general case, in which total cost decreases with acceleration till a certain point then starts increasing—CC, crash cost; NC, normal cost; LC, least cost; CD, crash duration; LCD, least-cost duration; ND, normal duration

We begin with the normal duration and the normal cost. Then, we start accelerating. At the beginning, the total cost decreases till it hits a minimum point, the least cost, with a corresponding **least-cost duration.** If cost is our priority, we must stop at this point. As we accelerate further, the cost increases till we either reach our desired duration or encounter the least possible duration, or **crash duration,** which has an associated **crash cost.**

As mentioned previously, the shape of the curve and the slope of the curve differ from one case to another. In some cases, the curve may start going up immediately (i.e., total cost starts increasing as soon as we start accelerating), as shown in Figure 8.9.

In other cases, the curve goes down then stops at the crash duration point, without going up anymore (see Figure 8.10). In this case, the crash duration point coincides with the least-cost duration point.

RECOVERY SCHEDULES

In real-life projects, schedules may slip. This situation may cause the owner concern, especially if the project deadline is critical. The owner may demand that the contractor adjust the work plan to enable him or her to finish on schedule. The

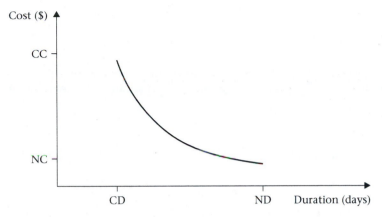

FIGURE 8.9   Effect of project acceleration on total cost: a special case, in which total cost starts increasing as soon as acceleration starts—CC, crash cost; NC, normal cost; CD, crash duration; LCD, least-cost duration; ND, normal duration

owner must be convinced that the contractor can feasibly do so, or the owner may fire the contractor and hire another contractor to ensure a timely finish. When the contractor adjusts the schedule, the result is a **recovery schedule.** It can be defined as a schedule prepared during construction, after the project has fallen behind (either the interim target has not been met or serious signs of failure to meet the deadline can be seen), with adjustments by the contractor that expedite the remainder of the project and ensure a timely finish. The recovery schedule may incorporate one or more of the techniques mentioned previously.

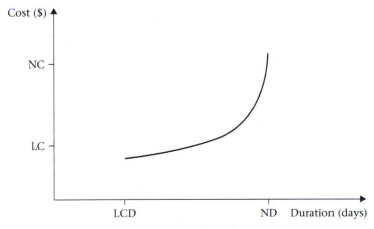

FIGURE 8.10   Effect of project acceleration on total cost: a special case, in which total cost keeps decreasing until the project is completely crashed—NC, normal cost; LC, least cost; LCD, least-cost duration; ND, normal duration

EXAMPLE 8.1

Calculate the normal, least-cost, and crash durations for the following project. Calculate the cost associated with each duration. Indirect (overhead) costs are $120 per day.

ACTIVITY	IPA[a]	DURATION (days) NORMAL	DURATION (days) CRASH	COST ($) NORMAL	COST ($) CRASH
A	—	5	4	500	600
B	A	7	5	350	500
C	A	8	5	800	920
D	A	11	7	1,200	1,400
E	B, C	6	4	600	700
F	C	4	4	500	500
G	D, F	7	5	700	1,000
H	E, F	6	5	300	420

[a]Immediately preceding activity.

Solution

This simple project has five paths (see Figure 8.11). They are listed next, along with their lengths in days:

PATH	DURATION (days)
ABEH	24
ACEH	25
ACFH	23
ACFG	24
ADG	23

Activity F is struck out because it cannot be accelerated. Let us prepare the time-cost trade-off calculation table (Figure 8.12). We have to start with the critical (longest) path: ACEH. We choose activity C because

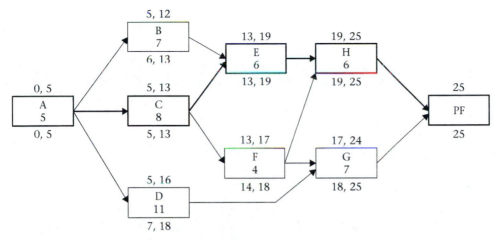

FIGURE 8.11 Precedence network for project in example 8.1—PF, project finish

it costs the least to crash, $40 per day. We cut the duration of C from 8 days to 7. This action affects three paths:

PATH	DURATION (days)	
ABEH	24	24
ACEH	~~25~~	24
ACFH	~~23~~	22
ACFG	~~24~~	23
ADG	23	23

This action increased the direct costs by $40 and decreased the indirect costs by $120. The total impact on the cost is a net savings of $80.

We now have two paths that tie at 24 days' duration: ABEH and ACEH. We can compress a shared activity (A, E, *or* H) or a combination of unshared activities (B *and* C). We choose activity E and compress it from 6 days to 5 at a cost of $50.

PATH	DURATION (days)		
ABEH	24	~~24~~	23
ACEH	~~25~~	~~24~~	23
ACFH	~~23~~	22	22
ACFG	~~24~~	23	23
ADG	23	23	23

■ The direct costs increased by $50 and the indirect costs decreased by $120. This results in a net decrease of $70 in the total cost.

Now we have four paths that tie at 23 days' duration: all but ACFH. We can compress a shared activity (A) or a combination of unshared activities (plenty of options exist). We choose activity A and compress it from 5 days to 4 at a cost of $100.* Activity A is now completely crashed.

PATH	DURATION (days)			
~~ABEH~~	24	~~24~~	~~23~~	22
~~ACEH~~	~~25~~	~~24~~	~~23~~	22
~~ACFH~~	~~23~~	22	~~22~~	21
~~ACFG~~	~~24~~	23	~~23~~	22
~~ADG~~	23	23	~~23~~	22

With this action, we spent an extra $100 in direct costs and saved $120 in indirect costs. The total cost decreased by $20 (we are still saving money, but the rate is decreasing).

Now we need to compress the same four paths using the least-cost combination. After simple mathematical inspection of the table, we find the best combination to be C, D, and E, with a total combined cost of $140. We compress *each* of these activities by 1 day to shorten the project duration from 22 days to 21 days.

PATH	DURATION (days)				
~~ABEH~~	24	~~24~~	~~23~~	~~22~~	21
~~ACEH~~	~~25~~	~~24~~	~~23~~	~~22~~	20
~~ACFH~~	~~23~~	22	~~22~~	~~21~~	20
~~ACFG~~	~~24~~	23	~~23~~	~~22~~	21
~~ADG~~	23	23	~~23~~	~~22~~	21

Note that path ACEH was cut by 2 days because it contains both C and E. Now, the total cost has increased by $20 ($140 increase in direct costs and $120 decrease in indirect costs). The next step is to

---

*If activity A could be crashed by more than 1 day, we could have crashed it to the limit since it is part of any path on the network. This means any day cut from activity A would automatically mean a day cut from the entire schedule.

find an alternative to activity E because it is completely crashed. The next least-cost combination is B, C, and D, at a total cost of $165. In this case, the total cost has increased by $45.

PATH	DURATION (days)					
ABEH	24	24	23	22	21	20
ACEH	25	24	23	22	20	19
ACFH	23	22	22	21	20	19
ACFG	24	23	23	22	21	20
ADG	23	23	23	22	21	20

Note that the critical paths may change in every round. Now, activity C is also completely crashed. Our next choice is the combination of B and G at a combined cost of $225, with a net increase of $105 in the total cost.

PATH	DURATION (days)						
ABEH	24	24	23	22	21	20	19
ACEH	25	24	23	22	20	19	19
ACFH	23	22	22	21	20	19	19
ACFG	24	23	23	22	21	20	19
ADG	23	23	23	22	21	20	19

Activity B is now completely crashed. All paths are tied at 19 days. The only remaining option is to combine activities G and H at a cost of $270, with an increase of $150 in the total cost.

PATH	DURATION (days)							
ABEH	24	24	23	22	21	20	19	18
ACEH	25	24	23	22	20	19	19	18
ACFH	23	22	22	21	20	19	19	18
ACFG	24	23	23	22	21	20	19	18
ADG	23	23	23	22	21	20	19	18

Now the entire project is completely crashed, with a duration of 18 days. The results may be summarized as follows:

- The normal duration is 25 days, at a total cost of $7,950.
- The least-cost is $7,780, at a duration of 22 days.
- The crash duration is 18 days, with a crash cost of $8,100.

Activity	Duration (days) Normal	Crash	Cost ($) Normal	Crash	Δ Cost ($)	Δ Days	Δ Cost / Δ Days	Days shortened						
A	5	4	500	600	100	1	100			1				
B	7	5	350	500	150	2	75					1	1	
C	8	5	800	920	120	3	40	1			1	1		
D	11	7	1,200	1,400	200	4	50				1	1		
E	6	4	600	700	100	2	50		1		1			
F	4	4	500	500	0	0	—							
G	7	5	700	1,000	300	2	150						1	1
H	6	5	300	420	120	1	120							1
Days cut							—	1	1	1	1	1	1	1
Project duration (days)							25	24	23	22	21	20	19	18
Increased cost/day ($)							—	40	50	100	140	165	225	270
Direct costs ($)							4,950	4,990	5,040	5,140	5,280	5,445	5,670	5,940
Indirect costs ($)							3,000	2,880	2,760	2,640	2,520	2,400	2,280	2,160
Total cost ($)							7,950	7,870	7,800	7,780	7,800	7,845	7,950	8,100

FIGURE 8.12   Time-cost trade-off calculation table for example 8.1

Notes

1. Accelerating can become complicated even in a small example. For larger projects, we use computers along with general guidelines.
2. Activity D is not completely crashed, which demonstrates an important point: To accelerate a project, we need not compress all activities. If we did, we would be wasting money for no benefit to the schedule.
3. We assumed linearity within each activity (e.g., it costs the same amount of money to compress activity C from 8 days to 7, from 7 days to 6, or from 6 days to 5). However, we see that the change in total cost for the project is not linear.
4. The project manager may choose a project duration between 22 days and 18 days to meet the contract-required finish date (22 days for least cost and 18 days for least duration).

ACCELERATING PROJECTS BY USING COMPUTERS

Real-life projects usually contain hundreds or thousands of activities. There may be tens or even hundreds of paths, each with 50, 60, or more than 100 activities. Performing calculations such as those done in example 8.1 would be too cumbersome. The practical approach is trial and error. However, nine guidelines follow:

1. Always make a backup copy of the schedule before you make any changes.

2. Focus on the critical path. A good idea is to sort activities by total float in ascending order. You may also apply a filter for activities with the least total float (zero or most negative).

3. Pick an activity on the critical path and reduce its duration by 1 day. Schedule the project (perform CPM calculations) and examine the impact on the project finish date. If the finish date is now 1 day earlier, move to step 5. If you are applying a filter, you may have to refresh the view.

4. If the project finish date did not change, at least one other critical path must exist, and you reduced only one. Go back to the list of activities with the least total float, pick one, and repeat step 3. Looking at the different paths on either a bar chart or a logic diagram can be helpful.

5. You have reduced the project duration by 1 day; you now need to reduce it by another day. Repeat step 3. You may find more activities that are critical now. This fact does not mean more options for you. On the contrary, you may have to compress several activities—simultaneously—to reduce the project duration by 1 day.

6. Repeat the same steps till you achieve the desired duration.

7. Avoid compressing any path by multiple days in one step unless you know the critical path is longer than the next one by several days. For example, if you compress an activity by 10 days, but the project finish date decreases by only 3 days, you have achieved nothing from the last 7 acceleration days (i.e., only the first 3 days of acceleration were effective). In this case, go back and replace the 10-day compression with 3 days (or the correct effective number).

8. If you are determining the least-cost duration, you may want to do the calculations manually (for every step, you calculate the total net savings by subtracting the increase in direct costs from the decrease in indirect costs). You may also create a simple spreadsheet that performs the calculations.

9. The project manager should give the scheduler the crash duration and crash cost information for the activities. The scheduler must then experiment with the accelerated schedule and submit the results to the project manager. After the project manager approves these results, the scheduler may implement the accelerated schedule.

CHAPTER 8 EXERCISES

1. What does the term *accelerating a project* mean?

2. Why would a project manager (or a contractor) accelerate a project?

3. A project manager may shorten the duration of a project in many ways. Mention six of these ways. Discuss each briefly, mentioning its pros and cons.

4. The decision to accelerate a project may be made early, before the project starts, or in the middle of it. The timing may limit your options for accelerating the schedule. Discuss this statement. Mention any example that comes to mind.

5. Discuss the pros and cons of fast tracking construction projects and using this concept as a means for accelerating projects.

6. Explain how accelerating a project works.

7. Would you advocate using overtime always, sometimes, or never? Explain your answer.

8. Give an example of accelerating a project by improving communications among the parties involved in the construction activities.

9. Your critical path is 128 days long. The next-longest path is 122 days long.

   a. If you extend the longest path by 5 days, the entire project duration will increase by 5 days. True or false?

   b. If you reduce the longest path by 5 days, the entire project duration will decrease by 5 days. True or false?

c. If you reduce the longest path by 10 days, the entire project duration will decrease by 10 days. True or false?

10. You are the project manager of a construction project. Your project is falling behind. You met with your team (including the scheduler) and discovered that accelerating the schedule to bring it back on track will cost you an additional $20,000. Would you do it? (*Hint:* You do not know enough to give a definite answer.)

11. You are the scheduler for a large commercial building project. The schedule you prepared (based on feedback from the project manager) falls 15 days short of the owner's deadline. The project manager decides to write a memo to all subcontractors requiring them to work 6 days per week, 10 hours per day. You ask the project manager to wait till you determine the most efficient way to crash the project. Outline your argument to convince him to go with a certain accelerating plan that focuses on the critical path and not all activities.

12. In general, what is the effect of accelerating an activity on the direct costs of a project. Why?

13. What is the effect of accelerating an activity on the indirect costs of a project? Why?

14. In general, what happens to the total cost of a project when you start accelerating and keep accelerating till you reach the least possible duration?

15. Explain your answer to the previous question graphically. Make sure you show the points of normal duration (ND), normal cost (NC), least cost (LC), least-cost duration (LCD), crash duration (CD), and crash cost (CC).

16. Visit a construction site and meet with the project manager. Ask the project manager what it would take to reduce the project duration by 5 days. Try to quantify the extra cost and benefits for such acceleration. Ask the project manager about the means he or she would use to achieve such acceleration.

17. What is a *recovery schedule?*

18. Calculate the normal, least-cost, and crash durations for the following project. Calculate the cost associated with each duration. Indirect (overhead) costs are $100 per day.

ACTIVITY	IPA	DURATION (days)		COST ($)	
		NORMAL	CRASH	NORMAL	CRASH
A	—	7	5	500	640
B	A	6	5	550	630
C	A	8	5	800	935
D	B	10	7	1,200	1,440
E	B, C	6	4	600	700
F	C	4	3	500	590
G	D, F	4	2	700	1,000
H	E, F	7	4	650	950
I	G, H	2	2	300	300

19. Calculate the normal, least-cost, and crash durations for the following project. Calculate the cost associated with each duration. Indirect (overhead) costs are $120 per day.

ACTIVITY	IPA	DURATION (days)		COST ($)	
		NORMAL	CRASH	NORMAL	CRASH
A	—	5	4	770	900
B	—	3	2	660	700
C	A	7	4	800	1,070
D	A, B	4	3	1,000	1,110
E	B	6	4	800	920
F	C, D	6	5	560	630
G	D	5	3	700	810
H	F	8	4	1,000	1,260
I	E, G	4	3	500	580
J	H, I	3	2	400	600

20. Calculate the normal, least-cost, and crash durations for the following project. Calculate the cost associated with each duration. Indirect (overhead) costs are $200 per day.

ACTIVITY	IPA	DURATION (days)		COST ($)	
		NORMAL	CRASH	NORMAL	CRASH
A	—	1	1	800	800
B	A	7	4	1,000	1,600
C	A	6	4	300	500
D	A	3	2	400	800
E	B	3	1	100	200
F	B, C	7	5	500	800
G	D	8	4	1,200	1,400
H	E	7	6	350	600
I	F	5	3	700	850
J	F, G	3	2	500	1,000
K	H, I, J	5	4	450	800

21. When you accelerate projects by using a computer, what steps do you follow?

22. Using *ENR* magazine and other resources, prepare a case study on the Northridge earthquake and C. C. Meyers' project. Determine how the contractor achieved these results (mention them as itemized factors).

Reports and Presentations

The Pinnacle, Sunny Isles, Florida. Courtesy of Smith Aerial Photos, Maitland, Florida.

Little John was excited about his new pair of pants, but they were a bit too long for him. He asked his oldest sister, Dorothy, "Would you please take 4 inches off my new pants?" "I would, but I have to go out now," she said. He asked his middle sister, Terry, "My beloved sister, would you please take 4 inches off my new pants?" With a sad smile, she replied, "I am so sorry I can't. I am too busy with house chores." He thought he would never ask his little sister, Lisa, but he had no choice. "I am really sorry, Johnny. I have tons of homework to do," she said. Little John went to bed, upset that he would not be able to wear his new pants to school the next day. Dorothy came back home early that evening. She wanted to surprise her little brother. She quietly went to his room and took the pants to her room. She was good at alterations. She altered them in no time and put them back in their place. Terry finished her house chores and still had some energy. "I feel so guilty letting my little brother down," she thought. Not knowing what her sister just did, she took 4 more inches off the pants. Lisa was sitting in her room doing homework and studying for an exam the next day. She was thinking of little John's disappointment at not being able to wear his new pants to school. Despite her not-so-friendly relationship with him, she closed her book and went to his room, took the new pants, and shortened them by yet 4 more inches. Next morning, the family was having an early breakfast when angry John came in with his new pants reaching barely below his knees and asked, "Who is the idiot who took a foot off my new pants?"

INTRODUCTION

Without a doubt, good communication is an essential component of the successful management effort. This means conveying the right (or proper) information to the right party at the right time and in the right form. Ten characteristics of good communication are as follows:

1. *Clarity.* The information must be clear to the receiving party. Ambiguous and subjective terms such as "as soon as possible," "good performance," and "the changes must be authorized by a responsible person in the architect's organization" must be avoided. Acronyms and abbreviations must not be used in the contract unless they are identified in the contract or they are standard in the industry. The speaker or writer must make sure the listener or reader understands exactly what is meant.

2. *Simplicity.* Simplicity helps improve understanding. If the information can be efficiently conveyed in one sentence, two sentences or a whole paragraph should not be used. The contract may contain phrases written by lawyers that may not be easy for the layperson to understand. However, project team members should use simple language in their daily communications.

3. *Preciseness and relevance to the subject.* Providing too much or irrelevant information may be confusing and counterproductive. An example of this is what the author of this book calls *lazy designer syndrome:* Some architects and engineers copy and paste information from the drawings and specifications of previous projects or boilerplates. Many sections, details, or paragraphs may not pertain to the current project. For instance, a contract may be written in New York or Chicago that has a clause about the frost line, which never applies in Miami or the Caribbean. Such information will only confuse and aggravate the contractor when he or she is trying to link it to the studied project.

4. *Legibility.* Some people have handwriting that is illegible or difficult to read. Sometimes only a person's secretary can read his or her handwriting. Such people should either type their communications on the computer or draft their notes and forward them to their secretaries, who can type or rewrite them.

5. *Proper support tools (pictures, tables, charts, statistics, etc.).* The old saying "A picture is worth more than a thousand words" proves to be true when we perform a simple task like assembling a bookshelf. Not only are pictures more helpful, they are unilingual: anyone can understand them. Tables, flowcharts, bar charts, organizational charts, and so forth are also helpful in conveying information. Current e-mail systems allow users to attach files, pictures, audio or video clips, and so forth to activities in a schedule or to an issue in project management software. When sending a file by e-mail, you must be concerned with two issues (other than the possibility of virus-infected files): the size of the attachments and software compatibility. Some users send e-mails with huge attachments that may clog or slow the recipient's e-mail system. Also, some users send file attachments that are not compatible with the recipient's software and cannot be opened. Some file types (e.g., .doc, .xls, .ppt, .mdb, .txt, .rtf, .pdf, .jpg, .gif, .exe) are universal, and almost any user of an IBM-compatible computer can open them. You should always check with the

recipient when the file attachment size is large or when the file type is uncommon.

6. *Proper level of detail.* The communicator must balance the amount of information in an intelligent way. Giving too little information or information that is too abstract may not convey the whole picture clearly, in which case one of two situations results: either the information recipient must contact the source to clarify the information, which takes precious time, or he or she must make assumptions to "fill in the blanks," which may lead to serious consequences. In contrast, providing too much information may overwhelm and confuse the receiving party. With a strict time limitation and the fact that we receive a multitude of mail, e-mail, fax, and telephone messages every day, we often discard information that does not seem important. The less information, the better the chance it will be read. A message containing too much information may be overlooked, not read, or trashed.* When a communication must include a large amount of information, one good idea is to include an abstract or a brief summary paragraph on the issue (the downside is that the recipient may feel content to read only the summary and may not read the details).

7. *Good organization and formality.* Good organization implies sorting and organizing the information so that it is easy for the viewer to read, follow, and retrieve. Formality means following the company's standard forms and procedures. Both aim at facilitating reading, searching, storing, and retrieving the information. Such facilitation is important in large companies, especially those with high employee turnover rates. Several software packages, such as Primavera Expedition (Primavera Systems, Inc., Bala Cynwyd, PA), Prolog Manager (Meridian Project Systems, Folsom, CA), and Project Management (Timberline, Beaverton,OR), were developed to help organize project documentation and communications.

8. *Conformance to industry standards.* As the world grows smaller, the industry is trying to find a common language. Many specifications were written years ago with descriptions of products and services no longer available or supported. The International Organization for

---

*An example of this is the contract for buying and financing a new car or for applying for a credit card. Contracts are often long and written in complex legal language. Most people sign such a contract without reading it.

Standardization (ISO)* is a worldwide federation of national standards bodies, one from each of more than 140 countries. ISO is a nongovernmental organization that was established in 1947. ISO's mission is to promote the development of standardization and related activities in the world with a view toward facilitating the international exchange of goods and services and toward developing cooperation in the spheres of intellectual, scientific, technological, and economic activity. ISO's work results in international agreements that are published as international standards.

Another organization, the International Alliance for Interoperability (IAI), a nonprofit organization, was formed on a much smaller scale, for the interoperability of the different software programs in the construction industry. Its mission statement is as follows: "To develop a standard universal framework to enable and encourage information sharing and interoperability throughout all phases of the whole building life cycle" (for more information, visit http://www.iai-na.org).

Whether or not the construction or design company follows ISO 9000, IAI, or other standards, it must make sure it conforms to the client's specifications, the local codes, federal standards, other components of the project, and general industry guidelines. For example, U.S. companies that do international work often have to convert their measuring units to the metric system.

9. *Retrievable.* We are no longer in the age of basements full of boxes and file cabinets containing information on archived projects. Fortunately, we can store, on a single compact disk (CD) or similar media, more than an entire file cabinet can hold. Not only is this possible, but the ease of searching and retrieving is incomparable. Retrieving information for live (current) projects may be performed easily by using computer search commands. Retrieving also includes resurrecting information on closed-out projects that were archived, which may be important in some legal cases.

10. *Transformable (from one form to another).* Transferring information from one program to another may not be as smooth as we would like. Information may get distorted or "chopped" when we go from one program to another or even from an old version to a new version of

---

*The term *ISO* is not an acronym for the name of the organization; it is derived from the Greek *isos*, meaning "equal," which is the root of the prefix *iso-* that occurs in a number of terms, such as *isometric*. For more details, go to http://www.iso.ch/iso/en/ISOOnline.frontpage.

the same program. Although software vendors make claims about the compatibility of their products with Microsoft (MS) Project, Primavera, and other products, glitches and discrepancies should always be expected. The problem may not be in the compatibility per se but in the different functions of and terminology in the two programs. For example, Primavera products allow combination relationships (start to start plus finish to finish). MS Project does not allow them. So, if you transfer a project from Primavera Project Planner (P3) format to MS Project format, some relationships may be dropped. In addition, products are frequently updated, so their compatibility may not remain intact. You must be careful with any transformation.

The ability to convert and open electronic files and to read the information is extremely important. For this reason, the author advises against using unknown software packages unless you are certain that such products communicate with more common products without problems.

THE DIFFERENCE BETWEEN REPORTS AND PRESENTATIONS

Although reports and presentations are both types of communications that aim at conveying information, one major difference exists between them. The written words of a report are the only vehicle for conveying information between the person preparing the report and the person receiving it. For this reason, it should be clear and complete. In contrast, a presentation focuses on the speaker's persuasive skills, although a written report (partial or complete, detailed or summarized) is often provided to the audience. The speaker focuses on certain points, using oral, visual, and written or printed tools. In addition, audiences usually have the opportunity to ask the speaker to elaborate on or to explain any point that is unclear to them.

Presentations are used for a variety of purposes, both within an organization and for outside parties. They may carry a lot of weight in influencing the audience's decision to buy a product or service. Four types of presentations are as follows:

1. *Contract candidate presentations.* Many owners require a presentation as part of the selection process for design, construction, or construction management professionals. The main focus of the presentation is to

convince the owner (or the decision maker) that the presenter not only can do the job, but also can do it better than other candidates can. This type of presentation should simply answer the owner's explicit or implicit question: "Why should I (we) hire you?" In many cases, contractors have won contracts from owners with the help of a brilliant presentation, even though they were not the lowest bidders.

2. *Sales and demonstration presentations.* A representative of a manufacturer or vendor may give a presentation to demonstrate a product (e.g., computer software, an office machine, specialized equipment).

3. *Project status presentations.* A project management team may give a presentation to upper management about a particular project and its status. Such presentations may be conducted both periodically and on an as-needed basis.

4. *Management presentations.* The management of a company may conduct a presentation to its staff to inform them about a new work plan, a new system, a new organization, or something else.

A sales presentation and an educational presentation are significantly different, although they have several characteristics in common. The first two types of presentations just described are mostly the sales type, even though they may have some educational content. A presentation on computer software does not aim at teaching its use to the audience. Rather, such a presentation focuses on the features and points of strength in the software. It attempts to impress rather than educate. It can be biased and subjective for the purpose of making a successful sale. The latter two types of presentations are mostly educational. Their objective is to inform the audience of a certain situation. We can argue that they are also "sales" presentations. In project status presentations, the project manager may try to impress the management for self-promotion purposes. In management presentations, the management is "selling" a new work plan or new system to the employees. Still, the main difference is that the last two types do not usually lead to a direct sale.

Another key difference between presentations and reports is the time constraint. Reports are submitted to a party who can read and review them at his or her own pace (within deadline restrictions). Presentations are time constrained. The information flows at the presenter's pace (within time-limit restrictions), not the receiver's. A large amount of information could be included in the presentation, but the presenter's challenge is to prioritize this information and focus on important issues that have more influence on the audience, particularly the decision maker. In many cases, the presenter refers the audience to a detailed report (which may be available with the presentation) or to an external source (e.g., an Internet Web site, a magazine).

Scientific seminars and short courses are not relevant to this discussion. Thus, they are not covered.

SKILLS NECESSARY FOR GIVING GOOD PRESENTATIONS

In addition to learning the characteristics of good communications described previously, presenters should develop seven skills for giving good presentations:

1. *Focus on the client's needs.* The presenter should present his or her product or service in the best way that serves the client. The product or service may have great features that are not relevant to the client's line of work. Elaborating on such features would be a waste of time. The presenter's main focus must be on how to meet the client's needs.

2. *Be honest.* Even though the presenter's ultimate goal—in most cases—is to sell a product or service, he or she should still be honest and objective, especially with regard to facts and numbers. For instance, making a statement such as "Our product is the best on the market" is easy to do, but backing up this statement with numbers, such as the sales volume, the number of clients served, and the results of a customer satisfaction poll, would make a better statement.

3. *Ensure that materials are visible.* The presenter must make sure the materials displayed on the screen are comfortably viewable and legible from all sides of the room. If possible, the presenter should test the display from several positions in the room before the presentation. During the presentation, the presenter should stand in a position not blocking the audience's line of sight.

4. *Speak clearly.* The presenter should speak clearly and with authority, occasionally interacting with the audience and sometimes using humor.

5. *Make eye contact.* The presenter should speak to the audience and not to him- or herself or to his or her notes. Eye contact with the audience is extremely important. Eye contact should be made with not just those in the front row or closest to the presenter, but everyone in the audience.

6. *Have a backup plan.* Some precautions should be taken in case something goes wrong. Items to have on hand include an extension cord; a signal cord; an electronic copy of the presentation on a disk, CD, flash drive,* or another medium; and a printout of the presentation. If the presenter is not using his or her personal computer, he or she must make sure the necessary software (e.g., Microsoft PowerPoint) is installed on the computer that will be used.

7. *Watch your body language.* Body language and hand and arm gestures are important. General advice on this topic and special advice about body language in certain cultures can be found in the many articles and books written on this subject.

Many references on teaching skills for good presentations are available. One of the best sources, which the author recommends, is Toastmasters International.[†]

THE POWER OF PRESENTATION

Current technology gives us powerful tools with which to create, manage, manipulate, present, and store data. When producing reports or presentations, we typically have many options for organizing and displaying information. Any cost estimating, scheduling, management, or other software has tens if not hundreds of standard reports. Users can also create and customize their own reports. Third-party software packages can provide even more reports. Each report has its own settings, rules, and options. Many features in these reports can be adjusted or turned on and off. Many users use these reports "as is," without paying careful attention to the default settings and consequently the output.

To create a good report, we should ask ourselves the following questions:

- Does the report include all the information the report user needs?
- Does it include any unneeded information?

---

*A removable little device that connects to the USB port of the computer. It is sometimes called a *thumb drive*, a *smart drive*, or a *pen drive*.

[†]Toastmasters International is a nonprofit organization that was established in 1924 to train people to have better communications and leadership skills. It has local clubs in almost every U.S. city and in many other locations worldwide. For more information about this organization, visit http://www.toastmasters.org/.

- Is the information clear and well organized?
- Is the information presented in the required format?
- Can the look of the report be enhanced?

The report must address the specific needs of the party receiving it. For example, if the report is for an upper-level manager who is responsible for tens or hundreds of projects, it should be brief and precise, containing a powerful summary that is not overly detailed. If the manager needs more information, he or she may request more details on a specific topic.

A progress payment report may not need to show bar charts or technical details such as total float, constraints, and so forth. Likewise, a report issued by the general contractor to one of his or her subcontractors may not show details of other subcontractors' activities that will not affect this subcontractor's work. The general contractor may not want to reveal the total float to subcontractors and, similarly, may not want to reveal certain information, such as the **actual cost,** when presenting a report to the owner.

The report should focus on one main issue or area. For example, the **Look-ahead schedule** shows the contractor what is supposed to happen in the next 2 weeks or month. Selecting activities with a total float of less than 3 days, for example, allows the contractor to focus on the critical path. When the project is large, it is divided into several areas, departments, or phases. The scheduler can then produce reports that cover a relatively small group of activities, grouped by building, floor, phase, and so forth; one group at a time. In some reports, the scheduler can show all areas, departments, and the like, summarized by a single bar per code. Use of software filters* and the organize function helps in choosing, sorting, and grouping activities efficiently.

Information comprises text and graphics. Graphics are an excellent tool if used properly. Graphics include bar charts, logic diagrams, flowcharts, pictures, video clips, and other items. Graphics are best used to support a result, a finding, or a recommendation or to just explain a situation (e.g., a bar chart for a project schedule). However, overuse or misuse of graphics may be counterproductive. Text should also be organized. Using tables, bullets, and short paragraphs helps the report reader separate and focus on specific issues.

Careful use of vivid colors can help the report user understand the report more easily. For example, red is customarily used for critical activities. Bars representing completed or underway activities should be clearly identified.

---

*A *filter* is a function in some computer scheduling programs, such as Primavera products. Its main function is to pick certain activities on the basis of specified criteria.

Black-and-white graphic reports may not be as powerful as color reports, even with varying grades of shading.

The size of report pages may be specified by the owner (the party to receive the report). Many schedulers print the schedule on regular letter-size $8\frac{1}{2}$-by-11-inch) paper, which will fit in a folder or binder with other project documents. However, project managers like to print a complete schedule on a large piece of paper (size D or E) and post it on the wall inside the project trailer. Regular inkjet and laser printers can handle paper as large as 11 inches by 17 inches. Plotters can handle larger sizes of paper.

Any report—text or graphic—should contain the following information:

- Name of the company and department or division; address of the company, especially if multiple offices; company logo
- Name of the person preparing the report and supervisor's approval (initials), if needed
- Name and location of the project
- Date
- Title of the report
- Attachments, if any
- Page numbering (if multiple pages) in a format such as "Page 2/6" so that missing pages can be replaced where they belong
- Legends to explain any graphics and colors in graphic reports
- Definitions of terms and acronyms or abbreviations that may not be known

In some cases, hiring a professional to prepare a report makes sense if the company does not employ someone who knows how or has the time to produce a high-quality professional report.

REVIEWING REPORTS BEFORE AND AFTER PRINTING

Since reports often comprise many pages and color printers may be slow, a report should be reviewed on the computer screen (Print Preview) to make sure it looks fine. If the report comprises many pages, the author recommends printing page 1 only: review and approve it, then print the rest of the report. Remember that, in many cases, what you see may not be what you get.

An error may occur in any report. It may be caused by the software, the hardware (computer or printer), or the user. Thus, the scheduler should be sure to review the report after printing it but *before* submitting it because errors may be found in a report even after it has been successfully reviewed on the computer screen.

GENERAL TIPS ON PRINTING REPORTS

In many cases, the scheduler must repeat the printing process several times because of errors or missing data. The result is multiple versions of the report. Although most software packages indicate the time and date on each report, the scheduler may become confused by all the versions and submit an incorrect copy of the report. For this reason, invalid copies of any report should be destroyed or recycled as soon as an error or omission is detected and the decision to reprint is made.

For some projects, certain reports must be printed with every update. Primavera software gives the user the opportunity to combine all these reports in a "series." In this case, the scheduler chooses one series rather than several individual reports.

While organizing the report, the person preparing the report should separate issues, areas, phases, and so forth, perhaps printing each on a page. However, the scheduler must be careful not to waste paper unnecessarily. Several ways to condense a report and save paper are as follows:

- Make sure only the needed activities and information are included. Use the software filter to help sort out unwanted information.
- Margins may be slightly reduced to allow more information per page.
- The choice between Portrait and Landscape may make a difference as to how many pages the report comprises.
- Using a smaller or a different font may help. However, make sure the report is comfortably legible.
- Use the Fit to One Page function in the Print menu.
- In limited cases, you may print on both sides of the paper.
- Most important, many reports and other types of communications may remain in electronic form and need not be printed.

SUMMARY REPORTS

The scheduler must relate the schedule information to the project manager not only as computer-generated colorful charts, but in clear language as well. For example, after a periodic update, the scheduler will likely produce standard Primavera or MS Project reports, including bar charts, cost tables, and so forth. Along with the reports, a document (written in plain text) summarizing the situation should be included. This summary report should contain the following information:

- The overall situation of the project: the total float for the critical path and the expected completion date
- The preceding information as compared with that in the last update: did we gain or lose any days?
- The new critical path, if it changed: what is delaying the project?
- Cost information (if applicable): cost this period, cost variance, cost to date, and cost to complete, along with the total planned budget (at the level of the entire project only)
- Any other information that may help the project manager identify trouble spots or make up for any lost time
- No unnecessary details, such as routine progress per activity, a slight delay in activities that have sufficient float, and so on

The summary report should not exceed one page. It should be written in the form of a memorandum as a simple word-processor document.

PAPER OR ELECTRONIC REPORTS?

Computers have become an essential part of our lives and businesses, including project management. Many documents are now sent electronically. Electronic signatures are even legally accepted in many situations. Nevertheless, some documents still must be printed on paper. Either way, the contractor, the design professional, the construction management firm, and the owner must be able to store, manage, and retrieve information efficiently. The software industry has developed several software packages for this purpose, such as Primavera Expedition, Meridian's Prolog Manager, and Timberline's Project

Management. This software helps organize the "paperwork": transmittals, submittals, purchase orders, payment requisitions, telephone logs, RFIs (requests for information), **requests for proposals (RFPs),** proposals, change orders, memos, invoices, notices, general correspondence, meeting minutes, daily reports, and any other document that relates to the project management. Such software also helps speed up the communications, including the review and approval processes. These software packages are becoming more and more powerful:

- They are continuously being expanded and more modules are being added to them to circumvent all facets of project management.
- They can be integrated with other programs (CAD, estimating, accounting, scheduling, etc.).
- They include many standard forms, including some third-party forms.
- They allow the user to tap into the software through their SDKs (software development kits) and to customize certain aspects or to export data.
- They allow project team members to go on the Web (Internet and intranet) and read and respond to documents from anywhere.
- They can be linked to external devices such as palmtops (PDAs).

Users of electronic media should follow certain precautions, such as the following eight:

1. Back up your documents periodically. If you are on a local server and are using the shared drive, be sure to back up your documents regularly. Keeping a backup copy in a place away from the company's building is also a good idea. Doing so is a precaution against fires, floods, hurricanes, theft, and other events that can destroy the records. Having all the information in one local location only, such as the scheduler's notebook computer, is dangerous and unwise.

2. Programs such as P3 and Primavera Enterprise (P3e) are disk based and not memory based. This means you cannot "undo" commands or "save as" a different file. Whatever you do will be permanent. For this reason, if you want to experiment with some "what-if" scenarios, make a copy of the schedule and leave the original intact. Once you finish experimenting, delete one of the two files or archive it so that the two files do not get mixed up and you use the incorrect file.

3. When the e-mail system is used for communication, print important e-mail messages or transfer them from the inbox to a permanent folder or box. Most e-mail systems automatically "clean up" the inbox periodically (e.g., every 6 months).

4. For projects that require periodic updating, always make a copy of the schedule before updating. The names of the schedules must follow a pattern that represents the company's policy. P3 allows only four characters for a file name. One good practice is to use two alpha characters to identify the project and two numerical characters to indicate the number of the update (starting with the baseline, 00). MS Project, Primavera's SureTrak Project Manager, and Primavera P3e do not have this limitation and allow almost as many characters as the user desires. All versions of a project schedule should be stored in an organized and systematic way. An example is as follows:

```
C:\Schedules\Tampa\OfficeBuilding\OB00
............................\OB01
............................\OB02
.............................

C:\Schedules\Tampa\ShoppingCenter\SC00
............................\SC01
............................\SC02
.............................

C:\Schedules\Orlando\SmithBuilding\SB00
............................\SB01
............................\SB02
.............................
C:\Schedules\Orlando\CityGarage\CG00
............................\CG01
............................\CG02
.............................
```

5. When making a copy of the schedule (or any project-related file) on a floppy disk or a CD, label or identify the disk or CD with the project name, version, and date.

6. Some users of simple programs such as word processors and spreadsheets "insert" the date rather than typing it. For example, MS Word

has an Update Automatically option that can be turned on or off. Serious problems may result if this option is unintentionally turned on. The document may have originally been created on 10/15/2004, but the project manager needs a copy of the document on 12/16/2004. The date that would appear on the document would be 12/16/2004, not the original date, 10/15/2004. Note that other software options that many users do not usually pay attention to may also have serious consequences.

7. It has been said that your hard drive is like your garage: no matter how large, it will soon be full of junk. For this reason, completed projects should be archived. Thanks to new technology, what formerly occupied several file cabinets can now be stored on a single CD. Because of the fragility of CDs and other electronic media, however, making duplicate CDs and storing them in different locations may be wise. Make sure the CDs are labeled properly.

8. Only professionals should be in charge of company technology. Computer viruses and hackers often cause serious damage. An overlooked or a careless action by an employee may cause the computer system in a company to shut down for a period or may erase important files, which may result in huge losses and inconvenience. For this reason, large companies usually dedicate a person or a department to taking care of information technology (IT) and filtering every electronic correspondence through the continuously updated antivirus program and firewalls.

E-REPORTS

Reports can be e-mailed, but the sender must make sure the receiver has the proper software with which to open them. Many computer programs offer the Save As option with several format options. One format that is becoming increasingly popular is the HTM or HTML format, which allows the user to view the report in Internet Explorer or Netscape Navigator, the two standard Internet programs. Several Primavera products call this option the *Publish* function. When the e-report has multiple files, the sender may want to "ZIP" them in one compressed, self-extracting file. The receiver may want to create a temporary folder in which to download the ZIP file, then extract it there. Large attachments should not be sent unless the receiver approves such an action. The sender should identify each report and include a table of contents with a brief description of each report.

COMMUNICATIONS IN THE INTERNATIONAL ENVIRONMENT

Technology has rendered the world smaller. Not only can project participants (owner, architect, structural engineer, mechanical engineer, general contractor, etc.) be located in different regions or countries, but also many companies now have a diversified workforce. Thus, making a mistake as a result of lacking knowledge about a local culture and work environment is easy, and possibly embarrassing and costly.

Many books and articles have been written and many seminars have been conducted on this subject. We cover only some scheduling-related issues:

1. In most countries, the date is written in the day/month/year format rather than in the customary U.S. date format of month/day/year. A date such as 11/8/2004 can cause a crisis if it is meant as the 11th day of August but is interpreted as the 8th day of November. For international projects, writing the name of the month, rather than its number, is recommended. The previous date can then be written as 11 August 2004. Alternatively, the month may be abbreviated by three letters, such as 11 AUG 2004.

2. Most of the Western world starts the workweek on Monday and takes Saturday and Sunday off as a nonwork weekend. This is not necessarily the case in other parts of the world such as the Middle and Far East. Thus, software defaults must be checked and adjusted accordingly.

3. Holidays differ from one country to another. They may have to be inserted as nonworkdays in the schedule.

4. In the daily work schedule, the number of workdays (5 or 6), start time, finish time, lunch break, "siesta time," and other breaks may also differ. Thus, productivity, and hence activity durations, may have to be recalculated.

5. Weather can have a significant impact on the schedule. The project management team must be fully aware of local weather, including seasonal floods, hurricanes, rain, and so forth.

6. The labor market and customs also differ from one place to another. In some countries, most of the skilled labor needed in construction projects is imported. In such countries, it is not unusual to see workers from different backgrounds (ethnicities, religions, cultures) working together. In some cases, workers on the same project do not speak a

common language and communications become a challenge to management.

7. Availability and methods of acquisition and delivery of materials and equipment may differ significantly. In some countries, rigid or slow customs procedures may cause major delays.

8. Permits and government procedures for approval may also differ and may require special consideration.

9. Communication among different cultures, even those using the same language, may result in misunderstandings. The same word may have two meanings to two people. Body language and hand gestures may have different—and possibly obscene—meanings in different cultures. In fact, a person may unintentionally insult another person because of a misunderstanding or a language or cultural difference.

10. Currency exchanges may create a nightmare for management. In some international contracts, the budget may be set in U.S. dollars but the materials and labor are paid in local currency. The exchange rate may differ from day to day. The management team must deal with such situations carefully.

CHAPTER 9 EXERCISES

1. List the characteristics of good communications. Briefly explain each.

2. Why do you think communications is an important issue? Can you mention a situation in which the lack of good communication resulted in negative consequences?

3. What is the *lazy designer syndrome?*

4. You are a new scheduler for a medium-size project. You joined the company after the project started. The project manager asks you to prepare a report that tells him "everything about the schedule." Does this statement provide sufficient instructions for you to create the report? If not, list the questions you will ask the project manager so that you will know exactly what you need to print out.

5. You were hired by a company that does not have a formal policy for managing schedule files. The schedules are currently on the project managers' laptops (created with SureTrak Project Manager software). What precautions do you recommend to ensure the uniformity and security of the schedules?

6. Mention and briefly describe the various types of presentations.

7. What are the major differences between reports and presentations?

8. Indicate which type of presentation is required for each of the following situations.

   a. The owner of a large project has a short list of three contractors. They all seem acceptable, but the owner wants each contractor to present the way he or she will build the project so the best contractor can be chosen.

   b. Primavera and Meridian are competing on a bid to provide project management software to a local government. Each provider will be given a 2-hour time slot in which to show the advantages of his or her software. Following this, the government will make its choice.

   c. The government in exercise b chose the software. Now, it hires a consultant to teach the use of the software to its employees.

   d. A large company changes its medical insurance provider. As a result, many terms of the insurance have changed. Linda, a human resources manager, will give a presentation explaining the new terms and procedures of the new medical insurance.

   e. A construction company is in financial trouble. A new president was appointed by the board of trustees. He lays out a recovery plan for the company. He will present this plan to the employees.

   f. Before the new president presents his plan in exercise e, he requires each project manager to give a presentation on the status of his or her projects to the upper management members.

   g. A large company is hiring a chief estimator. There are three top candidates. As part of the interview process, each candidate must give a presentation simulating the estimation of a real project.

9. List some tips for giving a successful presentation.

10. "The report must focus on certain issues." Discuss this statement and mention some helpful tips.

11. In addition to the main data in the report, what type of information should a report contain?

12. Why is it important to review a report before and after printing it?

13. Provide some tips on saving paper when you are printing reports.

14. You are the scheduler for a shopping center project. You just finished an update on many activities occurring in the project. You printed the

updated bar chart and cost tables, but you missed something important before submitting the report to the project manager. What was it? What kind of information must you include?

15. Your company is trying to "go electronic." It just bought new computers and a new server. You are given the task of writing a set of instructions for all project managers and their personnel on the procedures for storing and managing the projects. Outline your plan.

16. In the previous exercise, since you are the only "computer guru" in the company, you are also given responsibility for the company's information technology. Outline your plan to back up and secure the company's files.

17. Mention some tips for a project manager who will be taking over a new project in the Middle East. Bear in mind, this is the manager's first trip overseas.

18. Can you mention any situation in which not understanding a particular language or culture resulted in an embarrassment or a loss to a company? This experience does not need to be personal. You may use any real story.

Scheduling as Part of the Project Management Effort

Technology Center of the Americas, Miami, Florida. Courtesy of Smith Aerial Photos, Maitland, Florida.

INTRODUCTION

Construction project management comprises several components that are often interrelated. Typically, one person (the project manager, or PM for short) is responsible for running and managing the overall operations. Under the PM is the project management team, which may consist of a large number of professionals (assistant PM, project superintendent, project engineer, scheduler, estimator, safety manager, procurement manager, accountant, clerk, secretary, etc.) for large projects. Small projects typically have a smaller team, and some of the team members may be working on multiple projects.

The management team typically includes field personnel and office personnel. It may include team members who are dedicated exclusively to a particular project and others who are assigned to the project part time (they work on other projects as well) or serve on the project for only a temporary period. For example, a project scheduler may be dedicated to one large project even if he or she works in the main office. For smaller projects, the scheduler may distribute his or her time among assignments for the different projects.

Managing projects requires several skills. We must distinguish between managerial skills and technical skills. In some cases, a person who is top notch in his or her technical field may fail completely as a manager. Managerial skills are essential for a PM. An interesting statement is found in *Commentary on AIA Document A201-1997* (The American Institute of Architects 1999, 25): "A superintendent cannot build a project alone, but an incompetent superintendent can single-handedly ruin one." This statement applies even more so to the PM. It is outside the scope of this book to discuss the characteristics of a good manager. As far as technical expertise, construction is a diverse industry. Within each type of construction are many specialties, such as demolition, excavation, concrete, masonry, carpentry, structural steel, finishes, electrical, HVAC (heating, ventilation, and air-conditioning), plumbing, and many others. Within each specialty might be numerous subspecialties. Rarely, if ever, is a person an expert in all fields. A typical PM may be an expert in one or a few fields, but he or she must be familiar with all of them to manage the project competently. Each technical area is usually headed by a foreman, who must be an expert in that particular field.

Scheduling is one of the important pieces of the "project pie." It is a technical field concerned with time calculation and management. Scheduling interrelates with other components of the overall project management. In this chapter, we briefly discuss some of these interrelationships.

SCHEDULING AND ESTIMATING

Scheduling and estimating are closely related, and their relationship is probably one of the most important relationships in project management. These two areas intersect in many ways, such as the following eight:

1. The estimator needs to know how long the project will last in order to estimate certain costs, particularly overhead (management team, field office, utilities, etc.).

2. Estimating and scheduling departments collaborate to provide information to the procurement department. The estimating department tells which materials are needed and the scheduling department tells when they will be needed. This facilitates the procurement of labor, materials, and equipment.*

3. The scheduler sometimes estimates the durations of activities with help from the estimating department.

4. Many schedules are cost loaded. The cost must be imported (manually or electronically) from the cost estimate.

5. Earned value management, discussed in chapter 7 as part of project control, is an integrated approach to project cost and schedule control.

6. **Progress payments** depend on the schedule of values (prepared by the estimator) and the percent complete (prepared by a scheduler).

7. Resource allocation and resource leveling may be cost related, although they are scheduling issues.

8. Schedule compression always involves a balance between cost and time.

Other interrelationships exist between estimating and scheduling, as is shown in the following sections.

Evolution of a Cost Estimate and a Schedule for a Project

When a contractor considers a project for bidding or negotiation, he or she needs to know the cost and the time frame.† Owners usually specify the

---

*The project schedule might have an impact not only on the procurement schedule, but also on the estimate because the timing may affect the cost of labor, materials, and equipment.

†*Time frame* does not mean only the duration. It includes the time span during which the project will occur. For example, a project scheduled to occur during a winter season in Chicago will probably cost more than if it were built in the summer.

required finish date of a project in the bid documents or the contract. However, the contractor must calculate his or her own estimate of the project duration to ensure that he or she can meet the owner's stipulated date. If the contractor's schedule does not meet the owner's date, the contractor must either accelerate (crash, compress) the project to fit it within the given time interval or ask the owner to extend the time limit on the project.

Depending on the size and type of the project, as well as the contractual arrangement, the contractor may start with a rough estimate of the schedule (not necessarily a critical path method, or CPM, schedule, but an educated estimate of the time required to build the project). The contractor may use his or her previous experience and a "gut feeling" to estimate the duration of the major components of the project and build an initial schedule. After the contractor lays out an initial rough schedule, he or she uses the duration to estimate the indirect-cost items (overhead), such as the following:

- Project staff (PM, project superintendent, project engineer, receptionist or secretary, clerk, etc.)
- Office trailer
- Cars and trucks assigned to the project team
- Office equipment (copying machine, fax machine, computers, etc.)
- Temporary utilities (electricity, water, drinking water and ice, telephones, cell phones, gas, portable toilets, etc.)
- Other indirect project-related expenses

The cost of most, if not all, of these items is linearly proportional to time. This is why the estimator needs to know the duration of the project to assess the indirect expenses.

Schedules, like cost estimates, are created on the basis of available information. Reality (what will actually happen) is never fully known in advance. Thus, every cost estimate or schedule includes some assumptions and guessed information. A difference exists, though, between a situation in which 95% of the information is known and 5% is assumed, and a situation in which 20% of the information is known and 80% is assumed. Estimators use one major criterion to differentiate, in principle, between approximate estimates and detailed estimates. Detailed estimates are obtained by performing quantity takeoffs from the design drawings and using the specifications. These detailed quantities are then multiplied by unit prices set by the estimator. Indirect expenses are added to the calculated direct expenses to yield the grand total.

In contrast, approximate estimates are based on comparing the project under consideration with previous similar projects, then making adjustments according to the size, quality, location, and so forth. No work breakdown or quantity takeoff is used in approximate estimates. The main difference between the two methodologies is that we start with the known information, which is supposed to be the majority, for detailed estimates, then complement it with assumptions for the unknown. With detailed estimates, we can look at the estimate and identify the cost of one particular item, such as a window, paint, or even a single footing. With approximate estimates, such identification is generally not possible.

In scheduling, no such clear distinction exists between a "rough schedule" and a "detailed schedule," but the process is similar to that for cost estimating. We start with the known information and complement it with assumptions. One frequent practice of designers is to show a construction activity as one bar without details. Once a contractor is chosen, he or she will submit a detailed construction schedule that should fit within the time frame of the single bar. This detailed schedule is then integrated into the original schedule created by the designer and replaces the single Construction activity.

Summary schedules, rather than a lack of detailed information, may also be used for quickness. This approach is not generally used, and such schedules are not used for field implementation or project control. This approach is also similar to using approximate cost estimates when the contractor needs to give the potential client a ballpark cost estimate of the project without spending much time studying the design drawings and specifications.

When the design is finalized, performing detailed cost estimating and scheduling makes sense. This practice is used in the traditional delivery method, in which the project is completely designed, then a contractor is selected through the process of bidding or negotiation. In other delivery methods, a contractor may be selected* before the design is completed or even started, such as in design-build (D/B) or pure agency construction management (PCM) delivery methods. In this case, the design may come in stages, called **design development (DD).** Each stage specifies a completed percentage of the design. For example, if the design is called *DD30*, it

---

*In some contractual arrangements, there is no prime or general contractor. Instead, subcontractors may contract directly with the owner (e.g., construction management not-at-risk) or with the construction management professional (e.g., construction management at-risk).

is about 30% complete. In this case, when the contractor estimates the cost and duration of the project, he or she must use the available design information, then supplement it with assumptions. Doing so is exactly like solving a 100-piece puzzle with only 30 pieces available. Later, the designer provides a more detailed design (e.g., DD60, DD90, etc.). The design is still incomplete but contains more information than in the previous stage. The contractor refines the cost estimate and schedule by replacing some assumptions with new design information. If the project schedule changes, the cost estimate may be affected. If the scope changes, both the cost estimate and the schedule may change. This process continues until the final design is issued. The final design* will be the base for the contractor's final cost estimate and schedule.

Estimate-Generated Schedules

Some cost-estimating software packages can export information to scheduling programs or to a plain spreadsheet. In most of these cases, the result is a list of activities along with their durations but without any logical links (relationships). Before we discuss the **estimate-generated schedule,** let us briefly discuss how information is generated in cost-estimating programs. In short, with regard to labor and equipment costs, two methods for building the cost-estimate database items are used:

1. Provide the labor and equipment cost per unit. For example, if we are placing concrete for columns, using a pump, the cost is $17.55 per CY (cubic yard) for labor and $7.30 per CY for equipment. Although there is a basis for how we derived these numbers, the database does not contain this basis or any details about how we generated these numbers.

2. For the same item, suppose we are using Crew C-20,† and this crew can place 90 CY per day. The crew cost is usually listed as part of the resource information in the database and not for each item. In our case, Crew C-20 comprises the following:

---

*In the traditional delivery method, the final design is called the *construction document* and becomes part of the contract.

†This example was taken from *R. S. Means Building Construction Cost Data* (R. S. Means 2001).

RESOURCE	QUANTITY	COST/HOUR EACH ($)	TOTAL COST PER DAY ($)
Labor foreman	1	24.85	198.80
Laborer	5	22.85	914.00
Cement finisher	1	27.95	223.60
Equipment operator	1	30.35	242.80
Total Laborers	**8**		**1,579.20**
Gas engine vibrator	2	4.75	76.00
Concrete pump	1	72.50	580.00
Total Equipment	—		**656.00**
Total Crew C-20	—		**2,235.20**

If we check the numbers,

Cost/CY = Total daily cost/Total daily production,

so

Labor cost/CY = $1,579.20/90 = $17.55/CY

and

Equipment cost/CY = $656.00/90 = $7.29/CY

which are identical to the numbers obtained with the first method.

The second method has two advantages over the first:

1. If the labor or equipment rates change, you can make limited changes to the labor or equipment rate tables, assuming you are using a computer. Such changes should automatically adjust the prices of all items using these labor or equipment rates. In the first method, you must manually change every database item that uses the changed resources.

2. When you are deriving a schedule from the estimate, the first method does not indicate productivity and thus cannot provide the activity duration. The second method can provide the activity duration if you simply divide the total quantity by the daily production rate. For

instance, in the preceding example, if we must place 166 CY of concrete, the duration would be $166/90 \approx 2$ days. The PM may choose to use multiple crews or to adjust the productivity as a result of favorable or unfavorable conditions. Regardless, one source of productivity will feed both the estimate and the schedule.

Materials costs do not affect the productivity level, the durations, or the schedule.

The scheduler must be extremely careful about using estimate-generated information for three reasons. First, activities in such a schedule are defined by the estimator, not the scheduler. Second, the durations in such schedules are based on the productivity level built into the estimate items. In reality, the productivity level may need to be adjusted because of many factors, such as project size and complexity; crew size; skill level; weather conditions; site conditions; equipment size, type, and condition; overtime or the lack thereof; and management competency and experience. Formulas and adjustment tables and curves have been developed to allow productivity-level adjustments for individual factors such as weather and overtime (Oglesby, Parker, and Howell 1989).* Some authors have even suggested one formula that incorporates these factors for the productivity adjustment (Neil 1982). Third, and finally, in some activities, two or more crews may be working simultaneously (a common occurrence in large projects), which will reduce the duration accordingly.

After the scheduler has adjusted the productivity level, the logic must be built. The importance of such a step cannot be overemphasized.

Cost-Loaded Schedules

A **cost-loaded schedule** is a schedule in which each activity is assigned a dollar-amount budget. Similar to the two methods described previously for building the cost-estimate database items, two methods are used to assign a budget to activities in scheduling programs:

1. Assign a lump-sum amount without providing details about how this number is sliced or which resources use it. You may still be required to supply a cost account code in some software packages to help track the cost.

---

*See also the discussion on overtime in chapter 8.

2. Assign a number of units of certain resources (e.g., one foreman, one equipment operator, two common laborers, and one hydraulic excavator) to the activity. The schedule must contain a "resource dictionary," in which every resource is defined and priced. The program calculates the required resource quantities for the activity by multiplying the number of resources required by the activity by the duration of the activity. For example, if the activity requires 3 laborers and has a 4-day duration, the resource assignment is $3 \cdot 4 = 12$ labor-days, or $3 \cdot 4 \cdot 8 = 96$ man-hours. The program then calculates the budget for the activity by multiplying the resource assignment by the resource unit prices in the resource dictionary.

The second method has six advantages:

1. You can level your resources only when you assign resources to the activity. (Resource leveling is discussed in chapter 6.)

2. You can produce procurement reports specifying the resource need by type, quantity, date, and even price. You can link your schedule with the accounting (and estimating) system, match your demand with supply, and trace each expense in your project. In the first method, you can track only the budget.

3. This method aids in project control and earned value management.

4. If the cost or availability of a resource that is being used in one or more activities changes, the scheduling program can reflect the impact of this change at the entire project level.

5. You may be able to use a "resource calendar." This type of calendar is defined for a specific crew. For example, if a plumbing crew is available for a project Wednesday through Saturday only, when you assign the crew to an activity, the program will automatically schedule work only during the days the crew is available.

6. Under certain conditions, you may allow your resources to control the duration of an activity. For example, if an activity requires four painters for 10 days, the program calculates a total of 40 man-days, or 320 man-hours. Depending on the painters' availability, and within the schedule logic and constraints, the scheduling program may assign a fluctuating number of painters to the activity so that the job can be finished in the most efficient way (from a resource management perspective). The result may be an increase or a decrease in the duration, with the same bottom-line 320 man-hours. With scheduling software, this option may be turned off to retain the original duration.

One interesting scenario that relates to point 4 is when resources are priced through a certain date then increase after this date. Suppose a union contract specifies a carpenter's rate of $18 per hour through 6/30/04. After this, it will increase to $20 per hour. Assume a certain activity requires 128 carpenter man-hours and is scheduled to take place in June 2004. The total cost for carpenters for this activity is 128 · $18 = $2,304. Now, suppose the activity slips to July. The cost will increase by 128 · $2 = $256, for a new budget of $2,560. This cost may be in addition to other delay-related expenses. You must be careful in such cases as to whether to allow the resource dictionary to drive the budget or to treat the budget as a fixed amount.

ESTIMATING AND ACCOUNTING

Cost accounting is defined as "the systematic recording and analysis of the costs of materials, labor, and overhead incident to production" (Merriam-Webster 2004). Cost accounting involves checks and balances: matching actual spending with estimated or budgeted amounts. The actual cost of every work item must not exceed the estimated (budgeted) amount. In some cases, particularly in public agencies, accounting also involves different categories of money sources (funds). For example, a transportation project in a city may be funded by a combination of federal funds, state funds, local funds, grants, and special taxes or fees. Each fund has its limits and restrictions. Many grant funds have stipulations, such as the type of project, geographic location, type of expense, or type of subcontractor (e.g., minority, small business). The accountant must make sure the expenses met these stipulations.

As discussed in chapter 8, construction project costs are classified into direct and indirect expenses. Direct expenses include labor, materials, equipment, subcontracts, and others. Indirect expenses include job overhead, general overhead, profit, and contingency fees. When actual expenses are incurred, the accountant must link each expense to a specific work item. The expense must be categorized (labor, materials, equipment, overhead) and subcategorized (common labor, carpenter, concrete, crane, etc.). The accountant must make sure actual expenses do not exceed the estimated cost.

The contractor's accounting system maintains a list of vendors, suppliers, and subcontractors. At any time, the contractor should be able to track any material ordered from any particular supplier, including the following information:

- Total quantity ordered
- When it was ordered
- Delivery status
- Total cost, how much paid, the balance, and the due date for the balance
- Any problems with the materials and the action taken

The general contractor's accounting system should also include records of subcontractor's monthly payments: how much was requested, approved, authorized, paid, and retained.

The payroll (for hourly workers) is done regularly (weekly or biweekly). Workers' hours (regular and overtime) are also posted against specific work items. Accountants add burden expenses and benefits, then subtract the appropriate amounts from the payroll, such as federal and state withholding tax, FICA (Federal Insurance Contributions Act) fees, FICA medical fees, unemployment insurance contributions, union dues, medical insurance contributions, and so forth.

The general contractor collects the subcontractors' pay requests and incorporates them into his or her **request for payment** and submits it to the owner. A pay request goes through the usual steps: verification and approval by the owner, processing, and issuance of the payment (minus any retainage). Accountants must also keep track of each subcontractor: total contract, payments to date, retainage to date, and balance.

Every expense must be approved by an authorized person before it is accepted into the accounting system. Checks must also be signed by an authorized person.

SCHEDULING AND ACCOUNTING

Scheduling is related to accounting in basically one way. When the project is updated (statused), information is obtained on new work progress. The cost of this new work progress is then processed as described previously. If the schedule is cost loaded, it provides periodic information:

- Which activities have started (along with the start dates)
- The percent complete of such activities

- Which activities are finished (along with the finish dates)
- Total budget, cost this period, cost to complete, cost variance, and **cost at completion**
- Any other activity-related financial information

This information must be reviewed and approved by the PM and is then forwarded to the accounting department.

If the project is not cost loaded, the same procedure must take place through the accounting system. In this case, the percent complete for each activity must be entered for the pay period. The accounting system uses the schedule of values and calculates cost this period, cost to complete, cost variance, and cost at completion. After schedule approval, cost this period becomes the basis for monthly progress payments, as described previously.

SCHEDULING AND CHANGE ORDERS

Accounting, estimating, and scheduling departments also handle change orders (COs), each from its own perspective. In construction, COs are almost inevitable. However, well-planned and well-managed projects may have few or no COs. COs may be initiated by the contractor or the owner (and are discussed in more detail in chapter 12). In all cases, the contractor estimates the cost of the CO and the impact on the schedule, if any. The owner approves, rejects, or negotiates the contractor's request. Once the owner approves such a request, he or she issues the CO.

The contractor must then implement the CO in the estimating, scheduling, accounting, and other tracking systems. Managing COs may present a challenge to the contractor's staff. COs may—and usually do—affect existing items. For example, two additional floors in a mid-rise office building may require the engineer to redesign the columns, the foundation, the main HVAC unit, the type of elevators, and possibly other items. A deletion of a swimming pool will alter the amount of excavation and landscaping. If the contractor encounters "differing site conditions," his or her work plan may have to be delayed or altered.

What is important to scheduling and project control is implementing the changes in the baseline schedule (and estimate) so that measuring against the baseline will still be a fair and objective procedure. The original baseline should not be erased. Rather, it must be archived with the project records because it could be used in case of a later dispute.

PAPERLESS PROJECT MANAGEMENT

The construction industry, as well as other industries, is increasingly managing information electronically. As a result, the traditional use of paper has been minimized.

Any project usually starts with the design (architectural, civil, structural, mechanical, electrical, etc.). Many designers work with drafting or design software, such as AutoCAD (Autodesk, Inc., San Rafael, CA) or MicroStation (Bentley Systems, Inc., Exton, PA). The drawings (usually on paper) are given to the contractor,* along with the specifications. The contractor calculates quantity take-offs from these drawings then prices the job. Most contractors calculate takeoffs by using manual or electronic tools such as digitizer boards. These quantities are carried over to the spreadsheet or estimating program. Some software companies have developed computer software programs to perform computerized takeoffs directly from the CAD file to the estimating spreadsheet.

Project management software programs, such as Primavera Expedition, Meridian's Prolog Manager, and Timberline's Project Management, keep records of all project administration and communication documents. In an ideal situation, they link to the schedule, the cost estimate, and the accounting software. In addition, you can host all this information on an exclusive Web site (Internet or intranet) where project participants obtain access to the project, review documents, and correspond. The Web site administrator can control who sees what. This capability can tremendously expedite communications, such as design review, submittals, RFIs, and so forth, among project participants. Several leading companies in the construction software industry are trying to develop an "ultimate project management suite" in which all project management and administration components are available and communicating flawlessly. The author is unaware of any such existing product, but all signs indicate that the industry is moving in this direction.

PROCUREMENT MANAGEMENT

Procurement is the process of acquiring materials, equipment, and services from external sources for use in a project. Procurement is a process that usually starts long before the start of the construction process and ends with

---

*The design could be complete (construction documents) or incomplete (DD30, DD60, etc.). The contractor (or subcontractor) may look at the design before getting the job (for bidding or negotiation) or after getting the job.

project completion or **project closeout.** The procurement team must work in close coordination with both the estimating team and the scheduling team, all under the project management team. Depending on the company's functional hierarchy, the procurement manager or department may or may not be under the construction manager.* In most large companies, the PM is the highest authority within the project management team. Under this person is a construction manager, a procurement manager, a quality manager, a safety manager, and so forth.

The two objectives of procurement, from the general contractor's viewpoint, are as follows:

1. *To hire the subcontractors who will actually erect and assemble the project.* Doing so can be accomplished through bidding or negotiation. Such hiring is also subject to the contractual agreement between the general contractor and the owner. The general contractor must know when each subcontractor's role starts in the project. For this reason, the general contractor focuses on subcontracts on the critical path. Some subcontractors may not be hired until after the project starts. Again, such hiring is subject to the agreement between the owner and the general contractor.

2. *To purchase the materials called for in the contract.* This task may not be easy. First, the procurement team must have a list of all needed materials, along with their specifications, quantities, and dates of installation. Many times, if an ordered material does not exactly match its description in the specifications, confusion will arise on the job site. Second, the procurement team must find the best prices for the ordered materials. Finally, the procurement team must also balance between having a conservative attitude of buying the materials early and storing them (the inventory buffer theory) and having a liberal attitude of ordering the materials for just-in-time installation (the just-in-time theory). (Both theories are discussed in chapter 6.)

---

*The project organization may be a *pure project organization* (in which the team becomes almost autonomous), a *functional or departmental organization* (in which everyone works under his or her functional department in the main office), or a *matrix organization* (a combination of the preceding two types of organizations that leans more toward a pure project organization, more toward a functional organization, or somewhere between). For more details on this subject, refer to Meredith and Mantel (2000).

The purchasing cycle involves the procurement, estimating, scheduling, and accounting departments. The estimating department provides a list of the types and quantities of materials needed for a certain activity. The scheduling department predicts the date the activity is to start. The procurement team then makes sure the materials are ordered and to be delivered on time. It also verifies the cost of these materials against the cost estimate, then provides the actual cost to the accounting department. The contractor's project management team is responsible for receiving the materials and unloading, accepting, sorting, and storing them. The quality assurance department of both the contractor's and the owner's organizations may become involved to ensure that the materials comply with the specifications.

The purchase of some materials, such as ready-mix concrete, must be carefully coordinated. This type of concrete must be installed immediately upon delivery and cannot be stored. Other materials may be expensive and must be secured before and after installation.

MANAGEMENT OF SUBMITTALS

A **submittal** is a sample, manufacturer's data, a shop drawing, or another item submitted to the owner or the design professional by the contractor for approval or another action, usually a contractual requirement. Submittals are an important part of the schedule. In many cases, placement of a post-tensioned cable, reinforcement, structural steel detail, or framing cannot proceed until the shop drawing is approved. In the case of samples, such as types and colors of carpet or paint, the procedure includes the submittal of the samples and the owner's selection or acceptance of one or more of them.

In the case of shop drawings, the cycle consists of four steps:

1. Preparation of the shop drawings by the subcontractor or supplier
2. Submittal of the drawings to the contractor, then forwarding them to the A/E or the party responsible for reviewing them.
3. A review of the drawings by the appropriate party (engineer or architect) (typically, the drawings are accepted as is, rejected, or accepted with changes; if they are rejected, the subcontractor or supplier must redo and resubmit them)
4. After approval, fabrication of the work by the subcontractor or supplier

The formal chain of command should be specified in the contract. It usually restricts correspondence between parties who have a contractual agreement. For example,

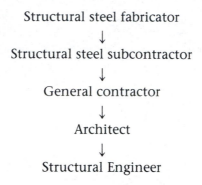

Structural steel fabricator
↓
Structural steel subcontractor
↓
General contractor
↓
Architect
↓
Structural Engineer

The direction of these arrows is reversed when the drawings are sent back after the review. This chain may be shortened, to speed up the process, by sending the drawings from the fabricator or subcontractor directly to the structural engineer. Such an arrangement requires the approval of the main contracting parties. Most likely, it also requires copying all parties between in both directions. Electronic correspondence helps expedite this process.

The submittal procedure in the contract must be precise in terms of time limits. Ambiguous expressions such as "the owner will review submittals within a reasonable period of time so as not to delay work progress" and "as soon as possible" must be avoided.

Another important point, from a scheduling point of view, is the possibility of rejection. If the shop drawing cycle is on a critical or a near-critical path, the contractor must be careful in handling the submittals. He or she should try to determine the results of the review as soon as possible so that he or she can plan for the next step.

THE MASTER SCHEDULE AND SUBSCHEDULES

In a typical construction project, many parties are involved: the general contractor, the owner, the architect or engineer (which could be several entities), subcontractors, government agencies, vendors, and so forth. There are two approaches to scheduling in this situation:

1. *Build a master schedule that includes several subschedules.* Each subschedule represents the activities belonging to one party involved in the project. The external relationships will show only in the master schedule. In this approach, when scheduling (performing the CPM calculations for) a subschedule, the scheduler must be sure to consider the external relationships because the software may ignore them. For instance, consider the three activities shown in Figure 10.1. Assume the relationship between activity GC230 and activity SDF1270 is external. If you schedule the SDF schedule alone, you may get early dates for activity SDF1270 as (35, 40) instead of (51, 56).

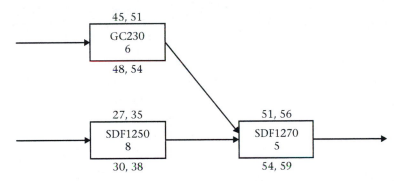

FIGURE 10.1   Subnet of a master schedule with two activities belonging to one subschedule and one activity belonging to a different subschedule.

2. *Include all activities in one schedule and assign a Responsibility code for each contracting party.* The scheduler can later apply a filter to show activities belonging to only one party. This way, the external relationships are always there, even if they do not show.

It is important to include external relationships for proper project management. For example, an owner's furnished kitchen equipment for a commercial project may have to be delivered after the structure has been erected and after mechanical and electrical rough-ins, but before doors and windows are installed and before mechanical and electrical finishing. Such operations may involve coordination among several entities.

In many situations, the master schedule is not the creation of one party (the general contractor or the construction manager). Contracting parties, such as subcontractors, create their own schedules (using the same or compatible software) and submit them to the general contractor (or construction manager). The general contractor (or construction manager) then assembles these subschedules, along with his or hers, in one master schedule, using one of the two approaches just mentioned.

MULTIPROJECT MANAGEMENT

In large corporations or government agencies, tens or hundreds of projects may have to be managed simultaneously. Typically, there are two levels of project management:

1. *Management at the individual project level (micromanagement).* The PM should be managing or monitoring all activities and all project details. The project is the focus of the PM. Depending on the size and complexity of the project, the management team can be composed of one part-time person to several people.

   For such a PM, the basic unit of control is the activity, with related information, such as duration, logic (predecessors, successors, lags), constraints, calendar, resources, budget, cost, notes, and so forth. The information may be rolled over to a WBS (work breakdown structure) level or other codes within the project. The highest level of rollup is the project itself, where only one unit shows, with the total duration, total budget, and so forth.

   In some governmental agencies (counties, municipalities, etc.), every project has two managers: the agency's (owner's) PM and the contractor's PM. The first monitors the project and makes sure the contractor is performing according to the terms of the contract. He or she also authorizes payments to the contractor. The contractor's PM is the "real" construction manager. He or she is responsible for the day-to-day construction operations in the project.

2. *Management at the corporate or enterprise level (macromanagement).* The corporate manager will look at all projects, with each project represented as one basic integral unit (usually represented by a single bar in a bar chart). The corporate manager may not get involved in the

details of individual projects (although he or she usually can, and will do so in certain cases). The basic unit in this case is the project. Projects can be grouped by organizational breakdown structure, such as department, section, program, and so forth.

Primavera P3e (or P3e/c), for example, is a product designed for the "enterprise," with a multiproject management capability.* It offers three breakdown structures:

a. The *EBS (enterprise breakdown structure)* is a breakdown for the corporation (enterprise). Typically, this structure includes the departments under the corporation. Each department can be broken down further into sections and so on, where projects reside.

b. The *OBS (organizational breakdown structure)* is a breakdown of the functional responsibility. Typically, you tie the EBS with the OBS to define people along with their departments (who does what).

c. The *WBS (work breakdown structure)* is a typical **project breakdown structure (PBS).** Unlike the EBS and the OBS, the WBS is at the project level and can differ from one project to another.

TIME CONTINGENCY AND MANAGEMENT OPTIONS

When a scheduler or PM creates a schedule, he or she must include a time contingency representing the expected nonworkdays. This time contingency includes two types of nonworkdays:

1. *Known dates such as holidays and planned shutdown days.* The scheduler must enter these days in the calendar of the computer program. The computer program will not allow any work on an activity on such days (provided the activity uses that calendar).

2. *Unknown dates.* A scheduler should typically expect some occurrences that will prevent work from taking place, such as severe weather conditions or accidents. For example, for a 1-year project, the scheduler allocates 18 nonworkdays. This 18-day **schedule contingency** can

---

*As mentioned in chapter 7, Microsoft has developed more-advanced products and solutions, such as Microsoft Office EPM (Enterprise Premier Solution), in which the solution is customized by selecting certain Microsoft or partner components to fit the client's needs.

be considered total float for the entire project, in addition to the calculated total float. It can be handled in one of the following two ways, or a combination of both can be used:

a. *Allow the crews to control this float.* In this case, the durations of all activities are stretched by a percentage that makes the entire schedule extend by these 18 days. As an alternative, the PM may assign these 18 days to certain activities according to his or her discretion.

b. *Give management control of these days and allow them to "be spent" as needed.* Management must be careful not to use such time contingency days to compensate for poor performance or low productivity. The challenge in this approach is how to implement such days in the baseline schedule. There are two ways to do so:

  i. *Distribute these days evenly along the duration of the schedule.* In this case, the scheduling program treats these days the same as holidays and scheduled nonworkdays. This approach may cause some problems in tracking the project when a certain day is shown on the schedule as a nonworkday when it is not. The advantage of this method is that the schedule is most realistic in the occurrence distribution of nonworkdays, although the specific date may be incorrect. As a remedy, the scheduler can adjust dates for nonworkdays during the update.

  ii. *Put the entire 18 days at the end of the project.* This method makes the actual schedule look worse than it is. As the project progresses, nonworkdays occur, but they are not reflected in the schedule, so the schedule looks behind till the end. At this point, the 18 contingency days start, and the negative float (as many as 18 days) disappears.

Besides using the nonworkdays, the contractor may create *hidden float.* Hidden float can be created either by inflating the duration of an activity or by manipulating the logic. For example, assume that the durations and logic in Figure 10.2a are correct, but the contractor wants to show that the project takes 25 days instead of 20. He or she can "fluff" the durations, as shown in Figure 10.2b, or add an unnecessary link to extend the critical path, and thus extend the duration of the project, as shown in Figure 10.2c.

The author strongly opposes the tactic used in Figure 10.2c. Phony logic should never be allowed in the schedule. Fluffing the duration is a controversial

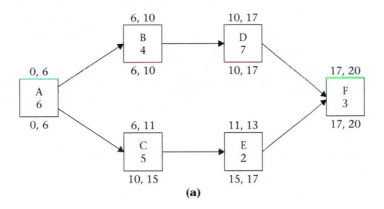

(a)

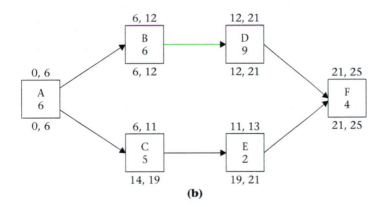

(b)

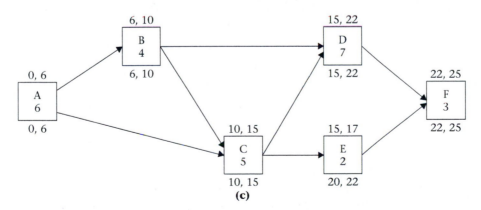

(c)

FIGURE 10.2 (a) Real durations; (b) "fluffed" durations; (c) manipulated logic.

subject. The danger of using a fluffed duration in project control and performance measurement is that it may skew the performance observations and conclusions, and subsequently future estimates.

CHAPTER 10 EXERCISES

1. Discuss three ways in which cost estimating and scheduling intersect.
2. Discuss the evolution of a cost estimate. How does this relate to the creation of the schedule?
3. What is an *estimate-generated schedule?* What precautions must the scheduler take before using such a schedule?
4. What is a *cost-loaded schedule?*
5. What are the two methods of loading cost into a schedule? Which method is more powerful? Why?
6. How does accounting relate to scheduling? Discuss briefly.
7. How do change orders affect a schedule? What should the scheduler do for objective project control when changes occur?
8. What is the "ultimate project management suite" computer program?
9. Define *procurement*. What are the main objectives of procurement?
10. How does procurement relate to scheduling?
11. Explain the cycle of submittal management.
12. What can the scheduler do to minimize time losses during the submittal cycle?
13. When you take on a large project made up of several smaller projects, how can you handle this in the schedule?
14. When using the "master project" and "subprojects" approach, what pitfalls may happen in the schedule? How do you deal with them?
15. In a highway project, both the contractor and the government schedulers must keep track of the schedule. However, their roles differ significantly. Explain.
16. The scheduler must include a time contingency in the schedule. How many ways can you implement such a contingency? What are the pros and cons of each method?
17. After you prepare a schedule for a shopping mall, the architect issues a design change in which an escalator is added inside one of the areas that

will be occupied by a major store in the mall. The subcontractor in charge of the escalator submits his schedule, showing that the work can be completed in 6 weeks. First, mention the work packages that will be affected (e.g., concrete, electrical, etc.). Second, do you believe that the master schedule will affect the escalator schedule, the escalator schedule will affect the master schedule, or both? Explain the potential interdependencies between the escalator work and other subcontractors' work. Why do you believe that the escalator work will take more than 6 weeks?

Other Scheduling Methods

Sunrise Harbor, Ft. Lauderdale, Florida. Courtesy of Smith Aerial Photos, Maitland, Florida.

INTRODUCTION

Although the critical path method (CPM) is the predominant method used for scheduling construction projects, other methods may be used for particular types of projects or in other industries. In this chapter, three of these methods are discussed. (*Note:* Some of the information discussed in this chapter requires basic knowledge of statistics.)

PROGRAM EVALUATION AND REVIEW TECHNIQUE (PERT)

Definition

The **program evaluation and review technique (PERT)** is an event-oriented network analysis technique used to estimate project duration when individual activity duration estimates are highly uncertain. PERT applies the CPM to a weighted-average duration estimate. PERT is considered a probabilistic, or stochastic, method.

Background

In the 1950s, the U.S. Navy had a budget overrun and a schedule delay of as much as 50% in the Polaris missile system project. The main problem was the lack of any relevant historical data. The project team—the U.S. Navy (the owner), Lockheed Aircraft Corporation (the prime contractor), and Booz Allen Hamilton (the management consultant team)—launched a joint research effort to develop a tool to assist in the planning of the Polaris project. The objective was to devise a method that predicts the completion date of a project with a certain likelihood using the theory of probability. In 1958, this tool was developed under the name *program evaluation and review technique* and later became known by its acronym, PERT.

The PERT system was adopted in its early days by the Department of Defense (DoD) under the name *program evaluation procedure (PEP)*. After that, PERT was modified several times and carried different names: PERT I, PERT II, PERT III, PERT/TIME, and PERT/COST. In June 1962, the DoD and the National Aeronautics and Space Administration (NASA) adopted a uniform approach of planning and controlling procedures for major weapon systems (Popescu and Charoenngam 1995).

Concept of PERT

Like the regular (deterministic) CPM, PERT uses logic networks to calculate the completion date of a project or the date of any other event in the schedule. In PERT, a probability (likelihood) is associated with any event date. This probability depends on uncertainty in the durations of the activities that lead to the desired event (e.g., project completion). PERT realizes that actual durations vary from those assigned, so it attempts to compensate for this variation with a "time range" during which activity durations may realistically occur. This topic is discussed in more detail after the details of PERT are covered.

How PERT Works

PERT uses a probabilistic approach, which requires a duration frequency distribution for each activity. In most cases, such distributions are unknown or unavailable. Because of this, PERT requires the user to set three durations that constitute the practical range of the duration for each activity. For example, Assembling and Erecting the Falsework for an Elevated Slab will most likely require 5 days. If all goes well, without interruption or snags, the duration may be cut to 4 days. However, in the practically worst-case scenario, this activity may take 8 days. These three durations give a "distribution" for the activity, and we can produce the statistical mean and variance for the duration of the activity.

When we need to compute the probability that a certain event, such as Substantial Completion of a building, will occur by a certain date, we need to take into account all preceding events, starting at the beginning of the project and including the continuous chain of activities till Substantial Completion. Using the **central limit theorem,** PERT treats the means of the durations of these activities as a **normal distribution,** no matter what distributions these durations followed. PERT then uses simple statistics to calculate the mean and variance (or standard deviation) of the time required to complete the chain of events leading to Substantial Completion. It calculates the probability that Substantial Completion will occur by a particular date, or, conversely, it calculates the date that the Substantial Completion event will happen with a certain level of confidence (probability).

PERT Calculations

As mentioned previously, the path (chain of activities or events) leading to the examined event (e.g., Substantial Completion) must be chosen. For each activity on that path, three durations must be estimated:

T_o: **Optimistic Duration**

T_m: **Most Likely Duration**

T_p: **Pessimistic Duration**

The preceding values are estimated by the scheduler or project manager, who uses his or her experience and good judgment to do so. The optimistic duration is the amount of time the activity will take if everything goes smoothly and efficiently. The pessimistic duration is the duration under the almost-worst-case scenario. Both values must be within the realistic, although perhaps unlikely, realm of expectations.

The mean weighted value for these three durations is called the **expected duration** (T_e). It is calculated as follows:

$$T_e = \frac{T_o + 4T_m + T_P}{6} \tag{11.1}$$

The weights assigned to these times (coefficients of T_o, T_m, and T_P) may be adjusted, but the denominator must equal the sum of all weights. The weights in equation 11.1 represent a population of durations made up of 16.7% (one-sixth) optimistic (T_o); 66.7% (four-sixths) most likely (T_m); and 16.7% (one-sixth) pessimistic (T_P).

Several symbols are used in other textbooks to represent the mean (arithmetic average), such as μ and $\overline{X}$.

The standard deviation for the expected duration (σ_e) is

$$\sigma_e = \frac{T_P - T_o}{6} \tag{11.2}$$

and the variance (V_e) is

$$V_e = \sigma_e^2 \tag{11.3}$$

Now, add the expected duration for all activities on the studied path (T_E),

$$T_E = \sum_{i=1}^{n} (T_e)_i \tag{11.4}$$

The variance (V_E) and standard deviation (σ_E) *for the entire path* are calculated as

$$V_E = \sum_{i=1}^{n} (\sigma_e^2)_i \tag{11.5}$$

and

$$\sigma_E = \sqrt{V_E} \tag{11.6}$$

With the information just calculated for the examined path, we can calculate the probability that an event will occur on or by a certain date (T_S) by using the normal distribution formulas:

$$Z = \frac{T_S - T_E}{\sigma_E} \tag{11.7}$$

where Z (called the **Z function**) represents the number of standard deviations (σ_E) away from the mean (T_E).

Plugging the Z value just calculated into the Z table (Table 11.1), we can find the probability.

PERT can also predict the date by which a certain event will be completed, with a certain level of confidence (i.e., probability). This date is calculated by using the set probability value (level of confidence) to find the corresponding Z value in the Z table. Rewriting equation 11.7, we get

$$T_S = \sigma_E * Z + T_E \tag{11.8}$$

These calculations are clarified further in the following examples.

Graphic Explanation

The **probability density function** of a normal distribution is represented by a bell-shaped curve. The area under the curve represents the **probability universe,** where all possibilities are covered, which is 1.00, or 100%. The probability that an event will occur by a certain date (i.e., on or before that date) is the area under the curve to left of that date. See Figure 11.1.

TABLE 11.1.   *Z* Table: Cumulative Probability of the Standard Normal Distribution

Z	.00	.01	.02	.03	.04	.05	.06	.07	.08	.09
0.0	.5000	.5040	.5080	.5120	.5160	.5199	.5239	.5279	.5319	.5359
0.1	.5398	.5438	.5478	.5517	.5557	.5596	.5636	.5675	.5714	.5753
0.2	.5793	.5832	.5871	.5910	.5948	.5987	.6026	.6064	.6103	.6141
0.3	.6179	.6217	.6255	.6293	.6331	.6368	.6406	.6443	.6480	.6517
0.4	.6554	.6591	.6628	.6664	.6700	.6736	.6772	.6808	.6844	.6879
0.5	.6915	.6950	.6985	.7019	.7054	.7088	.7123	.7157	.7190	.7224
0.6	.7257	.7291	.7324	.7357	.7389	.7422	.7454	.7486	.7517	.7549
0.7	.7580	.7611	.7642	.7673	.7704	.7734	.7764	.7794	.7823	.7852
0.8	.7881	.7910	.7939	.7967	.7995	.8023	.8051	.8078	.8106	.8133
0.9	.8159	.8186	.8212	.8238	.8264	.8289	.8315	.8340	.8365	.8389
1.0	.8413	.8438	.8461	.8485	.8508	.8531	.8554	.8577	.8599	.8621
1.1	.8643	.8665	.8686	.8708	.8729	.8749	.8770	.8790	.8810	.8830
1.2	.8849	.8869	.8888	.8907	.8925	.8944	.8962	.8980	.8997	.9015
1.3	.9032	.9049	.9066	.9082	.9099	.9115	.9131	.9147	.9162	.9177
1.4	.9192	.9207	.9222	.9236	.9251	.9265	.9279	.9292	.9306	.9319
1.5	.9332	.9345	.9357	.9370	.9382	.9394	.9406	.9418	.9429	.9441
1.6	.9452	.9463	.9474	.9484	.9495	.9505	.9515	.9525	.9535	.9545
1.7	.9554	.9564	.9573	.9582	.9591	.9599	.9608	.9616	.9625	.9633
1.8	.9641	.9649	.9656	.9664	.9671	.9678	.9686	.9693	.9699	.9706
1.9	.9713	.9719	.9726	.9732	.9738	.9744	.9750	.9756	.9761	.9767
2.0	.9772	.9778	.9783	.9788	.9793	.9798	.9803	.9808	.9812	.9817
2.1	.9821	.9826	.9830	.9834	.9838	.9842	.9846	.9850	.9854	.9857
2.2	.9861	.9864	.9868	.9871	.9875	.9878	.9881	.9884	.9887	.9890
2.3	.9893	.9896	.9898	.9901	.9904	.9906	.9909	.9911	.9913	.9916
2.4	.9918	.9920	.9922	.9925	.9927	.9929	.9931	.9932	.9934	.9936
2.5	.9938	.9940	.9941	.9943	.9945	.9946	.9948	.9949	.9951	.9952
2.6	.9953	.9955	.9956	.9957	.9959	.9960	.9961	.9962	.9963	.9964
2.7	.9965	.9966	.9967	.9968	.9969	.9970	.9971	.9972	.9973	.9974
2.8	.9974	.9975	.9976	.9977	.9977	.9978	.9979	.9979	.9980	.9981
2.9	.9981	.9982	.9982	.9983	.9984	.9984	.9985	.9985	.9986	.9986
3.0	.9987	.9987	.9987	.9988	.9988	.9989	.9989	.9989	.9990	.9990

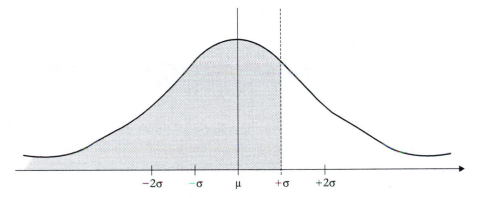

FIGURE 11.1   Probability density function curve (shaded area indicates the probability that an event will occur by a certain date)

EXAMPLE 11.1

In a CPM network, the critical path includes five activities. Their durations are tabulated next.

	DURATION (DAYS)		
ACTIVITY	OPTIMISTIC (T_o)	MOST LIKELY (T_m)	PESSIMISTIC (T_P)
A	2	4	7
B	5	8	14
C	4	6	8
D	2	2	2
E	7	10	21

Compute the following nine values:

1. The probability that the project will finish by the end of day 32
2. The probability that the project will finish by the end of day 34
3. The probability that the project will finish before day 30

4. The probability that the project will finish on the 32nd day
5. The probability that the project will finish no later than the 35th day
6. The probability that the project will finish at least 2 days early
7. The probability that the project will finish at least 2 days late
8. The probability that the project will finish on the 32nd day ±1 day
9. The completion date with at least a 90% confidence level

Solution

Before computing any of the nine values, we need to calculate the expected duration (T_E) and the standard deviation (σ_E) of the path ABCDE. We start by performing the calculations for the individual activities. For every activity, we calculate the expected duration (T_e) and standard deviation (σ_e) by using equations 11.1 and 11.2. After this, we calculate the variance (V_e) by using equation 11.3. We tabulate the results as shown next.

ACTIVITY	DURATION (DAYS)			EXPECTED DURATION (T_e)	STANDARD DEVIATION (σ_e)	VARIANCE ($V_e = \sigma_e^2$)
	OPTIMISTIC (T_o)	MOST LIKELY (T_m)	PESSIMISTIC (T_p)			
A	2	4	7	4.167	0.833	0.694
B	5	8	14	8.500	1.500	2.250
C	4	6	8	6.000	0.667	0.444
D	2	2	2	2.000	0	0
E	7	10	21	11.333	2.333	5.444
				$T_E = 32$		$V_E = 8.833$

The next step is to do the calculations for the entire path. We simply add the expected durations and variances, as explained in equations 11.4 and 11.5, to obtain T_E and V_E.

Next, take the square root of V_E (use equation 11.6) to find the standard deviation (σ_E) of the path:

$T_E = 32$ days

$V_E = 8.833$ days

and

$\sigma_E = \sqrt{8.833} = 2.972$ days

Note that $\sigma_E \neq \sum_{i=1}^{n} (\sigma_e)_i$

1. *The probability that the project will finish by the end of day 32.*
   Using equation 11.7, we find that

   $Z = (32 - 32)/2.972 = 0$

   From the Z table (Table 11.1), we find that

   $\Pr(T_S \leq 32) = 0.5 = 50\%$

   See Figure 11.2.

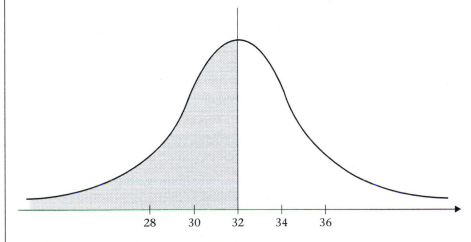

FIGURE 11.2   Solution to example 11.1, part 1

2. *The probability that the project will finish by the end of day 34.*

   $Z = (34 - 32)/2.972 = 0.67$

   From Table 11.1, we find that

   $\Pr(T_S \leq 34) = 0.749 = 74.9\%$

   See Figure 11.3.

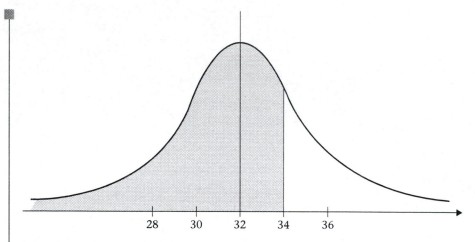

FIGURE 11.3   Solution to example 11.1, part 2

3. *The probability that the project will finish before day 30.* This probability is the same as the probability of finishing by the end of day 29:

$$Z = (29 - 32)/2.972 = -1.01$$

When $Z < 0$, take the probability that corresponds to the positive value of Z, then subtract it from 1.0 (100%):

$$\Pr(T_S \leq 29) = 1 - 0.844 = 0.156 = 15.6\%$$

See Figure 11.4.

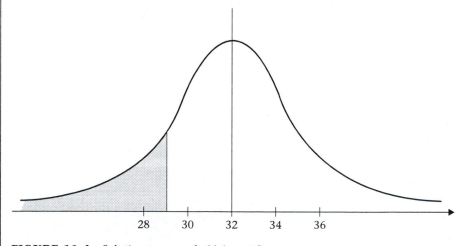

FIGURE 11.4   Solution to example 11.1, part 3

4. *The probability that the project will finish on the 32nd day.*

$$\Pr(T_S = 32) = \Pr(T_S \leq 32) - \Pr(T_S \leq 31)$$

We already calculated $\Pr(T_S \leq 32) = 0.5 = 50\%$ (part 1). For $\Pr(T_S \leq 31)$,

$$Z = (31 - 32)/2.972 = -0.34$$

$$\Pr(T_S \leq 31) = 1 - 0.633 = 0.367 = 36.7\%$$

and

$$\Pr(T_S = 32) = \Pr(T_S \leq 32) - \Pr(T_S \leq 31) = 50\% - 36.7\% = 13.3\%$$

See Figure 11.5.

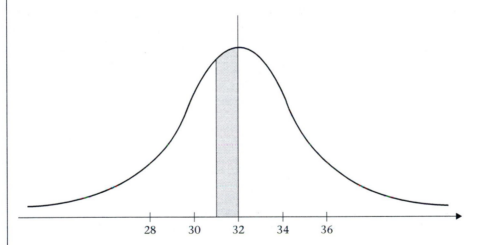

FIGURE 11.5   Solution to example 11.1, part 4

5. *The probability the project will finish no later than the 35th day.*
   This probability is the same as the probability that the project will finish by the end of day 35:

$$Z = (35 - 32)/2.972 = 1.01$$

and

$$\Pr(T_S \leq 35) = 0.844 = 84.4\%$$

See Figure 11.6.

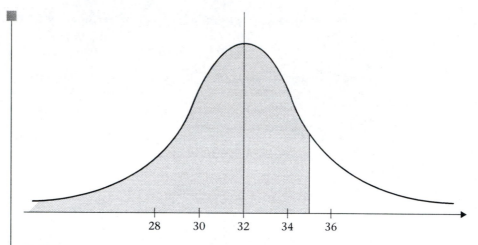

FIGURE 11.6   Solution to example 11.1, part 5

6. *The probability that the project will finish at least 2 days early.*
   This probability is the same as the probability of finishing on
   the 30th day or earlier, or the same as the probability that the
   project will finish by the end of day 30:

$$Z = (30 - 32)/2.972 = -0.67$$

and

$$\Pr(T_S \leq 30) = 1 - 0.749 = 0.251 = 25.1\%$$

See Figure 11.7.

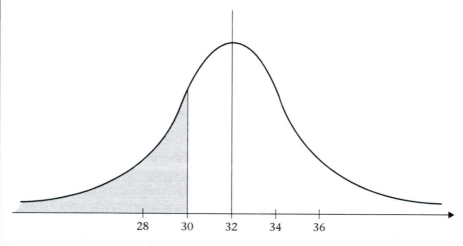

FIGURE 11.7   Solution to example 11.1, part 6

7. *The probability that the project will finish at least 2 days late.*
   This probability is the same as the probability of finishing by the 34th day or later, or the same as the probability that the project will finish after day 33:

   $$\Pr(T_S > 33) = 1 - \Pr(T_S \leq 33)$$

   For $\Pr(T_S \leq 33)$,

   $$Z = (33 - 32)/2.972 = 0.34$$

   and

   $$\Pr(T_S \leq 33) = 0.633 = 63.3\%$$

   Thus,

   $$\Pr(T_S > 33) = 1 - 0.633 = 0.367 = 36.7\%$$

   See Figure 11.8.

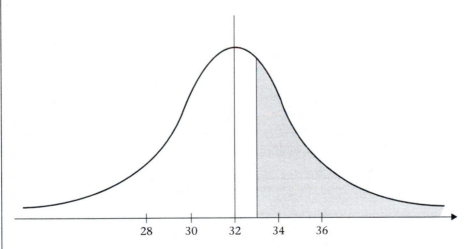

FIGURE 11.8   Solution to example 11.1, part 7

Note that if the instruction had said "the probability that the project will finish *more than* [rather than *at least*] 2 days late," it would have meant $\Pr(T_S > 34)$.

8. *The probability that the project will finish on the 32nd day ±1 day.* This means finishing on day 31, 32, or 33.

$$\Pr(T_s = 31, 32, 33) = \Pr(30 < T_s \leq 33) = \Pr(T_s \leq 33) - \Pr(T_s \leq 30)$$

and

$$\Pr(T_S = 31, 32, 33) = 0.633 - 0.251 = 0.382 = 38.2\%$$

See Figure 11.9.

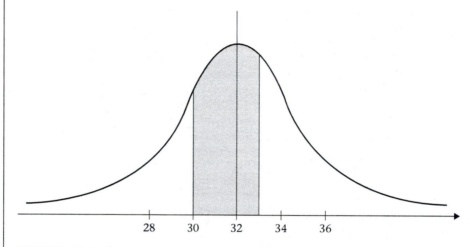

FIGURE 11.9   Solution to example 11.1, part 8

9. *The completion date with at least a 90% confidence level.* Go to Table 11.1 and pick a probability value close to (but not less than) 0.9. Read the corresponding Z value. You should read 1.28. Apply equation 11.8:

$$T_S = \sigma_E * Z + T_E = 2.972 * 1.28 + 32 = 35.8 \approx 36 \text{ days}$$

Difference Between "Most Likely" and "Expected" Durations

From a linguistic viewpoint, *most likely* and *expected* may be thought of as the same. However, in our context, they are different. The most likely duration is simply the duration that we believe has more likelihood of happening than any other duration. In our case, it is a user-defined amount; that is, we provide it along with other durations (optimistic and pessimistic) in the equation so that we can calculate the expected duration and the standard deviation. It does not represent the arithmetic mean or the median.

The expected duration is the amount of time we expect the project or path duration to take, considering the different durations (optimistic and pessimistic), their values, and their weights. It is a computed amount. For example, consider a case in which 6, 8, and 10 are the optimistic, most likely, and pessimistic durations, respectively. The expected duration will be equal to 8. In this case, it is equal to the most likely duration because the optimistic and pessimistic durations "deviate" by the same amount from the most likely duration (6 to 8 and 10 to 8). Now, suppose the pessimistic duration is 13 days, whereas the optimistic and most likely durations are still the same. The expected duration is calculated as 8.5 days, by using equation 11.1. The expected duration value increased as a result of the increase in the skewness of the pessimistic duration. Even though the probability of the occurrence of the pessimistic duration (or the weight) is still the same in both examples (one-sixth), the consequences worsened in the second case.

Is the Longest Path Still the Most Critical?

A typical network project has tens or hundreds (perhaps thousands) of paths. Typically, we define the critical path as the longest path from the start till the end of the network (see the definition of *critical path* in chapter 4). In addition to the duration, another factor must be considered in the criticality of the path in PERT. This factor is the "uncertainty" of the duration of the path, measured by the standard deviation. Let us look at the following example for an illustration.

EXAMPLE 11.2

Draw the network for the following project.

ACTIVITY	IPA[a]	DURATION (DAYS)		
		OPTIMISTIC (T_o)	MOST LIKELY (T_m)	PESSIMISTIC (T_p)
A	—	4	5	6
B	A	10	12	14
C	A	7	9	16

(continued)

ACTIVITY	IPA[a]	DURATION (DAYS)		
		OPTIMISTIC (T_o)	MOST LIKELY (T_m)	PESSIMISTIC (T_P)
D	B	14	17	22
E	B, C	10	15	30
F	C	4	7	13
G	D	12	20	40
H	D, E	10	12	15
I	F, H	8	9	10

[a] Immediately preceding activity.

Compare the three paths ABDHI, ABDG, and ABEHI. Calculate the expected duration and the standard deviation for each path. Considering all three paths, what is the duration of the project with at least 95% confidence?

Solution

With regular CPM calculations (using most likely durations), the critical path is ABDHI with 55 days, followed by paths ABDG and ABEHI at 54 and 53 days, respectively (Figure 11.10). Now, let us do the PERT calculations:

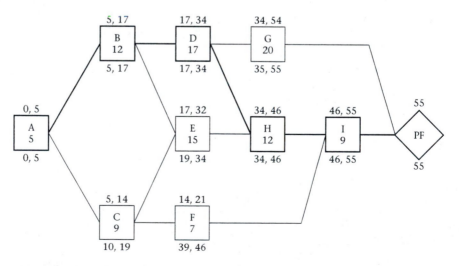

FIGURE 11.10 Solution to example 11.1, part 9—PF, project finish

ACTIVITY	DURATION (DAYS)			EXPECTED DURATION (T_e)	STANDARD DEVIATION (σ_e)	VARIANCE $(V_e = \sigma_e^2)$
	OPTIMISTIC (T_o)	MOST LIKELY (T_m)	PESSIMISTIC (T_P)			
A	4	5	6	5.00	0.33	0.11
B	10	12	14	12.00	0.67	0.44
C	13	9	16	9.83	1.50	2.25
D	20	17	22	17.33	1.33	1.78
E	10	15	30	16.67	3.33	11.11
F	4	7	13	7.50	1.50	2.25
G	12	20	40	22.00	4.67	21.78
H	10	12	15	12.17	0.83	0.69
I	8	9	10	9.00	0.33	0.11

With regard to path ABDHI,

$$T_E = 5.00 + 12.00 + 17.33 + 12.17 + 9.00 = \boxed{55.50 \text{ days}}$$

$$V_E = 0.11 + 0.44 + 1.78 + 0.69 + 0.11 = 3.14$$

and

$$\sigma_E = \sqrt{3.14} = 1.77 \text{ days}$$

To find the duration with a minimum level of confidence of 95%, find the Z values associated with probability of 0.95. From the table, this Z value is 1.645, and

$$T_S = \sigma_E \cdot Z + T_E = 1.77 \cdot 1.645 + 55.50 = \boxed{58.41 \text{ days}}$$

Applying the same calculations to path ABDG, we find

$$T_E = 5.00 + 12.00 + 17.33 + 22.00 = \boxed{56.33 \text{ days}}$$

$$V_E = 0.11 + 0.44 + 1.78 + 21.78 = 24.11$$

$$\sigma_E = \sqrt{24.11} = 4.91 \text{ days}$$

and

$$T_S = \sigma_E \cdot Z + T_E = 4.91 \cdot 1.645 + 56.33 = \boxed{64.41 \text{ days}}$$

Applying the same calculations again to path ABEHI, we find

$T_E = 5.00 + 12.00 + 16.67 + 12.17 + 9.00 = \boxed{54.83 \text{ days}}$

$V_E = 0.11 + 0.44 + 11.11 + 0.69 + 0.11 = 12.47$

$\sigma_E = \sqrt{12.47} = 3.53 \text{ days}$

and

$T_S = \sigma_E \cdot Z + T_E = 3.53 \cdot 1.645 + 54.83 = \boxed{60.64 \text{ days}}$

Let us discuss the results: When we look at the most likely durations (as single-value, or deterministic, durations), path ABDHI is the longest, at 55 days. When we look at the expected durations, path ABDG is the longest, at 56.33 (say, 57) days. When we consider the standard deviation and the 95% confidence level, the same path, ABDG, is longest (by a larger margin), at 64.41 (say, 65) days. Note also that in this case, path ABEHI is second in importance (at 60.64 days), after path ABDG and before path ABDHI. In other words, the path considered longest by the deterministic CPM calculations was superseded by two other paths considered by PERT to be more critical.

Note: The preceding calculations were done using an Excel spreadsheet. The answers were rounded for simplicity.

Example 11.2 illustrates the importance of considering near-critical paths, especially those with high uncertainty (a large standard deviation). Simulations may be used to determine which path is the most critical.

Using PERT to Calculate the Date of an Event with a Certain Level of Confidence

The main focus in PERT is the event, not the activity.* You can use the same probabilistic approach with any event (e.g., delivery of a custom item, the building is watertight, substantial completion). In this case, you consider the path from the start of the project until, and including, the event under consideration.

---

*The terms *event* and *activity* were introduced in chapter 3. An activity has a start date, a duration, and a finish date. An event has just one date (start or finish) with no duration. An event can be the start or finish of an activity.

EXAMPLE 11.3

Calculate the date of completion of activity F in example 11.2 with 90% confidence.

Solution
From the calculation table in example 11.2, we take the path ACF:

	DURATION (DAYS)			EXPECTED	STANDARD	
ACTIVITY	OPTIMISTIC (T_o)	MOST LIKELY (T_m)	PESSIMISTIC (T_P)	DURATION (T_e)	DEVIATION (σ_e)	VARIANCE $(V_e = \sigma_e^2)$
A	4	5	6	5.00	0.33	0.11
C	13	9	16	9.83	1.50	2.25
F	4	7	13	7.50	1.50	2.25
				$T_E = 22.33$		$V_E = 4.61$

$\sigma_E = \sqrt{4.61} = 2.15$ days

The Z value associated with a probability of 95% is 1.645, and

$T_S = \sigma_E \cdot Z + T_E = 2.15 \cdot 1.645 + 22.33 = 25.87$ days

Note: The preceding calculations were done using an Excel spreadsheet. The answers were rounded for simplicity.

Determining the Probability of a Certain Project Finish Date (Multiple Paths Considered)

In statistics and probability, the probability that two *independent* events will happen simultaneously is equal to the product of the two probabilities:

$$Pr(A \cap B) = Pr(A) \cdot Pr(B) \quad\quad\quad (11.9)$$

Equation 11.9 holds only if events A and B are independent. If they are dependent, the probability that both events will happen at the same time will depend on the correlation between the two events and cannot be defined in one simple equation. For example, in the network of Figure 11.10, paths BDG and CFI may be independent. The reason we say "may be independent" rather than "are independent" is that we cannot be sure until we know everything about them. Even though they are not linked with a logical relationship, they could be dependent, such as if activities on both paths are performed by the same crew or the materials used in activities on both paths will be delivered in one shipment.

Theoretically, if we need to calculate the probability that the project in Figure 11.10 will finish by a certain date, we need to consider all paths. In our small example, we have five paths: ABDG, ABEHI, ABDHI, ACEHI, and ACFI. Since they all share at least one activity, A, they have dependencies. Calculating the probability that the project will finish by a certain date requires not only complicated calculations, but also correlation factors between activities that may be difficult to obtain or estimate. In real-life projects, we may have tens, hundreds, or even thousands of paths in a CPM network. For practical reasons, we focus on one path at a time, as we did in the last example.

PERT and the Construction Industry

Even though PERT can be a good tool for predicting event dates, it is rarely, if ever, used in the construction industry. There are four reasons for this:

1. The main area of effective application for PERT is experimental projects with a great deal of uncertainty with regard to durations. In construction projects, even if the project design is new, the basic elements of the construction operations are usually well known. Project managers usually feel comfortable with the estimated durations they provide. A good project manager's estimates may be slightly over or under for the duration of individual activities, but the overall duration of the project should be fairly accurate.

2. As shown previously, PERT focuses on a single path. The scheduler must study different paths and analyze them for the highest uncertainty (least likelihood) of meeting a specific finish date. This process may be complicated and time consuming.

3. Project managers may have a problem providing three durations (optimistic, most probable, and pessimistic) for each activity. During a discussion with the author, one project manager said, sarcastically

"We can barely come up with one duration per activity and you want me to provide you with *three* durations?"

4. Many project managers adopt the practice of adjusting and correcting the durations (and possibly the logic) while updating the schedule. Even though we are required to do such adjusting and correcting while updating, this practice must not be an excuse for poor preparation of schedules. The project manager should always remember that the project schedule could be a legal and binding document, as part of the contract. In such a case, it may be used in court later to prove or disprove a delay claim.

PERT and Computer Project-Scheduling Software

Several computer software programs perform **Monte Carlo simulations,** generating random numbers that follow the distribution of individual activities (optimistic, most likely, and pessimistic, along with their weights). The program generates results for each run. It is typical to do 100 runs or more. The more runs we do, the more confidence we will have in the results. Some products run Monte Carlo simulations in a "generic" environment. Crystal Ball (Decisioneering, Inc., Denver, CO) performs risk analysis by using Monte Carlo simulations in MS Excel. Other products tie in with specific scheduling software. For example, Pertmaster Professional + Risk (Pertmaster Ltd., London, UK) runs risk analysis by integrating with Primavera scheduling products. You can assign an uncertainty to activity durations, costs, and resources, then determine the probability of completing the project on time and within budget. Risk+ (ProjectGear, Inc., Tacoma, WA) and @Risk (Palisade Corp., Newfield, NY) are compatible with MS Project for calculating risk and probabilities based on PERT calculations. Regardless of the product you use, you must ensure that it integrates with the scheduling program you are using.

Some software companies call precedence network diagrams *PERT*. In most cases, the displayed diagram is nothing but a precedence network applying the deterministic CPM calculations. Because of this, many people in the construction industry began to use the term *PERT* simply, and erroneously, to indicate a CPM logic diagram, as compared with a bar chart. The author has even observed this terminology error in some owners' specifications calling for "PERT reports" to be submitted. The author strongly recommends refraining from this use of the term *PERT*.

GRAPHICAL EVALUATION AND REVIEW TECHNIQUE (GERT)

The **graphical evaluation and review technique (GERT)** is a network analysis technique that allows for conditional and probabilistic treatment of logical relationships (that is, some activities may not be performed) (Project Management Institute 2000). GERT is similar to PERT but considers both deterministic and probabilistic branching. It incorporates both in the network analysis. GERT allows additional branching features not provided by CPM or PERT.

In deterministic branching, as shown in Figure 11.11a, we consider all activities leaving the node. In other words, activities A, B, and C in Figure 11.11a, will all take place. In probabilistic branching, as shown in Figure 11.11b, we consider one branch at any given time. For example, in Figure 11.11b, we consider either A or B. However, the sum of the probabilities for each branch leaving a probabilistic branching must equal 100% (Fair 1994).

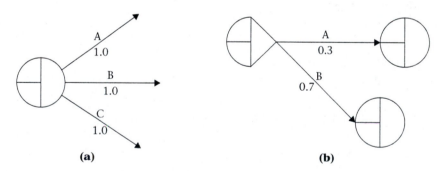

FIGURE 11.11   (a) Deterministic and (b) probabilistic branching

Furthermore, GERT allows looping, something both CPM and PERT do not allow. For example, Figure 11.12 shows three possible outcomes following activity A: activity B (with 30% probability), activity C (with 50% probability), *or* activity D (repeat of activity A, with 20% probability). We can think of activity A as Shop Drawing Submittal, activity B as Accepted As Is, activity C as Accepted with Changes, and activity D as Rejected; Resubmit.

GERT has not gained popularity in the construction industry. In fact, it did not gain any interest beyond some academic research.

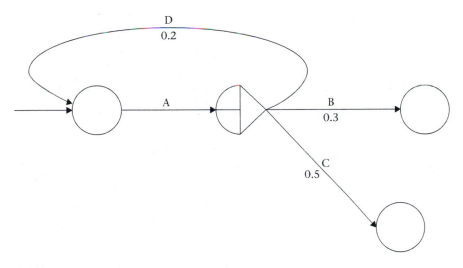

FIGURE 11.12   Three possible outcomes following activity A

LINEAR SCHEDULING METHOD (LSM)

Construction projects differ in type, size, and nature. Scheduling methods also differ in efficacy depending on the type of project they are serving. Bar charts are generally good for small, simple projects.* CPM networks are used for medium-size to large projects that consist of large numbers of small activities. Some construction projects consist of a few activities (usually with large quantities) that must be done in the same order or sequence, such as heavy construction projects such as roads, earthwork, or utility piping. Let us consider a project to lay down 5,000 linear feet (LF) of an underground utility pipe. The basic activities are Excavation, Prepare Subbase, Lay Pipe, Backfill, and Compact. If we are to use CPM networks for this project, we can take one of the following two approaches:

1. Create a project with only five large activities. Connect these activities with start-to-start (with lags) and finish-to-finish relationships.
2. Divide each major activity into a number of activities (e.g., 50 subactivities) in which each represents a distance of 100 LF.

---

*Unless used along with CPM networks, then they can be used for large projects to focus on a small group of activities or to present a few summary activities. Refer to the discussion in chapters 3 and 9.

Steps Required to Build a Schedule by Using the LSM

Three simple steps (similar to the first three steps in the CPM discussed in chapter 4) are necessary to build a schedule by using the LSM:

1. Determine the work activities. As mentioned previously, we expect only a few activities in LSM schedules.
2. Estimate activity production rates. Such estimation is similar to determining durations, but we are concerned with not only durations, but also the production rate.
3. Develop an activity sequence, similar to determining logical relationships. All relationships are start to start (with lags) with finish to finish.

Before applying the LSM, we must make sure it is the most appropriate method.

How the LSM Works

In the LSM, since the *x*-axis represents time and the *y*-axis represents distance, the slope represents the "speed," or rate, of production (Figure 11.13). When we have two or more activities, the production rate will differ from one to another. The horizontal distance between two lines represents the

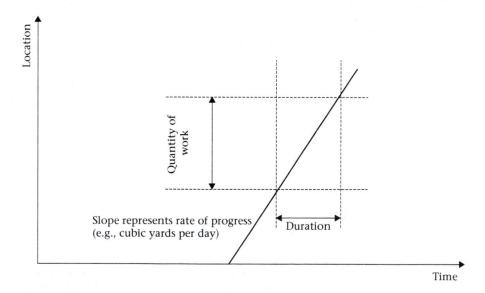

FIGURE 11.13   The linear scheduling method (LSM)

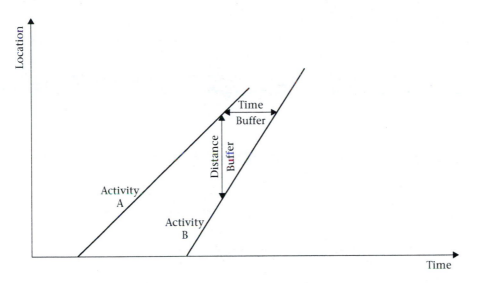

FIGURE 11.14   Time and distance buffers in the LSM

float of the earlier activity. In the LSM, we call it the *time buffer*. The vertical distance represents the distance separating the two operations. We call it the *distance buffer*. See Figure 11.14.

Lines are not allowed to intersect because an intersection literally means that the successor has gotten ahead of the predecessor, which is impossible (see Figure 11.15). Consider, for example, a carpentry crew installing and taping

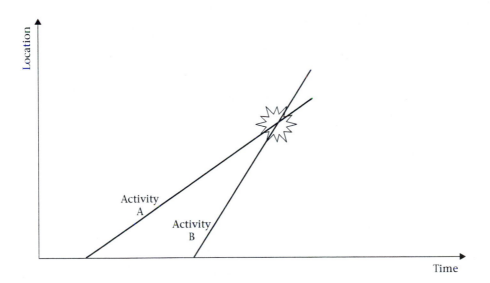

FIGURE 11.15   A successor's getting ahead of its predecessor: an illegal relationship

drywall for a total of 10,000 square feet (SF). The production rate for the crew is 500 SF per day for installation and taping. The painting crew is directly behind at a production rate of 800 SF per day. Assume the painting crew starts on day 2 (1 day after the carpentry crew started), then, at the end of day 3, the carpentry crew would have finished $500 \cdot 3 = 1,500$ SF, but the painting crew would have finished $800 \cdot 2 = 1,600$ SF, which is impossible. There are four solutions for this problem:

1. Speed up the rate of the carpentry crew.
2. Slow the rate of the painting crew.
3. Make the painting crew start later (calculate the time buffer).
4. Make the painting crew work in intervals: once they catch up with the carpentry team, they stop for a period and so on.

Solution 1 would increase the slope of activity A. Solution 2 would decrease the slope of activity B. Solution 3 would increase the starting time buffer. All three solutions aim at preventing the intersection of the two lines. Solution 4 would be represented in an LSM diagram as shown in Figure 11.16. The horizontal lines (slope = 0) represent an interruption time (no production). If the productivity of the crew changes, the slope changes too. Therefore, alternatively, instead of completely halting activity B during intervals, we can reduce the crew

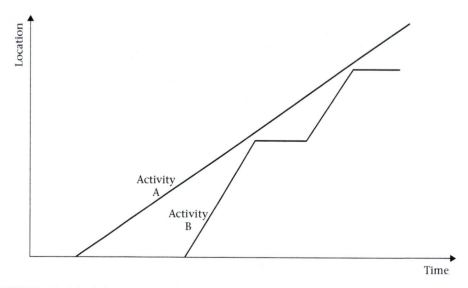

FIGURE 11.16   Solution 4 for avoiding an intersection in the LSM

size to slow the rate until there is a safe time buffer (a combination of solutions 2 and 4; see Figure 11.17).

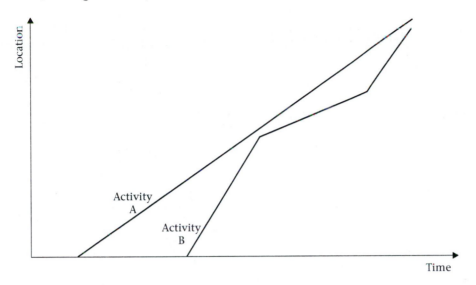

FIGURE 11.17   Combination of solutions 2 and 4 for avoiding an intersection in the LSM

The time buffer is necessary only if the rate of the successor is faster than the rate of the predecessor. If the rate of the successor is slower than that of the predecessor, the time buffer can start at zero. Naturally, the successor (activity B) will finish after the predecessor (activity A). See Figure 11.18.

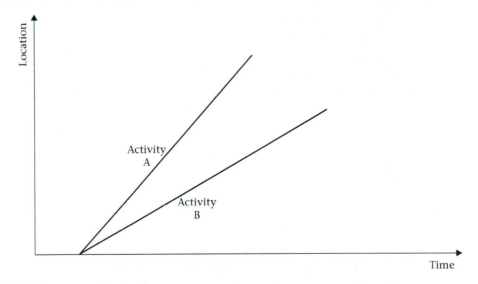

FIGURE 11.18   Rate of successor slower than rate of predecessor in the LSM

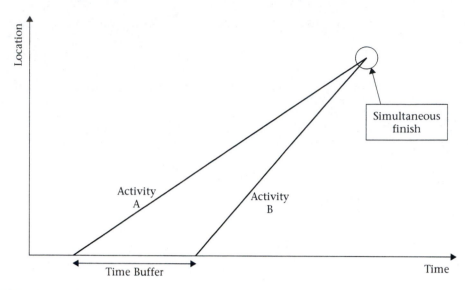

FIGURE 11.19   Time buffer calculation in the LSM

To calculate the time buffer (Figure 11.19), we start from the end: Allow activities A and B to finish simultaneously. Then,

$$\text{Duration A} = \text{Duration B} + \text{Time buffer}$$

or

$$\text{Time buffer} = \text{Duration A} - \text{Duration B} \qquad (11.10)$$

With multiple activities, you must consider two activities at a time. Starting from the beginning, do the following:

1. Compare the durations of activities 1 and 2. If activity 2 has a shorter duration, determine the time buffer from equation 11.10. If activity 2 has a longer duration, there is no need for a time buffer (practically, we need a minimum buffer because a predecessor and a successor cannot start at exactly the same time).

2. Repeat step 1 for activities 2 and 3 and so on.

EXAMPLE 11.4

A project consists of five activities:

A. Excavating a trench

B. Laying a subbase of gravel

C. Laying a concrete pipe

D. Backfilling

E. Compacting

Assume that the length of the pipe is 1,000 LF and that the productivity rates for the five activities are 100, 125, 75, 200, and 150 LF per day, respectively. Draw the project diagram, using the LSM. Leave a *minimum* 1-day time buffer.

Solution

First, determine the durations by dividing the total quantity, 1,000 LF, by the production rate for each activity. The following durations result: 10, 8, 14, 5, and 7 days for activities A through E, respectively.

If we start activity A on (end of) day 0, it will finish on day 10. Activity B lasts only 8 days and we must leave at least a 1-day time buffer so that we can finish this activity on day 11. Subtracting its duration of 8 days, we find the starting point: day 3. Activity C lasts 14 days, so we lag it by 1 day and start it on day 4. It will finish on day 18. Activity D can finish no earlier than day 19. It will start on day 14. Finally, activity E can start on day 15 and finish on day 22. See Figure 11.20.

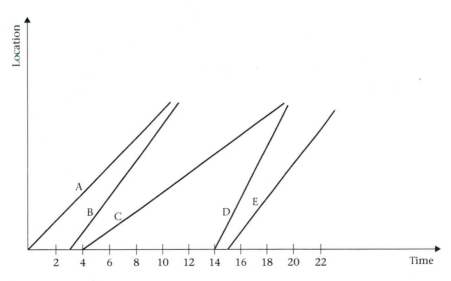

FIGURE 11.20 Solution to example 11.4

LSM Computer Software Programs

Despite its advantages, the LSM method has not been widely accepted in the construction industry. Only a few programs on the market use this method. One is TransCon XPosition, by TransCon, Richmond, Virginia. Another is PlaNet+, by Artemis, Finland.

CHAPTER 11 EXERCISES

1. What do the acronyms PERT, GERT, and LSM stand for?
2. What is the main concept of PERT?
3. How does the PERT method work?
4. What are the main differences between CPM and PERT?
5. In a CPM network, the critical path has five activities. Their durations are tabulated next.

	DURATION (DAYS)		
ACTIVITY	OPTIMISTIC (T_o)	MOST LIKELY (T_m)	PESSIMISTIC (T_P)
A	2	5	9
B	3	4	8
C	4	6	9
D	5	10	20
E	3	5	9

Compute the following:

   a. The probability that the project will finish by the end of day 32
   b. The probability that the project will finish by the end of day 34
   c. The probability that the project will finish before day 30

    d. The probability that the project will finish on the 32nd day

    e. The probability that the project will finish no later than the 35th day

    f. The probability that the project will finish at least 2 days early

    g. The probability that the project will finish at least 2 days late

    h. The probability that the project will finish on the 32nd day ±1 day

    i. The completion date with at least a 90% confidence level

6. In a CPM network, the critical path has five activities. Their durations are tabulated next.

	DURATION (DAYS)		
ACTIVITY	OPTIMISTIC (T_o)	MOST LIKELY (T_m)	PESSIMISTIC (T_P)
A	4	6	9
D	6	10	15
G	7	11	15
H	10	20	36
M	8	10	14
O	4	5	8

Compute the following:

    a. The probability that the project will finish by the end of day 64

    b. The probability that the project will finish by the end of day 65

    c. The probability that the project will finish before day 60

    d. The probability that the project will finish on the 62nd day

    e. The probability that the project will finish at least 6 days early

    f. The probability that the project will finish no more than 4 days late

    g. The completion date with at least a 95% confidence level

7. In a CPM network, the critical path has six activities. Their durations are tabulated next.

ACTIVITY	DURATION (DAYS)		
	OPTIMISTIC (T_o)	MOST LIKELY (T_m)	PESSIMISTIC (T_p)
B	2	3	5
D	4	8	13
F	5	6	8
K	3	3	3
N	7	10	15
S	3	5	8

Compute the following:

    a. The probability that the project will finish by the end of day 36
    b. The probability that the project will finish by the end of day 39
    c. The probability that the project will finish before day 38
    d. The probability that the project will finish on the 35th day
    e. The probability that the project will finish at least 3 days early
    f. The probability that the project will finish more than 4 days late
    g. The completion date with at least a 90% confidence level

8. Draw the network for the following project. Perform the CPM calculations on the basis of the most likely durations. Pick the longest three paths. Calculate the expected duration and the standard deviation for each path. Considering all three paths, what is the duration of the project with at least a 90% confidence level?

ACTIVITY	IPA	DURATION (DAYS)		
		OPTIMISTIC (T_o)	MOST LIKELY (T_m)	PESSIMISTIC (T_p)
A	—	4	6	11
B	—	3	4	6
C	—	6	9	15

(continued)

ACTIVITY	IPA	DURATION (DAYS)		
		OPTIMISTIC (T_o)	MOST LIKELY (T_m)	PESSIMISTIC (T_p)
D	A, B	3	4	11
E	B	5	7	10
F	D	4	5	8
G	D, E	7	10	16
H	C, F, G	6	8	10
I	C, G	3	3	5
J	H, I	2	2	2

9. What is the risk of using PERT and focusing on the critical path only?

10. What types of projects are best for the PERT application?

11. Is PERT popular in the construction industry? Why?

12. What is the main difference between PERT and GERT?

13. What types of projects are best for the LSM application?

14. What are the steps for preparing an LSM schedule?

15. Define *time buffer* and *distance buffer*. Use words and graphs to explain your answer.

16. Draw an LSM schedule for a 5-mile stretch of a road project. Consider the following activities:

Activity	Daily production (LF)
A. Excavation	500
B. Subbase	300
C. Base	240
D. Paving	1,000
E. Striping and Signage	1,500

17. Draw an LSM schedule for a 2-mile road-resurfacing project. Consider the following activities:

Activity	Daily production (LF)
A. Milling	2,000
B. Structural Course	1,000
C. Friction Course	800
D. Striping and Signage	1,200

Construction Delay Claims

Marriott World Center, Orlando, Florida. Courtesy of Smith Aerial Photos, Maitland, Florida.

INTRODUCTION AND DEFINITION

Construction delay claims and their resolution is a complicated subject. Many attorneys retain consulting engineers and other experts to assist them in understanding the technical issues that arise in construction-related cases. Some attorneys have even returned to college to obtain engineering and construction degrees to acquire technical knowledge in addition to their legal knowledge. Many books, seminars, and organizations have been dedicated to this topic.

In this chapter, we merely touch on the subject by discussing some commonsense concepts and providing some general guidelines. The author strongly recommends that readers refer to specialized books and sources, such as those listed in the Construction Scheduling Law section of the Bibliography, for a more detailed study.

The simplest definition of a **delay** (in the construction management context) is an event or a condition that results in finishing the project later than stipulated in the contract. A delay may also pertain to starting or finishing a specific activity later than planned. A **claim** is a request from one contracting party (usually the contractor) to another party for additional compensation, a time extension, or both. If we put the two terms together, a *delay claim* simply means a claim related to a delay.

As is well known, construction projects involve many risks because real life and plans rarely, if ever, coincide. As a result, claims have become an almost-inevitable part of construction projects.

Claims may be initiated by any project participant against any other participant. An architect may file a claim against an owner or vice versa. A supplier may file a claim against the contractor or the owner, and so on. Since the contractor is usually responsible for performing the physical work of the project and he or she does not traditionally have a contracting relationship with the designer (architect or engineer), most claims are initiated by the contractor against the owner.

Note, however, that a claim is not always a negative action, nor does it automatically indicate a confrontation. Many claims are legitimate and are routinely resolved to the satisfaction of both parties.

DELAY CLAIMS AND CHANGE ORDERS

A delay claim may ask for a time extension, monetary compensation, or both. Delays that result in claims are classified as excusable, nonexcusable, and concurrent, as explained subsequently.

A claim for only monetary compensation often forms the basis for a change order (CO). A CO may be initiated at the request of the owner, contractor, subcontractor, and so on. For example, an owner may want to change the color of the brick, the type of floor tile, or the type of light fixtures from that specified in the contract. Such a CO may be initiated by the owner's submitting a **request for quotation (RFQ).** This request could be an owner's decision (a directive) or a "what-if" inquiry. In the latter case, the owner sends an RFQ,* along with relevant architectural or engineering details (drawings or specifications), if necessary, to the contractor. The contractor evaluates the new changes, including their impact on his or her work plan and issues the owner a quotation. The quotation typically includes a cost estimate but may also include the impact on the schedule. In response, the owner accepts, rejects, or negotiates this quotation. Once the owner and the contractor agree on the price or schedule change, the owner issues a CO. The CO signals the owner's acceptance of the cost and other terms already agreed on with the contractor, and it authorizes the contractor to do the work. A CO can be for an addition to, a deletion from, or a substitution to the original contract. An example of a deletion CO is an owner's deleting a swimming pool from a contract to build a house. In such cases, most contractors issue partial credit that is less than the amount originally estimated in the contract for the item.

For this reason and to minimize the number of COs, owners should do a thorough job of defining the scope of the project and selecting a competent designer. Many projects suffer from **scope-creep syndrome,** in which COs keep adding to the project budget and put it at levels far beyond what the owner originally planned. From the contractor's perspective, COs, although a source of headaches, can be a source of extra income. Many experts contend that if all COs were taken into consideration prior to designing a project, the total cost to the owner would be significantly less. Some owners, when not sure about certain major items, obtain project bids with alternatives. For our example, the base bid may be the house without a swimming pool but with the alternative of adding a pool. In this case, the bidder must provide a base bid price and an additional amount for the pool in case the owner decides to add it. Conversely, if the owner is leaning more toward including the pool, he or she may include the pool in the base bid but with an alternative to omit it.

The timing of the changes also makes a significant difference. The later the change is made, the more expensive (and perhaps more time consuming)

---

*Some contractors call it a *request for price;* however, it should not be abbreviated as RFP, which is an industry abbreviation for request for proposal.

it becomes. Consider a simple example: An owner decides to change a few doors from 2 feet 8 inches wide to 3 feet wide. Now, consider the following five scenarios along with the cost associated with each:

Scenario 1. The owner makes the change before the design is complete. The extra cost is nothing (other than the difference in the door prices).

Scenario 2. The owner makes the change after the design is complete but before bidding. A small extra cost is associated with the architect's reworking some of the drawings and specifications.

Scenario 3. The owner makes the change after signing the construction contract but before doors are delivered and work on this portion of the project has started. The extra cost is still small, but this request has become a CO. The contractor may try to make some "extra profit" as a result of this change.

Scenario 4. The owner makes the change after the door openings have been framed (in masonry walls) but before the walls have been finished. The change includes the cost of widening the door openings (i.e., demolition of part of the masonry walls) and installing new door frames. If the doors have been delivered, the owner will be charged extra for delivery and restocking.

Scenario 5. The owner makes the change after everything is finished. This request is a major CO that includes widening the door openings (i.e., demolition of part of the masonry walls covered by drywall and painted) and installing new door frames. Extra costs will result from redoing the masonry walls, drywall, paint, and cleanup. Because the doors are painted, they may not be returnable, so their cost will be added to the total loss.

Scenarios 4 and 5 may affect the project schedule.

In certain cases, the CO process may be shortened, such as when trust exists between the owner and the contractor, when the owner is constrained because of lack of time, or when the CO has a minimal economic impact. In these cases, the owner may issue a directive to the contractor before verifying the price: the contractor performs the work then charges the owner later.

REASONS FOR DELAY CLAIMS

Claims usually occur because of unexpected events or developments, regardless of who is at fault. Unlike projects in other industries, no two construction projects are the same. Even when two projects have the same design and are performed by the same company, they may differ with regard to site conditions, climate, regulations, subcontractors, market conditions, and team members. Consequently, anticipating every event that will affect a construction project is difficult, even when the projects are substantially similar. A claim may arise during any construction project for several reasons.

Differing Site Conditions

A contractor may initiate a claim if the actual site conditions differ from those mentioned in the contract documents. For example, a contractor may encounter underground water that was not mentioned in the contract documents. Soil types may also differ from what was mentioned in the geologic (soil) report. In one case known to the author, a contractor encountered soil contamination that was not known or mentioned in the contract.

One possible reason for differing site conditions is when the architect or engineer uses old site plans that may not reflect recent activities. For instance, the contractor may find a temporary structure that needs to be demolished or a utility pole that needs to be relocated, neither of which is shown in the design drawings. Therefore, the contractor should always visit the site before mobilization—and even before bidding.

The risks of dealing with unknown site conditions are usually addressed in the contract documents in a provision known as the *differing site conditions clause.* This clause typically imposes on the contractor the duty of site investigation and the assumption of responsibility for bearing the cost of conditions that a bidder performing a reasonable prebid investigation would encounter. However, the differing site conditions clause does allow the contractor to recover for unknown site conditions that differ from the contract documents or are unusual. The owner often bears the cost of dealing with matters that fall within the terms of the differing site conditions clause.

Design Errors or Omissions

Errors or omissions in the design may, and usually do, require the contractor to perform additional work than originally contemplated. However, not all design errors or omissions form the basis for a compensable claim. Judges have rejected some claims when an error or omission was patently obvious and a construction professional could have discovered it during the bidding or negotiation phase. For example, if floor joist spacing is shown as 16′ rather than 16″ on center, this error should be recognizable as a typographical error. Also, if the structural drawings did not show any reinforcement in a concrete column or beam section, the contractor should know that such a member must have rebar. In general, the contractor must inquire about obvious design errors before submitting a bid (*Blinderman Construction Co. v. United States*, 17 Cl. Ct. 860 [1989]).

Changes in Owner's Requirements

Changes in the owner's requirements may constitute a change in the contract and provide a foundation for COs. As discussed previously, owners are always encouraged to know exactly what they want within their budgetary limits.*

Unusually Adverse Weather

Most contracts allow for certain expected weather delays without allowing time extensions to the contract time (The American Institute of Architects 1997). A contractor who is rained out 5 or 6 days in July in Tampa, Florida, will probably not get a time extension from the owner because such delays are common for that location during that part of the year. In contrast, a weather condition that is unusual for the geographic area during that time of the year may provide grounds for the contractor to file a time-extension claim. Likewise, a hurricane or tornado may be regarded as force majeure (this term is defined subsequently), which provides grounds for a time extension even if the area is known for hurricanes or tornadoes.

---

*In a project the author was involved in, a city municipality asked an architect about the possibility of designing a parking garage in a certain location with a capacity of 280 cars within a budget of $2.5 million. The architect confirmed on the basis of a "plain" design with a simple finish and no fancy options. The contractor's estimate for the design was just below $2.5 million. During the detailed design phase, the city started adding options, such as a sprinkler system, a security system, retail space, planters, pavers, trees and some landscaping, an extra half-floor that increased the capacity to about 325 cars, and so forth. These additions increased the cost till it topped $4.2 million. The city liked the design but was shocked to see the contractor's price tag. It told the architect, "We thought we were getting the parking for about $2.5 million." The architect replied, "You can't get a Cadillac for the price of a Chevy!" The city had to go back and remove many of the added options but still insisted on some. The project was eventually constructed for slightly more than the original budget.

Miscellaneous Factors

Factors that may not be the claimant's fault include failure of the owner to provide a project site, a late notice to proceed (NTP), labor strikes,* a delay in the delivery of the owner's furnished equipment, events that can be classified as force majeure, and problems deemed to be the owner's responsibility.

Force Majeure

The term *force majeure* (also sometimes spelled incorrectly as *force majure*) originated in 1883 from French and means "superior force" (August 2003; Houghton Mifflin 2000; Merriam-Webster 2003, http://www.dictionary.com). In the context of construction projects, this term usually involves three important elements:

1. Something that is superior, overwhelming, or overpowering (i.e., cannot be prevented)
2. Something that is unexpected or cannot be reasonably anticipated or controlled
3. Something that has a destructive or disruptive effect on the construction process

Force majeure usually means that an event satisfying all three criteria has occurred and the contractor is excused from certain contractual requirements as a result. Examples of force majeure are earthquakes, hurricanes, tornadoes, wars, labor strikes, and acts of sabotage or terrorism.

Another contractual term with a similar meaning is *vis major,* which is Latin for "act of God." However, the term *force majeure* is probably more appropriate than *act of God* in this context because it indicates an event that could not have been prevented with reasonable human effort. Although the term *act of God* has been construed to mean the same thing as force majeure, it may be interpreted differently according to an individual's religious beliefs or philosophy. In extreme cases, some people may even argue that every action that happens in this world is an "act of God," whether or not we have control over it or responsibility for it.

---

*In some cases, judges have ruled that when the contractor signs the construction contract and a labor strike is looming, such a strike is not grounds for a time extension.

All the preceding factors may entitle the contractor to monetary compensation, a time extension, both, or neither. The contract usually specifies the conditions under which the contractor is entitled to remedies when such factors occur.

TYPES OF DELAYS RESULTING IN CLAIMS

Delay claims pertaining to the construction schedule are usually the result of three types of delays (Bramble and Callahan 2000):

1. *Excusable delays*. An **excusable delay** entitles the contractor to additional time to complete the contract work. Excusable delays usually stem from reasons beyond the contractor's control. These delays can be further classified as follows:
   a. **Noncompensable delays.** These delays are beyond the control, and not the fault, of the owner—such as unusual weather conditions, natural disasters (earthquakes, floods, hurricanes, etc.), wars or national crises, and labor strikes. Most likely, these delays entitle the contractor to a time extension but not monetary compensation.
   b. **Compensable delays.** These delays are caused by the owner or the designer (architect or engineer). They usually entitle the contractor to a time extension, recovery of the costs associated with the delay, or both.
2. *Nonexcusable delays*. By definition, a **nonexcusable delay** does not entitle the contractor to either a time extension or monetary compensation. Typically, a nonexcusable delay is any delay that is either caused by the contractor or not caused by the contractor but should have been anticipated by the contractor under normal conditions. Examples of the first group include slow mobilization, contractor cash-flow problems (e.g., the contractor committed him- or herself to more financial obligations than he or she could afford), poor workmanship, labor strikes due to unfair labor practices, and accidents on the project site caused by the contractor's negligence or lack of preparation. Examples of the second group include late delivery of the contractor's furnished materials and equipment, contractor cash-flow problems (e.g., the bank refused to issue a loan to the contractor after he or she was preapproved), adverse weather conditions that can be expected for the location during that time of year, and a lack of skilled labor.

3. *Concurrent delays.* A **concurrent delay** involves a combination of two or more independent causes of delay during the same period. Often, a concurrent delay involves an excusable delay and a nonexcusable delay. For example, the one case the author was involved in, the contractor was working slowly and increasingly falling behind schedule. Around midproject, the owner issued a major, or cardinal, CO. The contractor requested a 120-day time extension because of this CO. To prove his point, he presented two schedules: the original (baseline) schedule and an impacted schedule. After analyzing the situation, the author found that the CO justified a 56-day delay. The other 64 days were nonexcusable. The contractor was trying to hide the nonexcusable delay within the delay caused by the owner's CO.

Note: Just because additional work may require time to perform, the contractor is not automatically entitled to a time extension. He or she may have to demonstrate that the additional work affects the critical path of the project. The use of critical path method (CPM) schedules and scheduling experts is often necessary to prove or disprove such claims.

In the case of a CO, the contractor may be entitled to extra monetary compensation in lieu of a time extension, even if he or she finished by the original finish deadline. This situation is called *constructive acceleration.* Typically, the extra payment covers the contractor's effort, above and beyond that outlined in the original contract plan, for accelerating the schedule. Such effort may include overtime payments and extra labor or equipment. In such cases, when an owner issues a schedule-affecting CO or causes a delay, the contractor may negotiate with the owner to finish on time in exchange for extra payment.

DELAY-CLAIMS PREVENTION

Construction projects take months or years to finish and involve numerous people and events. In many cases, people are replaced in the middle of the project for myriad reasons. Inevitably, project participants will forget details about what occurred during the project. Therefore, the importance of diligently maintaining daily reports, journals, and the like cannot be overemphasized. Many a case or claim has been won or lost on the basis of the quality of the record keeping for the project.

One of the most important documents in delay-claims prevention is the baseline schedule (defined and discussed in chapter 7). It indicates the manner in which the contractor planned to perform the work and the owner's acceptance of that plan. The 1997 version of The American Institute of Architects (AIA) Document A201 requires the contractor to submit a schedule that complies with the contract completion date. Most contract forms currently used by public and private owners also require a schedule prepared by the contractor and accepted by the owner. Such a schedule, once adopted as the baseline schedule in the contract, becomes an important document because it is the yardstick for measuring any variation. Because of lack of knowledge or experience, negligence, or other reasons, many contractors commit errors or submit faulty schedules. Following is a list of nine frequent scheduling mistakes contractors may make:

1. *Baseline schedules that do not show logic.* Some contractors use spreadsheets or simple bar charts as schedules. Spreadsheets are not scheduling programs, and they are used merely as "color tapes" to indicate when the contractor intends to start and finish each activity. A problem occurs when an activity is delayed or shifted. Such "bar chart schedules" do not show the impact on other activities.

2. *Baseline schedules with dates rather than logic.* Some schedules, even if built with computer scheduling programs, use events rather than activities. For example, instead of showing Excavation as a 20-day activity, the schedule shows two milestones (events): Start Excavation and Finish Excavation. This approach causes several problems. First, most contractors use constraints to "fix" the date of an event, which disallows the introduction of logic into the schedule. Second, this approach deprives the control manager (on both the contractor's and the owner's sides) of evaluating the percent complete of an activity.

3. *Overuse of constraints.* Sometimes the contractor "schedules" activities by assigning them start and finish dates, usually by using constraints. As in the previous case, activities "get nailed" with such constraints and become inflexible because they are not tied by logic. Often in construction, activities are delayed, finished early, omitted, or adjusted. Such changes may have an impact on succeeding activities, which will not be apparent if activities are constrained. (Some computer programs introduce different types of constraints: some are subject to logic and some override logic.)

4. *"Erasing footprints."* A contractor may build or update the schedule as the project proceeds, without keeping a copy of the original or previous updates. This schedule is an *as-built schedule.* It shows how the

project was actually built, not how the contractor intended to build it. This conduct leaves no footprints to track and no baseline with which to compare progress.

5. *Unrealistic baseline schedules.* Some contractors do not realize that a baseline schedule approved by the owner may be a legal and binding document. Later, during construction, contractors cannot get relief by complaining about an unrealistic duration or unrealistic logic in the schedule unless a change in work circumstances warrants such relief.

6. *Schedules with logic errors.* Errors may render the schedule useless and, during litigation, cause it to be thrown out by the judge (*Fortec Constructors v. United States,* 8 Cl. Ct. 490 [1985]). The schedule must be prepared by a construction professional. Contractors without scheduling skills usually hire CPM consultants. Note that the reliability and correctness of the schedule may have nothing to do with the contractor's field of practice. The contractor may deviate from the schedule, but the schedule is still evaluated on its own merits.

7. *Skipping periodic updates.* Skipping periodic schedule updates because "things are going just fine" often yields a baseline schedule and an updated schedule that reflects work progress long (e.g., 6 months) after the start of construction. The large gap between the two schedules makes tracing events during that period difficult. Courts may not accept schedules to prove delays unless they are regularly updated (*Wilner v. United States,* 26 Cl. Ct. 260 [1992]).

8. *Lack of proper documentation.* Lack of proper documentation can have serious repercussions. When updating, the scheduler should record any unusual events. For example, if an excavation activity finished 1 week after its scheduled finish date, the scheduler should record the reason for this delay. Most scheduling programs provide "note" or "log" functions at both the activity level and the project level.

9. *Lack of a reasonable time contingency.* Contractors must have a reasonable amount of time contingency built into the schedule for delays (such as expected bad-weather conditions). One commonly overlooked scenario is the possibility of submittal rejection. A contractor may allocate only 10 days for shop-drawing review and approval in a tight schedule. If the drawings are rejected, they must be corrected and resubmitted for approval. This process will likely take more than 10 days and may cause a delay in the schedule. In most cases such as this, the contractor must absorb the delay, without relief from the owner.

PROJECT SCHEDULE DOCUMENTATION

The characteristics of good communications, both oral and written, were discussed in chapter 9. Written communications include both text and graphic reports. We cannot overestimate the importance of good communications. Most construction companies list good communications skills as one of the top conditions for hiring project management personnel. *Communications* generally means conveying information from one party to other parties within the organization or across organizations. In contrast, *documentation* generally means saving the information in an organized manner for possible future retrieval. Communications and documentation must both contain clear information, provide the proper amount of detail, and be stored efficiently so that the information can be retrieved easily.

Project documentation includes both home-office and field-office documentation. Since many types of information may be documented in the home office or on-site, we list all the information to be documented wherever it is documented. With advances in communications technology, home-office and field-office information is becoming more and more integrated into one comprehensive project database. Construction companies are using several software packages for this purpose.* These are packages continually improving, becoming more powerful and more capable of being integrated with other systems such as drafting, scheduling, estimating, accounting, Web publishing, and e-mail communications.

For delay-claims prevention and resolution, the following 14 pieces of information must be documented:

1. *The project baseline schedule that the owner accepted.* Both an electronic copy and a printed report (bar chart, predecessors-successors table, etc.) must be kept in both the main office and the field office.
2. *Periodic schedule updates.* The scheduler must name and store projects in a clear and consistent fashion. Copies of these updates should also be kept in the main office. Updates should include both the printout (bar chart and other reports) and an electronic copy of the CPM schedule.
3. *Change orders.* The administrative and technical correspondence should be included with the COs.

---

*The author is familiar with Primavera Expedition, Meridian's ProLog Manager, and Timberline's Project Management.

4. *Project manager's daily log.* Although the trend is to use electronic logbooks, many project managers still use a traditional daily logbook. Many types of logbooks are available commercially (Prentice Hall 2000). Alternatively, many companies print their own official logbooks. A typical logbook should include daily information such as the following:

   a. Weather conditions, such as temperature, humidity, precipitation, wind, lightning, and so forth

   b. Work performed during that day (including any disruptions such as accidents or unforeseen conditions)

   c. The number of workers on-site and the entities that employ them (including the number of work hours, especially overtime hours)

   d. Equipment on-site and its condition (working or not)

   e. Any material delivered to the site and an inspection record

   f. Materials used and materials stored on-site

   g. Any telephone calls made by the project manager or other field personnel that are relevant to the project

   h. Any visitors to the site, their time of visitation, and the organization they represented

   i. Any accidents that occurred on-site

   j. Any other events that may be related to the project, especially problems that may cause delays
   Nonworkdays (including weekends) should be marked as "no work" in the book. Every page must reflect the project name and date at the top of the page and be signed by the project manager. Typically, logbook pages are numbered consecutively so that if a page is ripped out, this fact is easy to recognize.

5. *Job diary.* A job diary is like an informal daily logbook. It may contain the accounts of the project manager or superintendent without following a certain format. It may also contain personal observations, suggestions, and opinions. Because of their informality and subjectivity, such diaries may not be used as evidence in the court of law but may be used to refresh someone's memory about a certain event.

6. *Submittal records, such as shop drawings and material samples.* In addition to shop drawings and material samples, the records must contain a log showing the dates and actions (accepted, rejected, etc.) taken for any submittal.

7. *Records of any transmittals.* Such records include but are not limited to requests for information (RFIs), requests for clarification, test lab results, warranties, and certificates.

8. *Correspondence with the owner, architect or engineer, subcontractors, vendors and suppliers, and other contracting parties.* The record must include the topic of the communication, the person with whom the project manager (or his or her staff) communicated, and the date of the communication.

9. *Correspondence with the home office.*

10. *Meeting minutes.* These should include the typical information in any meeting minutes (subject, date, location of meeting, names of people attending and absent people, etc.).

11. *Procurement records.* Such records include materials and equipment orders and delivery tickets; equipment maintenance records; any quotations for materials, labor, and the like; receipts for any purchases or payments; and any other record that deals with the acquisition of labor, materials, or equipment.

12. *Government records.* Such records include permits, code nonconformance reports, and Occupational Safety and Health Administration (OSHA) forms and citations.

13. *Record of payments (owner to general contractor and general contractor to subcontractors and vendors).* Such records should include the total amount billed, the total amount paid, the retainage, and other financial details. The general contractor must also keep lien releases signed by subcontractors (and the owner must keep lien releases signed by the general contractor).

14. *Photos of important events.* Any picture must have the date printed on its back or front. Digital cameras are effective because the picture can be downloaded to a computer then attached to a document or to the project management software.

In a good documentation system, the information is stored in a well-organized fashion and can be efficiently and easily retrieved, not only by the people who originally stored the information, but also by anyone else. One major challenge to anyone filing a delay claim is to retrieve all the information in an accurate manner, then re-create past events in the correct sequence. Keeping a good record helps refresh the memory of any party involved, which not only may help in case of a dispute, but also may help prevent such disputes from emerging.

DELAY-CLAIMS RESOLUTION

Most contracts contain clauses for claim dispute resolution. The process usually starts with the simplest and quickest procedure, then proceeds to the next level, and so on. Since court cases are lengthy, costly, and complicated, alternative dispute resolution methods have been used. The following five methods are usually used in resolving claims:

1. *Negotiation.* **Negotiation** is the most direct method for resolving any type of construction claim. In many cases, the "truth" may not be entirely known or acknowledged, and "fairness" is seen differently by the disputing parties. Negotiation requires certain skills that reduce the gap between the negotiating parties. Although negotiation occurs basically between the disputing parties, independent experts or consultants may be asked to give opinions on certain issues. Negotiation starts with parties at the project management level, but higher-level officers may become involved if the lower-level team fails to reach an agreement. Although complete satisfaction may never be attained, the objective of negotiation is to reach a solution that might be acceptable to both parties.

2. *Mediation.* When negotiation does not work, either because of a lack of trust or a lack of skills, **mediation** may be an option. A mediator may become involved to bring the disputing parties together. The mediator may be an individual or a team. The mediator usually starts by explaining his or her role in bringing the parties to an agreement. He or she must demonstrate neutrality and patience and must collect all the facts before making any recommendations. Typically, the mediator spends time with each party individually, but, if the atmosphere is encouraging, may bring the parties together in a meeting. The mediator, like the negotiator, must be skilled at narrowing the gap between the disputing parties and focusing on the positive side of any proposed solution. For example, although the dispute may be about financial issues between a general contractor and his or her subcontractor, the mediator may sense that the subcontractor is concerned about security and future work. The mediator may then convince the subcontractor to accept a lesser financial **settlement** in exchange for an extended relationship with the general contractor.

3. *Dispute review boards.* Rather than waiting until the end of a project to settle claims, **dispute review boards (DRBs)** resolve disputes as

they arise. The owner and the contractor select an independent, neutral panel with construction experience when the contract is signed, and the parties agree to call on the neutral panel to assist them in resolving any disputes that arise during construction. Since some cases involve large, complicated, and lengthy projects, collecting all the information may be difficult for the parties. The DRB technique was created to aid this process by involving the neutral panel from the early stages of the project. DRB members often visit the construction site periodically to become familiar with work progress and to provide assistance in the early stages of disputes (Gould and Joyce 2003).

Negotiation, mediation, and DRBs are *nonbinding,* which means the solution changes its shape, like a piece of dough, during the process until it reaches an acceptable form to both parties. Neither party is under obligation until it accepts the proposed solution.

4. *Arbitration.* **Arbitration** is usually a formal process performed by an independent professional arbitrator. It is defined by the American Arbitration Association (AAA) as a "referral of a dispute to one or more impartial persons for final and binding determination. Private and confidential, it is designed for quick, practical, and economical settlements (Peña-Mora, Sosa, and McCone 2003, 181). In construction, arbitration is usually performed by experts in the construction industry, such as architects, engineers, or construction management professionals. Some states grant design professionals quasi-judicial immunity when they act as judge. Although arbitration is usually binding to both parties, arbitrators do not have the enforcement power of judges. If necessary, an arbitration award in binding arbitration may be reduced to an enforceable judgment by a court of law.

   Unlike litigation (discussed subsequently), arbitration is voluntary, at least until the parties accept it in the contract or later, after the dispute arises. Arbitration does not require the use of lawyers, although parties arbitrating important matters often do use them. Not being subject to the complicated procedures and restrictions of the court system gives the arbitrator more freedom and makes the arbitration process faster. The power given to an arbitrator differ from state to state. For example, in many states, arbitration does not allow for an effective method of *discovery,* the process by which attorneys in litigation can obtain evidence from the other party to prepare for the hearing (Sweet 1999).

Mediation and arbitration can be combined in a two-stage process: the disputing parties select a mediator and agree that the same third party will become the arbitrator if the parties fail to reach a mediated settlement within a specific time frame (Peña-Mora, Sosa, and McConc 2003).

5. *Litigation.* When none of the previous processes work and parties cannot reach a settlement, the complaining party sues the other party in a court of law. Construction **litigation** is usually complicated, lengthy, and expensive. Many plaintiffs spend more money on attorney's fees than they later recover by the court's judgment. Note that in many contracts, arbitration is specified as a binding process if negotiation and mediation fail. As mentioned previously, unlike judges, arbitrators cannot enforce their judgments. If a party refuses to comply with the arbitrator's judgment, the other party may need to seek the court's intervention. Most state arbitration statutes specify grounds for reviewing an arbitrator's award, such as proof of corruption or fraud, evidence of an arbitrator's partiality, or proof that the arbitrator exceeded his or her powers (Sweet 1999).

THE IMPORTANCE OF CPM SCHEDULES IN DELAY CLAIMS

Resolving a delay claim may be a complicated and challenging task. Several concurrent factors might be involved in affecting the schedule. A concurrent delay means more than one delay contributed to the project delay; however, it does not necessarily mean that the delays occurred at the same time. A concurrent delay may occur during the same period as another delay, but a concurrent delay also includes any delay that has contributed to the overall project delay, whether or not the delay overlaps with another (Callahan, Quackenbush, and Rowings 1992). For example, the owner may have caused a 1-month delay, but the contractor claims that this delay pushed the start of the schedule to the rainy season, which caused an additional delay. A delay of only 1 day by the architect or engineer reviewing and approving the shop drawings may cause the cancellation of placement of concrete on a suspended slab, and the contractor may not be able to reschedule the concrete delivery for another week or so. Concurrent delays may also involve two or more factors that occurred at the same time, in which case, isolating the impact of each may be difficult for the investigator. Such isolation is particularly important when one factor is the contractor's fault and the other is not, such as if the materials delivery was delayed because of the contractor's negligence and severe weather occurred concurrently. Likewise, as mentioned previously, a contractor may be late, because of his or her own fault, then the owner issues a CO, so the contractor tries to hide his or her delay in a CO time-extension claim. The investigator must try to verify the effect of one factor at a time. Theoretically, doing so involves isolating other factors, which in reality might be difficult if not impossible.

CPM schedules are important in delay claims because, on the one hand, the claimant usually provides at least two CPM schedules—one without the impact of the change and one with the impact—in an attempt to prove that the change caused the claimed delay. On the other hand, the investigator builds several CPM schedules, each representing one factor isolated from other factors, to show exactly how much of the alleged delay, if any, can be attributed to the change.

METHODS OF SCHEDULE ANALYSIS

As-Built Schedule

As the name implies, the as-built schedule should reflect what actually happened in the field. Activities are plotted by their real start and real finish, disregarding any logic (usually, as-built schedules have no logic ties). This schedule may also contain real budget and real resources numbers. Investigators usually build the as-built schedule from project records such as daily logs, diaries, project correspondence, and so forth. Building such a schedule may require considerable effort, and some gaps in the schedule may need to be filled by the project manager's memory recollection and the investigator's judgment. Again, in such cases, documentation proves valuable for retrieving information that helps rebuild the case for proving or disproving a delay claim.

Updated Impacted Schedule

The U.S. Corps of Engineers modified the as-built method by creating an as-built schedule or updated schedule from the start of the project only to the point just before the delay occurred. The "original," or baseline, schedule is updated with progress information and then compared with the impacted completion date on another schedule on which a delay is included (Callahan, Quackenbush, and Rowings 1992).

As-Planned Schedule

The as-planned schedule describes the manner in which the contractor intended to build the project. This schedule is usually the same as that submitted by the contractor to the owner and later becomes the baseline schedule (Popescu and Charoenngam 1995). However, in some cases, the originally submitted schedule may contain some errors and need to be corrected (O'Brien and Plotnick 1999, 480). When no CPM schedule was required or when it was required but was not submitted or was submitted but was not formally approved, the investigator may need to develop a revised or prototype schedule, using the best and most credible information available, to reflect the original plan and intentions (Wickwire, Driscoll, and Hurlbut 1991, 377).

Comparison Schedule

The original schedule (usually the as-planned schedule) is revised to incorporate any claimed delays. Typically, for a delay claim, the contractor submits two schedules: one without the causative factors (factors allegedly causing the schedule delays) and one with the causative factors (called the **impacted schedule**). By comparing the two schedules, the contractor hopes to prove that the delay is caused by the alleged factors. The contractor may lump more than one factor in the delay claim. The investigator may then build an impacted schedule for each factor.

Accelerated Schedule

An **accelerated schedule** is a schedule, usually submitted by the contractor, implementing some adjustment to the project schedule so that the project can finish by the contract finish date. By doing this, the contractor attempts to collect the cost associated with the acceleration of the project.* The owner tries to make sure the contractor has used all available float before any schedule is crashed.

---

*Review the cost of schedule compression in chapter 8.

Recovery Schedule

A recovery schedule (as discussed in chapter 8) is similar to an accelerated schedule in the sense that, in both, adjustments are made to compress the schedule (or the remainder of it) to ensure project completion by the contract finish date. However, the main difference is in the reason for the delay that triggered this compression. Recovery schedules are mainly used when the contractor causes the delay and the owner becomes concerned about the contractor's ability to complete the project by the contract finish date. The owner may then demand that the contractor make adjustments and submit a recovery schedule that demonstrates a timely completion. The contractor usually prepares accelerated schedules when delays occur that the contractor alleges are caused by the owner, force majeure, or a third party.

FLOAT OWNERSHIP

Float (sometimes called **slack**) may be defined technically as the maximum amount of time an activity can be delayed from its early start date without delaying the entire project.[†] From a practical point of view, float is regarded as the time contingency associated with a path or chain of activities (Wickwire, Driscoll, and Hurlbut 1991). Some contracts give the owner the right to use the float in case of a delay. In this case, the contractor may not be entitled to a time extension or compensation until and unless the float is entirely exhausted. If the contract does not grant the owner float ownership, the contractor has, for each noncritical activity, a range of time between the early and late dates. The contractor may choose specific dates within this range for efficient resource allocation or other reasons.

EXAMPLE 12.1

In the construction project represented by the logic network shown in Figure 12.1, the owner issued a work order to the contractor that would delay the start of activity E till day 16 (i.e., its late start date). Would the contractor be entitled to a time extension, compensation, both, or neither?

[†]This is the definition of total float. See the definitions in chapter 4.

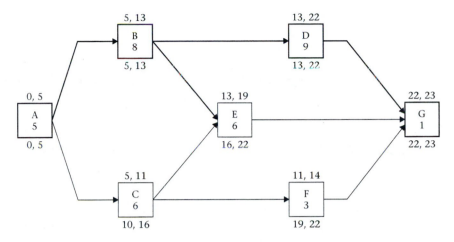

FIGURE 12.1 Logic network for example 12.1

Solution

As we see in Figure 12.1, activities C, E, and F have total floats equal to 5, 3, and 8 days, respectively. Let us redraw the schedule as a bar chart, showing the amount of float, if any, for each activity. See Figure 12.2.

The contractor may choose not to start noncritical activities on their early dates. Assume these three activities require the same crew. For the most efficient use of the crew, the contractor chooses the plan shown in Figure 12.3. According to this plan, all activities are critical, some by logic constraints and others by resource constraints. If we start activity C 1 or 2 days earlier than shown in Figure 12.3, we then have to hire the crew for an extra day or two (since we cannot start activity E earlier).

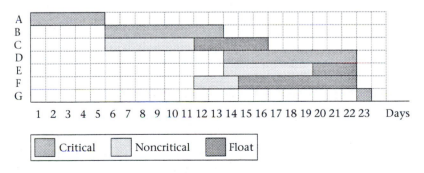

FIGURE 12.2 Bar chart for example 12.1, showing float

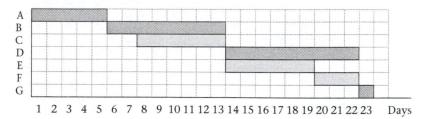

FIGURE 12.3   Final plan for example 12.1

Now assume the owner caused a delay of 3 days in the start of activity E (so it starts on its original late dates). The owner can use the argument that activity E had 3 days of total float, thus the contractor does not qualify for a time extension or compensation. The contractor argues that this delay will force him or her either to hire a second crew on days 20, 21, and 22 or to finish the project 3 days late. For this reason, the contractor requests extra pay and/or a time extension for 3 days.* The answer to this argument generally lies in the contract agreement. If the contractor granted the owner float ownership, the owner can use the float to absorb any delay. If the contractor owns the float, he or she may be entitled to a time extension or compensation if he or she can prove that the delay disrupted his or her resource allocation plan, even though it affected a noncritical activity and did not delay the entire project.

---

*We said "extra pay *and/or* a time extension" because even with a 3-day time extension, the contractor still needs to hire the crew for 3 extra days (8th through the 25th instead of 8th through the 22nd), unless the crew can do other work during the delay time (i.e., the 14th, 15th, and 16th). The alternative is to hire a second crew and do E and F concurrently (finish them both by the end of day 22).

Conclusions About Delays and Float

The subject of float is complicated and cannot be adequately covered in this simple discussion. In chapters 4 and 5, several types of float, not just total float and free float, were described. Types such as interfering float and independent float (see chapter 4) may not mean anything to field personnel or even the project manager. However, these terms could be used in a dispute to illustrate the dependency and distribution of the float. Total float (TF), as defined previously, is more like a path-shared float (if the float for an activity at the beginning of the path is used, the rest of the activities on the path will be affected). A simple example is the network shown in Figure 12.1. If the 5 days of float for activity C are used, activity E becomes critical and the total float for activity F shrinks from 8 days to 3 days. Free float (FF) is the portion of total float that would not affect the succeeding activities. However, free float is still subject to an impact from the preceding activities. For example, for activity E, $FF = TF = 3$ days, but this float will disappear if the float for activity C is used. The difference between total float and free float is interfering float (Int. F.), which is the part of the total float that will affect the succeeding activities. Independent float (Ind. F.) is the portion of free float that cannot be affected by preceding activities, nor can it affect succeeding activities. In other words, it is the only float that truly belongs to that activity. We do not usually deal with these definitions on a daily basis in the construction industry, but experts may have to understand and deal with them in some delay-claims cases.

Since we defined both total float and free float as a characteristic that may be shared among activities, and since many activities in construction projects are performed by different companies, the crucial question is this: who owns the float? We mentioned that the owner and the general contractor may agree on this point in their contract. Nevertheless, the issue may not be resolved. Disputes may still arise between the general contractor and a subcontractor, between two subcontractors, or between a vendor and the general contractor or subcontractor. In general, if the language in the contract specifies obligations of the general contractor to the owner, such obligations automatically become applicable to any subcontractor. Thus, if the general contractor grants float ownership to the owner, the owner then owns the float for all activities, whether performed by the general contractor or a subcontractor. The case may not be so simple when the general contractor owns the float. He or she may reach an agreement with a subcontractor for the distribution of the float. In some jurisdictions, the distribution of float has been determined through case law, legislation, or contracts, and in others, it has not. Researchers have studied this topic extensively and have devised many suggestions and algorithms for distributing float. Yet, no "industry standard" has been adopted for this issue, so contracting parties must make sure this issue is discussed and agreed on before signing the contract.

CHAPTER 12 EXERCISES

In addition to completing the following exercises, refer to appendix A, which contains a computer project for a two-story commercial building. This project includes assignments that are consistent with the subjects discussed in this chapter.

1. Define a construction *delay claim.*
2. Who can initiate a construction delay claim?
3. How can owners minimize the number of change orders?
4. The earlier the owner decides on a change, the less cost and trouble. Can you elaborate on this statement and provide a practical example?
5. What are the major reasons for change orders?
6. Define *force majeure.*
7. What are the types of delays resulting in claims?
8. If the owner adds additional work items to the project, would this action automatically entitle the contractor to a time extension? Explain.
9. What can the scheduler—as part of the project management team—do to prevent delay claims or help resolve them? List the items that you must document.
10. List the methods usually used to resolve claims. Briefly explain each. Classify them as binding and nonbinding methods.
11. Why is the CPM important in proving or disproving construction delay claims?
12. Define the following:

    a. As-built schedule

    b. As-planned schedule

    c. Comparison schedule

    d. Accelerated schedule

13. If a subcontractor's activity has 5 days of total float, does he or she have the authority to use the float however he or she likes? Explain your answer.
14. Can the owner require float ownership in the contract? If yes, can he or she add a 3-day work item to a path that has 5 days of total float without giving the contractor a time extension? (*Hint:* The answer is not a simple yes or no.)

Computer Project

You are scheduling a project: a two-story concrete office building with an area of about 4,000 square feet (SF) per floor. The first floor has a slab on a grade (SOG). The second floor is made of a cast-in-place (CIP) concrete slab, carried by both concrete columns and concrete masonry unit (CMU) walls. The roof is made of wood trusses topped with sheathing and asphalt shingles. The schedule logic includes many simplifying assumptions.

GENERAL GUIDELINES

1. This is an individual project, but group discussion is allowed and encouraged.
2. Your work will be mainly on the computer. Some written parts may be required. Make sure your reports are marked clearly with your name, the date, the report name, the page number, and so forth.
3. Write down any assumptions you make. Submit a written copy with your report.

4. The recommended software is Primavera Project Planner (P3), Primavera Enterprise (P3e), Primavera P3e/c, or Primavera's SureTrak Project Manager. Alternatively, you may use Microsoft (MS) Project, but if you do, remember that combination relationships will not work in this program.

5. The project comprises no more than 60 activities so that the student version of Primavera software can be used.

6. The assignments pertain to topics covered in the body of this book. Be sure to keep an electronic copy of each assignment.

7. Make the start date 8/2/04. Leave the finish date open.

8. In all calendars, enter the following as nonworkdays: New Year's Day (January 1), Martin Luther King Day (3rd Monday of January), Memorial Day (last Monday of May), July 4, Labor Day (1st Monday of September), Thanksgiving (4th Thursday of November) and the day after, and Christmas (December 25). If a holiday falls on a non-workday, take the nearest workday as a holiday. In addition, enter 2 rain days per month. Try to distribute these rain days as evenly as possible.

9. The general contractor (GC) will be doing mainly the structural work, using his or her own work-force, but he or she will use the following subcontractors for other work:

NICKNAME	FULL NAME	TYPE OF WORK
ACAL	All Seasons AC & Heating	HVAC[a]
WALL	Wall to Wall	Drywall, stucco, and paint
MART	Master Art Landscape	Site work and landscaping
MASE	Mase & Company	Masonry
ROSS	Ross Carpentry & Framing	Wood framing
PLMX	Plumbing Experts	Plumbing
RABT	Rabbit-the-Roofer	Roofing
TACO	Tile and Carpet Co., Inc.	Flooring
WINT	Windows & Doors NT	Doors and windows
ZAPP	Zapp Electric Co.	Electrical

[a]Heating, ventilation, and air-conditioning.

10. Four areas are designated in the project: ALL (for all of the project), 1ST (for first-floor activities), 2ND (for second-floor activities), and ROOF (for roof activities).

ACTIVITY ID	ACTIVITY TITLE	DURATION (days)	IPA[a]	REL. TYPE[b]	LAG (days)	RESP[c].	AREA
1000	NTP[d]	—	—			GC	ALL
1010	Mobilization	3	1000			GC	ALL
1020	Clear & Grub	12	1010			GC	ALL
1030	Excavation	7	1020	SS	4	GC	ALL
1040	Foundation	15	1030	SS	3	GC	ALL
			1030	FF	1		
1050	Fill, Compact, and Treat Soil	3	1040			GC	ALL
1060	1st-Floor Plumbing Rough-In	3	1050			PLMX	1ST
1070	SOG	4	1060			GC	1ST
1080	1st-Floor Columns	7	1050			GC	1ST
1090	1st-Floor External CMU Walls	10	1070			MASE	1ST
1100	1st-Floor Internal CMU Walls	14	1070			MASE	1ST
1110	2nd-Floor Suspended Slab	8	1080, 1090, 1100			GC	2ND
1120	2nd-Floor Plumbing Rough-In	3	1110	SS	1	PLMX	2ND
			1110	FF	− 1[e]		
1130	1st-Floor Electrical Rough-In	4	1090, 1100, 1280	SS	2	ZAPP	1ST
			1090, 1100, 1280	FF	2		
1140	1st-Floor HVAC Ductwork/ Rough-In	6	1110			ACAL	1ST
1150	1st-Floor Door & Window	5	1090, 1100, 1280	SS		WINT	1ST
			1090, 1100, 1280	FF			
1160	2nd-Floor Columns	7	1110		3	GC	2ND
1170	2nd-Floor External CMU Walls	12	1110			MASE	2ND
1180	2nd-Floor Internal CMU Walls	16	1110		2	MASE	2ND
1190	Roof Trusses	8	1160, 1170, 1180			ROSS	ROOF
1200	2nd-Floor Electrical Rough-In	4	1170, 1180, 1280	SS	2	ZAPP	2ND
			1170, 1180, 1280	FF	2		
1210	2nd-Floor HVAC Ductwork/ Rough-In	6	1190			ACAL	2ND
1220	2nd-Floor Door & Window Frames	5	1170, 1180, 1280	SS		WINT	2ND
			1170, 1180, 1280	FF			
1230	Roof Sheathing	5	1190			ROSS	ROOF

(continued)

ACTIVITY ID	ACTIVITY TITLE	DURATION (days)	IPA[a]	REL. TYPE[b]	LAG (days)	RESP[c].	AREA
1240	Roof Felt	1	1230			RABT	ROOF
1250	Building Dry-In[f]	—	1240			GC	ALL
1260	Soffit & Fascia	3	1250			ROSS	ROOF
1265	Roof Shingles	6	1240			RABT	ROOF
1270	Roof Insulation	2	1250			ROSS	ROOF
1280	Internal Partition Framing	12	1250			ROSS	ALL
1290	1st Floor: Hang Doors & Windows	10	1150, 1280			WINT	1ST
1300	1st-Floor Drywall	8	1280			WALL	1ST
1310	1st-Floor HVAC Air Handler	5	1140, 1300			ACAL	1ST
1320	1st-Floor Suspended Ceiling	8	1300			WALL	1ST
1330	1st-Floor Plumbing: Install Fixtures	2	1060, 1300			PLMX	1ST
1340	1st-Floor Paint/Wall Covering	10	1320	SS	4	WALL	1ST
			1330				
1350	1st-Floor Electrical Finish	6	1130, 1320			ZAPP	1ST
1360	1st-Floor Flooring	12	1340, 1350			TACO	1ST
1370	2nd Floor: Hang Doors & Windows	10	1220, 1280			WINT	2ND
1380	2nd-Floor Drywall	8	1300			WALL	2ND
1390	2nd-Floor HVAC Air Handler	5	1210, 1380			ACAL	2ND
1400	2nd-Floor Suspended Ceiling	8	1270, 1380			WALL	2ND
1410	2nd-Floor Plumbing: Install Fixtures	2	1120, 1380			PLMX	2ND
1420	2nd-Floor Paint/Wall Covering	11	1400	SS	4	WALL	2ND
			1410				
1430	2nd-Floor Electrical Finish	6	1200, 1400			ZAPP	2ND
1440	HVAC: Install Equipment	1	1310, 1390			ACAL	ALL
1450	2nd-Floor Flooring	10	1420, 1430			TACO	2ND
1460	Stucco & Paint to Ext. Walls	8	1260			WALL	ALL
1470	Site Work	15	1020, 1090	g		MART	ALL
1480	Plumbing Finish	2	1330, 1410			PLMX	ALL
1490	HVAC Thermostat & Test	1	1350, 1430, 1440			ACAL	ALL
1500	Electrical Final	4	1340, 1350, 1420, 1430			ZAPP	ALL

ACTIVITY ID	ACTIVITY TITLE	DURATION (days)	IPA[a]	REL. TYPE[b]	LAG (days)	RESP[c].	AREA
1510	Building Cleanup	2	1265, 1290, 1360, 1370, 1450, 1460, 1480, 1490, 1500			GC	ALL
1520	Final Check/CO[h]	1	1470, 1510			GC	ALL

[a]Immediately preceding activity.
[b]Relationship type: SS, start to start; FF, finish to finish. If blank, the relationship is FS, finish to start.
[c]Responsibility.
[d]Notice to Proceed. Make this activity a start milestone.
[e]The negative lag means 2nd-Floor Plumbing Rough-In must finish 1 day before completion of 2nd-Floor Slab. Note also that the start of this activity lags 1 day behind the start of the slab activity. This makes the plumbing activity completely contained within the slab activity.
[f]Make this activity a finish milestone.
[g]Insert a constraint so that Site Work will not finish till about 1 week before the end of the entire project.
[h]**Certificate of occupancy.**

Assignment 1

Do the following:

1. Create the project and call it "Tampa Office Building–01."* You may choose the name you like. Enter the specified start date. Enter the nonworkdays in the calendar. Enter the Responsibility and Area codes and values.
2. Enter all the activities listed in the preceding table, along with their information (duration, relationships, lag, responsibility, and area).
3. Schedule the project. Make sure there are no errors. Check all dates.
4. Determine the calculated finish date. Go back to the Site Work activity and put in the appropriate constraint.
5. Schedule again. Print the scheduling report. As an option for a better-looking report, save the report, then open it in your word processor. Work on improving its looks.

---

*If you are using Primavera Project Planner (P3), you must select a name with four characters. You may choose TOB0.

6. Print the following:

   a. The scheduling report. Record the expected finish date (should be 11-MAR-05) for use in the next assignments.

   b. A tabular report listing all activities, ordered by Activity ID. Compare this with the preceding table to make sure nothing is missing.

   c. A tabular report listing all activities, ordered by ES (early start), TF (total float). This report shows all early and late dates and total float.

   d. A tabular report similar to the previous one. Mask late dates and total float. Check if the program automatically renames early dates as scheduled dates. If not, do so yourself.

   e. A tabular report for activities scheduled to start during the month of September 2004.

   f. A bar chart showing all activities, organized by Area, ordered by ES, TF.

   g. A bar chart showing all activities, organized by Responsibility, ordered by ES, TF.

   h. A bar chart showing only critical or near-critical ($TF \leq 3$) activities. Do not organize. Sort by ES, TF. Display relationships.

   i. A logic diagram. In each box (node), show the activity ID; also show the early dates, the late dates, and the original duration. You may have to work on the size of the box so that the writing inside is legible and the report is not enormous.

   j. A logic diagram for the activities under the electrical subcontractor only.

7. Make at least one backup copy of the project on an external medium (e.g., floppy disk, CD, flash drive).

COST LOADING

In this exercise, the GC is cost loading his or her schedule but will follow two approaches. For self-performed activities, the GC will resource load them (i.e., assign the proper amount of labor and equipment, plus add the cost of materials, if any).* For subcontracted activities, the GC will add only the cost of these activities (no resource loading).

---

*In some computer scheduling programs, this must also be achieved by adding a resource called *Lump Sum,* which is used for cash amounts only.

| ACTIVITY ID | ACTIVITY TITLE | RESOURCES[a] | | | | COST[b] |
		LABORER	FOREMAN	CARPENTER	EXCAVATOR	($)
1000	NTP	—	—	—	—	0
1010	Mobilization	3	1	—	1	2,000
1020	Clear & Grub	4	1	—	2	0
1030	Excavation	3	1	—	1	0
1040	Foundation	3	1	2	1	5,000
1050	Fill, Compact, and Treat Soil	2	1	—	1	1,000
1060	1st-Floor Plumbing Rough-In					2,500
1070	SOG	2	1	1	—	1,500
1080	1st-Floor Columns	2	1	2	—	1,200
1090	1st-Floor External CMU Walls					9,200
1100	1st-Floor Internal CMU Walls					7,800
1110	2nd-Floor Suspended Slab	2	1	2	—	3,000
1120	2nd-Floor Plumbing Rough-In					2,500
1130	1st-Floor Electrical Rough-In					6,000
1140	1st-Floor HVAC Ductwork/Rough-In					7,000
1150	1st-floor Door & Window Frames					3,500
1160	2nd-Floor Columns	2	1	1	—	1,200
1170	2nd-Floor External CMU Walls					11,500
1180	2nd-Floor Internal CMU Walls					8,500
1190	Roof Trusses					10,000
1200	2nd-Floor Electrical Rough-In					6,000
1210	2nd-Floor HVAC Ductwork/Rough-In					7,000
1220	2nd-Floor Door & Window Frames					2,600
1230	Roof Sheathing					3,500
1240	Roof Felt					400
1250	Building Dry-In	—	—	—	—	0
1260	Soffit & Fascia					2,500
1265	Roof Shingles	—	—	—	—	8,000
1270	Roof Insulation					4,000
1280	Internal Partition Framing					4,500
1290	1st Floor: Hang Doors & Windows					5,200

(continued)

| ACTIVITY ID | ACTIVITY TITLE | RESOURCES[a] | | | | COST[b] |
		LABORER	FOREMAN	CARPENTER	EXCAVATOR	($)
1300	1st-Floor Drywall					6,500
1310	1st-Floor HVAC Air Handler					4,000
1320	1st-Floor Suspended Ceiling					7,500
1330	1st-Floor Plumbing: Install Fixtures	—	—	—	—	7,500
1340	1st-Floor Paint/Wall Covering					5,700
1350	1st-Floor Electrical Finish					15,000
1360	1st-Floor Flooring					11,000
1370	2nd Floor: Hang Doors & Windows					4,200
1380	2nd-Floor Drywall					7,000
1390	2nd-Floor HVAC Air Handler					4,000
1400	2nd-Floor Suspended Ceiling					7,500
1410	2nd-Floor Plumbing: Install Fixtures					7,500
1420	2nd-Floor Paint/Wall Covering					5,400
1430	2nd-Floor Electrical Finish					17,000
1440	HVAC: Install Equipment					22,000
1450	2nd-Floor Flooring					8,500
1460	Stucco & Paint to Ext. Walls					7,000
1470	Site Work					30,000
1480	Plumbing Finish					4,500
1490	HVAC Thermostat & Test					5,000
1500	Electrical Final					9,500
1510	Building Cleanup	3	1	—	—	200
1520	Final Check/CO	1	1	—	—	0

[a]Resources for the GC's self-performed activities. The author has used only three labor categories and one equipment category for simplicity.

[b]When used for self-performed activities, cost reflects the GC's materials cost only (total cost excluding labor and equipment). For subcontracted work, cost includes all expenses.

Assignment 2

Do the following:

1. Make a copy of the Tampa Office Building–01 project. Call it "Tampa Office Building–02." Add all the information mentioned in the preceding table to the schedule.

2. Print the following reports:

   a. A tabular report showing the quantity of each resource used by each activity. You may need to use a filter to select activities with resources (Responsibility = GC).

   b. A tabular report showing the cost (in dollars) for all activities. Organize by Responsibility.

   c. A tabular report showing the cost (in dollars) for all activities. Summarize by Responsibility.

   d. A tabular report showing cost per month. Organize by Responsibility.

UPDATING THE PROJECT

On 9/1/04, the project manager is doing the first update, with Data date = 8/31/04 and the following information:

Activities 1000 NTP and 1010 Mobilization were finished on time.

Activity 1020 Clear & Grub started on time. It finished on 8/27/04.

Activity 1030 Excavation started on 8/16/04. As a result of unexpected hard soil, the contractor had to acquire different equipment. Excavation was finished on 8/27/04.

Activity 1040 Foundation started on 8/19/04. As of the data date, the percent complete for this activity is 44%. The expected remaining duration is 10 days.

Activity 1110 2nd-Floor Suspended Slab was modified by the engineer and will require 10 days' duration.

Assignment 3

Do the following:

1. Make a copy of the Tampa Office Building–01 project. Call it "Tampa Office Building–03."

2. In the new copy, update activity progress according to the preceding list. Schedule the project with new Data date = 31-AUG-04.

3. Print the following reports:

   a. A tabular report listing all activities, ordered by ES, TF. Note that every finished event has one date (i.e., actual date) instead of the range (Early – Late) it had before. Also, float disappears from any finished activity.

   b. A bar chart showing all activities, organized by Responsibility, ordered by ES, TF. Note how a new vertical line now separates completed items from future items. This line represents the data date.

4. Now go back to the project data (function name differs depending on your software) and assign a finish date equal to the date you originally obtained in assignment 1 (11-MAR-05).

5. Reprint the tabular report from step 3a. Note the negative float that appeared with many activities. Print this report.

6. Print a report similar to the previous one, but apply a filter to include only activities with negative float.

CHANGE ORDER

The owner issued a change order to add a vault. The vault will be built on the first floor but will require a thickened SOG and concrete walls. The additional work will include the following new and modified activities:

ACTIVITY ID	ACTIVITY TITLE	DURATION (days)	IPA	REL. TYPE	LAG (days)	RESP.
1070	SOG	5	1060			GC
1080	1st-Floor Columns	7	1050			GC
1085	FRP Vault Walls	6	1070			GC
			1080	FF		GC
1087	Vault Door	2	1085			WINT
1110	2nd-Floor Suspended Slab	8	1080, 1085, 1090, 1100			GC
1300	1st-Floor Drywall	8	1087, 1280			WALL

In addition to the preceding information, the following table provides the resources and costs for the new and affected activities:

ACTIVITY ID	ACTIVITY TITLE	RESOURCES				COST ($)
		LABORER	FOREMAN	CARPENTER	EXCAVATOR	
1070	SOG	2	1	1	—	2,000
1080	1st-Floor Columns	2	1	1	—	900
1085	FRP Vault Walls	2	1	1	—	800
1087	Vault Door	—	—	—	—	3,000
1110	2nd-Floor Suspended Slab	2	1	2	—	3,000
1300	1st-Floor Drywall					7,000

Assignment 4

Do the following:

1. Make a copy of the Tampa Office Building–01 project. Call it "Tampa Office Building–04."
2. Add the new activities listed in the previous table and make any needed adjustments to existing activities.
3. Schedule the project and record the calculated finish date; compare it with the date you obtained in assignment 1. The difference, if any, is due to the change order.
4. Print the following:

   a. The scheduling report.
   b. A tabular report listing all activities, ordered by Activity ID.
   c. A tabular report listing all activities, ordered by ES, TF. Make sure you show all early and late dates, and total float.
   d. A bar chart showing all activities, organized by Responsibility, ordered by ES, TF.
   e. A tabular report showing the quantity of each resource used by each activity.
   f. A tabular report showing the cost (in dollars) for all activities. Organize by Responsibility. Reschedule the project.

RESOURCE LEVELING

Assignment 5

Using the resource information given in assignment 2, do the following:

1. Make a copy of the Tampa Office Building–01 project. Call it "Tampa Office Building–05."
2. Assign resources to the appropriate activities (as mentioned in assignment 2).
3. Apply a filter to include only the GC's activities.
4. Print a resource usage profile for each of the four resources (i.e., units of the resource used per day).
5. Level the Laborer resource to a limit of 7 without delaying the project. Print another resource usage profile for Laborer.
6. If the GC has only 6 laborers, what solution would you suggest? (Print a report.)
7. Level the Foreman resource to a limit of 2 without delaying the project. Print another resource usage profile for Foreman. (Print a report.)
8. On what date do you need to have carpenters on the job site? What is the minimum number of carpenters you can hire without delaying the project?
9. Can you help the contractor find a plan to do the job with only 2 excavators? Outline your plan. (Print a report.)

SCHEDULE COMPRESSION

Assignment 6

Assume the cost of overhead for the project is $500 per day. This cost is not included in the following table, so it must be added manually after you calculate the project duration. Do the following:

1. Make a copy of the Tampa Office Building–01 project. Call it "Tampa Office Building–06."
2. Enter the normal cost for each activity as shown in the following table. Calculate the total cost (with normal duration).

Note: Some of this assignment will force a split of some activities (i.e., an interruption and resumption at a later date). In most cases, you must do this manually.

ACTIVITY ID	ACTIVITY TITLE	DURATION (DAYS)		COST ($)	
		NORMAL	CRASH	NORMAL	CRASH
1000	NTP	—	—	—	—
1010	Mobilization	3	2	4,000	5,000
1020	Clear & Grub	12	6	12,000	16,000
1030	Excavation	7	5	14,000	17,020
1040	Foundation	15	11	22,000	30,000
1050	Fill, Compact, and Treat Soil	3	2	4,000	4,500
1060	1st-Floor Plumbing Rough-In	3	2	2,500	2,800
1070	SOG	4	3	10,000	11,000
1080	1st-Floor Columns	7	5	7,000	7,800
1090	1st-Floor External CMU Walls	10	6	9,200	11,800
1100	1st-Floor Internal CMU Walls	14	8	7,800	9,200
1110	2nd-Floor Suspended Slab	8	6	12,000	13,600
1120	2nd-Floor Plumbing Rough-In	3	2	2,500	2,800
1130	1st-Floor Electrical Rough-In	4	2	6,000	7,400
1140	1st-Floor HVAC Ductwork/Rough-In	6	4	7,000	7,500
1150	1st-Floor Door & Window Frames	5	3	3,500	4,100
1160	2nd-Floor Columns	7	5	7,000	7,800
1170	2nd-Floor External CMU Walls	12	7	11,500	13,300
1180	2nd-Floor Internal CMU Walls	16	9	8,500	10,100
1190	Roof Trusses	8	6	10,000	11,000
1200	2nd-Floor Electrical Rough-In	4	3	6,000	6,200
1210	2nd-Floor HVAC Ductwork/Rough-In	6	4	7,000	7,500
1220	2nd-Floor Door & Window Frames	5	3	2,600	3,000
1230	Roof Sheathing	5	3	3,500	4,100
1240	Roof Felt	1	1	400	400
1260	Soffit & Fascia	3	2	2,500	3,000
1265	Roof Shingles	6	4	8,000	10,000
1270	Roof Insulation	2	1	4,000	4,200
1280	Internal Partition Framing	12	9	4,500	5,300
1290	1st Floor: Hang Doors & Windows	10	5	5,200	6,100
1300	1st-Floor Drywall	8	6	6,500	6,900
1310	1st-Floor HVAC Air Handler	5	3	4,000	4,400
1320	1st-Floor Suspended Ceiling	8	5	7,500	8,000
1330	1st-Floor Plumbing: Install Fixtures	2	2	7,500	7,500
1340	1st-Floor Paint/Wall Covering	10	6	5,700	6,300
1350	1st-Floor Electrical Finish	6	4	15,000	15,800
1360	1st-Floor Flooring	12	8	11,000	12,000
1370	2nd Floor: Hang Doors & Windows	10	5	4,200	4,800
1380	2nd-Floor Drywall	8	6	7,000	7,600

(continued)

ACTIVITY ID	ACTIVITY TITLE	DURATION (DAYS)		COST ($)	
		NORMAL	CRASH	NORMAL	CRASH
1390	2nd-Floor HVAC Air Handler	5	3	4,000	4,400
1400	2nd-Floor Suspended Ceiling	8	5	7,500	8,000
1410	2nd-Floor Plumbing: Install Fixtures	2	2	7,500	7,500
1420	2nd-Floor Paint/Wall Covering	11	7	5,400	6,000
1430	2nd-Floor Electrical Finish	6	4	17,000	17,400
1440	HVAC: Install Equipment	1	1	22,000	22,000
1450	2nd-Floor Flooring	10	7	8,500	9,100
1460	Stucco & Paint to Ext. Walls	8	6	7,000	7,800
1470	Site Work	15	11	30,000	32,000
1480	Plumbing Finish	2	2	4,500	4,500
1490	HVAC Thermostat & Test	1	1	5,000	5,000
1500	Electrical Final	4	3	9,500	9,700
1510	Building Cleanup	2	1	1,000	1,400
1520	Final Check/CO	1	1	400	400

3. Accelerate the project by 2 days. When accelerating by 2 days, you may have to do so 1 day at a time. Record the total cost. When compressing an activity, reflect the increase in its direct cost as an extra cost (acceleration cost) in its budget in the scheduling program. You may have to create an Excel spreadsheet to calculate the total cost.

4. Accelerate the project by an additional 2 days. Record the total cost.

5. Accelerate the project 1 extra day at a time. Determine the least cost and least-cost duration. Print a tabular report and a bar chart displaying all activities, along with their durations, organized by Responsibility.

6. Keep accelerating until the project is completely crashed. Determine the crash duration and the associated crash cost.

7. On a separate page, record the following:

   a. Normal duration (number of days and date) and normal cost

   b. Least-cost duration and least cost

   c. Crash duration and crash cost

SCHEDULE COMPRESSION 2

Assignment 7

The GC is trying to accelerate the schedule by requiring certain crews to work on Saturdays. Most likely, this will

*increase the indirect cost — because of overtime pay — but we
will not calculate cost in this exercise. Do the following:*

1. Make a copy of the Tampa Office Building–01 project. Call it "Tampa Office Building–07."
2. Create a new calendar called "Six-Workday Week." Maintain the same holidays and rain days as on the regular calendars.
3. Choose certain activities to switch to the "Six-Workday Week" calendar. Start with critical activities. Make sure this change will contribute to an earlier project completion date. This process will start simple but become more complicated as you accelerate the schedule.
4. Keep working on the acceleration until the project calculated finish date is no later than 20-FEB-05.
5. Print a tabular report and a bar chart. Add a column in each report showing the calendar.

DELAY CLAIM 1: UNFORESEEN CONDITIONS

While excavating, the contractor discovered contaminated soil that forced him or her to change plans. He or she incurred an extra cost because of the hauling and disposal of the contaminated soil. In addition, excavation took 12 workdays rather than 7 workdays. The contractor issued a claim to the owner, requesting the following:

1. A 1-week (5-workdays) time extension.
2. An extra $23,600 (to cover extra excavating, hauling, and disposing of contaminated soil, plus the GC's overhead for the extra week of duration).

Assignment 8

*Do you think the contractor's claims are legitimate? Analyze
both claims (time and cost) separately. Explain your answers.*

DELAY CLAIM 2: CHANGE IN OWNER'S REQUIREMENTS

(*Note:* This delay claim is independent of delay claim 1.)

The owner decided to add an awning at the building entrance. It will require three activities:

ACTIVITY ID	ACTIVITY TITLE	DURATION	IPA (days)	REL. TYPE	LAG (days)	RESP.	COST ($)
1103	Embed Awning Attachments to Wall	1	1090	FF		MASE	500
1105	Decorative Posts (to support awning)	1	1070			AWNE	2,000
1107	Hang Awning	1	1103, 1105, 1460			AWNE	7,500

Assignment 9

Do the following:

1. Make a copy of the Tampa Office Building–01 project. Call it "Tampa Office Building–09."
2. Add the preceding activities to the project. You must add AWNE as a new Responsibility code with the description "Annie's Awnings." Make activity 1510, Building Cleanup, a successor to activity 1107. Also, activity 1107 becomes an additional predecessor to activity 1470, Site Work.

The GC is requesting, in addition to the cost of the change order ($10,000), a 3-day time extension because the change order "disrupted his plans and affected other activities." The owner disputed the time extension.

3. Argue from the contractor's viewpoint: Why is this a legitimate request? What supporting argument would you present? Make any necessary assumptions to support your point (e.g., contract language, timing of the change order).
4. Argue from the owner's viewpoint: Why is this request unacceptable? What supporting argument would you present? Make any necessary assumptions to support your point.

Sample Reports

The sample reports in this appendix were produced by using Primavera P3e/c and Primavera's SureTrak Project Manager software. In these reports, an asterisk next to a date indicates a constraint.

TABULAR REPORTS

REPORT 1:   Report 1 (Figure B.1) is a list of activities with information such as the original duration, remaining duration, percent complete, early start, early finish, late start, late finish, and total float.

For new projects that have not started yet, the remaining duration and percent complete may be omitted. Note that when an event (start or finish) happens, the early and late dates for the event are replaced with the actual date (followed by *A* in the report). Obviously, total float disappears from completed activities.

Milestones are represented by a single date: start or finish.

TAMPA OFFICE BUILDING—UPDATE AS OF 5/31/04

RESPONSIBILITY

ACTIVITY ID	ACTIVITY TITLE	ORIG DUR	REM DUR	%	EARLY START	EARLY FINISH	LATE START	LATE FINISH	TOTAL FLOAT
General Contractor		**96**	**57**		**01-Apr-04 A**	**17-Aug-04**	**31-May-04**	**17-Aug-04**	**0**
0990	NTP	0	0	100	01-Apr-04 A				
1000	Mobilization	2	0	100	01-Apr-04 A	02-Apr-04 A			
1010	Clear & Grub	8	1	87.5	06-Apr-04 A	31-May-04	31-May-04	31-May-04	0
1020	Excavation	7	0	100	12-Apr-04 A	27-Apr-04 A			
1030	Foundation	15	0	100	19-Apr-04 A	12-May-04 A			
1050	SOG	3	0	100	17-May-04 A	31-May-04 A			
1060	1st-Floor Columns	7	0	100	20-May-04 A	31-May-04 A			
1070	2nd-Floor Suspended Slab	5	1	80	27-May-04 A	31-May-04	01-Jun-04	01-Jun-04	1
1130	2nd-Floor Columns	7	7	0	04-Jun-04	14-Jun-04	07-Jun-04	15-Jun-04	1
1140	Roof Slab	5	5	0	15-Jun-04	21-Jun-04	16-Jun-04	22-Jun-04	1
1210	Building Dry-In	0	0	0		05-Jul-04		17-Aug-04	31
1410	Building Cleanup	2	2	0	13-Aug-04	16-Aug-04	13-Aug-04	16-Aug-04	0
1420	Final Check	1	1	0	17-Aug-04	17-Aug-04	17-Aug-04	17-Aug-04	0
Masonry & Associates		**32**	**23**		**18-May-04 A**	**30-Jun-04**	**31-May-04**	**09-Aug-04**	**28**
1100	1st-Floor Int. Walls	14	10	28.57	18-May-04 A	11-Jun-04	08-Jun-04	21-Jun-04	6
1090	1st-Floor Ext. Walls	10	7	30	20-May-04 A	08-Jun-04	31-May-04	08-Jun-04	0
1160	2nd-Floor Int. Walls	15	15	0	03-Jun-04	23-Jun-04	04-Jun-04	24-Jun-04	1

ID	Activity Description	OD	RD	%	Early Start	Early Finish	Late Start	Late Finish	TF
1150	2nd-Floor Ext. Walls	12	12	0	09-Jun-04	24-Jun-04	09-Jun-04	24-Jun-04	0
1190	Roof CMU Parapets	4	4	0	25-Jun-04	30-Jun-04	04-Aug-04	09-Aug-04	28
Plumbing Expert		**58**	**43**		**12-May-04 A**	**28-Jul-04**	**21-Jul-04**	**03-Aug-04**	**4**
1040	1st-Floor Plumbing Rough-In	3	0	100	12-May-04 A	14-May-04 A		27-Jul-04	40
1080	2nd-Floor Plumbing Rough-In	3	2	30	31-May-04 A	02-Jun-04	23-Jul-04	27-Jul-04	9
1280	1st-Floor Plumbing Finish	5	5	0	08-Jul-04	14-Jul-04	21-Jul-04	27-Jul-04	4
1360	2nd-Floor Plumbing Finish	5	5	0	22-Jul-04	28-Jul-04	28-Jul-04	03-Aug-04	4
Zapp Electrical Company		**37**	**37**		**14-Jun-04**	**03-Aug-04**	**19-Jul-04**	**03-Aug-04**	**0**
1110	1st-Floor Electrical Rough-In	4	4	0	14-Jun-04	17-Jun-04	19-Jul-04	22-Jul-04	25
1170	2nd-Floor Electrical Rough-In	4	4	0	25-Jun-04	30-Jun-04	23-Jul-04	28-Jul-04	20
1270	1st-Floor Electrical Finish	4	4	0	15-Jul-04	20-Jul-04	23-Jul-04	28-Jul-04	6
1350	2nd-Floor Electrical Finish	4	4	0	29-Jul-04	03-Aug-04	29-Jul-04	03-Aug-04	0
AC & Heating All Season		**38**	**38**		**14-Jun-04**	**04-Aug-04**	**27-Jul-04**	**12-Aug-04**	**6**
1120	1st-Floor HVAC Ductwork	6	6	0	14-Jun-04	21-Jun-04	27-Jul-04	03-Aug-04	31
1180	2nd-Floor HVAC Ductwork	6	6	0	25-Jun-04	02-Jul-04	30-Jul-04	06-Aug-04	25
1230	1st-Floor HVAC Finish	3	3	0	30-Jun-04	02-Jul-04	04-Aug-04	06-Aug-04	25
1310	2nd-Floor HVAC Finish	3	3	0	13-Jul-04	15-Jul-04	09-Aug-04	11-Aug-04	19
1370	HVAC Test	1	1	0	04-Aug-04	04-Aug-04	12-Aug-04	12-Aug-04	6
Rabbit-the-Roofer		**3**	**3**		**01-Jul-04**	**05-Jul-04**	**10-Aug-04**	**12-Aug-04**	**28**
1200	Roofing	3	3	0	01-Jul-04	05-Jul-04	10-Aug-04	12-Aug-04	28
Windows & Doors NT		**21**	**21**		**14-Jun-04**	**12-Jul-04**	**22-Jun-04**	**12-Jul-04**	**0**
1220	1st-Floor Doors & Windows	12	12	0	14-Jun-04	29-Jun-04	22-Jun-04	07-Jul-04	6
1300	2nd-Floor Doors & Windows	12	12	0	25-Jun-04	12-Jul-04	25-Jun-04	12-Jul-04	0

(continued)

ACTIVITY ID	ACTIVITY TITLE	ORIG DUR	REM DUR	%	EARLY START	EARLY FINISH	LATE START	LATE FINISH	TOTAL FLOAT
Stucco & Paint Works		**29**	**29**		**18-Jun-04**	**28-Jul-04**	**28-Jun-04**	**12-Aug-04**	**11**
1240	1st-Floor Drywall	8	8	0	18-Jun-04	29-Jun-04	28-Jun-04	07-Jul-04	6
1250	1st-Floor Paint/Wall Covering	10	10	0	24-Jun-04	07-Jul-04	02-Jul-04	15-Jul-04	6
1390	Stucco & Paint to Ext. Walls	8	8	0	25-Jun -04	06-Jul-04	03-Aug-04	12-Aug-04	27
1320	2nd-Floor Drywall	8	8	0	01-Jul-04	12-Jul-04	01-Jul-04	12-Jul-04	0
1330	2nd-Floor Paint/Wall Covering	11	11	0	07-Jul-04	21-Jul-04	07-Jul-04	21-Jul-04	0
1260	1st-Floor Suspended Ceiling	5	5	0	08-Jul-04	14-Jul-04	16-Jul-04	22-Jul-04	6
1340	2nd-Floor Suspended Ceiling	5	5	0	22-Jul-04	28-Jul-04	22-Jul-04	28-Jul-04	0
Tile & Carpet Co.		**17**	**17**		**21-Jul-04**	**12-Aug-04**	**04-Aug-04**	**12-Aug-04**	**0**
1290	1st-Floor Flooring	7	7	0	21-Jul-04	29-Jul-04	04-Aug-04	12-Aug-04	10
1380	2nd-Floor Flooring	7	7	0	04-Aug-04	12-Aug-04	04-Aug-04	12-Aug-04	0
Master Art for Landscape		**15**	**15**		**16-Jul-04**	**06-Aug-04**	**27-Jul-04**	**16-Aug-04**	**7**
1400	Site Work	15	15	0	16-Jul-04	06-Aug-04	27-Jul-04	16-Aug-04	7

FIGURE B.1 Report 1. Asterisk indicates a constraint on the activity.

Activity codes may be used to group (organize) activities. In this case, we grouped by Responsibility. When grouping, you may use the software Subtotal function, which provides summary information per grouping code at the top of the group (or you may choose the bottom of the group). Note, however, that you must read these subtotals with caution. They include what you see and exclude any activities that were filtered out.

REPORT 2:   Report 2 (Figure B.2) is a list of activities such as those in report 1, but we hid the late start, late finish, and total float. Note that the early start and early finish were renamed as just "Start" and "Finish." We grouped by department (with a subtotal at the bottom) and listed the activity code Responsibility and the calendar that each activity will follow.

REPORT 3:   Report 3 (Figure B.3) is a list of activities with their predecessors and successors. Note that the list does not specify the type of relationship or the lag (if any). Other information may be listed, such as Activity Status.

REPORT 4:   Report 4 (Figure B.4) is an earned value report that shows earned value versus actual and planned costs. Also note the totals.

REPORT 5:   Report 5 (Figure B.5) is a resource analysis showing budgeted units, actual units, and other data per resource.

GRAPHIC REPORTS

REPORT 6:   Report 6 (Figure B.6) is a bar (Gantt) chart that shows the original duration, early dates, late dates, and total float in the tabular section. The bar chart shows the float bar. The user may opt to hide it. The report is grouped by primary code (phase) and secondary code (department).

REPORT 7:   Similar to report 6, report 7 (Figure B.7) has an addition and a deletion. We added the remaining duration and percent complete (since the project has already started) and omitted the late dates and total float. We also hid the float bar in the bar chart section. In both reports 6 and 7, relationship lines may be displayed in the bar chart section.

REPORT 8:   Report 8 (Figure B.8) is a logic diagram grouped by phase. Note that completed activities are shown as boxes with two diagonal lines. Boxes representing in-progress activities are designated with one diagonal line. Activities that have not started do not have diagonal lines.

REPORT 9:   Report 9 (Figure B.9) looks like a tabular report since the bar chart was hidden. The report shows activity status and budget information.

REPORT 10:   Similar to report 9, report 10 (Figure B.10) shows the bar chart. Such a report should be printed on wider paper, or the font size will be too small.

REPORT 11:   Report 11 (Figure B.11) is a bar chart that contains a resource usage profile.

APEX PROJECT – LIST OF ACTIVITIES

DEPARTMENT

ACTIVITY ID	ACTIVITY NAME	ORIG DUR	REM DUR	%	CALENDAR	RESP	START	FINISH
Engineering Department								
CS300	System Design	30	30	0	Conveyor System Calendar 1	MF	01-Apr-03*	12-May-03
CS310	Review and Approve Design	8	8	0	Conveyor System Calendar 1	MF	13-May-03	22-May-03
CS430	Prepare Drawings for Conveyors	10	10	0	Conveyor System Calendar 1	MF	23-May-03	05-Jun-03
CS440	Review and Approve Drawings for Conveyors	7	7	0	Conveyor System Calendar 1	MF	06-Jun-03	17-Jun-03
BA400	Design Building Addition	23	0	100	Office Building Addition Calendar 1	GG	04-Jun-02 A	04-Jul-02 A
BA469	Assemble Technical Data for Heat Pump	3	0	100	Office Building Addition Calendar 1	GG	18-Jul-02 A	22-Jul-02 A
BA470	Review Technical Data on Heat Pump	10	0	100	Office Building Addition Calendar 1	GG	23-Jul-02 A	05-Aug-02 A
BA501	Review and Approve Designs	9	0	100	Office Building Addition Calendar 1	GG	05-Jul-02 A	17-Jul-02 A
BA530	Review and Approve Brick Samples	10	0	100	Office Building Addition Calendar 1	JN	23-Jul-02 A	05-Aug-02 A
BA560	Review and Approve Flooring	10	0	100	Office Building Addition Calendar 1	LH	30-Jul-02 A	12-Aug-02 A
AS100	Define System Requirements	14	0	100	Automated System Calendar 1	KL	04-Jun-02 A	21-Jun-02 A
AS101	System Design	30	0	100	Automated System Calendar 1	KL	24-Jun-02 A	02-Aug-02 A
AS102	Approve System Design	5	0	100	Automated System Calendar 1	KL	05-Aug-02 A	09-Aug-02 A
AS204	Prepare Drawings for Temp. Control Equipment	14	0	100	Automated System Calendar 1	KL	22-Jul-02 A	08-Aug-02 A
AS205	Review and Approve Temp. Control Equipment	5	0	100	Automated System Calendar 1	KL	09-Aug-02 A	15-Aug-02 A
AS216	Prepare Drawings for System Controller	4	0	100	Automated System Calendar 1	KL	22-Jul-02 A	25-Jul-02 A
AS217	Review and Approve System Controller	5	0	100	Automated System Calendar 1	KL	26-Jul-02 A	02-Aug-02 A
	Subtotal	**270**	**55**				**04-Jun-02 A**	**17-Jun-03 A**

FIGURE B.2 Report 2. Asterisk indicates a restraint on the activity.

LIST OF ACTIVITIES WITH PREDECESSORS & SUCCESSORS

ACTIVITY ID	ACTIVITY NAME	ORIG DUR	ACTIVITY STATUS	PREDECESSORS	SUCCESSORS
BA702	Begin Structural Phase	0	Completed	BA710	
BA712	Floor Decking	14	Completed	BA710	BA730
BA720	Erect Stairwell and Elevator Walls	10	Completed	BA730	BA732, BA860
BA730	Concrete First Floor	15	Completed	BA712	BA720, BA731, BA810, BA735
BA731	Concrete Basement Slab	10	Completed	BA730	BA732
BA732	Structure Complete	0	Completed	BA720, BA731	BA750
BA735	Concrete Second Floor	15	Completed	BA730	
BA741	Close-In Phase Begins	0	Not Started	BA750	
BA750	Brick Exterior Walls	7	Not Started	BA600, BA732	BA741, BA770, BA780
BA770	Install Door and Window Frames	1	Not Started	BA750	BA790
BA780	Insulation and Built-Up Roofing	10	Not Started	BA750, BA790	BA800
BA790	Install Exterior Doors and Windows	2	Not Started	BA770	BA780, BA800
BA800	Building Enclosed	0	Not Started	BA780, BA790	BA830, BA831, BA850, BA890, BA913
BA809	Rough-In Phase Begins	0	Completed	BA810	
BA810	Set Mechanical and Electrical Equipment	15	Completed	BA730	BA809, BA820
BA820	Install HVAC Ducts	10	Completed	BA810	BA830, BA840
BA830	Insulate Ducts	2	Not Started	BA800, BA820	BA831
BA831	Set Heat Pump	5	Not Started	BA550, BA800, BA830	BA870, BA983
BA840	Rough-In Plumbing/Piping	1	Not Started	BA820	BA850
BA850	Install Wiring and Cable	15	Not Started	BA800, BA840	BA870
BA860	Install Elevator Rails and Equipment	1	Not Started	BA720	BA880
BA870	Connect Equipment	3	Not Started	BA831, BA850	BA871
BA871	Startup and Test HVAC	1	Not Started	BA870, BA983	BA880

FIGURE B.3 Report 3

352

EARNED VALUE REPORT

WBS

ACTIVITY ID	ACTIVITY NAME	ACTIVITY STATUS	PLANNED COST (BCWS)	ACTUAL COST (ACWP)	EARNED VALUE (BCWS)	COST VARIANCE	VARIANCE AT COMPLETION
Caprini Corporation							
Apex Project							
Apex Construction							
Office Building Addition							
Design and Engineering							
BA400	Design Building Addition	Completed	$5,520.00	$5,520.00	$5,520.00	$0.00	$0.00
BA469	Assemble Technical Data for Heat Pump	Completed	$720.00	$720.00	$720.00	$0.00	$0.00
BA470	Review Technical Data on Heat Pump	Completed	$2,400.00	$2,400.00	$2,400.00	$0.00	$0.00
BA501	Review and Approve Designs	Completed	$0.00	$1,800.00	$0.00	($1,800.00)	($1,800.00)
Subtotal			**$8,640.00**	**$10,440.00**	**$8,640.00**	**($1,800.00)**	**($1,800.00)**
Foundation							
BA630	Begin Building Construction	Completed	$0.00	$0.00	$0.00	$0.00	$0.00
BA640	Site Preparation	Completed	$3,096.00	$532.69	$3,096.00	$2,563.31	$2,563.31
BA650	Excavation	Completed	$1,720.00	$14.58	$1,720.00	$1,705.42	$1,705.42
BA660	Install Underground Water Lines	Completed	$1,320.00	$6.11	$1,320.00	$1,313.89	$1,313.89
BA670	Install Underground Electric Conduit	Completed	$1,280.00	$5.93	$1,280.00	$1,274.07	$1,274.07
BA680	Form/Pour Concrete Footings	Completed	$13,160.00	$394.95	$13,160.00	$12,765.05	$11,965.05
BA681	Concrete Foundation Walls	Completed	$9,960.00	$409.33	$9,960.00	$9,550.67	$8,750.67
BA690	Form and Pour Slab	Completed	$5,940.00	$147.59	$5,940.00	$5,792.41	$5,392.41
BA700	Backfill and Compact Walls	Completed	$728.00	$1.87	$728.00	$726.13	$726.13
BA701	Foundation Phase Complete	Completed	$0.00	$0.00	$0.00	$0.00	$0.00
Subtotal			**$37,204.00**	**$1,513.05**	**$37,204.00**	**$35,690.95**	**$33,690.95**

FIGURE B.4   Report 4

353

APEX PROJECT—RESOURCE CONTROL—SUMMARY BY RESOURCE

RESOURCE ID	BUDGETED UNITS	UNITS % COMPLETE	ACTUAL UNITS	ACTUAL THIS PERIOD UNITS	REMAINING UNITS	AT COMPLETION UNITS
Jeff Young	121.00	100	121.00	-203.00	0.00	121.00
Wendy Resner	562.00	38.71	200.74	-287.26	317.83	518.57
Paul Kim	600.00	86.67	520.00	-60.00	80.00	600.00
Ed Wood	308.00	10.39	32.00	-65.00	276.00	308.00
Oliver Rock	260.00	98.46	256.00	203.00	4.00	260.00
Ace Corp	1,768.00	84.62	1,496.00	1,496.00	272.00	1,768.00
Field Eng-Senior	744.00	22.38	166.47	166.47	577.53	744.00
Field Engineer	439.00	43.41	190.23	190.23	248.00	438.23
Field Eng-Assistant	136.00	23.25	31.62	-0.38	104.38	136.00
Hardware Specialist	223.00	81.89	182.62	182.62	40.38	223.00
Programmer	168.00	0	0.00	0.00	168.00	168.00
Software Engineer	40.00	0	0.00	0.00	40.00	40.00
Elevator Installer	24.00	0	0.00	0.00	24.00	24.00
Electrician	403.00	58.31	235.00	235.00	168.00	403.00
Excavator	240.00	100	240.00	144.00	0.00	240.00
Floor and Carpet Layer	40.00	0	0.00	0.00	40.00	40.00
Finisher	256.00	100	256.00	256.00	0.00	256.00
Finishes Carpenter	328.00	0	0.00	0.00	328.00	328.00
Ironworker	672.00	100	672.00	672.00	0.00	672.00
Laborer-Construction	504.00	79.37	400.00	400.00	104.00	504.00
Mason	136.00	58.82	80.00	80.00	56.00	136.00
Operating Engineer	264.00	75.76	200.00	200.00	64.00	264.00
Plumber	168.00	85.71	144.00	144.00	24.00	168.00
Painter	144.00	0	0.00	0.00	144.00	144.00
Rough Carpenter	400.00	100	400.00	400.00	0.00	400.00
Heating Ventilation & AC Technician	120.00	66.67	80.00	80.00	40.00	120.00
Machinist	48.00	100	48.00	48.00	0.00	48.00
100-ft Crane	8.00	0	0.00	0.00	8.00	8.00
Piping Material	40.00	80	32.00	32.00	8.00	40.00
No Resource ID Name	128.00	0	0.00	0.00	128.00	128.00
Total	—	**64.7**	—	—	—	—

FIGURE B.5 Report 5

Act ID	Description	Orig Dur	Early Start	Early Finish	Late Start	Late Finish	Total Float
Design and Engineering Phase		193	13AUG99	15MAY00	17SEP99	15MAY00	0
Engineering Department							
BA469	Assemble Technical Data for Heat Pump	3	13AUG99	17AUG99	04NOV99	08NOV99	58d
BA470	Review Technical Data on Heat Pumps	10	18AUG99	31AUG99	08NOV99	22NOV99	58d
AS217	Review and Approve System Controller	10	20AUG99	02SEP99	17SEP99	30SEP99	19d
CS900	System Design	40	24JAN00 *	20MAR00	24JAN00	20MAR00	0
CS310	Review and Approve Design	15	21MAR00	10APR00	21MAR00	10APR00	0
CS430	Prepare Drawings for Conveyors	20	11APR00	08MAY00	11APR00	08MAY00	0
CS440	Review and Approve Drawings for	5	09MAY00	15MAY00	09MAY00	15MAY00	0
Procurement Phase		251	20AUG99	15AUG00	01OCT99	15AUG00	0
Engineering Department							
BA530	Review and Approve Brick Samples	10	20AUG99	02SEP99	13OCT99	26OCT99	37d
BA580	Review and Approve Flooring	10	24AUG99	07SEP99	11FEB00	25FEB00	120d
Purchasing Department							
BA411	Prepare and Solicit Bids for Heat Pump	3	01SEP99	03SEP99	23NOV99	29NOV99	58d
BA213	Prepare and Solicit Bids for System	5	03SEP99	10SEP99	01OCT99	07OCT99	19d
BA421	Prepare and Solicit Bids for Brick Exterior	3	03SEP99	08SEP99	27OCT99	29OCT99	37d
BA412	Review Bids for Heat Pump	2	07SEP99	08SEP99	30NOV99	01DEC99	58d
BA407	Prepare and Solicit Bids for Flooring	5	06SEP99	14SEP99	29FEB00	03MAR00	120d
BA413	Award Contract for Heat Pump	1	09SEP99	09SEP99	02DEC99	02DEC99	58d
BA422	Review Bids for Brick	3	09SEP99	13SEP99	01NOV99	03NOV99	37d
BA550	Fabricate and Deliver Heat Pump and	90	10SEP99	17JAN00	03DEC99	07APR00	58d
AS214	Review Bids for System Controller	4	13SEP99	16SEP99	08OCT99	13OCT99	19d
BA423	Award Contract for Brick	4	14SEP99	14SEP99	04NOV99	04NOV99	37d
BA408	Review Bids for Flooring	3	15SEP99	17SEP99	09MAR00	09MAR00	120d
BA600	Deliver Brick	60	15SEP99	09DEC99	05NOV99	31JAN00	37d
AS215	Award Contract for System Controller	1	17SEP99	17SEP99	14OCT99	14OCT99	19d
AS218	Fabricate and Deliver System Controller	60	20SEP99	14DEC99	15OCT99	10JAN00	19d
BA409	Award Contract for Flooring	1	20SEP99	20SEP99	08MAR00	08MAR00	120d

Start date 15JUL99
Finish date 08FEB01
Data date 13AUG99
Run date 22JUN04
Page number 1A
© Primavera Systems, Inc.

Acme Motors
Plant Expansion and Modernization

Legend: Early bar · Early start point · Early finish point · Total float bar · Progress bar

FIGURE B.6 Report 6. Asterisk indicates a restraint on the activity. (Reprinted with permission from Primavera Systems, Inc. Primavera® and P3e/c™ are either trademarks or registered trademarks of Primavera Systems, Inc.)

355

Act ID	Description	Orig Dur	Rem Dur	% Compl	Early Start	Early Finish
Design and Engineering Phase		212	193	47	19JUL99 A	15MAY00
Engineering Department						
BA400	Design Building Addition	20	0	100	19JUL99 A	27AUG99
AS100	Define System Requirements	10	0	100	20JUL99 A	04AUG99
AS101	System Design	20	0	100	03AUG99	31AUG99
BA469	Assemble Technical Data for Heat Pump	3	3	0	13AUG99	17AUG99
AS204	Prepare Drawings for Temp Control	10	0	100	17AUG99	31AUG99
BA470	Review Technical Data on Heat Pumps	10	10	0	18AUG99	31AUG99
AS217	Review and Approve System Controller	10	10	0	20AUG99	02SEP99
AS216	Prepare Drawings for System Controller	10	5	50	23AUG99	19AUG99
BA501	Review and Approve Designs	14	0	100	30AUG99	20SEP99 A
AS102	Approve System Design	10	0	100	31AUG99	13SEP99 A
AS205	Review and Approve Temp Control	5	0	100	31AUG99	13SEP99 A
CS300	System Design	40	40	0	24JAN00 *	20MAR00
CS310	Review and Approve Design	15	15	0	21MAR00	10APR00
CS430	Prepare Drawings for Conveyors	20	20	0	11APR00	08MAY00
CS440	Review and Approve Drawings for	5	5	0	09MAY00	15MAY00
Procurement Phase		256	256	5	20AUG99	15AUG00
Engineering Department						
BAS30	Review and Approve Brick Samples	10	10	0	20AUG99	02SEP99
BA560	Review and Approve Flooring	10	10	0	24AUG99	07SEP99
Purchasing Department						
BA411	Prepare and Solicit Bids for Heat Pump	3	3	0	01SEP99	03SEP99
AS213	Prepare and Solicit Bids for System	5	5	0	03SEP99	10SEP99
BA421	Prepare and Solicit Bids for Brick Exterior	3	3	0	03SEP99	08SEP99
AS200	Prepare and Solicit Bids for Temp Control Equip	5	0	100	07SEP99 A	16SEP99 A
BA412	Review Bids for Heat Pump	2	2	0	07SEP99	08SEP99
BA407	Prepare and Solicit Bids for Flooring	5	5	0	06SEP99	14SEP99
BA413	Award Contract for Heat Pump	1	1	0	09SEP99	09SEP99

Start date 15JUL99
Finish date 08FEB01
Data date 13AUG99
Run date 22JUN04
Page number 1A
© Primavera Systems, Inc.

Acme Motors
Plant Expansion and Modernization

Legend:
Early bar
Early start point
Early finish point
Total float bar
Total float point
Progress bar

FIGURE B.7 Report 7
(Reprinted with permission from Primavera Systems, Inc. Primavera® and P3e/c™ are either trademarks or registered trademarks of Primavera Systems, Inc.)

356

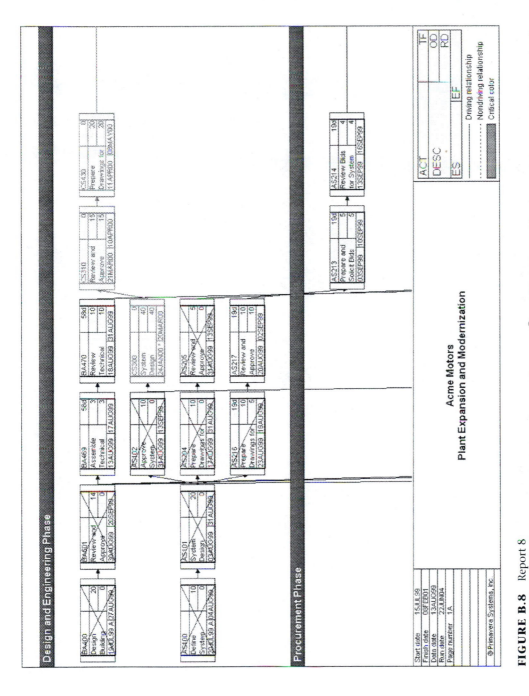

FIGURE B.8 Report 8

(Reprinted with permission from Primavera Systems, Inc. Primavera® and P3e/c™ are either trademarks or registered trademarks of Primavera Systems, Inc.)

Plant Expansion and Modernization

Act ID	Description	Orig Dur	Rem Dur	% Compl	Early Start	Early Finish	Late Start	Late Finish	Total Float	Budg Cost	Act Cost to Date	Cost at Compl	Cost Var
		399	360	7	19JUL99 A	08FEB01	19JUL99 A	08FEB01	0	1,397,047.90	43,863.20	1,398,147.90	-822.00
BA400	Design Building Addition	20	0	100	19JUL99 A	27AUG99	19JUL99 A	27AUG99	0	9,600.00	9,600.00	9,600.00	0.00
AS100	Define System Requirements	10	0	100	20JUL99 A	04AUG99	20JUL99 A	04AUG99	0	2,960.00	3,300.00	3,300.00	-340.00
AS101	System Design	20	0	100	03AUG99	31AUG99	03AUG99	31AUG99	0	16,640.00	16,640.00	16,640.00	0.00
BA469	Assemble Technical Data for Heat Pump	3	3	0	13AUG99	17AUG99	04NOV99	08NOV99	58d	540.00	0.00	540.00	0.00
AS103	Install Robot Base	18	18	0	17AUG99	10SEP99	25AUG99	20SEP99	6d	4,824.00	0.00	4,824.00	0.00
AS104	Run Sealant, Air, and Water Piping	13	13	0	17AUG99	02SEP99	14SEP99	30SEP99	19d	3,432.00	0.00	3,432.00	0.00
AS204	Prepare Drawings for Temp Control Equipment	10	0	100	17AUG99	31AUG99	17AUG99	31AUG99	0	1,760.00	1,936.00	1,936.00	-176.00
AS315	Install Electrical Power	24	24	0	16AUG99	20SEP99	17AUG99	20SEP99	0	12,288.00	0.00	12,288.00	0.00
BA470	Review Technical Data on Heat Pumps	10	10	0	16AUG99	31AUG99	09NOV99	22NOV99	58d	600.00	0.00	600.00	0.00
AS217	Review and Approve System Controller	10	10	0	20AUG99	02SEP99	17SEP99	30SEP99	19d	3,426.00	0.00	3,426.00	0.00
BA530	Review and Approve Brick Samples	10	10	0	20AUG99	02SEP99	13OCT99	26OCT99	37d	240.00	0.00	240.00	0.00
AS216	Prepare Drawings for System Controller	10	5	50	23AUG99	19AUG99	23AUG99	16SEP99	19d	1,760.00	880.00	1,760.00	0.00
BA560	Review and Approve Flooring	10	10	0	24AUG99	07SEP99	11FEB00	25FEB00	120d	240.00	0.00	240.00	0.00
BA501	Review and Approve Designs	14	0	100	30AUG99	20SEP99 A	30AUG99	20SEP99 A		1,680.00	1,500.00	1,500.00	180.00
AS102	Approve System Design	10	0	100	31AUG99	13SEP99 A	31AUG99	13SEP99 A		2,546.00	2,546.00	2,546.00	0.00
AS205	Review and Approve Temp Control Equipment	5	5	0	31AUG99	13SEP99 A	31AUG99	13SEP99 A		2,826.00	2,930.00	2,930.00	-104.00
BA411	Prepare and Solicit Bids for Heat Pump	5	3	3	01SEP99	03SEP99	23NOV99	29NOV99	58d	384.00	0.00	384.00	0.00
AS213	Prepare and Solicit Bids for System Controller	5	5	0	03SEP99	10SEP99	01OCT99	07OCT99	19d	784.00	0.00	784.00	0.00
BA421	Prepare and Solicit Bids for Brick Exterior	3	3	0	03SEP99	08SEP99	27OCT99	29OCT99	37d	384.00	0.00	384.00	0.00
AS200	Prepare and Solicit Bids for Temp Control Equip	5	0	100	07SEP99 A	16SEP99	07SEP99 A	16SEP99 A		1,080.00	1,080.00	1,080.00	0.00
BA412	Review Bids for Heat Pump	2	2	0	07SEP99	08SEP99	30NOV99	01DEC99	58d	128.00	0.00	128.00	0.00
BA407	Prepare and Solicit Bids for Flooring	5	5	0	08SEP99	14SEP99	28FEB00	03MAR00	120d	640.00	0.00	640.00	0.00
BA413	Award Contract for Heat Pump	1	1	0	09SEP99	09SEP99	02DEC99	02DEC99	58d	32.00	0.00	32.00	0.00
BA422	Review Bids for Brick	3	3	0	09SEP99	13SEP99	01NOV99	03NOV99	37d	96.00	0.00	96.00	0.00
BA650	Excavation	10	10	0	09SEP99	22SEP99	09SEP99	22SEP99	0	13,760.00	0.00	13,760.00	0.00
BA550	Fabricate and Deliver Heat Pump and Controls	90	90	0	10SEP99	17JAN00	03DEC99	07APR00	58d	2,300.00	0.00	2,300.00	0.00
AS214	Review Bids for System Controller	4	4	0	13SEP99	16SEP99	08OCT99	13OCT99	19d	659.80	0.00	659.80	0.00
AS240	Installation Begins	0	0	100	14SEP99		14SEP99 A	13OCT99	19d	0.00	0.00	0.00	0.00
AS310	Site Preparation	10	2	80	14SEP99 A	16AUG99	14SEP99 A	16AUG99	0	680.00	590.00	680.00	-46.00

Start date	15JUL99
Finish date	08FEB01
Data date	13AUG99
Run date	22JUN04
Page number	1A
© Primavera Systems, Inc.	

Legend:
- Early bar
- Early start point
- Early finish point
- Total float bar
- Total float point
- Progress bar

Acme Motors
Plant Expansion and Modernization

FIGURE B.9 Report 9

(Reprinted with permission from Primavera Systems, Inc. Primavera® and P3e/c™ are either trademarks or registered trademarks of Primavera Systems, Inc.)

Plant Expansion and Modernization

Act ID	Description	Orig Dur	% Compl	Early Start	Early Finish	Budg Cost	Act Cost to Date	Cost at Compl	Cost Var
		399	7	19JUL99 A	08FEB01	397,047.90	43,863.20	396,147.90	-822.00
BA400	Design Building Addition	20	100	19JUL99 A	27AUG99	9,600.00	9,600.00	9,600.00	0.00
AS100	Define System Requirements	10	100	20JUL99 A	04AUG99	2,960.00	3,300.00	3,300.00	-340.00
AS101	System Design	20	100	03AUG99	31AUG99	16,640.00	16,640.00	16,540.00	0.00
BA469	Assemble Technical Data for Heat Pump	3	0	13AUG99	17AUG99	540.00	0.00	540.00	0.00
AS103	Install Robot Base	18	0	17AUG99	10SEP99	4,824.00	0.00	4,824.00	0.00
AS104	Run Sealant, Air, and Water Piping	13	0	17AUG99	02SEP99	3,432.00	0.00	3,432.00	0.00
AS204	Prepare Drawings for Temp Control	10	100	17AUG99	31AUG99	1,760.00	1,936.00	1,936.00	-176.00
AS315	Install Electrical Power	24	0	17AUG99	20SEP99	12,288.00	0.00	12,288.00	0.00
BA470	Review Technical Data on Heat Pumps	10	0	16AUG99	31AUG99	600.00	0.00	600.00	0.00
AS217	Review and Approve System Controller	10	0	20AUG99	02SEP99	3,426.00	0.00	3,426.00	0.00
BA530	Review and Approve Brick Samples	10	0	20AUG99	02SEP99	240.00	0.00	240.00	0.00
AS216	Prepare Drawings for System Controller	10	50	23AUG99	19AUG99	1,760.00	880.00	1,760.00	0.00
BA560	Review and Approve Flooring	10	0	24AUG99	07SEP99	240.00	0.00	240.00	0.00
BA501	Review and Approve Designs	14	100	30AUG99	20SEP99 A	1,680.00	1,500.00	1,500.00	180.00
AS102	Approve System Design	10	100	31AUG99	13SEP99 A	2,546.00	2,546.00	2,546.00	0.00
AS205	Review and Approve Temp Control	5	100	31AUG99	13SEP99 A	2,826.00	2,930.00	2,930.00	-104.00
BA411	Prepare and Solicit Bids for Heat Pump	3	0	01SEP99	03SEP99	384.00	0.00	384.00	0.00
AS213	Prepare and Solicit Bids for System	5	0	03SEP99	10SEP99	784.00	0.00	784.00	0.00
BA421	Prepare and Solicit Bids for Brick Exterior	3	0	03SEP99	08SEP99	384.00	0.00	384.00	0.00
AS200	Prepare and Solicit Bids for Temp Control	5	100	07SEP99 A	16SEP99 A	1,080.00	1,060.00	1,060.00	0.00
BA412	Review Bids for Heat Pump	2	0	07SEP99	08SEP99	128.00	0.00	128.00	0.00
BA407	Prepare and Solicit Bids for Flooring	5	0	08SEP99	14SEP99	640.00	0.00	640.00	0.00
BA413	Award Contract for Heat Pump	1	0	09SEP99	09SEP99	32.00	0.00	32.00	0.00
BA422	Review Bids for Brick	3	0	09SEP99	13SEP99	96.00	0.00	96.00	0.00
BA650	Excavation	10	0	09SEP99	22SEP99	13,760.00	0.00	13,760.00	0.00
BA550	Fabricate and Deliver Heat Pump and	90	0	10SEP99	17JAN00	2,300.00	0.00	2,300.00	0.00
AS214	Review Bids for System Controller	4	0	13SEP99	16SEP99	659.80	0.00	659.80	0.00
AS240	Installation Begins	0	100	14SEP99 A		0.00	0.00	0.00	0.00
AS310	Site Preparation	10	80	14SEP99 A	16AUG99	680.00	590.00	680.00	-46.00

Start date 15JUL99
Finish date 08FEB01
Data date 13AUG99
Run date 22JUN04
Page number 1A
©Primavera Systems, Inc.

Acme Motors
Plant Expansion and Modernization

Legend:
- Early bar
- Early start point
- Early finish point
- Total float bar
- Total float point
- Progress bar

FIGURE B.10 Report 10
(Reprinted with permission from Primavera Systems, Inc. Primavera® and P3e/c™ are either trademarks or registered trademarks of Primavera Systems, Inc.)

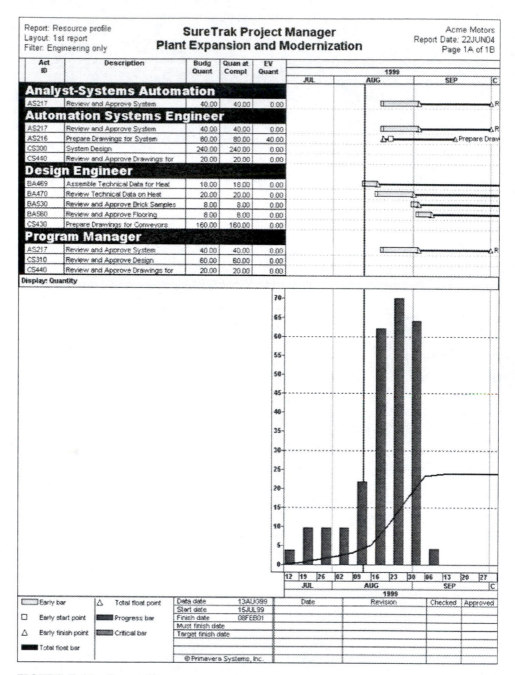

FIGURE B.11 Report 11
(Reprinted with permission from Primavera Systems, Inc. Primavera® and P3e/c™ are either trademarks or registered trademarks of Primavera Systems, Inc.)

GLOSSARY

accelerated schedule. A schedule submitted, usually by the contractor, implementing some adjustments to the project schedule so that the project can finish by the contract finish date.

acquisition. The obtaining of supplies, services, or property to meet the needs for a project.

activity. A basic unit of work, as part of the total project, that is easily measured and controlled. It is time and resource consuming. Also called a *task*.

activity description. A short phrase or label used in a project network diagram describing the scope of work and sometimes the location of the activity.

activity duration. The number of time units (weeks, days, hours, etc.) required to complete that activity. There are three types of duration: *original duration, actual duration,* and *remaining duration*.

activity on arrow (AOA) networks. Network diagrams showing a sequence of activities, in which each activity is represented by an arrow connecting two circles, or nodes, each node representing an event.

activity on node (AON) network. A network diagram in which activities are represented by boxes (nodes) linked by lines representing logic dependencies.

actual cost. See *actual cost for work performed (ACWP)*.

actual cost at completion. Total costs incurred (direct and indirect) in the overall completion of the assigned work.

actual cost to date. The actual cost incurred from the beginning of construction activities to the current data date.

actual cost this period. The actual cost incurred between the previous data date and the current data date. It is equal to actual cost to date minus actual cost reported in the last payment request.

actual cost for work performed (ACWP). Total costs incurred (direct and indirect) while work is being performed during a given time period.

actual duration. The number of time units consumed to complete the activity, if completed, or consumed on the activity so far, if not completed yet.

addenda. Plural of *addendum*.

addendum. A document describing an addition, a change, a correction, or a modification to contract documents. An addendum is issued by the design professional or owner to all bidders during the bidding period but prior to awarding the contract. Addenda become part of the contract documents.

alternate dispute resolution (ADR). Any procedure or combination of procedures voluntarily used to resolve a dispute without going to court. These procedures may include, but are not limited to, assisted settlement negotiations, conciliation, facilitation, mediation, fact finding, minitrials, and arbitration.

applications for payment. See *payment requests.*

arbitration. The process by which parties agree to submit their disputes to the determination of a third, impartial party (referred to as the *arbitrator*) rather than pursuing their claims before a judge and jury in a court of law. The parties often agree in advance to binding arbitration of disputes, either as a clause in the contract or at the occurrence of a dispute. This method of avoiding litigation can save both time and money.

arrow diagramming method (ADM). See *activity on arrow (AOA) network.*

as-built schedule. A schedule prepared after the project has started that reflects what happened in the field rather than what was planned to happen. Activities are plotted by their real start date and real finish date, disregarding any logic (usually, as-built schedules have no logical relationships).

as-of date. See *data date.*

As Late As Possible. A constraint in some computer scheduling programs that forces the maximum delay in starting an activity without delaying the succeeding activities. Also called the *Zero Free Float* constraint.

as-planned schedule. The schedule submitted by the contractor—as usually required by the contract—and approved by the owner before the start of the project (and sometimes before the signing of the contract).

backward pass. The process of navigating through a network from finish to start and calculating late dates for all activities. This, along with the forward-pass calculations, helps identify the critical path and the float for all activities.

backward resource leveling. Leveling resources, starting from the project finish and going backward through all project activities, fulfilling their resource requirements and maintaining the total resource use within the set limits. With such restrictions, the project may require longer than originally allowed, and the project start date may have to occur before the scheduled date.

bar chart. "A graphical representation of project activities shown in a time-scaled bar line with no links shown between activities" (Popescu and Charoenngam 1995, 96). Originally developed by Henry L. Gantt in 1917. Also called Gantt Charts.

baseline. The original approved plan for a project, including approved changes. It usually includes the baseline budget and the baseline schedule. It is used as a benchmark for comparison with actual performance (see *project control*).

baseline budget. The original approved budget for the project, including any approved changes.

baseline schedule. A schedule usually prepared by the contractor before the start of the project and approved by the owner. Typically used for performance comparison.

beginning-of-day convention. When any date mentioned for an activity means the start of the day. Usually used only by computer software for start dates.

beneficial occupancy. The use of a premises (or a portion of it) for its intended purposes, even though the project work may not be complete. This term is almost the same as *substantial completion*. See also *certificate of substantial completion.*

beta distribution. A continuous probability with a probability density function defined on the interval [0, 1]. It is used in PERT with three time estimates for the completion of an activity: the optimistic duration, the most likely duration, and the pessimistic duration. Using these three durations, the beta distribution allows the calculation of the means and variances of activity completion times. The beta distribution also has an advantage over the normal distribution in that it can be skewed right (toward the pessimistic duration), can be skewed left (toward the optimistic duration), or can be symmetrical.

budget at completion (BAC). The sum of the total budgets throughout the completion of a project or an activity. Not to be confused with *estimate at completion (EAC)*.

budgeted cost for work performed (BCWP). The sum of the approved cost estimates (including any overhead allocation) for activities (or portions of activities) completed during a given period (usually project to date). See also *earned value*.

budgeted cost for work scheduled (BCWS). The sum of the approved cost estimates (including any overhead allocation) for activities (or portions of activities) scheduled to be performed during a given period (usually project to date).

calculated finish date. The completion date of the project calculated using the critical path method.

calendars. Calendars show the days on which work on activities may be performed.

calendar unit. The smallest unit of time used for activity duration and scheduling the entire project.

central limit theorem. A theorem that demonstrates that in large-enough samples, the distribution of sample means approximates a normal curve, regardless of the shape of the distribution of the population from which they were drawn. The larger the sample size, the better the approximation to the normal distribution.

certificate of completion. A written document forwarded to the general contractor by the architect, engineer, or owner stating that construction is complete according to the contract agreement (approved plans, specifications, change orders, etc.).

certificate of occupancy. A written document issued by a local governmental agency stating that the building or facility is in a condition to be occupied (i.e., is in compliance with public health and building codes).

certificate of substantial completion. A written document forwarded to the general contractor by the architect, engineer, or owner indicating that the project is substantially complete. This document initiates the time period for the final payment to the contractor.

change in the critical path. A partial or complete change in the critical path of a CPM schedule that was caused by a change in the duration of one or more activities and/or a change in the schedule logic. Practically, the critical path changes if a near-critical path increases to exceed the original critical path or if the original critical path decreases to become shorter than another path in the schedule.

change orders (COs). Formal written documents, signed by the owner, directing the contractor to make changes to the original contract. A change order can be used for adding, deleting, or substituting work items. A change order usually—but not always—has an impact on the project cost and schedule.

claim. A request from one contracting party (usually the contractor) to another party (usually the owner) for additional compensation, a time extension, or both.

combination relationship. Two activities related (or connected) by two logical relationships, usually start-to-start and finish-to-finish.

comparison schedule. The original (usually as-planned) schedule revised to incorporate any claimed delays. Typically for a delay claim, the contractor submits two schedules: one without the causative factors (factors allegedly causing the schedule delays) and one with the causative factors (called the *impacted schedule*). By comparing the two schedules, the contractor hopes to prove that the delay is caused by the alleged factors.

compensable delays. Project delays, caused by the actions or inactions of another party (usually the owner), that entitle the contractor to a time extension, monetary compensation, or both.

concurrent delay. A combination of two or more independent causes of delay during the same period.

constraint. An externally imposed factor affecting when an activity can start and/or finish. Constraints may conflict with logical relationships. Individual scheduling programs provide the user with a variety of constraint types, some of which can override logic and some of which are subject to logic.

constructability. "The optimum use of construction knowledge and experience in planning, design, procurement, and field operations to achieve overall project objectives" (Construction Industry Institute 1986a, 2).

constructive acceleration. A schedule acceleration by the contractor that occurs when a delay takes place beyond a contractor's control, yet the owner expects the project to be completed by the original contract completion date. The contractor usually files a claim for this acceleration after the completion of the contract.

contiguous activities. Activities that cannot be split or paused. Once work starts on a contiguous activity, it must continue until its completion.

contingency fees. Amounts included in the construction budget to cover the cost of unforeseen events that will most likely occur during the life of the project. Such fees are estimated or calculated directly proportional to the risk taken in the project.

contract. A legally binding agreement that obligates one party (the architect, engineer, constructor, etc.) to offer products or services under certain terms (budget, schedule, specifications) and obligates the other party (owner) to pay for these products or services.

contract closeout. The completion and settlement of the contract, including resolution of any open items. From a financial management standpoint, closeout involves settling all financial and accounting matters between the contractor and the owner.

contractor-created float. Schedule float created because the contractor's work was done in a shorter-than-planned period. This float may be created by shorter actual durations for performed activities, a change in the logic, different calendars (a 6- or 7-day week rather than a 5-day week), or a combination of these factors. This float is not a part of the total float calculated in the original baseline schedule.

cost accounting. "The systematic recording and analysis of the costs of materials, labor, and overhead incident to production" (Merriam-Webster 2004).

cost breakdown. See *schedule of values*.

cost to complete. See *estimate to complete (ETC)*.

cost at completion. See *actual cost at completion.*

cost to date. See *actual cost.*

cost-loaded schedule. A CPM schedule in which each activity has a cost figure assigned to it. In some software packages, the user may assign resources (labor, equipment, materials) to each activity, then the software calculates the cost using the cost of these resources.

cost performance index (CPI). The ratio of the earned value of an activity to its actual cost (AC). $CPI = BCWP/ACWP$ or $CPI = EV/AC$.

cost ratio. A method of measuring percent complete for an activity (or a project) by distributing (linearly or using other curves) the cost over the duration of the activity (or project). Percent complete = Actual cost/Total cost. This method works well for activities with a fixed budget and fixed duration, such as a salaried staff member.

cost/schedule control system criteria (C/SCSC). A formal planning and control reporting system developed by the Department of Defense for its contractors to use. It is used for reporting project schedule and financial information. This system was later simplified and modified to what is currently known as *earned value management.*

cost this period. See *actual cost this period.*

cost variance (CV). The difference between the earned value of an activity and its actual cost (AC). $CV = BCWP - ACWP$ or $CV = EV - AC$.

crash cost. Total cost of a construction project (direct and indirect), including the impact of crashing (maximum compression of) the schedule.

crash duration. The least possible duration for a construction project schedule. It is usually achieved by maximum schedule compression.

critical activities. Activities on the critical path. Any delay in the start or completion of a critical activity will result in a delay in the entire project.

critical path. The longest path in a network, from start to finish.

critical path method (CPM). A scheduling technique using networks for graphic display of the work plan. The method is used to determine the length of a project and to identify the activities critical to project completion.

cumulative distribution function. A function used to compute probabilities for a continuous random variable having values up to a certain value x: $F(x) = \Pr(X \leq x)$.

current finish date. The current (updated) estimate of the point in time when the project (or a specific activity) will be completed.

damages. A measure of monetary compensation that a court or an arbitrator awards to a plaintiff for loss or injury suffered by the plaintiff's person, property, or other legally recognizable rights.

dangling activities. Activities tied from only one end (start or finish). A dangling activity does not have either predecessors or successors.

data date. The date as of which all progress on a project is reported.

degressing an in-progress schedule. Reversing all progress reflected on the schedule to go back to the starting point. This practice is used when there is no baseline schedule but there is a need to create one after construction has started.

delay. An event or a condition that results in work activity starting, or project completion, later than originally planned, or an interruption or a hindrance to planned progress.

delay claims. Claims for a time extension, monetary compensation, or both as a result of a delay caused by the actions of another party. Delay claims can be classified as excusable, nonexcusable, and concurrent.

dependency. See *logical relationship*.

design development. The second phase of a designer's basic services (the first phase is schematic design), which includes developing all engineering and architectural drawings, specifications, and cost estimates. This phase usually occurs in stages, and each stage is defined by a certain percent complete. For example, DD30 means design development is 30% complete, which indicates that about 30% of the information in the design is defined. Potential contractors have to assume the remaining 70% is undefined information. Further stages follow with increased percentages (e.g., DD60, DD90). Final design is the third and final phase of the design process. It follows design development.

direct costs. Costs directly associated with a specific activity or work item. They typically include labor, materials, equipment, and subcontractors.

dispute review boards (DRBs). A panel of three experienced, respected, and impartial reviewers organized before construction begins that meets periodically at the job site. The board is usually formed by the owner's selection of a member for approval by the contractor, the contractor's selection of a member for approval by the owner, and the chosen two selecting the DRB chair to be approved by both parties. The board becomes familiar with the project and its development. It helps prevent and resolve disputes between the contracting parties.

dissolve an activity. A function in Primavera software that deletes an activity but assigns its predecessors to its successors so that there will not be an interruption in the schedule logic.

double-restricted float (DRF) (in precedence networks). The amount of time we must delay the rest of the work in an activity after it has started, then finish on time without delaying the entire project.

dummy activity. A fictitious activity with zero duration used in *activity on arrow networks* to maintain correct logic or distinguish the identities of activities.

durations. See *activity duration*.

early dates (for an activity). The early start date and early finish date of an activity.

early finish (for an activity) (EF). The earliest date on which an activity can finish without violating the schedule logic.

early start (for an activity) (ES). The earliest date on which an activity can start.

earned value (EV). See *budgeted cost for work performed (BCWP)*.

earned value analysis (EVA). Analysis of project progress in which the actual money budgeted and spent are compared with the value of the work achieved.

earned value management (EVM). A method of integrating the project scope, the project schedule, and the project budget for measuring project performance. It compares the amount of work that was planned with what was actually earned and with what was actually spent to determine whether cost and schedule performance are as planned.

effort-driven activity. See *resource-driven activity*.

end-of-day convention. A convention adopted by most schedulers in which the day (date) mentioned implicitly means the *end* of that day. An end of a day is equivalent to the beginning of the next day. For this reason, network calculations start on day 0 (i.e., end of day 0), which practically means the beginning of day 1.

estimate at completion (EAC). The expected total cost of an activity or a project when the defined scope of work is completed. EAC = Actual cost (AC) + Estimate to complete (ETC).

estimate to complete (ETC). The projected cost to complete the activity or project from its present state.

estimate-generated schedule. A list of project activities along with their durations generated by the cost-estimating software. The list does not form a CPM schedule because it lacks logic links (relationships) and other schedule attributes. It may help form the foundation of a schedule.

event. A point in time marking a start or an end of an activity. In contrast to an activity, an event does not consume time or resources. In computer software, events with significance can be created as milestones, and they are either start milestones, such as Notice to Proceed, or finish milestones, such as Substantial Completion.

excusable delay. A delay that entitles the contractor to additional time to complete the contract work. Excusable delays usually stem from reasons beyond the contractor's control.

exemplary damages. See *punitive damages*.

expected duration. The amount of time we expect the project or path duration to take, considering the different possible values (optimistic, most likely, and pessimistic durations) and their weights. It is the mean (mathematical average). It is calculated by using the following equation:

$$T_e = \frac{T_o + 4T_m + T_P}{6}$$

which is a form of the general equation

$$\mu = \frac{1}{n} \sum_{i=1}^{n} x_i$$

fast-track project. A project for which the construction process is started while the design is still underway (i.e., overlapping the design and construction of a project).

finish-to-finish (FF) relationship. A logic restraint that does not allow for the completion of one activity (the successor) until another activity (the predecessor) is completed.

finish-restricted float (in precedence networks). The amount of time we can delay the start of work of an activity, or the rest of it if it has started, then finish on time without delaying the entire project.

finish-to-start (FS) relationship. A logic restraint that does not allow for the start of one activity (the successor) until another activity (the predecessor) is completed.

float. The maximum amount of time an activity can be delayed without violating certain conditions, depending on the type of float. See the specific type of float for an exact definition. Float is sometimes called *slack* or *leeway*.

force majeure. An event or effect that cannot be reasonably anticipated or controlled. Usually entitles the contractor to relief from a contractual obligation. Such relief is often a time extension for the completion of the project.

forecasted cost variance (FCV). The expected cost variance (CV) of an in-progress activity or a project after its completion, assuming the continuation of productivity and job conditions without change.

forecasted schedule variance (FSV). The expected schedule variance (SV) of an in-progress activity or a project after its completion, assuming the continuation of productivity and job conditions without change.

forecasting. Extrapolating actual performance for the remaining portion of a project.

forward pass. The process of navigating through a network from start to finish and calculating the early dates for each activity and the completion date of the project.

forward resource leveling. Leveling resources, starting from the project start and going forward through all project activities, fulfilling their resource requirements and maintaining the total resource use within the set limits. With such restrictions, some activities must be delayed until resources are available, and the project duration may be longer than planned, which will cause the finish date to occur later than originally scheduled.

free float (FF). The maximum amount of time an activity can be delayed without delaying the early start of the succeeding activities.

frequency of updating. The time interval between two regular schedule updates.

front-end loading the cost. Overestimating early work activities and underestimating the later work activities while maintaining the same overall contract sum. A practice some contractors use to get early money. Owners dislike and often dispute this practice.

Gantt chart. See *bar chart*.

general overhead. See *indirect costs*.

graphical evaluation and review technique (GERT). A network analysis technique that allows for conditional and probabilistic treatment of logical relationships (i.e., some activities may not be performed).

I–J method. See *activity on arrow (AOA) networks*.

impacted schedule. A schedule similar to the original (usually as-planned) schedule but incorporating the causative factors (factors allegedly causing the schedule delays). By comparing the two schedules (original and impacted), the contractor hopes to prove that the delay was caused by the alleged factors.

imposed finish date. The required project completion date, typically specified in the contract by the owner.

independent float (Ind. F). The maximum amount of time an activity may be delayed without delaying the early start of the succeeding activities and without being affected by the allowable delay of the preceding activities.

indirect costs. Expenses that cannot be directly associated with a specific activity or work item, such as overhead, profit, or insurance. If an indirect cost can be attributed to a specific project, it is job overhead; otherwise, it is general overhead.

interfering float (Int. F). The maximum amount of time an activity may be delayed without delaying the entire project but causing a delay to the succeeding activities. It is the part of the total float that remains after free float is deducted. Mathematically speaking, *Int. F = TF − FF*.

interruptible activities. Activities that may be performed in two or more separate segments. They are activities that may be interrupted or paused.

inventory buffer theory. A theory in materials management that calls for all materials to be purchased, delivered, and stored on-site prior to installation.

job overhead. See *indirect costs*.

just-in-time theory. A theory in materials management that calls for delivering materials at the time of installation only. Thus, no materials are stored on-site.

lag. A minimum waiting period between the finish (or start) of an activity and the start (or finish) of its successor.

late dates (for an activity). The late start date and late finish date of an activity.

late finish (for an activity) (LF). The latest date on which an activity can finish without extending the project duration.

late start (for an activity) (LS). The latest date on which an activity can start without extending the project duration.

lead. A negative lag.

least-cost duration. See *least-cost schedule*.

least-cost schedule. A CPM schedule accelerated to reach the point at which the total cost of the project (direct and indirect) is least. If the duration of the schedule increases or decreases, the total cost will increase.

linear scheduling method (LSM). A scheduling method that consists of a simple diagram showing the location and time at which a certain crew will be working on a given operation. It is most suited for construction projects with few activities (usually with large quantities) that must be done in the same order or sequence (e.g., heavy construction projects such as roads, earthwork, or utility piping).

liquidated damages. A stipulation in the contract of a monetary amount that must be paid by the contractor if he or she fails to satisfactorily complete the project by the contract finish date. Liquidated damages are usually assessed per day of delay, and they may increase after a certain amount of days (e.g., $1,000 per day for the first week then $1,500 per day for the second week, and on).

litigation. The process of carrying on a legal contest by judicial process. The parties submit their disputes to the jurisdiction and procedures of federal or state courts for resolution.

logical relationship. The interdependency of the activities in a network: one activity (the predecessor) must finish (or start) before another (the successor) can start (or finish), with or without a lag. There are four types of logical relationships: *finish-to-start, start-to-start, finish-to-finish, and start-to-finish.*

logic loop. A circular logical relationship between two activities in a network (i.e., each one is a predecessor and a successor to the other). A loop is an error that must be corrected or CPM calculations (whether manual or computerized) will stop.

logic network. Diagram showing project activities and their logical relationships (interdependencies). Often incorrectly referred to as a *PERT diagram*.

look-ahead schedule. A segment of the overall schedule that includes only activities that have work planned during a certain period, such as the next month or the next 2 weeks. Project managers may use look-ahead schedules to focus on activities in the immediate future.

loop. See *logic loop*.

man-hour ratio. A method of measuring percent complete for an activity (or a project) by distributing (linearly or using other curves) the budgeted man-hours over the duration of the activity (or project). Percent complete = Actual man-hours/Total man-hours. This method is similar to the cost ratio method, except man-hours are used instead of dollars.

master schedule. A CPM schedule that includes more than one *subschedule.* Typically, a general contractor requires his or her subcontractors to submit their schedules then incorporates them as subschedules in the master schedule, which shows all work items in the project. Relationships in a master schedule may be internal (i.e., within the same subschedule) or external (i.e., between activities from two subschedules).

materials management. The planning and controlling of all necessary efforts to ensure that the correct quality and the correct quantity of materials and equipment are appropriately specified in a timely manner, are obtained at a reasonable cost, and are available when needed.

mediation. A method of trying to resolve a dispute by the use of an impartial intermediary to suggest ways to settle the dispute, rather than imposing a decision on the parties.

milestones. An event with special significance, such as Notice to Proceed (NTP) or Substantial Completion.

Monte Carlo simulations. The technique used by project management applications to estimate the likely range of outcomes from a complex random process by simulating the process many times.

most likely duration. The amount of time that we believe an activity is more likely to take than any other duration.

negotiation. When two or more parties with competing interests discuss an issue with the aim of reaching an agreement.

network. A logical and chronological graphic representation of the activities (and events) composing a project. Network diagrams are basically of two types: arrow networks and node networks. Arrow networks are also called the *arrow diagramming Method (ADM), activity on arrow (AOA) networks,* or the *I–J method.* Node networks are also called *activity on node (AON) networks* or the *node diagramming method.* Precedence diagrams and the precedence diagramming method (PDM) are an advanced form of node networks.

noncompensable delays. Project delays beyond the control, and not the fault, of the owner—such as unusual weather conditions, natural disasters (earthquakes, floods, hurricanes, etc.), wars or national crises, and labor strikes. Such delays usually do not entitle the contractor to monetary compensation but most likely entitle him or her to a time extension.

nonexcusable delay. A delay that does not entitle the contractor to either a time extension or monetary compensation.

nonworkdays. Days on which no work is performed, such as holidays, rain days, shutdowns, and the like.

normal cost. The cost of a project that is performed under normal duration.

normal distribution. A probability distribution forming a symmetrical bell-shaped curve.

normal duration. The amount of time required to finish the project under ordinary circumstances without any deliberate delay or acceleration.

optimistic duration. The amount of time an activity will take if everything goes smoothly and efficiently within the realistic (although perhaps unlikely) realm of expectations.

original duration. The number of time units estimated to complete an activity that has not started yet.

overhead. See *indirect costs*.

payment requests (pay requests, payment requisitions). Formal written requests for payment by a contractor or subcontractor for work completed on a contract and, if allowed for in the contract, materials purchased and stored on the job site or in a warehouse. Subcontractors submit their payment requests to the general contractor, who combines them with his or hers in one total payment request to the owner. Typically, this process is done monthly.

pessimistic duration. The amount of time an activity will take under the almost-worst-case scenario within the realistic (although perhaps unlikely) realm of expectations.

planned value (PV). See *budgeted cost for work scheduled (BCWS)*.

precedence diagramming method (PDM). A node network (see *activity on node [AON] network*) that allows for the use of four types of relationships: (1) finish-to-start (FS) relationship, (2) start-to-start (SS) relationship, (3) finish-to-finish (FF) relationship, and (4) start-to-finish (SF) relationship.

precedence networks. See *precedence diagramming method (PDM)*.

predecessor activity. Any activity that must finish (or start) before the next activity or activities can start (or finish). It has also been defined as an activity that has some measurable portion of its duration logically restraining a subsequent activity or activities (theoretically, this portion can be zero, but practically it must be greater than zero).

probability density function. A function used to compute probabilities for a continuous random variable at a certain value. The area under the curve of a probability density function for an interval represents the probability (chance of occurrence): $f(x) = \Pr(X = x)$.

probability distribution. A function or mathematical model that describes all the values that a random variable can have and the probability (chance of occurrence) associated with each. Also called a *probability function*.

probability universe. The set of the values of all possible outcomes for a random variable.

procurement. The process of acquiring materials, equipment, and/or services from external sources for use in a project. It is a process that usually starts long before the start of the construction process and ends with project completion or project closeout.

professional engineer (PE). An engineer licensed by an authority (usually the government of the state) after he or she fulfills certain requirements (minimum education and experience and passing an examination).

pro forma. A projection or an estimate of the cost-benefit ratio or rate of return on an investment. Project owners and investors usually use a pro forma to help them decide whether or not to carry out a project. Typically, a pro forma includes all expected costs (initial, recurring, and occasional) and expected revenues throughout the life cycle of the project, then calculates the rate of return.

program evaluation and review technique (PERT). An event-oriented network analysis technique used to estimate project duration when individual activity duration estimates are highly uncertain. PERT applies the critical path method to a weighted-average duration estimate. PERT is considered a probabilistic method. The term *PERT diagram* is sometimes used incorrectly in the construction industry to denote a logic network.

Progress Override. An option used in Primavera scheduling software to ignore a logical relationship between two activities after actual work has violated this logic (e.g., if activity A is a predecessor [with an FS relationship] to activity B but activity B has started before activity A is finished). See the other option, *Retained Logic*.

progress payments. Periodic (usually monthly) payments made by the owner to the general contractor (and from the general contractor to the subcontractors) upon approval of the payment request. Owners usually retain a portion of the progress payment (typically 5–10%) till the successful completion of the project.

project. "A temporary endeavor undertaken to produce a unique product or service" (Project Management Institute 2000, 204).

project breakdown structure (PBS). A task-oriented family tree of activities that organizes, defines, and displays the work to be accomplished.

project close-out. The full completion of a project signed off by all responsible parties and the finalization of all paperwork and payments.

project control. The continuous process of monitoring work progress from schedule (time) and budget standpoints, comparing it with the baseline schedule and the baseline budget (what was supposed to happen or what was planned), finding any deviations (where and how much) and analyzing them to determine the causes, then taking corrective action whenever and wherever necessary to bring the project back on schedule and within budget.

project cost breakdown. See *schedule of values*.

project management team. The individuals involved in the management of a project. This involvement can be in different capacities, at different levels, or at different times. The team is usually led by the project manager (PM).

project manager (PM). The individual responsible for managing a project.

project monitoring. A term sometimes used to mean project control. Technically, it includes the first three functions of project control (monitoring, comparing, finding).

project planning. The process of choosing the one method and order of work to be adopted for a project from all the various ways and sequences in which it could be done. Project planning serves as a foundation for several related functions, such as cost estimating, scheduling, project control, quality control, safety management, and others.

project tracking. See *project control*.

punch list. A list made near the completion of a project, showing the remaining work items that must be finished to complete the project scope.

punitive damages. Damages awarded by a judge to a plaintiff in excess of those required to compensate the plaintiff for losses incurred. Used to punish the defendant for wrongful conduct and to show the plight of the defendant as an example to potential wrongdoers.

rain days. The number of days (per month) that work on the project is expected to be suspended because of weather delays.

recovery schedule. A schedule prepared during construction, after the project falls behind (either fails to meet its interim target or shows serious signs of failure to meet its deadline), with adjustments made by the contractor that expedite the remainder of the project and ensure a timely finish.

redundancies. Duplications in depicting logical relationships. For example, if A and B are predecessors to C but A is a predecessor to B, then the relationship between A and C is redundant. Redundancies often occur when a scheduler inserts activities after the logic network has been built. Unlike logic loops, redundancies are not errors and will not halt CPM calculations.

remaining duration. The number of time units estimated to complete an in-progress activity.

request for change (RFC). A request initiated by the owner, or the party representing the owner, authorizing the contractor to change the scope of the contract. The request is usually—but not always—preceded by an agreement on the impact of the change on the cost and schedule of the project.

request for information (RFI). This term is used for a wide variety of purposes in many industries, generally indicating a party—contracted or not—requesting certain information on a particular issue of mutual interest between the party requesting the information and the party providing the information. In construction, the most frequent use is a request issued by the contractor or a subcontractor to the owner or design professional (A/E) for clarification of design information or to present any question pertaining to contract requirements.

request for payment. See *payment requests*.

request for proposals (RFPs). A formal invitation by the owner or (his or her representative) to potential bidders, containing a scope of work, that seeks a formal response (proposal) describing both the methodology and the compensation to form the basis of a contract.

request for quotation (RFQ). A formal invitation to submit a price for goods and/or services as specified.

resource allocation. The assignment of the required resources to each activity, in the required amount and timing.

resource constraint. A type of constraint that subjects the start and continuity of an activity to the availability of required resources. See *resource allocation, resource-driven activity, resource-driven schedule,* and *resource leveling.*

resource-driven activity. An activity for which its duration is calculated on the basis of the availability of required resources. Typically, several activities compete for limited resources and the scheduler must set the priority rules among them.

resource-driven schedule. A CPM schedule with *resource-driven activities*. Logical relationships still apply in addition to resource constraints.

resource histogram. A display of the number of units required (for future work) or consumed (for past work) of a specific resource during a specified period. The user can view the use per unit of time or the cumulative use. The user can compare the resource use with the resource limit (availability). The histogram may plot the resource use in terms of number of units or cost.

resource leveling. Minimizing the fluctuations in day-to-day resource use throughout the project. It is usually done by shifting noncritical activities within their available float. It attempts to make the daily use of a certain resource as uniform as possible.

resource loading. See *resource allocation*.

resources. Any measurable effort or substance required or consumed by work activities in a project. In the context of construction projects, resources are labor, materials, and equipment.

resource usage profile. See *resource histogram*.

restraint. See *constraint*.

Retainage. A portion of the eligible progress payment that is held by the owner until the contractor fulfills his or her contractual obligations. The contract usually specifies the amount (percentage) and conditions of a retainage. In contracts for some large projects, it is customary to decrease the retainage percentage after a significant portion of the project has been completed.

Retained Logic. Maintaining a logical relationship between two activities even though the successor activity has started before the predecessor activity has finished. In other words, the rest of the successor activity will still have to wait till the rest of the predecessor activity is completed.

roll-up schedule. See *summary schedule*.

schedule. A display of project activities and events, along with their timing, plotted chronologically against a calendar. A schedule may or may not be based on the critical path method.

schedule acceleration. See *schedule compression*.

schedule compression. Shortening the project schedule without reducing the project scope. Schedule compression usually increases the project cost and may not always be possible to compress the schedule to the desired point.

schedule contingency. An amount of time included in the construction schedule to account for the unforeseen events that will most likely occur during the life of the project and cause delay.

schedule crashing. See *schedule compression*.

schedule performance index (SPI). The ratio of work performed to work scheduled. $SPI = BCWP/BCWS$ or $SPI = EV/PV$.

scheduler. A project-scheduling professional in charge of preparing and updating CPM schedules for a construction project. The scheduler is also responsible for producing reports pertaining to the schedule that are required by the management.

schedule updating. Reflecting actual performance information—including time of occurrence and amount (or percentage) of work completed—on the schedule and indicating on the schedule any changes to future work, then recalculating the expected project completion date and the early and late dates for incomplete activities.

schedule of values. A listing of elements, systems, items, or other subdivisions of the work, each of which is assigned a monetary value, the total of which equals the contract sum when multiplied by the estimated quantities. The schedule of values is used for establishing the cash flow of a project and serves as the basis for payment requests (R. S. Means 2000). Also called *project cost breakdown* or, simply, *cost breakdown*.

schedule variance (SV). The difference between work performed and work scheduled. $SV = BCWP - BCWS$ or $SV = EV - PV$.

scheduling. The determination of the timing and sequence of operations in the project and their assembly to give the overall completion time. Scheduling focuses on one part of the planning effort.

scope-creep syndrome. The gradual expansion of the scope of a project (e.g., size, area, design, materials) after the contract has been signed, as a result of multiple and successive owner-issued change orders. Scope creep indicates that the owner is not adequately managing the scope of the project or does not have a clear definition of the scope in mind.

S curves. An S curve is a cumulative curve plotting work progress against time. Work progress may be expressed in terms of units of work, budget, man-hours, percent complete, or other units. The curve looks like the letter *S* because work typically starts on a small scale then expands toward the middle of the project, and finally winds down toward the end of the project. This curve is sometimes called the *lazy-S curve*.

sequestering the float. Eliminating or reducing the float of an activity or activities by inserting unnecessary logical relationships, inserting unnecessary lags, inflating durations, or a combination of these procedures. This is a technique practiced by some contractors in order to maintain implicit ownership of float. Most owners dislike this practice and insert a "no sequestering the float" clause in the contract to prevent such practice.

settlement. An agreement by which the parties consent to settle a dispute between them.

single-restricted float. Single-restricted float is either start restricted or finish restricted. It is the amount of time we can delay a portion of an activity, not including its start, if this float is start restricted, or its finish, if this float is finish restricted, without delaying the project.

slack. See *float*.

standard normal distribution. A normal distribution with the parameters $\mu = 0$ and $\sigma = 1$. The random variable for this distribution is denoted by Z. The Z tables (values of the random variable Z and their corresponding probabilities) are widely used for normal distributions.

start-to-finish (SF) relationship. A logic restraint that does not allow for the completion of one activity (the successor) until another activity (the predecessor) is started. This relationship is rarely—if ever—used in construction project scheduling.

start-restricted float (in precedence networks). The amount of time we can delay the rest of the work in an activity after it has started without delaying the entire project.

start-to-start (SS) relationship. A logic restraint that does not allow for the start of one activity (the successor) until another activity (the predecessor) has started.

status date. See *data date*.

store period performance. A function in Primavera software that adds the latest cost this period to the cost to date then makes cost this period zero. The scheduler must do this every time there is a schedule update along with a payment request.

submittal. A sample, manufacturer's data, a shop drawing, or another such item submitted to the owner or the design professional by the contractor for approval or another action, usually a requirement of the contract documents.

subschedule. Generally, a subschedule is a portion of a larger schedule. It is a common practice to refer to the schedule reflecting the work of one subcontractor or another single participant in the project as a *subschedule*. A subschedule may have a starting date, a completion date, and/or a duration different from those of the master schedule.

substantial completion. The point at which the project is ready for use by the owner for the purpose intended and is so certified. See *certificate of substantial completion.*

successor activities. Activities that cannot start (or finish) until another task has finished (or started).

summary schedule. A schedule (usually a bar chart) in which activities are summarized by a certain criterion such as responsibility, phase, or area. If a work breakdown structure (WBS) is used, it is possible to summarize (roll up) the schedule at any higher level. Summary schedules are usually used to inform upper management about the overall project situation without too much detail.

sunk cost. A cost already incurred that could not be avoided even if the project were to be terminated. It cannot be recovered regardless of future events.

target schedule. See *baseline schedule.*

task. See *activity.*

time contingency. See *schedule contingency.*

time ratio. A method of measuring percent complete for an activity (or a project) by dividing actual duration by total duration. This method works well for activities with uniform work over its duration. The method includes a variety of ways of performing calculations, discussed in chapter 7.

time-scaled logic diagrams (or bar charts with relationships). A bar chart with logical relationships depicted.

total float (TF). The maximum amount of time an activity may be delayed from its early start without delaying the entire project.

units completed. A method of measuring percent complete for an activity that comprises similar repetitive units of work. Percent complete = Completed units/Total units. This method can be applied to the entire project if the project can be divided into similar repetitive units of work (e.g., road construction or earthmoving projects).

unrestricted float (in precedence networks). The amount of time we can delay all or part of an activity without delaying the entire project.

upated impacted schedule. A method developed by the U.S. Corps of Engineers for helping resolve delay claims. The concept is to create an as-built schedule or an updated schedule from the start of the project only to the point just before the delay occurred. The "original," or baseline, schedule is updated with progress information, then compared with the impacted completion date on another schedule on which a delay is included.

Updated schedule. "A revised schedule reflecting project information at a given data date regarding completed activities, in-progress activities, and changes in the logic, cost, and resources required and allocated at any activity level" (Popescu and Charoenngam 1995, 566).

value engineering (VE). A science that studies the relative value of various materials and construction techniques. Value engineering considers the initial cost of construction, coupled with the estimated cost of maintenance, energy use, life expectancy, and replacement cost.

work breakdown structure (WBS). A task-oriented, detailed breakdown of activities that organizes, defines, and graphically displays the total work to be accomplished to achieve the final objectives of a project. The WBS breaks the project down into progressively detailed levels. Each descending level represents an increasingly detailed definition of a project component. In CPM scheduling, the components at the lowest WBS level are used as activities to build the project schedule.

workdays. Days on which work is performed or can be performed. Calendars usually, but not always, follow a 5-day workweek.

work package. A well-defined scope of work that terminates in a deliverable product or completion of a service.

Zero Free Float. See *As Late As Possible*.

Zero Total Float. A constraint in Primavera software that forces the activity's late dates to be same as its early dates. This constraint strips the activity of its total float and makes it critical.

Z function. See *standard normal distribution*.

REFERENCES

Ahuja, H. N., S. P. Dozzi, and S. M. Abourizk. 1994. *Project management.* 2nd ed. New York: Wiley.

The American Institute of Architects. 1997. *General conditions of the contract for construction.* Document A201, ¶ 4.3.7.2. Washington, DC: The American Institute of Architects.

The American Institute of Architects. 1999. *Commentary on AIA document A201-1997.* Washington, DC: The American Institute of Architects.

Antill, J. M., and R. W. Woodhead. 1990. *Critical path methods in construction practice.* 4th ed. New York: Wiley.

August, R. 2003. *International law dictionary and directory.* Pullman, WA: Ray August.

Blinderman Construction Co. v. United States, 17 Cl. Ct. 860 (1989).

Bramble, B. B., and M. T. Callahan. 2000. *Construction delay claims.* 3rd ed., § 1.01A, B, D. New York: Aspen.

The Business Roundtable. 1980. *Scheduled overtime effect on construction projects.* Report C-2. New York: The Business Roundtable.

Callahan, M. T., D. G. Quackenbush, and J. E. Rowings. 1992. *Construction project scheduling.* New York: McGraw-Hill.

Cho, A. 1997. Packing more road into parkway. *Engineering News-Record (ENR),* May 12, 30–32.

Construction Industry Institute. 1986a, July. *Constructability: A primer.* Publication no. 3-1. Austin, TX: Construction Industry Institute.

Construction Industry Institute. 1986b, November. *Costs and benefits of materials management systems.* Publication no. 7-1. Austin, TX: Construction Industry Institute.

Construction Industry Institute. 1987a. *Guidelines for implementing a constructability program.* Publication no. 3-2. Austin, TX: Construction Industry Institute.

Construction Industry Institute. 1987b. *Project control for construction.* Publication no. 6-5. Austin, TX: Construction Industry Institute.

Construction Industry Institute. 1988a, November. *Concepts and methods of schedule compression.* Publication no. 6-7. Austin, TX: Construction Industry Institute.

Construction Industry Institute. 1988b, November. *Project materials management primer.* Publication no. 7-2. Austin, TX: Construction Industry Institute.

Construction Industry Institute. 1993, May. *Constructability: Implementation guide.* Publication no. 34-1. Austin, TX: Construction Industry Institute.

Fair, M. L. 1994. A comparative study of critical path method (CPM), program evaluation and review technique (PERT), and graphic evaluation and review technique (GERT). Master's thesis, Indiana University of Pennsylvania.

Fortec Constructors v. United States, 8 Cl. Ct. 490 (1985).

Gould, F. E., and N. E. Joyce. 2003. *Construction project management.* 2nd ed. Upper Saddle River, NJ: Prentice Hall.

Harris, R. B. 1978. *Precedence and arrow networking techniques for construction.* New York: Wiley.

Hendrickson, C., and T. Au. 1989. *Project management for construction.* Upper Saddle River, NJ: Prentice Hall.

Houghton Mifflin. 2000. *The American heritage dictionary of the English language.* 4th ed. Boston: Houghton Mifflin.

Larew, R. E. 1998. Are any construction overtime "studies" reliable? *Cost Engineering,* 40 (9).

R. S. Means. 2000. *Means illustrated construction dictionary.* 3rd ed. Kingston, MA: R. S. Means.

R. S. Means. 2001. *R. S. Means building construction cost data.* Note R01100-100. Kingston, MA: R. S. Means.

Meredith, J. R., and S. J. Mantel, Jr. 2000. *Project management.* 4th ed. New York: Wiley.

Merriam-Webster. 2003. *Merriam-Webster's collegiate dictionary.* 11th ed. Springfield, MA: Merriam-Webster.

Merriam-Webster. 2004. *Merriam-Webster dictionary online.* Retrieved, April 21, 2004, from http://www.m-w.com

Neil, J. M. 1982. *Construction cost estimating for project control.* Upper Saddle River, NJ: Prentice Hall.

Oberlender, G. D. 2000. *Project management for engineering and construction.* 2nd ed. New York: McGraw-Hill.

O'Brien, J. J., and F. L. Plotnick. 1999. *CPM in construction management.* 5th ed. New York: McGraw-Hill.

Oglesby, C., H. Parker, and G. Howell. 1989. *Productivity improvement in construction.* New York: McGraw-Hill.

Pasiphol, S., and C. M. Popescu. 1994. Qualitative criteria combination for total float distribution. In *1994 AACE transactions,* DCL.03.1–DCL.03.6. Morgantown, WV: American Association of Cost Engineers International.

Peña-Mora, F., C. E. Sosa, and D. S. McCone. 2003. *Introduction to construction dispute resolution.* Upper Saddle River, NJ: Prentice Hall.

Ponce de Leon, G. 1986. Float ownership: Specs treatment. *Cost Engineering,* 28 (10): 12–15.

Popescu, C. M., and C. Charoenngam. 1995. *Project planning, scheduling, and control in construction: An encyclopedia of terms and applications.* New York: Wiley.

Prentice Hall. 2000. *Construction project log book.* Upper Saddle River, NJ: Prentice Hall.

Project Management Institute. 2000. *A guide to the project management body of knowledge: PMBOK guide.* Newtown Square, PA: Project Management Institute.

Rosenbaum, D. B. 1994. Contractor finishes early. *Engineering News-Record (ENR),* July 18, 9.

Rosenbaum, D. B. 1995. Fast quake recovery redeemed state transportation department. *Engineering News-Record (ENR),* January 16, 33.

Rosta, P. 1994a. Contractor drops bridges. *Engineering News-Record (ENR),* March 21, 13.

Rosta, P. 1994b. Fast work earns big bonus. *Engineering News-Record (ENR),* April 18, 12.

Sweet, J. 1999. *Legal aspects of architecture, engineering and the construction process.* 5th ed. Eagan, MN: Thomson West.

Tulacz, G. J. 1994. Penhall: Not just a wrecking crew. *Engineering News-Record (ENR),* July 11, 28.

Wickwire, J. M., T. J. Driscoll, and S. B. Hurlbut. 1991. *Construction scheduling: Preparation, liability, and claims.* New York: Wiley.

Wilner v. United States, 16 Cl. Ct. 260 (1992).

BIBLIOGRAPHY

PLANNING, SCHEDULING, AND PROJECT CONTROL

Antill, J. M., and R. W. Woodhead. 1990. *Critical path methods in construction practice.* 4th ed. New York: Wiley.

Associated General Contractors of America. 1994. *Construction planning and scheduling.* Alexandria, VA: Associated General Contractors of America.

Burke, R. 2001. *Project management: Planning and control techniques.* 3rd ed. New York: Wiley.

Callahan, M. T., D. G. Quackenbush, and J. E. Rowings. 1992. *Construction project scheduling.* New York: McGraw-Hill.

Cho, A. 1997. Packing more road into parkway. *Engineering News-Record (ENR),* May 12, 30–32.

Dreger, J. B. 1992. *Project management: Effective scheduling.* New York: Van Nostrand Reinhold.

Feigenbaum, L. 2002. *Construction scheduling with Primavera Project Planner.* 2nd ed. Upper Saddle River, NJ: Prentice Hall.

Harris, P. E. 1999. *Planning using Primavera Project Planner P3 version 3.0.* Melbourne, Australia: Eastwood Harris.

Harris, R. B. 1978. *Precedence and arrow networking techniques for construction.* New York: Wiley.

Hinze, J. W. 1998. *Construction planning and scheduling.* Upper Saddle River, NJ: Prentice Hall.

Horsley, F. W. 2004. *Means scheduling manual.* 3rd ed. Kingston, MA: R. S. Means.

Hutchings, J. F. 2004. *Project scheduling handbook.* New York: Dekker.

Kelley, R. M. 1998. *Planning techniques (basic and advanced).* Kettering, OH: Kelley Communication Development.

Lewis, J. P. 2000. *Project planning, scheduling, and control.* 3rd ed. New York: McGraw-Hill.

Marchman, D. A. 2002. *Construction scheduling with Primavera Project Planner.* 2nd ed. Clifton Park, NY: Delmar.

Moder, J. J., C. R. Phillips, and E. W. Davis. 1995. *Project management with CPM, PERT and precedence diagramming.* 3rd ed. Middleton, WI: Blitz.

O'Brien, J. J., and F. L. Plotnick. 1999. *CPM in construction management.* 5th ed. New York: McGraw-Hill.

Pasiphol, S., and C. M. Popescu. 1994. Qualitative criteria combination for total float distribution. In *1994 AACE Transactions,* DCL.03.1–DCL.03.6. Morgantown, WV: American Association of Cost Engineers International.

Patrick, C. 2004. *Construction project planning and scheduling.* Upper Saddle River, NJ: Prentice Hall.

Pierce, D. R., Jr. 2004. *Project scheduling and management for construction.* 3rd ed. Kingston, MA: R. S. Means.

Ponce de Leon, G. 1986. Float ownership: Specs treatment. *Cost Engineering,* 28 (10): 12–15.

Popescu, C. M., and C. Charoenngam. 1995. *Project planning, scheduling, and control in construction: An encyclopedia of terms and applications.* New York: Wiley.

Rosenbaum, D. B. 1994. Contractor finishes early. *Engineering News-Record (ENR),* July 18, 9.

Rosenbaum, D. B. 1995. Fast quake recovery redeemed state transportation department. *Engineering News-Record (ENR),* January 16, 33.

Rosta, P. 1994. Contractor drops bridges. *Engineering News-Record (ENR),* March 21, 13.

Rosta, P. 1994. Fast work earns big bonus. *Engineering News-Record (ENR),* April 18, 12.

Samad, S. A., ed. 1999. *Planning and scheduling.* Professional practice guide (PPG) #4. Morgantown, WV: American Association of Cost Engineers International.

Stevens, J. D. 1990. *Techniques for construction network scheduling.* New York: McGraw-Hill.

Tulacz, G. J. 1994. Penhall: Not just a wrecking crew. *Engineering News-Record (ENR),* July 11, 28.

Wiest, J. D., and F. K. Levy. 1977. *A management guide to PERT/CPM.* 2nd ed. Upper Saddle River, NJ: Prentice Hall.

Willis, E. M. 1986. *Scheduling construction projects.* New York: Wiley.

PROJECT AND CONSTRUCTION MANAGEMENT

Ahuja, H. N., S. P. Dozzi, and S. M. Abourizk. 1994. *Project management.* 2nd ed. New York: Wiley.

Angus, R. B., N. A. Gundersen, and T. P. Cullinane. 1999. *Planning, performing, and controlling projects.* 3rd ed. Upper Saddle River, NJ: Prentice Hall.

Barrie, D. S., and B. C. Paulson. 1992. *Professional construction management.* 3rd ed. New York: McGraw-Hill.

Bennett, F. L. 2003. *The management of construction: A project life cycle approach.* Boston: Butterworth-Heinemann.

The Business Roundtable. 1989. *Scheduled overtime effect on construction projects.* Report C-2. New York: The Business Roundtable.

Certo, S. C. 2002. *Modern management.* 9th ed. Upper Saddle River, NJ: Prentice Hall.

Clough, R. H., and G. A. Sears. 2000. *Construction project management.* 4th ed. New York: Wiley.

Collier, K. 1994. *Managing construction: The contractual viewpoint.* Albany, NY: Delmar.

Construction Industry Institute. 1986, July. *Constructability: A primer.* Publication no. 3-1. Austin, TX: Construction Industry Institute.

Construction Industry Institute. 1986, November. *Costs and benefits of materials management systems.* Publication no. 7-1. Austin, TX: Construction Industry Institute.

Construction Industry Institute. 1987. *Guidelines for implementing a constructability program.* Publication no. 3-2. Austin, TX: Construction Industry Institute.

Construction Industry Institute. 1988, November. *Concepts and methods of schedule compression.* Publication no. 6-7. Austin, TX: Construction Industry Institute.

Construction Industry Institute. 1988, November. *Project materials management primer.* Publication no. 7-2. Austin, TX: Construction Industry Institute.

Construction Industry Institute. 1993, May. *Constructability: Implementation guide.* Publication no. 34-1. Austin, TX: Construction Industry Institute.

Fisk, E. R. 2003. *Construction project administration.* 7th ed. Upper Saddle River, NJ: Prentice Hall.

Gould, F. E., and N. E. Joyce. 2003. *Construction project management.* 2nd ed. Upper Saddle River, NJ: Prentice Hall.

Graham, R. J. 1989. *Project management as if people mattered.* Bala Cynwyd, PA: Primavera Press.

Hegazy, T. 2002. *Computer-based construction project management.* Upper Saddle River, NJ: Prentice Hall.

Hendrickson, C., and T. Au. 1989. *Project management for construction.* Upper Saddle River, NJ: Prentice Hall.

Kerzner, H. 2000. *Project management: A systems approach to planning, scheduling and controlling.* 7th ed. New York: Wiley.

Levy, S. M. 2000. *Project management in construction.* 3rd ed. New York: McGraw-Hill.

Meredith, J. R., and S. J. Mantel, Jr. 2000. *Project management.* 4th ed. New York: Wiley.

Naylor, H. 1995. *Construction project management: Planning and scheduling.* Albany, NY: Delmar.

Neil, J. M. 1982. *Construction cost estimating for project control.* Upper Saddle River, NJ: Prentice Hall.

Nunnally, S. W. 2001. *Construction methods and management.* 5th ed. Upper Saddle River, NJ: Prentice Hall.

Oberlender, G. D. 2000. *Project management for engineering and construction.* 2nd ed. New York: McGraw-Hill.

Pilcher, R. 1992. *Principles of construction management.* 3rd ed. New York: McGraw-Hill.

Pinto, J. K., and O. P. Kharbanda. 1995. *Successful project managers.* New York: Van Nostrand Reinhold.

Project Management Institute. 2000. *A guide to the project management body of knowledge: PMBOK guide.* Newtown Square, PA: Project Management Institute.

Ritz, G. J. 1994. *Total construction project management*. New York: McGraw-Hill.

Rosenau, M. D., Jr. 1998. *Successful project management*. 3rd ed. New York: Wiley.

CONSTRUCTION SCHEDULING LAW

Blinderman Construction Co. v. United States, 17 Cl. Ct. 860 (1989).

Bramble, B. B., and M. T. Callahan. 2000. *Construction delay claims*. 3rd ed., § 1.01A, B, D. New York: Aspen.

Fortec Constructors v. United States, 8 Cl. Ct. 490 (1985).

Heuer, C. R. 1989. *Means legal reference for design and construction*. Kingston, MA: R. S. Means.

Peña-Mora, F., C. E. Sosa, and D. S. McCone. 2003. *Introduction to construction dispute resolution*. Upper Saddle River, NJ: Prentice Hall.

Stokes, M. 1980. *Labor law in contractors' language*. New York: McGraw-Hill.

Sweet, J. J. 1993. *Avoiding or minimizing construction litigation*. New York: Wiley.

Sweet, J. 1999. *Legal aspects of architecture, engineering and the construction process*. 5th ed. Eagan, MN: Thomson West.

Wickwire, J. M., T. J. Driscoll, and S. B. Hurlbut. 1991. *Construction scheduling: Preparation, liability, and claims*. New York: Wiley.

Wilner v. United States, 16 Cl. Ct. 260 (1992).

Wilson, R. L. n.d. *Construction claims . . . Their prevention and resolution*. Seminar. Glen Head, NY: Wilson Management Associates.

OTHER

The American Institute of Architects. 1997. *General conditions of the contract for construction*. Document A201, ¶ 4.3.7.2. Washington, DC: The American Institute of Architects.

The American Institute of Architects. 1999. *Commentary on AIA document A201-1997*. Washington, DC: The American Institute of Architects.

August, R. 2003. *International law dictionary and directory*. Pullman, WA: Ray August.

Barba-Arkhon International. 1996. *Schedule delay and loss of productivity analysis*. 11th annual construction superconference. Mount Laurel, NJ: Barba-Arkhon International.

Bent, J. A. 1982. *Applied cost and schedule control*. New York: Dekker.

The Business Roundtable. 1989. *Scheduled overtime effect on construction projects*. Report C-2. New York: The Business Roundtable.

Construction Industry Institute. 1986, Nov. *Costs and benefits of materials management systems*. Publication no. 7-1. Austin, TX: Construction Industry Institute.

Construction Industry Institute. 1986. *Project control for engineering*. Publication no. 6-1. Austin, TX: Construction Industry Institute.

Construction Industry Institute. 1986. *Scope, definition, and control*. Publication no. 6-2. Austin, TX: Construction Industry Institute.

Construction Industry Institute. 1987. *Project control for construction*. Publication no. 6-5. Austin, TX: Construction Industry Institute.

Construction Industry Institute. 1988, Nov. *Concepts and methods of schedule compression*. Publication no. 6-7. Austin, TX: Construction Industry Institute.

Construction Industry Institute. 1988, Nov. *Project materials management: Primer*. Publication no. 7-2. Austin, TX: Construction Industry Institute.

Construction Industry Institute. 1988. *Work packaging for project control*. Publication no. 6-6. Austin, TX: Construction Industry Institute.

Construction Industry Institute. 1990. *The impact of changes on construction cost and schedule*. Publication no. 6-10. Austin, TX: Construction Industry Institute.

Construction Industry Institute. 1991. *Organizing for project success*. Special publication no. 12-2. Austin, TX: Construction Industry Institute.

Construction Industry Institute. 1993, May. *Constructability: Implementation guide*. Publication no. 34-1. Austin, TX: Construction Industry Institute.

Dell'Isola, A. 1997. *Value engineering: Practical applications*. Kingston, MA: R. S. Means.

Fair, M. L. 1994. A comparative study of critical path method (CPM), program evaluation and review technique (PERT), and graphic evaluation and review technique (GERT). Master's thesis, Indiana University of Pennsylvania.

Fleming, Q. W., and J. M. Koppelman. 2000. *Earned value project management*. 2nd ed. Newtown Square, PA: Project Management Institute.

Haltenhoff, C. E. 1999. *The CM contracting system: Fundamentals and practices*. Upper Saddle River, NJ: Prentice Hall.

Houghton Mifflin. 2000. *The American heritage dictionary of the English language*. 4th ed. Boston: Houghton Mifflin.

Larew, R. 1995. Are any construction overtime "studies" reliable? *Cost Engineering*, 40 (9).

Locher, W. D., and A. Civitello, Jr. 2002. *Contractor's guide to change orders*. Anaheim, CA: BNi Building News.

R. S. Means. 2000. *Means illustrated construction dictionary*. 3rd ed. Kingston, MA: R. S. Means.

R. S. Means. 2001. *R. S. Means building construction cost data*. Note R01100-100. Kingston, MA: R. S. Means.

Merriam-Webster. 2003. *Merriam-Webster's collegiate dictionary*. 11th ed. Springfield, MA: Merriam-Webster.

Merriam-Webster. 2004. *Merriam-Webster dictionary online*. Retrieved, April 21, 2004, from http://www.m-w.com

Morrisey, G. L., T. L. Sechrest, and W. B. Warman. 1997. *Loud and clear: How to prepare and deliver effective business and technical presentations*. 4th ed. New York: Perseus Books.

Neil, J. M. 1982. *Construction cost estimating for project control*. Upper Saddle River, NJ: Prentice Hall.

Oglesby, C., H. Parker, and G. Howell. 1989. *Productivity improvement in construction*. New York: McGraw-Hill.

Peurifoy, R. L., and W. B. Ledbetter. 1985. *Construction planning, equipment, and methods*. 4th ed. New York: McGraw-Hill.

Prentice Hall. 2000. *Construction project log book*. Upper Saddle River, NJ: Prentice Hall.

Stumpf, G. R., ed. 1999. *Earned value*. Professional practice guide (PPG) #5. Morgantown, WV: American Association of Cost Engineers International.

Thomas, P. I. 1999. *The contractor's field guide*. Anaheim, CA: BNi Building News.

Thompson, P., and J. Perry, eds. 1992. *Engineering construction risks: A guide to project risk analysis and risk management*. London: Telford.

INDEX